THE CALOR BOOK OF PUB CATERING

THE LICENSEE'S COMPLETE GUIDE TO RUNNING A SUCCESSFUL FOOD OPERATION

DAVID & GLYNIS BEST

MARTIN BOOKS

Produced by Martin Books
Simon & Schuster International Group
Fitzwilliam House
32 Trumpington Street
Cambridge
CB2 1QY

In association with
Calor Gas Limited
Appleton Park
Slough
SL3 9JG

First published 1990
ISBN 0 85941 617 8

© David and Glynis Best, 1990

Conditions of sale
All rights reserved. No part of this publication may be reproduced, stored in a retrieval system or transmitted, in any form or by any means, electronic, mechanical, photocopying, recording or otherwise, without the prior permission of the copyright owners.

All possible care has been taken over the legal information given in this book, but for specific matters readers should seek expert legal advice.

Design: Ken Vail Graphic Design
Illustrations: Richard Jacobs, John Erwood, Andrew Sharpe and Sam Vail
Cartoons: David Lock
Photography on pages i – iv: Huw Evans
Food preparation for photography: Glynis Best and Tracy Phelan
Typesetting: Goodfellow & Egan Ltd, Cambridge
Printed and bound in Great Britain by: Richard Clay Ltd, Bungay, Suffolk

Acknowledgments
We would like to thank the following for their invaluable help, and in some cases, for kindly providing material used in the book: the Health Education Authority; Leslie Wilkinson of the Vegetarian Society; Bill Cooke of Cinders Barbecues; Barrowford Hotel Supplies, for the wine glass material (page 61); Peter Ibbotson, David Parker, Tony Sullivan et al of Whitbreads, West Pennines, for general help and for allowing us to reproduce their Wine and Spirit Retail Price Calculator (page 62); the Wine Development Board (page 64/65); Whitbreads & Co PLC (page 70); the Catering Centre, Blackburn (pages 83, 84 and 85); Jane Hildred and Verne George of Merrychef; the Environmental Health Office, Preston, who could not have been more helpful; Mr E Lake, Manager, Midland Bank, Preston, for the information on acceptable currency; the Association of Payment Clearing Services (page 112); the Inland Revenue, Preston; HM Customs and Excise (VAT), Lytham, (and central office page 119); Chris Parker of Parker Blake & Co., Stocktakers, Blackburn, and Roger Smith, Varley Edmondson & Co., Accountants, Clitheroe, for checking the information in the bookkeeping, stock-taking and staff chapters; Microsimplex; Mr Beedling of the Wages Inspectorate; ACAS, for patiently answering all our endless questions; Elizabeth Jordan, for allowing us to 'pinch' ideas from her excellent staff seminars; HMSO for the Crown copyright table (page 148); the Brewers' Society for all the information they provided including the Pub Facilities Symbols (page xvi); Don Moore of the Lancashire Constabulary, the Federation of the Retail Licensed Trade Association, Northern Ireland, the Scottish Licensed Trade Association (Chapter 15); and finally our parents, Fred and Connie, and the long-suffering staff at the Bushells Arms, without whom this book would never have been written.

The cutlery and crockery used in the photographs on page i – iv was kindly provided by Steelite International, Orme Street, Stoke-on-Trent ST6 3RB. The photographs on the front cover and page viii (bottom) were reproduced courtesy of *Pubcaterer* magazine. Thanks to Zanussi CLV Systems Ltd for the use of the equipment shot on page v (top); to Falcon Catering Equipment, page v (bottom), vi (top); to Stott Benham Ltd, pages vi (bottom), vii, viii (top); and to Cinders Barbecues, pages ix and x. The photographs on page xi, xii and xiii (bottom) were kindly provided by Calor Gas Ltd; those on pages xiii (top) and xiv: Whitbread and Co PLC; those on page xv: Courage Ltd.

Contents

Acknowledgments 2

Foreword by Victor Ceserani 5

Introduction 6

1 Pub food 8
2 Setting up the operation 10
3 Choosing the menu 19
4 Catering for vegetarians 38
5 Convenience foods 41
6 Functions, theme nights and barbecues 45
7 Wine – a brief introduction 60
8 Promotion and publicity 75
9 Kitchen layout 80
10 Equipment 87
11 Public health and hygiene 101
12 Bookkeeping and account management 111
13 Menu costing, stock-taking and suppliers 123
14 Staff 137
15 Licensing law 151
16 Recipes 159
    Glossary of culinary terms 189
    Index 190

Foreword

My first recollections of pub food are as a small boy growing up in the 1920s and my very first memory is of peeping around the door of the public bar and seeing on the counter three large glass jars. One contained large thick arrowroot biscuits, another, packets of Meredith & Drew cheese sandwich biscuits, and the third, packets of Smiths crisps. In those days Smiths were considered the best crisps by most youngsters of my acquaintance; there was only one flavour, the natural potato, and every packet contained salt in a twist of blue paper. That was all the catering you would expect to find in pubs in the thirties.

I worked with *Caterer & Hotelkeeper* magazine for several years; then when *Pubcaterer* magazine was launched I assisted with the planning and judging of the first Pub Caterer of the Year competition, and almost all the other numerous competitions that the magazine and various sponsors have run and continue to run today. The standards for winning the competitions are those that all publicans should fulfil if they want a very successful food operation. David and Glynis Best, who won the best pub meal section in 1987, do just that, and in *The Calor Book of Pub Catering* they show you how to do the same. All these standards should be achieved:

- ☐ Variety of choice – not necessarily large but interesting: include both old favourites and contemporary and original dishes, with a choice for the healthy-food-conscious and the vegetarian.
- ☐ Presentation – attractive and appetising, not over-garnished or garish but neat, clean, simple and mouthwatering.
- ☐ Ease of service – comfortable seating with table space to be able to put down a plate and use a knife and fork.
- ☐ Quality of the food and cooking – does the food taste good? Would you want to order that dish again on a subsequent visit? Also, size of portion and value for money.
- ☐ Overall hygiene – of the food, crockery, cutlery, tables, the food-server, the kitchen, food store and the toilets.
- ☐ Overall feeling of ease in the pub – did you feel comfortable and at ease when you entered the pub and with the attitude of the staff? Did you feel relaxed during your stay for the meal? Is it a pub that you would go out of your way to return to and to recommend to others?

It has been interesting and rewarding to see how the standard of the Pub Caterer of the Year competition has improved over the years. This year, 1989, in particular was outstanding. The standard of the second- and third-placed competitors was so high that in several of the previous years they could have gained the top prize.

So in this sort of climate, do not feel alone in aiming for excellence in your catering. Drink sales are shrinking and may continue to do so in the future as motoring legalisation is toughened, but food sales can and inevitably will rise, provided that the pub caterer offers good quality food at a fair price. The only way is up, as far as standards of pub catering are concerned.

In many pubs today the quality, choice and value for money of the food on offer can put many three- and four-star hotels to shame.

After reading this book I was pleased to be able to write a foreword, because I consider that David and Glynis Best have produced a thoroughly sound and most helpful manual, which is so comprehensive that anyone who aspires to run a successful and respected pub cannot fail to find it useful. Furthermore, as it has been written from experience, it will help you to avoid making the inevitable mistakes that I'm sure David and Glynis made in the early days (as we all do) when they started as rookies. Combining as it does a wealth of information with many years of practical experience, this book is a 'must' for any serious pub caterer.

Victor Ceserani

Introduction

In recent years, pub catering has not only come of age, it has reached its maturity in more senses than one, being by far the largest single area of growth in the catering industry. Running parallel with this increasing demand for food in pubs is a diminishing demand for alcohol in its more traditional form, that is, beer, whereas sales of wine and soft drinks are booming. Together, these trends present an interesting situation as they signal the birth of a new era for pubs, and something akin to an earthquake for the 'established' catering industry. As with anything else, there is probably no single reason which could account for this change of events and the likelihood is that the causes are many and varied. The conclusions of the 1989 Monopolies and Mergers Committee report may give licensees more opportunities than ever before, but there may also be new hazards ahead.

A tremendous increase in foreign travel and holidays abroad has done much to widen the horizons of the average family and has given them a taste for eating out, eating foreign food and drinking wine. This is where the pub comes into its own. Good, imaginative food at the right price in a relaxed and informal atmosphere make the pub a natural first choice for people who want to eat out more than once in a blue moon.

In order that pub caterers may take their rightful place in the vanguard of the catering industry, they have to make sure that they are professionally up to scratch. So far, the catering 'establishment' have been slow, to say the least, in recognising the true worth of pub catering. What this boils down to is that there is almost no guidance for aspiring pub caterers from people who are qualified to give such guidance. Until now that is!

All these various factors point to one thing: a real and urgent need for a pub catering manual written by people who have experience at first hand. We feel that this book will fit the bill and provide solutions to many of the vexing problems which are part and parcel of any catering operation. More than that, *The Calor Book of Pub Catering* is intended to provide help and reassurance with the day-to-day running of a pub catering business and, if used properly, should become something of a real friend. With such help close at hand, you will be able to get on with increasing your business, secure in the knowledge that you are doing things properly.

So how did the book come about? We have been in pub catering for some 16 years now and are both Members of the British Institute of Innkeeping and jointly qualified in City and Guilds and the Wine and Spirit Education Trust's Higher Certificate. Over the years we have been winners and finalists in most of the national pub catering competitions. We mention these things not by way of blowing our own trumpet but more by way of reassurance – we really do know about the sharp end of the business, and we are certainly not what might be described as armchair advisers.

During our early years in the trade we encountered all the pitfalls it is possible to encounter and we made mistakes, trying to put into practice ideas that didn't work because we did not have the knowledge to plan them properly. Incorrect profit margins meant we had made very little money at the end of the year and the sheer volume of information that is needed to run a small business overwhelmed us.

In order to save ourselves some time and energy we started to collate the information in

Introduction

a more logical fashion, rather than just rummaging through all the VAT and PAYE documents every time a query arose. We attended as many courses and seminars as we could manage and shamelessly picked any brains that were available. What we lacked as 'naturals' we made up for with tenacity. To put all this information into book form seemed a natural progression.

Calor have always supported the catering industry, so the connection with them happened very easily. We have always found them not only pleasant to work with but also very professional, so it has been a comfortable partnership.

We have tried to cover as many aspects of our trade as possible; we have gone into some aspects in great detail and with some we have merely tried to point the way. Pub catering can be hard work, it is 7 days per week and usually 50 weeks a year. If this book can help in any way to alleviate some of the work load, then we will have succeeded.

You will notice that most names and addresses in the acknowledgements section are in the north west of England. The reason for this is that we felt, rightly or wrongly, that if we were exhorting people to use local offices, the information should be there; so we tested the system we were advocating. With only one exception, the response was amazing – everyone was very, very helpful.

David and Glynis Best

1 Pub food

In days gone by, public houses were described variously as inns, hostelries, taverns, coaching houses and ale houses, and so deeply rooted is the pub in the British way of life, that these terms are still with us today. Originally, these different names probably distinguished places with slightly different functions, whereas nowadays they are used mainly on signs and letterheads to suggest a feeling of well being and warmth. They all have one thing in common though: they are all public houses. Look in any dictionary and you will discover that inns, taverns, hostelries, public houses – call them what you will – are all expected to provide food as well as drink.

Today, more than ever before, pubs are doing just that. The growth in demand for food in pubs has been enormous in recent years and has provided a new dimension for licensees. This demand clearly presents a challenge and should be taken advantage of: pubs are not restricted to providing bread and cheese and ham sandwiches, as one catering writer imperiously suggested in a clumsy attempt to ensure that pubs remember their place. The author of that remark would do well to remember the words of George Bernard Shaw who said, 'the golden rule is that there are no golden rules'. Those words are particularly true when applied to catering in pubs: there is no rule which ties pub caterers to provide only the simplest of fare. On the contrary, they are free to provide whatever food they think will be most successful.

We can see, then, that pub catering, because of its diversity, defies a definition. This, in itself, is no problem as a definition is not needed anyway. What is needed, though, is to be aware of certain trump cards which pub caterers are fortunate enough to have in their possession:

- [ ] Pubs are basic to our national way of life.
- [ ] Pubs exude warmth, cheerfulness and optimism.
- [ ] Pubs are aware of local traditions.
- [ ] Pubs are part of the community.
- [ ] Pubs have a reputation for offering better value for money than many other catering outlets.
- [ ] Pubs are more relaxed and less formal than many other outlets.

All these things together add up to an extremely powerful formula for a successful catering operation.

Just stop and think for a minute and ask yourself what sort of place people like to dine at when they are on holiday. Obviously, the sort of place which has attributes similar to those above, or the Greek taverna would not be half as popular as it is. The only thing missing from the formula so far is food, and this is an area where we can really score!

As we have said and contrary to what some people think, pubs are not restricted in any way regarding the sort of food they offer. Pub caterers have an ideal chance, for instance, to offer local or regional specialities and so keep traditions alive. It is also quite a sound idea commercially, as people travelling through the area, as well as local residents, are attracted to the idea of sampling local dishes. Casseroles and stews can be very impressive and they, too, are ideally suited to a pub catering operation. The same can be said of fish, which is enjoying an upsurge in popularity, being fat-free and healthy, and fish can be cooked to perfection in minutes with the help of a microwave oven.

Having established that the choice of what food to provide is very wide, it is essential to remember that the food offered to customers must be good, a principle which applies to all catering outlets but one which is often forgotten. If you are just beginning to set up a catering operation in your pub, this means cooking what you are best at. If your family thinks, for instance, that your liver and onion casserole is absolutely wonderful, you can be sure that it will be a winner with your customers too. Provide good, honest food and your customers will love it.

Pub catering is different from other forms of catering. This is not to imply that pub catering is in any way inferior – it is certainly not – but there are differences and if you recognise these, you can capitalise on them.

- [ ] Catering in a pub is a portion of the business not the whole of it. Unlike restaurants which depend entirely on the sale of food, pubs have their bar trade to fall back on.
- [ ] Pubs which offer food do so at lunch-time as well as in the evening, whereas a good proportion of restaurants do not. In this respect it is as well to remember that most people have only a limited amount of time for their lunch so the service at lunch-time must be quick and efficient. Those restaurants which do open at lunch-time very often try to emulate the style and price of food available in pubs!
- [ ] Service in pubs is generally much more relaxed than in hotels and restaurants, which like to provide what is known as silver service. However, some pubs that are lucky enough to have a separate dining room provide silver service in there, with more informal service in

the rest of the pub. To operate silver service, though, more staff are needed and as staff cost money this obviously has to be reflected in the prices on the menu.
- ☐ As a general rule, pubs see no disgrace in providing snacks for their customers, whereas most restaurants would blanch at the very idea - except perhaps at lunch-time! The provision of snacks is a good idea and it goes a long way towards promoting the rest of the menu, so long as such items are of good quality and are presented attractively.

So far, so good! We now know that pub catering covers a wide range of styles and that it differs from other forms of catering because pubs, by their very nature, have deep-rooted traditions. Why should you bother though? Why should you go to all that trouble when you could simply sit back and sell the booze and provide the odd sandwich from time to time? Here's why.
- ☐ There is a great deal of profit to be made in a pub catering operation, provided that the food which is offered is wholesome, imaginative and attractive.
- ☐ People who like to eat in pubs also like to drink in them and, what is more, they bring other people with them. In other words, a successful pub catering operation will also increase wet sales (sales of drink).
- ☐ As overheads continue to spiral ever upwards and the demand for alcohol continues to decline, a successful pub catering operation is now something of a necessity if you wish to make a profit.
- ☐ With the exception of a very small percentage of public houses (usually brewery managed houses), the days of the 'boozer' are numbered. This has been clearly demonstrated in recent years by the alarming number of licensees who have been forced out of business due to a decline in wet sales coupled with substantial increases in overheads.
- ☐ Food in pubs is a very trendy concept and the vast majority of people love to dine out. If they choose to eat out in pubs – and more and more are doing just that – it means that they can afford to indulge themselves more often as the prices in pubs are generally much more reasonable than elsewhere.
- ☐ Job satisfaction: pub catering is a very pleasurable way to make a living. People are at their best when they are relaxing over a meal and a bottle of wine. With time and effort, it is even possible to be included in the guidebooks or to win national catering competitions. When that happens, the sense of pride in achievement is enormous, to say nothing of all the free publicity!

The following chapters will reveal how all this can be achieved, but in the meantime, try ruminating on this. Why put all your energies into a frantic effort to increase wet sales which you know are declining when you have barely scratched the surface of what is essentially the other half of the trade?

Remember –

PUB CATERING = MORE TRADE = MORE PROFIT.

Get it?

2 Setting up the operation

Basically, there are two main ways of setting up a pub catering operation. Initially, it is possible to start by just serving simple food such as soup and sandwiches and gradually developing the concept by moving on to salads and one or two complementary hot dishes. This is the way that many pub caterers, including ourselves, started out. However, that was in the past, when fewer pubs were serving food and those that did had novelty value. Those days are gone!

The ideal way is perhaps the approach that the breweries adopt with their 'themed' pub. They close the place down, alter it to their requirements, then open up in a blaze of publicity with everything ready: menus printed, staff trained and the pub fully operational. Most licensees cannot mount such an operation. For a start, the pub may not be in such a prime position as the brewery-managed houses, nor can many afford the time or the expense of closing the pub down for several weeks. Often, too, licensees just have not got the expertise or experience to organise and operate a sophisticated catering operation without a little 'practice'.

So a 'softly, softly' approach does have advantages until you are in a position to evaluate the full potential of the pub and yourselves. Everyone goes into a new pub full of enthusiasm: even if you have done only a modicum of market research, you may think the area is ripe for development or may have fallen in love with the building or location. This last point is not to be sneezed at because you have to like a place in which you are to spend seven days per week for fifty-two weeks in the year!

Sometimes, people move and, without any local knowledge, take a pub in an area that is completely new to them, so time is needed to assess the full potential of the market. Even if you do know the area, you will still need to analyse the potential market if you are to have a chance of succeeding. Do allow yourselves this time, and do get the information down on paper in a logical and concise way so that you can refer or add to it at a later date. You will find a projection or presentation such as this very useful for your own purposes but also of immense value if you are aproaching a brewery or a bank for help, in that it demonstrates that you are pursuing your aim to succeed in a logical and business-like manner.

Whatever you do, it is important that you don't just drift in the general direction of catering or you will find yourselves left at the starting blocks. Here, then, are some points to consider for inclusion in your projection:

- [ ] **The pub itself** Does it have a kitchen other than the one in your private quarters? If not, is there room for one downstairs and how would its creation be funded? If there is an existing catering kitchen, list all the items of equipment which are already there and make a note of their general condition. What sources of power are available? Not just electric plug sockets but other forms of power such as Calor gas or natural gas. Where will you serve the food you intend to offer? Are the tables and seating arrangements adequate for the purpose? How many covers (place settings) are there room for? Is there any room to expand if your catering operation really takes off? Also have a look at pages 16–18.
- [ ] **Location** This is dealt with fully on pages 12–16.
- [ ] **Population** You need to know the population density of the area. Contact your local planning officer: he should be able to help and also let you know whether there are any development schemes or other plans scheduled for your area.
- [ ] **Competition** You need to know how many catering outlets or potential catering outlets there are in the area. Purchase a large-scale map of the area and, using a pair of compasses draw circles at half-mile intervals with your premises at the centre. Attach the map to a board and use coloured pins to mark each outlet, using a different colour for each different type: e.g. red for pubs, blue for restaurants, green for cafes and snack bars, and yellow for hotels. This same map can be used for other purposes, too, as you will be able to see at a glance what population you have to draw on and you will be able to highlight any local attractions which could provide you with valuable spin-off trade.
- [ ] **Yourselves** Are you up to the task of catering for the public? If you have a catering qualification and have some experience, you should have no problem, but if you are not qualified or experienced, how are you going to ensure that you can cope? We hope that this book will be a tremendous help, obviously, but it would do no harm to consider attending a part-time course at your local catering college or school such as those which are advertised in the catering press.
- [ ] **Capital** If you are going to need capital to set up your catering operation or to buy additional equipment or furnishings, where is it going to

Setting up the operation

Assessing the competition – a map showing local catering outlets

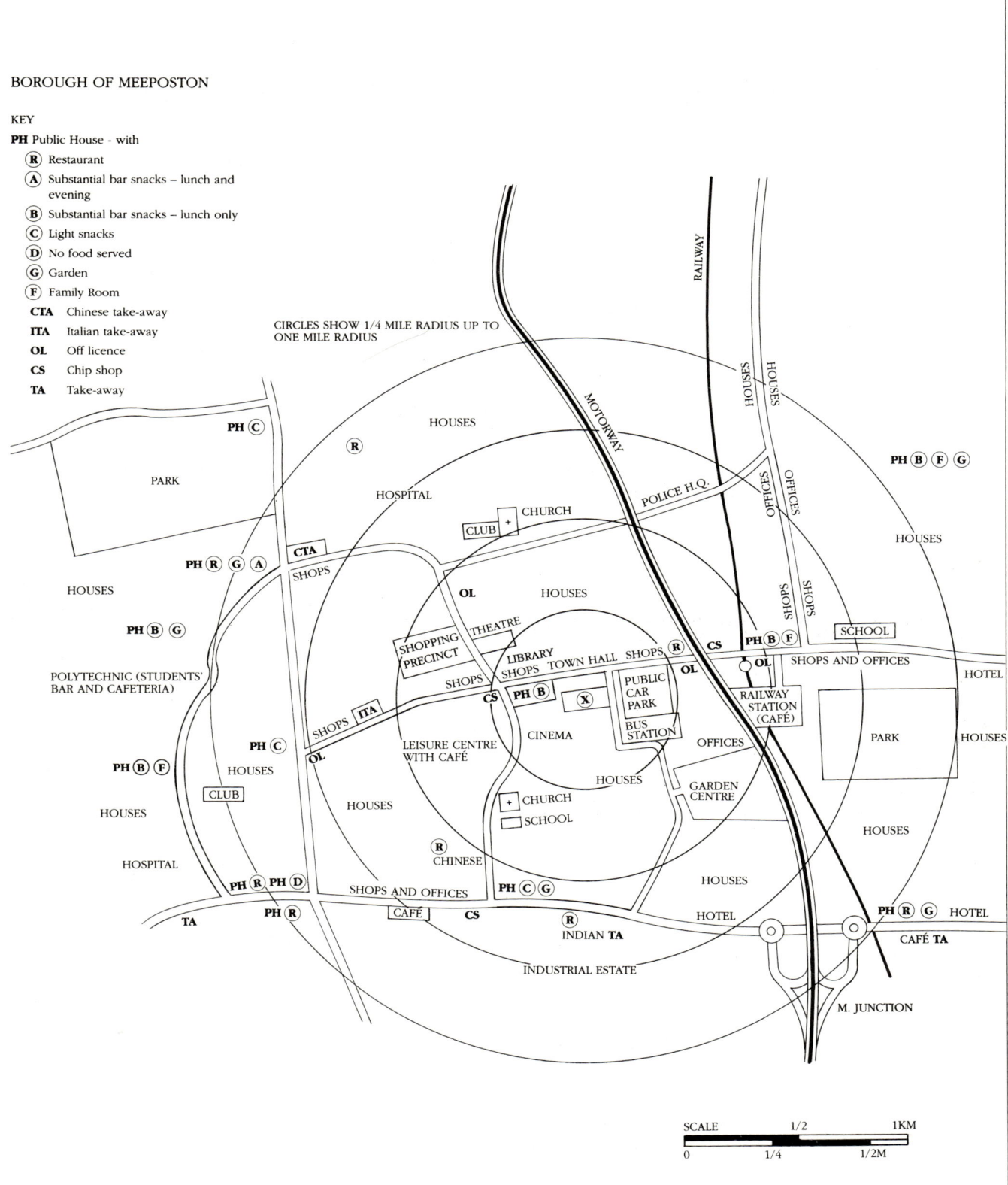

Setting up the operation

come from? If you have some spare capital of your own, that's fine, but if you have not, you may have to consider approaching your bank to help you. If such is the case, a well-thought out projection, complete with map would go a long way towards enlisting that help.

There is clearly plenty to consider before you can begin to make a realistic assessment. No doubt you will be able to think of other items which could be included in your projection, after all, you are on the spot. If you do, write them all down.

When your projection is complete, don't just file it and sit back: use it! Keep it handy so that you can read and re-read it and this way you will become more familiar with the task in hand. Keep it up to date by adding to the map any new features which have appeared in the locality and erasing any which have disappeared. If, at some time in the future, you wish to make provision for, say, a function room or some other additional feature, you can simply add another section to the existing projection and so build up an informative and helpful dossier on your aspirations and achievements. Don't forget to include failed projects either, so that you can analyse why you think the project failed and so that you have a reminder not to make the same mistake again!

The location

Some years ago, a very successful restaurateur told us that, as far as he was concerned, location was unimportant and that if you do things right, customers flock in regardless of where you are situated. Having said that, he, of course, had already set up his hotel and restaurant in just about the most stunning spot in the whole of the English Lakes!

What he said though, is true to a certain extent, even for those people who do not have the chance to select such a flamboyant location. What you must do is to identify first of all into which category your location falls, after which you can see more clearly just what level of business you can achieve with a little thought and planning.

As a rough guide, location can be divided into four main categories:
- ☐ **Urban** In or near a town or city centre, close to offices, shops, universities, polytechnics and industry.
- ☐ **Suburban** On the outskirts of a town or city, in a mainly residential area but possibly with some light industry or perhaps a trading estate.
- ☐ **Semi-rural** This could be a large village or the country section of a main or arterial road or even a 'green belt' area.
- ☐ **Rural** In a small village or isolated in the countryside.

All types of location have potential but it is important to ensure that the services and facilities you are offering complement that location. For instance, a juke box, pool table, video games and beefburgers would probably sit uncomfortably in an 'olde worlde' pub in the Derbyshire Dales as might classical music and silver service in an urban pub which is surrounded by industry.

Having said all that, there is no need to fall into the same old traps. Juke boxes, pool tables and videos are by no means compulsory, nor are they necessarily beneficial to trade, especially in a catering context. Have a good look around and if all the other pubs in the area are already doing that sort of thing, use your imagination and do something different; that way you generate your own business. After all, there has got to be more to life than a juke box, pool table and videos! You will also see as we go through the different categories of locations that there can be differences within those categories.

Urban

The main and most obvious point about towns and cities is the high concentration of people. However, things may not be as straightforward as they may seem. Right at the centre of a city, a pub could well be busy during the day but virtually dead at night. Within any town or city, there are areas which are absolutely booming because of new shop and office developments and pedestrian precincts which bring with them new life and opportunity. There are also areas which have been savagely hit by the phenomenon known as urban blight – depressed spots whose only source of warmth and optimism might be the local pub. Both have their advantages and disadvantages.

An example will illustrate this point. It would seem at first sight that a pub which is situated close to a busy shopping or office area just could not fail. A closer look, though, would reveal a different picture: in this sort of location, the competition can be quite fierce. Other traders are not blind to such potential, hence the rash of cafeterias, pizzerias, burger houses and restaurants. Nowadays, even the large stores have their own

Setting up the operation

restaurants and snack bars. And the difficulties do not end there: there are other factors to consider. Most town-centre pubs are Victorian or Edwardian buildings and, because of modern redevelopment, are now located outside the development area. Their design, too, makes it difficult to see what they are like inside without actually going in, and many people find that this rather off-putting. The modern purpose-built eating places which can be found in the nearby precinct or newly developed area all have large windows which allow easy visual access to potential customers, as well as making the buildings light and airy.

There are areas within a town centre where there is a predominance not of shops and department stores but offices and businesses. In such an area, lunch-time is the busiest time of day, and whilst there is a general trend away from 'fast food', people do like to be served quickly, especially if they have a limited amount of time. In a situation such as this, the modern, purpose-built pizza house or snack bar would have a distinct edge.

Couple all that with the fact that a town or city centre can be almost deserted at night and you can see that things are not quite as straightforward as they may at first have seemed.

All that might seem rather gloomy, but finding the right 'slot' is a prerequisite to any successful catering operation. In certain situations, disadvantages can be spotlighted and then analysed and used to advantage with a little thought and imagination. In town and city centres, for example most of the trade will be done during the day and early evening, so all day opening is an absolute boon. The only thing to decide is how early you wanted to start. If the location is close to a railway or coach station or near a market, breakfasts would be well worth considering, as would morning coffee, lunches, afternoon teas and evening meals. If you wished to simplify things, you could even serve the same menu throughout the day. If all the other catering outlets in the area are doing a booming trade, why not make full use of your premises and do likewise?

Just as modern, purpose-built premises have their advantages, so do pubs but for opposing reasons. Not everyone likes to sit in a shop window while they have a meal or drink a cup of coffee. Modern, open plan piazzas too can be cold and draughty on all but the hottest of days, and we all know how often they occur! This is where town-centre pubs can really score. Many women like to combine their shopping trips with meeting friends. What could be better, then, than going into a pub which has proper loos where they can freshen up comfortably and then settle down in a warm and cosy alcove to a cup of coffee, a spot of lunch and a good old natter?

Even in town and city centres, not everyone wants to bolt down their lunch and fly. Professional people very often have business lunches which can last for two hours or more, other people may have some reason to celebrate, whilse some people like a leisurely pub lunch as a once-a-week treat.

Most people who commute to a large town or city these days do not choose to use their own transport, and those who do, are reluctant to move their cars once they have parked them. The nearest pub which serves good food and is within reasonable walking distance of their place of work would obviously be the place they would head for at lunch-time. Pubs which are close to universities, polytechnics or industrial complexes have similar potential and can choose between catering for students and young workers with juke boxes and cheap, fast food and catering for mature students, lecturers and management with a wider variety of imaginative and healthy food. Again, have a look around, see what markets the other catering outlets in the area are aiming at and if they are all doing fast food for the youngsters, go for the more mature market, kick out the juke box and replace it with some softer, background music, put a menu in the window and generally make sure that the sort of customer you are aiming for is attracted by what you have to offer.

Pubs which are situated in the outer areas of towns and cities but which are not quite in the suburbs, are enjoying something of a revival. As the high-rise horrors of the Sixties are being demolished and replaced by new properties, the old-style communities are beginning to re-emerge, and the pub is resuming its role as a meeting place. This very welcome situation is further strengthened by the growing reluctance of people to drive after drinking. In this type of situation, the main advantage of serving attractive and varied food is that it spreads out the day's trading more evenly and can add a completely new dimension to those pubs which previously have not done any catering. A pub in this type of location, offering a good selection of food at a reasonable price could well find people calling in for lunch instead of going to the 'chippy'. Darts players, too, might decide to have a meal at their local, prior to the weekly darts match. Traditional food would probably be the most successful but with tastes becoming more and more catholic, a daily 'special' could be a real attraction.

Setting up the operation

Suburban

Most suburban pubs have large car parks and, situated as they are on the outskirts of large towns or cities, they have the advantage of being fairly near to the centre but of being unhampered by traffic congestion. They also have the advantage of being surrounded by quite a high density of population. Situated in the more up-market residential areas, they are a favourite for people who wish to have a run out for lunch or an evening meal. People who live close by can very often call in for their evening meal on their way home from work. Working people very often find that it is cheaper and less troublesome to eat in the pub than to prepare a meal at home after a hard day's work.

The potential for a catering operation is so great that many suburban pubs even support a separate restaurant in addition to serving food throughout the rest of the premises. In fact, food can often account for 60 or even 70 per cent of the turnover. The actual location of the pub need not be especially attractive as there are always large groups of people, practically on the doorstep, who are prepared to call in for good or different food.

This is the type of pub which can pin-point different markets and go for them. Morning coffee with croissants or biscuits could be very successful if there was a shopping area or a primary school nearby, with mothers dropping their children and stopping for a chat. Remember, though, that come the school holidays, that trade will disappear. Retired people — and there are more and more of them — can boost the lunch-time trade, as can couples in the evening and families at weekends. The blessing of such a location is that trade does not fluctuate very much and a steady all-year-round trade is the norm, which is a distinct advantage when it comes to planning.

Unless it is close to an office or industrial site, it is true that the suburban pub can lose out on working people popping in for lunch, as a ten-minute car journey each way can make a nonsense of a one hour lunch break. But there are ways round even this sort of problem: menus can be given out and orders can be telephoned in so that there is no wait when the customers arrive.

Semi-rural

A decent-sized pub with a large car park, situated on a busy arterial road, close to a motorway junction and set in beautiful countryside is perhaps the dream of all licensees. Trade could start with good, traditional breakfasts followed by morning coffee with hot croissants. Lunches could be served in the restaurant in addition to light meals in the bar. Afternoon teas could be served while staff prepare for the evening's trade, with dinners in the restaurant and lighter meals in the bar.

This type of pub could be so busy that staff would have to work shifts and the licensees would never have to sweat it out in the kitchen unless there was an emergency. This is the sort of pub which ambitious licensees dream about. Such places do exist, although they are usually brewery-owned, managed houses. Some are superbly run while others belong to the 'oh, what I could do with this place' category, but no matter which category they fall into, they simply cannot fail because of their superb position.

Not quite so lucky are the pubs which are to be found in the larger villages or situated just off the main drag. It is absolutely vital for pubs in this sort of location to get the food absolutely right. Food has got to be the only reason which would compel people to travel some distance to an area which is not that attractive and which, in any case, leads nowhere. If such a pub is to succeed, every effort must be made to capture what potential custom there is. As they do to suburban pubs, retired people will venture out to these pubs at lunchtime, but there will also be 'groups' in the area. By this, we mean housewives who regularly lunch together, teachers from the local schools, staff from health centres and other similar groups who get together on a regular basis over a glass of wine and lunch. Such groups can also go a long way to building up evening trade and are well worth cultivating. It really is amazing just how many groups of people actually exist in areas which are devoid of industry and commerce. Some local authorities publish a list of all the different societies and organisations which operate in their area. Lists such as these are invaluable when it comes to generating new trade.

Offering the pub as a venue for meetings with lunch or coffee is an excellent way of introducing people to the pub. Small industrial concerns and cottage industries are springing up all over the country and one of their features is that they do not have the same facilities as larger organisations. Some pubs have managed to supplement their lunch-time trade by providing a delivery service to small firms which do not have a canteen. This can be done by the firm ringing in a daily order, but a much better way is to negotiate a fixed or minimum price contract to provide lunches for all the staff.

Rural

There was a time when, if you went to the Lake District, the Highlands of Scotland or the Cornish Riviera in winter, you would find them just about deserted. Not so these days; more and more people frequent these places and others like them all the year round. Today, people are much more mobile and many would think nothing of motoring a couple of hundred miles in the course of a day trip. More flexible holiday arrangements have allowed for one or even two, extra holidays per year, and these are usually spent in the United Kingdom. Popular holiday venues are becoming increasingly congested which is forcing people to look further afield. This is obviously good news for the rural pub.

Unlike its suburban or semi-rural counterparts, the rural pub will have seasonal variations as a rule and despite an increased winter trade, most are only ticking over until spring. It is vital then, for the rural pub to cash in on any trade that is available. Afternoon teas, for instance, for so long a feature of Devon and Cornwall, are beginning to catch on elsewhere and are well worth considering. High teas, too, are increasing in popularity as a means of catching the traveller on the way home. Many travellers, and particularly those with young children, do not want to hang around until dinners start but are more than happy to delay their homeward journey if a good meal is available in the late afternoon or early evening.

Rural pubs have a dual function in that they serve as a meeting place for the surrounding community and provide a pleasant diversion for the day or evening tripper who wishes to absorb a little of the rustic atmosphere. Locals will not always want food and may even resent 'their pub' being taken over by 'outsiders', but unless the licensee can afford to run the pub purely for amusement, the wishes of one section of the community will have to be balanced against the needs of the other. To be fair, this can usually be achieved quite amicably, as visitors will provide most of the lunchtime and early evening trade, leaving the dart board free for locals at night. Also, as the increased trade begins to provide part-time or even full-time employment, any initial animosity will quickly diminish.

Although the countryside is a draw in its own right, unless it is an area of outstanding natural beauty, an added incentive is needed as a means to pull in the crowds. This could well be a large country house which is open to the public, an ancient monument such as a ruined castle or abbey, a canal or river or even a successful market garden. Anything which gives large

Setting up the operation

numbers of people a reason for visiting the area will provide the enterprising licensee with much needed spin-off trade.

And now for something completely different!

The seaside and other busy tourist locations.
Strictly speaking, pubs which are located at the seaside or at any other busy, seasonal location such as the English Lakes could be included under one of the four categories mentioned above. The reason why we are mentioning them separately here is because the conditions which prevail in such locations are unique. The vital point is that trade is markedly seasonal and this seasonal factor has a knock-on effect:

- ☐ Lots of extra staff are needed during the season.
- ☐ Those extra staff have to be fired when the season finishes.
- ☐ Because of this constant hiring and firing, staff loyalty can be non-existent which leads to …
- ☐ … a high turnover of staff, which means that…
- ☐ … you are more prone to stock deficiencies, which makes it necessary for you to
- ☐ … stock-take every week or 10 days.

In such a location, all-day opening is obviously a boon as both food and drink can be served non stop from 11 a.m. through to 11 p.m., but to be successful, you need to be aware of visitors' needs. For instance, if your pub was located on Blackpool's famous Golden Mile, there would be little point in providing haute cuisine entrées when the milling throng outside was screaming for cheap, fast food either to eat on the premises or to take away. In such circumstances, a cafeteria-style operation with a take-away counter would be much more appropriate or even essential, as would be the provision of a family room and a beer garden or patio.

What about when the season finishes, though? This is the time when the local residents come out of hiding and it presents an opportunity to run a normal operation. A different, out-of-season food operation could be devised to cater for the different, out-of-season trade. In such a way, the massive drop in trade generally experienced at the end of a season could be lessened.

If the points we have made in this chapter seem a little obvious, it is by way of reinforcing what we pointed out earlier, which is that a detailed analysis must be undertaken before any food operation is set up. If you can think of other points which you think you should look at, fine: include them on your personal research list, because the more information you accumulate, the better.

The pub itself

This chapter concerns the actual pub building and any garden area it has with it, i.e. what you have to work with and how it can be put to the best use.

We have all seen or been to pubs where both the interior and the exterior provoke the thought, 'what a dump!' Places which seem to be at war with themselves due to a total conflict of ideas and misguided concepts. It really is a terrible shame when you consider that a pub is to a licensee what a ship is to her captain. In other words, if it is no good, you go under! Such pubs are not confined to towns and cities by any means; they can present themselves in any of the four different categories of locations discussed earlier and can range from the smallest to the largest. Even pubs which have had quite a bit of money spent on them don't always work out, at least not for any length of time.

Perhaps the main thing to remember is also the most obvious: a pub is a pub. It is not a disco, or a youth club or an amusement arcade and it is certainly not, perish the thought, all three at once. Large pubs, it is true, may have the space to provide a games room or a separate disco or both, but for the smaller pub which is essentially one large room, the inclusion of such facilities could be counterproductive, especially in a catering context.

The exterior

Let us start with the outside of the pub. The exterior, after all, is what people see first. Go outside and stand across the road. Have a good, long look at the exterior and ask yourself these questions:

- ☐ Is the area in front of the premises clean and tidy and free from waste paper, weeds and other unmentionables which customers could bring in on their shoes?
- ☐ Does the building need decorating?
- ☐ Are the windows clean and bright?
- ☐ Are all the exterior lights in good working order?
- ☐ If the building is finished in brick or stone, would it benefit from being cleaned professionally?
- ☐ Are the exterior signs all present and correct or

Setting up the operation

do they need refurbishing or replacing?

☐ Do you like what you see? Does it look warm-hearted and inviting? If it was not your pub, would you want to go in for a meal and something to drink?

If you do not like what you see or you feel that there could be some improvement, *do something about it*. Make a list of the jobs which need doing and include it as a separate section in your project file. This way you will be more likely to remember everything and you can make notes about jobs which have been completed, neglected or left unfinished, as the case may be. Exactly the same method can be applied to the interior.

The interior

Basically the same method can be applied to the interior. But before you can make an assessment of the interior, you will need a plan, preferably up-to-date and to scale. If such a plan is not available to you, get someone to draw one up for you or make one yourself. Once armed with a plan, you will be able to see clearly just what space you have to work with and how it relates to the other facilities. Even if you are already living on the premises, a plan is extremely useful, but if you are simply looking at the premises as a possibility, it is absolutely vital.

The first consideration is to work out how many covers (place settings) you could do and where they would be located. Bums on seats, is after all, the name of the game. Then decide how you might use the different parts of the space available. A pub which is open plan more or less means that the matter has been decided for you, i.e. the same menu would be served throughout the premises.

Many pubs, however, have other, separate rooms which can be put to good use. Family rooms are increasing in popularity these days and can provide valuable extra trade for the enterprising caterer. Parents would, of course, pick what they wanted off the main menu, whilst their children could pick what they wanted from a special children's menu. See Chapter 15 for an outline of the law concerning children in pubs.

If there is a games room where your locals play darts and pool in the evenings, you could encourage them to stay by putting on suppers. People who play darts and pool feel the pangs of hunger just the same as anyone else and experience has shown that a really good Indian-style curry (see page 172) or a shepherd's pie proves impossible for them to resist, especially if it is served later in the evening, say at about 10 p.m. If you were busy, you could even restrict it to that time. Why watch them dash off to the fish and chip shop or to the Chinese take-away? That business could be yours!

If there are other rooms, have a really good think about how productive they are. A decent-sized room which is not used for anything special except perhaps as an overspill area could easily be transformed into a dining room and as such, you could apply for a Supper Hour Certificate (see Chapter 15) and serve alcoholic drinks with table meals all day on Sunday.

Another room could be earmarked for meetings and small functions when required, and again, our experience has shown that such rooms are in great demand by all the different groups, societies and organisations which like to meet in private. Some pubs find that the provision of a meeting or functions room, even though it may be comparatively small, can generate substantial extra income, not just over the bar, but through the provision of meals, buffets, finger buffets, morning coffees and afternoon teas. The possibilities are enormous.

Having decided on a plan of campaign to make maximum use of your premises, the need for coordination cannot be stressed too strongly. A few years ago, a lovely old Edwardian pub near us had an interior 'job' done on it and was described by a retired merchant marine officer of our acquaintance as the nearest thing he had seen to the first-class gents toilets on the QE2! All chrome rails, plastic ferns and mirrors! Quite apart from the fact that the revamp had cost a small fortune, it was patently obvious that the whole idea was totally out of keeping with the building. True, it did have a certain novelty value for about six months, but afterwards it simply flopped. The trick is to realise that all pubs are different, in the way that fingerprints are: there are no two alike and they are peculiarly individual. Any theme which is planned – and a theme can be important, be it Victorian, Modern, Olde Worlde, Edwardian or Romantic, to name but a few – should be in keeping with the building and the food should complement the whole.

Making the most of your premises need not necessarily mean the outlay of vast sums of money for a complete rehash. Provided that the facilities are in order – adequate central heating and toilet facilities, etc. – perhaps the only thing which is needed is redecoration, or perhaps the seating covers need bringing back to their former Edwardian plushness, or maybe that door is a really beautiful door underneath all those coats of chipped paint. In the fullness of time, when funds allow, your attention could be turned to carpets, curtains, pictures and light fittings so that your pub is eventually restored to its original style.

Outside

Moving on, what about the rear of the premises? Is there room for a beer garden or a terrace where your customers can relax over a drink and a bite to eat during the summer months? The provision of outside facilities is increasing in popularity and can double your trading capacity. Don't worry if you do not have a lawn; lawns need cutting, and a nicely paved area will do just as well and is much easier to maintain. In any case, a terrace or a courtyard can be a good deal more effective than a straightforward beer garden and can be more conducive to the sale of really good food.

If you do have a beer garden, you might like to give some consideration to a children's play area if space allows. This would encourage families to stay on fine days, would fit in nicely if you had a children's menu and would be a natural outdoor extension to your family room. The classified advertisements in most of the trade papers and journals abound with equipment which is suitable for a children's play area; but do shop around, as this sort of equipment can be expensive.

The question of what sort of furniture you will need for use outdoors needs a little thought. If the main area is a lawn, normal tables and chairs will sink into the ground. For this reason, the majority of licensees choose wooden tables with integral bench seats. Even these have their drawbacks, though, as they have to be maintained on a regular basis or they will rot. They are also fairly expensive to buy and are difficult to keep clean and to store. We got round this problem by creating several flagged areas in the lawn, rather like islands, and chose PVC tables and stacker chairs, which are a dream to keep clean and are easily stored during the winter months. They are versatile, too, in that they would be equally at home on a terrace or in a courtyard and they can be moved around with ease because they are so light.

If you are to achieve a degree of success with your outdoor area, it is not sufficient simply to provide tables and chairs. The area has to be attractive, otherwise, people will not bother to use the facility. If you don't really care about it, why should they? Borders and flower beds can easily be planted with attractive flowers and shrubs, and courtyards and terraces can be transformed by the imaginative use of tubs or gaps in the paving which you can plant up with the trees, shrubs and flowers of your choice. Try also to include some kitchen herbs such as rosemary, sage, thyme and hyssop: they have beautiful flowers, their perfume is a delight and you can use them in the kitchen. Herbs can be used on a barbecue to provide a tantalising flavour and aroma as well as that really professional touch. The question of barbecues is fully dealt with in Chapter 6 but for the purpose of this chapter, suffice to say that a professionally run barbecue can make a great deal of profit, so it would be wise to include one in your plans. Having gone to the expense and effort of creating an outdoor facility, why not fill it to capacity?

3 Choosing the menu

As we have seen in the previous chapters, market research is an essential factor when planning a pub catering operation. As much information as possible should be gathered in before any attempt is made to choose the actual menu. Chapter 2 deals in full with all the points which need to be considered and gives advice on how to collate all the information in the form of a projection.

Of course, we all know of catering operations which work the other way round. These are more often than not brewery 'themed' pubs where a set menu is chosen, after which, location, premises and decor are selected to match. As a rule, they belong to the 'in this spot, you simply cannot fail' category and are run by very experienced managers. Even if they do fail – and surprisingly some of them do – there is sufficient capital available to alter either the 'theme' or the operation to ensure that they do succeed. Most licensees are not so fortunate and must spend their limited capital wisely.

To begin, let us first consider the size of the menu, i.e. the number of different items on offer. If you read through the 'guides', you will notice that one point which is continually stressed is that they are more impressed by a limited menu of high quality than by an extensive menu offering indifferent food. This view has not been arrived at by chance: a menu which is too large and fragmented can actually create the problems which lead to a decline in standards and profitability:

- ☐ Higher staffing levels are needed and staff cost money.
- ☐ It actually takes longer to get food out to the customer due to the greater diversity of items being prepared. This in turn leads to customer dissatisfaction.
- ☐ There is more wastage.
- ☐ There is a greater risk of health hazards due to a slower turn-over on certain items.
- ☐ There can be too much pressure on limited equipment.
- ☐ Unless you are very experienced, too extensive a menu can result in too much pressure being placed on you and your staff.
- ☐ More equipment is needed, not just for the actual cooking but for preparation and storage too.
- ☐ Shopping expeditions can become lengthy and expensive.
- ☐ More and more capital is tied up in stock.

There was a time when food in pubs could be split into two distinct categories: the posher places, which were more like a restaurant than a pub and the rest, which offered very low-key bar snacks. Thankfully, these days, that division is becoming less distinct as more and more licensees are discovering that good and imaginative food can dramatically increase their turnover.

Today, provided of course that the market is there, pubs can serve whatever type of food in whatever manner they choose, due to the fact that customers' tastes have become far more wide-ranging. Even so, it is important for those who are new to catering, to learn to walk before they set off at a gallop. Start with a small but attractive menu to ensure that you do not overtax your equipment and yourself. Increase the choice gradually as your confidence and expertise grow.

Let us look, then, at the different basic types of foodstuffs which we have at our disposal:

- ☐ **Meat** Beef, lamb and pork.
- ☐ **Fish** Sea fish and freshwater fish.
- ☐ **Poultry** Chicken, turkey and duck or duckling.
- ☐ **Game** Venison, partridge, grouse, hare, rabbit, pheasant and the like.
- ☐ **Offal** Liver, heart, kidney, tripe and so on.
- ☐ **Dairy produce** Cheese, eggs, cream, milk and yogurt.
- ☐ **Butchers' produce** Sausages, puddings, brawn and potted meat.
- ☐ **Vegetables** A massive range of vegetables is available nowadays from all over the world.
- ☐ **Salad stuffs** Again, a truly impressive range of salad stuffs is available all the year round.
- ☐ **Fruit** Apples, oranges, lemons, pears, grapefruit, peaches, apricots, avocados, mangoes, grapefruit, figs, plums, nectarines, greengages and many, many more are freely available.
- ☐ **Dry goods** Flour, rice, peas, beans, lentils, barley, oats, corn, pasta and so on.

Basically, only you can decide what you are going to offer your customers, and hopefully, you should base your decision on the results of your market research and your own ability. You should also bear in mind some other considerations which need to be taken into account.

Balance A menu which consists solely of red meat dishes is not balanced. Even a small menu should ideally be made up of a variety of different foodstuffs:

- ☐ One red meat dish.
- ☐ One poultry dish.
- ☐ One fish dish.
- ☐ One salad.
- ☐ One vegetarian dish.

Choosing the menu

Colour on the plate is vital. Visual appeal is part and parcel of the joy of eating good food. A plate of poached halibut served with boiled potatoes, cauliflower, parsnips and braised celery might be extremely nourishing but, as far as visual appeal is concerned, it is a total whitewash. Bear this in mind when you go shopping.

Variety Even with a small menu which consists of only four or five different items, it is possible to provide variety and so expand it slightly. For instance, if the fish you have chosen for your fish dish happens to be salmon, you could consider the following:

- ☐ Gravlax as a delicious and unusual starter.
- ☐ For main courses, you could offer Russian-style Fish Pie and Salmon Salad.
- ☐ Off-cuts and bits could be made into salmon pâté.

You can see that what started out possibly as poached salmon steaks developed into an interesting selection and solved the wastage problem before it even occurred!

Individuality Your own trade mark or that extra something which makes the operation uniquely yours is vital if you wish to attract custom and make your business grow. In due course, you will achieve this in your own way, but here are some ideas to start you off:

- ☐ Make sure that what you offer is the best. If you decide to put a T-bone steak on the menu, for instance, make sure that it is a real whopper, the biggest in the area. Who wants a small T-bone steak anyway?
- ☐ Presentation, i.e. colour and layout on the plate, are to the caterer what a finished canvas is to the artist.
- ☐ Regional dishes or local specialities can be a real winner especially as most restaurants are inclined to disregard them as they do not fit their image. We have found them to be really good sellers. You can easily find out local dishes from the library or the local history society.
- ☐ Health food is another possibility and one which is currently very trendy.
- ☐ Ethnic food can be interesting, exciting, colourful and delicious. Ethnic food recipes are not secret and you have the whole globe to try! Why not give it a spin?
- ☐ Do remember that chips and peas are not the only things which can accompany a meal. Make

use of all the vegetables as they become available and consider cooking them to a recipe. Try ringing the changes with potatoes too: O'Brien Potatoes, Lyonnaise Potatoes and Bakery-style Potatoes (see pages 178–179) are well worth considering. Pasta, noodles and rice can also be used to great effect. Rice is now available precooked to different recipes and frozen in individual portions and needs only a minute or so in the microwave.

- ☐ Make full use of your own skills and those of your staff. For instance, if you are a dab hand at making beautiful and authentic curries, make them for the pub. Similarly, if you or a member of your staff can make fabulous sweets and puddings, it would be ridiculous to buy them in just so that you have the time to prepare other items which you do less well.

Basically, when choosing a menu, the choice you have to make is between snacks or meals on the one hand and between cold or hot food on the other. The reality, however, might well be a combination of all four.

If, in the course of your research, you have discovered that the lunch-time trade is completely different from that in the evening, there may be a case for offering, say, a set lunch-time menu but à la carte in the evening. Alternatively, you might think that snacks would fit the bill at lunch-time whereas more substantial food is needed in the evening. In our pub, we have just the one menu but find that customers prefer lighter food at lunch-time. Because of this, we have extended our range of starters so that they can also be served on their own as snacks.

When planning the menu, the workload too should be spread evenly, not only between the different items of equipment but also between the staff. It totally defeats the object of the exercise if you have plenty of waiting on staff but only one harassed cook or chef. Again, it is a question of getting the right balance.

We know that, as far as menus go, the pundits tell us that small is beautiful, but customers do, nevertheless, like choice. Additional choice can be provided by the inclusion of a daily 'special' or by frequently changing a small menu. The trouble with choice is that no matter how much of it you provide, there will always be someone who wants something other than what is on offer. Unfortunately, there are times when you simply have to say no. We have found over the years that these little 'asides' or distractions can create more problems than they are worth. Typical problem areas are sandwiches, omelettes and children's portions other than those which are on the menu. The reason why these are problem areas is not because we are ratty or unconcerned but because someone has to stop what they are doing to get them out and this causes a delay in the serving of items from the main menu.

It is this very same reason which often causes us to feel guilty when one of the staff or an interested customer suggests that we include a particular dish on the menu and we have to turn them down. It may be perfect in the home and absolutely delicious but impossible to get out during a busy session. They may argue that it only takes 5 minutes to cook, but during a hectic session, a dish which requires the undivided attention of a cook for even 5 minutes can create a snarl up. Just think what would happen if you got five of such orders in a row!

Those of you who have been in the trade for some time, will be only too conscious of the fact that even the most carefully planned menu and food operation will have problems from time to time. We had one such occasion on a Tuesday lunch-time in February. The weather was foul, and on top of our normal trade, two or three large parties turned up, all at the same time, all unannounced and all on their lunch hour. The result was absolute chaos and we are still twitching!

Healthy eating

Surely no-one can have failed to notice the trend towards more healthy eating habits which is being promoted by both official bodies and public opinion. It should be welcomed by the pub caterer as it presents us with an ideal opportunity to increase the range of food that can be offered. Healthy food is no longer the sort of thing that is peculiar to cranks and oddballs as it used to be in days gone by. People from all walks of life are demanding healthier food and their numbers are increasing at a tremendous rate. Healthy food is here to stay and it is big business.

The problem is that, to many members of the public, pubs conjure up an image of fast, greasy and stodgy food, largely because that is the sort of food which most pubs have been serving. It is up to the licensees to change that image and move with the times. In order to achieve this, it is necessary to understand about healthy food and a well-balanced diet, and to help us, the government-backed 'look after your heart' and 'look after yourself' campaigns have conveniently produced a

Choosing the menu

Look after your HEART!

inexpensive. Dried beans, peas and other pulses, which have also increased in popularity, but are nearly as rich in protein as meat, and are an excellent source of B vitamins and iron. As such, their high nutritional value makes them an obvious choice for many vegetarian recipes.

One outcome of this popular trend towards healthy eating, is a growing awareness that far too much meat is being eaten and that vegetarian food is not just for vegetarians. The type of meat which we should all regulate our consumption of is red meat, which is high in saturated fat; fish and poultry are not. Even so, a growing number of people are reducing the amount of meat they eat, so it makes good sense for the pub caterer to provide a selection of good, tasty and imaginative vegetarian food.

wide selection of free, informative and interesting leaflets. Copies can be obtained from the Health Education Authority or the British Heart Foundation (see Useful addresses, page 37) or from your local health education unit (District Health Authority).

The use of natural foods in cooking has enjoyed a great revival over the last few years so that now we hear and see the terms 'wholefood' and 'natural food' every day, but what do they mean? The terms 'wholefood' and 'natural food' mean foods which are virtually unprocessed and do not contain any artificial colourings, flavourings or preservatives. These foods retain their natural flavour and most of their nutrients. Wholefoods are preferably eaten raw or very lightly cooked so as to preserve their valuable vitamin and mineral content.

Nutritionally, whole grains are an ideal source of many of our dietary requirements such as proteins, carbohydrates, oils, vitamins, minerals and fibre. The grain starches are broken down during the process of digestion to form glucose, which provides a constant supply of energy to the body. The fibre in whole grains provides the intestine with essential roughage. Vegetables and fruit also contain fibre but it differs from that which is contained in cereals. The two should provide a healthy and well-balanced diet without any need for supplementary vitamin pills.

Natural foods such as wholewheat bread and flour products, whole grains, pure honey, fresh fruit, fresh vegetables, fresh salads, dried fruit, nuts and natural yogurt are increasingly available and are now relatively

Vegetables and salads

It is possible to make pub menus more healthy very simply and without any need for drastic restructuring. For instance, why not serve fresh vegetables instead of frozen ones? The main complaint levelled against fresh vegetables is that they take too long to prepare and that time, after all, is money. This problem is largely a thing of the past as there are now many suppliers who provide ready-prepared, fresh vegetables. These usually arrive vacuum-packed and prepared in any way you want. The cost is about the same as frozen vegetables and wastage is cut to an absolute minimum. Any uncooked vegetables which have not been used up can be added to soups and casseroles. The range on offer is quite extensive but it is wise to remember that vegetables which are out of season are usually more expensive. It is said that vacuum-packed vegetables are not quite as valuable nutritionally as their freshly prepared counterparts because vegetables do begin to lose some of their nutrients as soon as they are peeled or cut into. This is only marginal, however, and as these firms deliver on a daily basis, it is only a relatively minor consideration.

As farming methods improve and the world becomes effectively smaller, more and more is imported into the country, not just from Europe but from all around the world. The effect that this has on the range of vegetables, salad stuffs and fruit is truly amazing. More than ever before, caterers can make use of different colours, shapes and flavours not only to make their food more interesting but also to give it their individual stamp.

So why not take advantage of all this to make salads more interesting, appetising and delicious? Lettuce, for instance, comes in many colours, shapes and flavours these days, so use them to good advantage. Red, green, yellow and white capsicums, or peppers as they are more commonly known, are now available, and are a useful addition to all sorts of salads. Surely nothing can be more depressing than the piece of limp green lettuce, wedge of tomato, slices of cucumber curling at the edges and the ailing egg which for generations have masqueraded as a salad in this country. It is small wonder that people grew to hate salad. With only a modicum of care and imagination a salad can be so different. Why not try slivers of raw mushroom, slices of crisp apple, celery, your own home-made potato salad and a sprinkling of fresh herbs to liven things up? None of these things adds much to the overall cost – and, even if they did, the price could justifiably be increased a little – but they go a long way to making a salad a joy to look at and a delight to eat.

Pulses and grains

Pulses (the edible dried seeds from podded plants) are, from the health point of view, the perfect food: they are high in fibre, full of protein and carbohydrates, vitamins and minerals and, best of all, they contain no fat. On their own, it has to be said, they can be a rather tasteless, but they can be used to make many interesting and delicious dishes, if cooked with almost any herbs and spices. A word of warning, though: pulses do have something of a reputation for causing what we must politely call flatulence, but this phenomenon can be greatly reduced by throwing away the water in which they were soaked and any cooking liquor which produces a surface scum. The inclusion of some of the 'digestive' spices such as asafoetida, ginger and caraway, which are known for their treatment of colic, will also help.

One point to note is that certain pulses, such as red kidney beans, are toxic in their raw state and so, after soaking, they need fast boiling for at least 10 minutes. Instead of trying to memorise which have this toxic quality and which do not, it is probably better to assume that this rule applies to them all.

Messy and time-consuming are just two of the complaints levelled against pulses and it is true that they do need to be soaked overnight (although soaking time is greatly reduced by the use of boiling water) and they do take longer to cook than many foods. But even chick-peas, which take the longest, are ready in 1 to 2 hours. Of course, the use of a pressure cooker greatly reduces the cooking time anyway.

An advantage of pulses and grains for the caterer is that they provide inexpensive bulk as well as being healthy and versatile. The addition of split peas, lentils, barley or beans to a soup will transform it into a nourishing and sustaining broth. Similarly, added to a casserole, not only will they create interest and flavour but they will also make the more expensive meats go further.

Be careful where you buy your pulses: some of the smaller or poorer shops may sell pulses and grains which have not been properly screened. This is not a problem if you are aware of it and have the time to do the sifting and cleaning personally but, either way, it has

Choosing the menu

to be done at some stage. Apart from small stones which can easily damage teeth if chewed, pulses which have not been properly screened can sometimes contain grain weevils and such like. We had one such problem ourselves when, after purchasing some pine kernels, we discovered that they were infested with tiny weevils. Unfortunately for us, we made the discovery too late as the little blighters had gone forth and multiplied, infesting the rest of our stock. We were forced to destroy all our pulses, grains and nuts and enlist the services of a well-known pest control agency just to be on the safe side. All that, as you can imagine, cost us several hundred pounds. To be fair, that was some time ago. These days, imported pulses and grains are continually scrutinised so you can be pretty sure that any such goods marketed by well-known firms will be of high quality and cleanlinesss.

Grains include rice, which must be one of the most useful foods available. Even in its white form it supplies plenty of nourishment, although brown rice, which contains the whole grain, is much healthier. The more nutty flavour of brown rice is not universally popular but as tastes change, more and more people are eating it. For the pub caterer, brown rice has advantages; it is more filling than white rice and so portions may be justifiably reduced. It does require more water and a longer cooking time, but another advantage, is that even if accidentally overcooked, the grains usually remain separate. Precooked wholegrain rice is available frozen, in both large bags and individual portions and may be microwaved to order from frozen in a matter of seconds. This cuts down on wastage and cooking time dramatically and we think that brown rice lends itself more to this method of cooking than its white counterpart.

Burghul (also known as cracked wheat, bulgar or pourgouri) is already partially cooked when purchased and so needs very little preparation. Popular throughout the Middle East, it makes a welcome change from rice and it could not be easier to prepare. We have included recipes for burghul and for the larger-grained wholewheat in Chapter 16.

Couscous is an exotic-sounding name for a type of semolina that is used throughout North Africa and is usually cooked in the steam of the stew with which it is served. Coarse-ground semolina is also the main ingredient of halva, a delicious pudding with honey, nuts and fruit which bears no resemblance to the tired semolina pudding of our school days. Do try these things: you will find the recipes simple to follow and the ingredients easy to obtain. If you like very spicy food, it is worth noting that Middle Eastern food, while nourishing and healthy, can sometimes be rather bland but unless absolute authenticity is required, the flavour can easily be adjusted by the careful addition of herbs and spices.

Fats

We hear so much about fats these days that it can be a little confusing, to say the least. Everyone needs some fats: in adddition to providing a concentrated source of energy (hence their high calorie rating), they also assist in transporting the fat-soluble vitamins around the body. Fats take longer to digest than other foods and so delay the onset of hunger after a meal. One reason for the complaint that Chinese food leaves you hungry two hours after you have eaten it is that it is low in fat and so is digested quickly. We have all heard by now of the controversy of saturated versus unsaturated, fats but few people know so much about the detail. As more and more people are becoming more and more conscious of the need for a healthy diet, it is essential for pub caterers to understand the matter more fully.

Choosing the menu

The main difference between saturated and unsaturated fats lies in their chemical structure, which we do not need to concern ourselves with at this stage. What we do have to look at, though, is the effect they have on the human body and here cholesterol must be introduced. Cholesterol is a fat-like substance which is produced naturally in our bodies and although it is essential to our well-being, we do not need to eat any to stay healthy. On the contrary, if we have too much cholesterol in our bloodstream, it may lead to the build-up of fatty deposits in arteries. These deposits restrict the blood supply to the heart and can, in turn, lead to a heart attack. Consistently high levels of cholesterol in the food that we eat can lead to increased blood pressure and all its ills. However, this level of cholesterol is based not so much on the amount of fat that we eat, so much as the type. Foods which contain saturated fats can increase the blood cholesterol level.

Saturated fats are hard fats. This is an easy, although not foolproof way to differentiate between the two. Saturated fats include animal fats such as butter, lard, dripping, meat and are contained in eggs. Hard cheese, full-fat cream cheese, hard margarines which remain solid at room temperature, cream and full-cream milk are also high in saturated fats.

Olive oil, groundnut oil and the like are described as mono-unsaturated fats and are often pointed out as being one of the reasons for the lower incidence of heart disease in the Mediterranean and other areas, where they are the main source of fats. Polyunsaturates are so soft that they will not solidify even when refrigerated. These are the other oils and soft margarines such as sunflower oil and margarines made from sunflower oil. Invisible sources of polyunsaturates are most nuts, with the exception of coconuts and cashews. While the debate continues, one thing to bear in mind is that *all* fats are high in calories. Armed with this knowledge, it is a good idea to cut down on the total fat content of meals offered to our customers and, where fats are used, the mono-unsaturates and polyunsaturates are preferable.

Potatoes

There was a time, not so long ago, when the humble potato was the Cinderella of the nutritionist's world but fortunately, fairy godmother arrived in the guise of progress and rescued it. Potatoes, skins left on please, are an excellent source of vitamins, roughage and energy-giving carbohydrate. If it is necessary to peel them at all, it is better to do so as thinly as possible as many of the nutrients lie just under the skin.

Ask your merchant about the various types of potatoes – there are many – and what they are most suited for. The Potato Marketing Board are most helpful and have prepared a number of free leaflets concerning potato types, suppliers, advice on cooking methods, recipes and so on. Potatoes are now marketed not only by type but by size as well, so even in winter, small boiled potatoes in their jackets can be served as a facsimile of new ones and very tasty they are too. Also, try smaller jacket potatoes instead of large ones as a replacement for chips, with a blob of good thick yoghurt, they are delicious and are a healthier alternative. Another tip is that if nice crispy skins are called for, why not start them off in the oven to crisp off the skin and then finish them in the microwave. That way there is a saving on time and valuable space.

Bread

Over the past few years, the quality and variety of bread available has improved no end. Wholemeal bread, which is the best, contains vitamins B, C and E in addition to calcium, iron and lots of dietary fibre. In itself, bread, like potatoes, is not fattening, although it is filling, and the more tasty the bread is, the better it complements a plain salad or cottage cheese filling.

Nothing draws customers in like the smell of freshly baked bread and it is not as time-consuming to bake your own as you might imagine. In Chapter 16 you will find a recipe for Irish Soda Bread which can be made with skimmed milk, buttermilk or, as we make it, with yogurt. It is made from wholemeal flour and it contains virtually no fat. This leads us nicely on to flour.

Flours

Basically, the main nutritional difference between flours is in their dietary fibre content:
- ☐ Wholemeal or wholewheat flours are made from the whole of the wheat grain.
- ☐ Brown flours have some of the bran and germ removed.
- ☐ White flours consist almost entirely of the starch endosperm of the grain; in other words, they have had just about all the goodness taken out.

Choosing the menu

Check what a flour contains by looking at the panel on the side of the package. If you are buying in large quantities, ask your supplier, who will have all the information.

Wholemeal pastry is not difficult to make and is well worth experimenting with. It would be a pity not to make use of the wide range of flours now available as they are quite easy to obtain. There are proprietary brands of wholemeal puff and shortcrust pastry on the market now and some of them are quite good. The Flour Advisory Bureau (see Useful addresses, page 37) produces a selection of leaflets explaining all about the different types of flours and breads and how the caterer may maximise their use. Some of their recipes and tips can be found in Chapter 16.

Salt

Everyone needs some salt, but The Health Education Authority (see Useful addresses, page 37) recommends that people do not need more than 1 gramme (1 g) per day. This means that so long as you eat a good variety of food, you will get all the salt you need without adding extra and so reduce the risk of high blood pressure. Obviously, no-one would dream of insisting that our customers refrain from adding salt to their food once it has reached the table. But it is sensible to reduce the amount of salt used in the actual preparation of food. The Lancashire dialect word 'wallah' is used to describe food that is bland and tasteless. A popular misconception is reducing the salt used in cooking automatically makes the food become 'wallah'. Nothing could be further from the truth, and the addition of herbs, spices, lemon juice or mustard, to name but a few, will flavour food in a much more healthy and subtle way. Vegetables cooked in a microwave or steamer do not need any added salt at all, as the cooking method ensures that the natural salts are to a large extent retained and therefore sufficient.

Proprietary brands of stock usually contain monosodium glutamate or (MSG) for short. MSG is high in salt so do try to make your own stock – it tastes better any way. Many tinned and most packet soups also have a high salt content, so if you are using them, try adding some fresh, unsalted vegetables or pulses to offset the effect, or again, better still, make your own. It will not take as long as you think and if you are short of ideas, look at the Recipes section.

There are now many salt substitutes on the market but they all contain sodium chloride. Sea salt, which is supposed to be more healthy, does contain traces of minerals that ordinary salt does not, it is true, but it is basically the same old salt. Low sodium salts are high in potassium and we do not yet know what excessive potassium can do to the human body so, as with fats, the best advice is to be on the safe side and cut down on all salts.

Cooking methods

One way you can provide more healthy food is by changing some of the methods of cooking. Fats, as stated earlier, are probably the most unhealthy factor in a pub catering menu. Deep frying allows the food to absorb a high quantity of fat (especially in the case of crinkle-cut chips) so when you do fry, drain off as much of the fat as possible.

Dishes such as moussaka are always confined to the NO sections of diet books because the aubergines are fried in oil as part of their preparation. They absorb a tremendous amount. One quick tip to reduce the amount of oil that aubergines and courgettes absorb during frying is; after salting them for 30 minutes or so, wash them thoroughly and dry off as much as possible, then put them in the microwave on medium power for about 1 minute before adding them to the oil. You will be amazed at the difference it makes: the absorption rate is reduced by half.

Alternative methods of cooking are available. Many of the batters which coat the proprietary brands of fish are now suitable for oven baking; as are some of the crumb coatings. You can also buy a range of convenience foods with a wholemeal crumb coating. If these are not readily available in your area, it is quite a simple task to make your own.

Oven and microwave chips are now on the market and although they do not taste quite the same as deep-fried chips, their flavour this will no doubt improve in time as did their counterpart, frozen chips. There is an oven that uses a forced air convection system to cook oven chips and they do taste rather good cooked in this way. It can be used to cook anything that is prepared with an oven batter or, in the case of oven chips, with an oil coating. It will be interesting to see how the concept develops. However, one sideline of the 'healthy eating' trend is the emergence of customers who now regard chips as a treat: they no longer eat them at home!

Choosing the menu

If you wish to seal meat prior to casseroling, use very little oil and reduce the heat; this way you will, in effect, sweat the meat in its own juice rather than saute it. The end result will not alter the flavour very much, but it will reduce the fat content. We seal chicken joints and chops by grilling them prior to casseroling. Try wherever possible to skim the fat off gravy or juices, but be aware that there is a health risk in repeatedly cooling food down and then reheating it. A good tip is to throw a handful of ice cubes on to the surface of the liquid causing the fat to cling to the ice which can then be easily lifted out. This method will not remove all of the fat but it is particularly successful with fatty meats such as lamb and pork. Remember, though, to ensure that the food is thoroughly reheated after any cooling.

Thickening gravies, sauces and soups can also present a problem as it it all too easy to whack in the cream and egg yolks, but again, there are healthier alternatives. These alternatives are not new by any means and in the north of England are probably used with more frequency than in other parts. The use of cow heel and pig's trotters for thickening stews and casseroles is a method which has been successful for many generations and produces a really tasty and satisfying result. For soups, the addition of pulses and grains, especially barley, results in a lovely creamy texture for only a fraction of the price of cream and eggs. Finally, when thickening sauces, why not try simply reducing them over a fast flame, stirring as you go?

Healthy alternatives

As stated above, cream has a very high fat content, so these days we think twice before adding it to dishes. If cream is essential, we choose one with the lowest fat content possible and even then use it sparingly. British dairy produce shows the fat content in terms of grams (g) of fat per 100 ml, whereas imported European dairy products show it as a percentage. Confusing, isn't it? Don't rush to the conversion tables; simply regard them all as a straight percentage and you will not be far wrong. For example, double cream has 47 grams of fat per 100 ml or roughly 47%; single cream has 19.3 g per 100 ml or roughly 20%; whipping cream has 37.8 g per 100 ml so say 40%. This way, even if the conversion is not strictly accurate, it becomes apparent immediately that cream is high in fat and consequently high in calories. So before reaching for the cream to make a sauce for meat, fish or vegetables, think first about using the cooking juices just as they are or reduced to a simple glaze. This can be done by fast boiling until the liquor becomes thicker and slightly shiny, and the flavour becomes more concentrated, but don't forget to skim the fat off first.

There was a time when yogurt was offered as the universal alternative to cream but yogurt can be difficult to work with. The problem is that yogurt needs to be stabilised before it is used in cooking or it will separate. Stabilisation can be achieved in a number of ways such as mixing it beforehand with a little cornflour, potato flour or egg, but even then, it can easily curdle. Perhaps the surest way is to add it to the dish at the last minute and not allow it to come to the boil. Another disadvantage is that not all dishes lend themselves to the rather sharp taste of yogurt, which can mask flavours even more than cream. Even so, yogurt should not be discounted. It has a very low fat content in comparison to cream: and even the most thick and creamy Greek-style yogurt has only a 10% fat content and the fat content of the low-fat yogurts is minimal.

Instead of looking at yogurt as a compromise, consider using it in its own right. Greek-style yogurt or other thick yogurts which can be obtained from the many Asian or health food shops as well as supermarkets, have a rich and creamy texture and a flavour which is delicious with hot and cold puddings. This type of yogurt can be used with cold vegetables as a starter or made into dips which can be used instead of mayonnaise. Similarly, a blob added to jacket potatoes not only complements the flavour but is also much healthier than butter. The simple addition of fresh fruit or honey will make an interesting and inexpensive pudding. We use a blob of yogurt to top servings of goulash and certain curries, where, liberally sprinkled with chopped herbs or nuts, it not only adds to the flavour but also looks attractive. The thinner type of yogurt, watered down, will also add extra flavour to scones and soda bread.

There is no real substitute for proper mayonnaise which is notoriously high in calories, but there are proprietary brands available on the market which are calorie-reduced. The flavour, is not the same, but if you are using it as a base with other ingredients or using it in cooking, this does not matter too much.

Microwaves and steamers (see Chapter 10) cook fresh vegetables very quickly, retaining their colour and crispness and a lot of their nutrients. Prolonged soaking and cooking destroy the vitamin content of vegetables, so it is a pointless waste to leave large pans of vegetables simmering away endlessly. Fresh vegetables should be served only lightly cooked and with some of their crunchiness still left – 'al dente', as the Italians say – and not with all the goodness and texture boiled out of them. To do this, we use smaller pans, with a back-up continually ready during busy sessions. You may get the odd complaint about the vegetables not being cooked enough, but these days most people prefer their vegetables crisp, fresh and only lightly cooked.

In the bar, you will no doubt be offering low calorie-drinks, so why not offer low-calorie dressings too? There is no need to buy large quantities and if you have no room to display them, the serving staff can always mention that these alternatives are available. As an extension to this, we always keep a few dispensers of artificial sweeteners for customers who are cutting out sugar.

One final alternative which we find sells well is decaffeinated coffee. You can buy the instant variety but we have found that customers seem to prefer the one-cup filter. These are easy to serve and there is no wastage whatsoever.

Marketing

There is a temptation to change over completely to health foods but this would be a mistake unless you were absolutely sure that a sufficient market exists. It is a much more realistic idea to ease health foods into the existing menu gradually until a stage is reached where a satisfactory balance of choice is achieved. However, it is prudent to keep customers informed: wherever an item is oven-baked, as opposed to fried for instance, or something is suitable for slimmers, say so on the menu; it is not a secret and you will probably sell even more. One proven successful method of achieving this is to symbolise low-fat or particularly healthy dishes by placing a red heart symbol next to them. If this is done, however, it is vital to get it right – there must be no cheating. Just as vegetarians do not want meat stock in an allegedly vegetarian dish, so people who have to watch their diet for health reasons do not want something there that should not be. It is unprofessional to cheat and can be very dangerous! Bear in mind that there are many people these days who have restricted diets, so make sure that staff whose duty it is to take orders are fully briefed as to the ingredients of the dishes offered on the menu. Someone with an allergy to white flour needs to know whether dishes contain white flour. A reply of, 'oh, I don't think so' to their query could result in serious illness, whereas a positive and truthful answer accompanied by constructive advice will go a long way to ensuring that that customer returns.

As the public becomes more and more interested in healthy eating, it makes sound economic sense to provide as much healthy food as the market will stand. In this respect, the pub caterer has the advantage over the restaurateur because in the more relaxed atmosphere of a pub, customers are not as stifled by protocol and it is therefore much easier to talk to them and promote a particular item. Remember, the healthier your customers are, the longer you will have them!

Herbs and spices

There is a tremendous amount of renewed interest in herbs and spices which has been brought about largely by increased foreign travel. This, in turn, has caused the media to focus on the culinary art from all corners of the globe so that articles and documentaries on foreign and spicy food have become commonplace.

The Industrial Revolution and two successive World Wars had the combined effect of reducing British cooking to a bland, uninteresting version of its former self. This was compounded by the growing need for wives and mothers to go out to work, with the result that meals became merely an interruption rather than the focal point of the day. Herbs and spices were quick to disappear and the urge was to get meals over with as quickly as possible. The result was a whole generation brought up on stodgy, uninteresting food, the most exciting thing on the dinner table being the bottle of brown sauce or ketchup.

It was not always like that, as any student of medieval cookery will confirm. The range and quantity of herbs and spices used in days gone by was truly phenomenal and, along with the rest of Europe, the British had for centuries cherished a love of tasty, spicy food. The British Empire and in particular the Raj in India helped to keep this interest alive. Since those times, it is only recently, with this revival of interest and the growth of ethnic shops, that herbs and spices have become readily available once more. The old tale that herbs and spices were used only to mask the taste of rotten meat may have had some credibility in the past, but any cook worth his salt will tell you that herbs and spices, when properly used, will bring out the flavour of the food rather than mask it.

There is also a growing awareness of herbs and spices with regard to healthy eating as more and more people are avoiding the purchase of foodstuffs which contain liberal quantities of artificial additives and preservatives. Monosodium glutamate (MSG) is a prime example: sometimes referred to as 'flavour enhancer' – a misnomer if ever there was one – its taste is unmistakably chemical and leaves a nasty bitterness in the mouth. It can also make some people very ill indeed. Why ruin good food with artificial additives?

Modern factory farming methods have done much to increase the quantity of produce available but have served only to impair the flavour of much of our food. As the general public become more concerned about the quality of the food they eat, they are also looking for more natural ways of bringing out the food's full flavour, and that is precisely where herbs and spices come in. They are both HEALTHY and NATURAL, two words to keep in mind!

Herbs

For most people, a fully stocked, formal herb garden is something which is seen only in the gardens of stately homes, in books or on television. This is the case with most caterers too, as they scarcely have the time to look after one. There are ways, though, of easily acquiring all the herbs that you could possibly need.

Fresh herbs, it must be said, are undoubtedly better and much more delicate in flavour than their dried counterparts, which can be a little on the harsh side. Mercifully, there are now many herb farms which specialise in supplying to the catering trade and their fresh herbs can be purchased directly by post or through normal trade outlets. One thing to beware of, though, is that certain herbs, when out of season – in winter, for example – although available, can be *very expensive*.

For those who are not used to using herbs and wish to do a little experimenting, most fruit and vegetable wholesalers carry a range of fresh herbs, as do the larger supermarkets such as Sainsbury's and Asda. They usually stock all the more common varieties, but do make sure before buying them that they are fresh. Any signs of limpness or browning indicate that they are past their best and that their flavour will be impaired.

If you have a spare patch of garden, it is well worth considering planting a few herbs, especially those which you are likely to use most frequently. Many herbs are extremely decorative and are well worth growing for that reason alone. They can also be very fragrant on a balmy summers evening so they really are a winner all round. If incorporated into a beer garden, you will be amazed at the interest they create. Ecologically they are very sound too, as butterflies and bees adore them.

If no space is available in the garden, don't worry, herbs can be grown just as successfully in tubs or window-boxes, and with so many excellent books on herbs now available, their cultivation should not pose any problem either. The main thing to remember is that most herbs which are used for culinary purposes hail from sunny climes and, as a result, grow best in well-drained soil in a sunny and sheltered position. With one or two notable exceptions, they do not like to grow with their roots in waterlogged ground and, indeed, in winter, when that moisture turns to ice, it will surely kill them.

Having decided to grow some herbs for the kitchen but without wishing to go to extremes and create a fully stocked and formal herb garden, which herbs should you grow? Probably the most worthwhile are mint, thyme, sage, basil and rosemary, but you might also consider chives, parsley and tarragon.

Listed below are the herbs we feel are the most useful. The recipes in Chapter 16 use some more ideas for herbs in cooking.

Mint

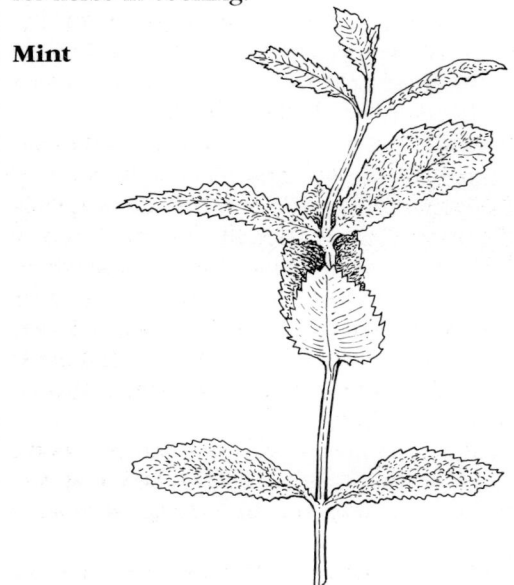

Mint is a must for your herb garden. We find that apple mint produces the best flavour. As with any other type of mint, it is a good idea to grow it in a container of some sort, even though that container may be sunk into the ground, as left to its own devices, it will quickly spread out of control. We grow ours in a large tub which doubles as the kitchen door stop. This does have certain disadvantages as it is always being knocked over and, being so handy for use, it has been mercilessly hacked down but still it survives. Only the winter frosts seem to kill it off but the first sign of spring produces a mass of new shoots. Unlike most other herbs, mint does not relish strong sunlight and a well-drained soil but prefers moisture and some shade so it is ideal for that corner of the garden where nothing else will grow happily.

Cooking hints Most people will be familiar with the ubiquitous mint sauce which is generally served with roast lamb, but if wine is to be drunk with the meal, the vinegar-based sauce and the wine do not go well together. It is far kinder to the palate and the lamb to use mint jelly or to fill any crevices in the lamb with a generous helping of freshly chopped mint leaves. Alternatively, a mixture of chopped mint, breadcrumbs and the zest and juice of a lemon could be put to the same use. Another method is to make a paste of finely chopped mint, honey and lemon juice which you then spread all over the lamb before cooking. This method imparts a delicious flavour and at the same time counteracts the fattiness of the meat, to say nothing of the wonderful gravy it makes!

Many root vegetables also benefit from the addition of a little mint. Most people will no doubt be familiar with minted new or boiled potatoes – and most delicious they are too – but have probably never considered trying the addition of a little chopped fresh mint to other root vegetables such as carrots and turnips. Garden peas, too, can be given a lift by the addition of a sprig or two of mint in the pan when they are being cooked.

The uses that mint can be put to are almost endless as it is an extremely versatile herb. For instance, added to a blend of finely chopped cucumber, onion and yogurt and served as a dip with fingers of hot toast or pitta bread, it immediately conjures up thoughts of the Middle East; added to a straightforward Hollandaise sauce, it adds a completely new dimension to a trusted old friend.

Thyme

Thyme is a small sturdy, ground-hugging, evergreen. It is very easy to grow, it is quite decorative and there are many varieties. Originating from the Mediterranean area, it revels in full sun and a well-drained soil, which makes it ideal for rockeries and the tops of walls, but grown in a pot or trailing over the side of a window-box, it will thrive just as well.

Cooking hints: Common thyme is one of the main ingredients of a bouquet garni which will be familiar to most people, and a bunch of thyme will add flavour to most soups and casseroles, but do use it with caution or you may find the flavour overpowering. Lemon thyme has a lighter flavour and is a little more astringent. Used in sauces and even in baked custard, it can impart a somewhat fruity flavour. Be particularly careful when using dried thyme as the flavour is very strong.

Sage

Sage is a rather leggy sort of plant which, when allowed to do so, develops into a small bush. It is therefore not really suitable for planting in window-boxes but it can be grown in a decent-size tub. The best place for sage is a sunny and sheltered, well-drained border where it will burgeon with masses of new growth. It needs renewing every 3 years or so as it becomes rather woody with age, but this is no problem. Cuttings taken from the parent plant in late summer will strike easily and when these are established, the old plant can be dug out.

Cooking hints: One of the claims of the French is that the British – but more likely the English in particular – only know of one herb and that herb is sage. It is true that sage and onion stuffing is a traditional accompaniment to goose, chicken and turkey, but there is nothing wrong with tradition. In many ways, sage is a much-maligned herb but it probably got its reputation from people who did not know how to use it properly. One of its main properties is that it will counteract the fat content of rich meat, but in order to do so, it must be used fresh. Its generic name, *Salvia,* means to save or heal, and although the herb will do more good than harm to the body, its culinary use can do more harm than good to food in the hands of an incautious cook.

Basil

Basil is known as the king of herbs and with some justification. The word basil comes from the Greek word meaning king and its uses are almost limitless. It does, however, have one major drawback for anyone wishing to grow it: it is extremely tender and delicate and not at all easy to grow in colder and wetter climates such as ours and the slightest whiff of frost will kill it.

Basil is not merely a sun lover, it is a sun worshipper, and will thrive in a spot which receives the full glare of the sun from morning until night, providing that spot is sheltered from wind and is so well drained that any water merely passes the roots on its way to somewhere else. Even on really hot summer days, Basil likes to be watered at its roots at midday so that there is no chance of any moisture staying for any length of time. If there is no such spot in the garden, large pots, small tubs or even window-boxes will do.

All this might seem to be a tall order and not worth the trouble, but your own basil, freshly picked, is streets ahead of any you can buy and the saving on cost is phenomenal.

Do give it a try, but make sure that the seeds or small plants which you purchase are those of sweet basil. The other variety, bush basil, is not, as its name implies, a bush, it is a small and insignificant plant and you would need acres of it to provide you with a sufficient quantity.

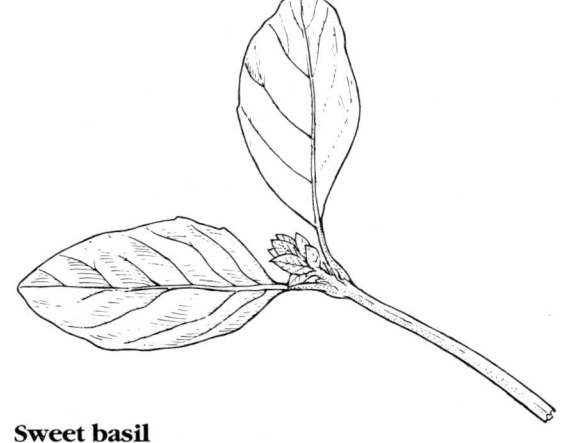

Sweet basil

If you wish to have a supply of fresh basil all the year round, you will have to keep some pots indoors on a sunny windowsill. This is a good idea anyway, as basil is very fragrant and discourages flies. Alternatively, you could use dried, but we find that dried basil is harsh and bitter in comparison to fresh.

Cooking hints: The uses of basil are almost limitless, although it is perhaps somewhat delicate in flavour for the heavier stews or casseroles. We use it in pâtés and dishes which do not require prolonged cooking.

Without a doubt, though, basil is at its absolute best when it has not been cooked at all, and the fresh, young leaves, roughly chopped, can be sprinkled liberally on to salads and fish. Lighter meats also benefit greatly from its delicate flavour.

One point to bear in mind is that basil has a reputation for being a solo performer so be careful if you are thinking of mixing it with other herbs as it might not turn out as you thought.

Rosemary

Rosemary, unlike basil, is a herb which is easy to grow. Like the other Mediterranean herbs, it prefers full sun and a well-drained soil. It is an asset in any garden and gives an interesting spiky quality to a sunny border; it blooms quite well and is extremely fragrant when touched or brushed against. It is for this last reason that some people like to grow a shrub of rosemary in a tub by the door: when anyone brushes past, the fragrance follows them.

Cooking hints: Rosemary has a strong and distinctive flavour whether fresh or dried. Probably the best and most familiar use for rosemary is with lamb, but it can be used equally well with fish or beef and makes a perfect stuffing with veal. Used sparingly and with discretion, it imparts a delicious aroma.

The only tiresome quality about rosemary is that, when used in sprigs – for example, laid on the top of a leg of lamb for roasting – the individual leaves or needles do come away from the stalk and invade the rest of the dish. This can be easily overcome by placing the sprigs in a piece of muslin or cheesecloth so that they can be removed after cooking.

Bay leaves

Dried bay leaves are a standard ingredient of bouquets garni and are useful in casseroles and stews. For a stronger flavour, you may like to try the powdered variety, but remember that a little goes a long way, so do not buy too much at once.

In the milder areas of the country, bay trees will grow successfully outside, and a small one in a tub or half barrel would look most attractive on a pub terrace.

Chives

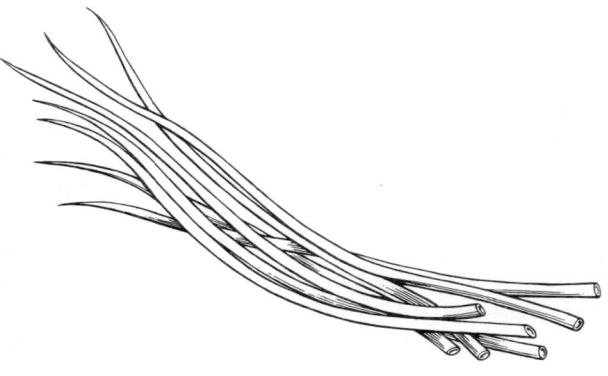

Chives have a delicate onion flavour which is largely destroyed in cooking. They are therefore more effectively used as a garnish or added to sauces after they have cooled somewhat. They do not dry or freeze especially well, although both may now be purchased. If you really cannot grow your own, a better substitute would be the freshly chopped leaves of scallions, or spring onions as they are better known.

Choosing the menu

Coriander

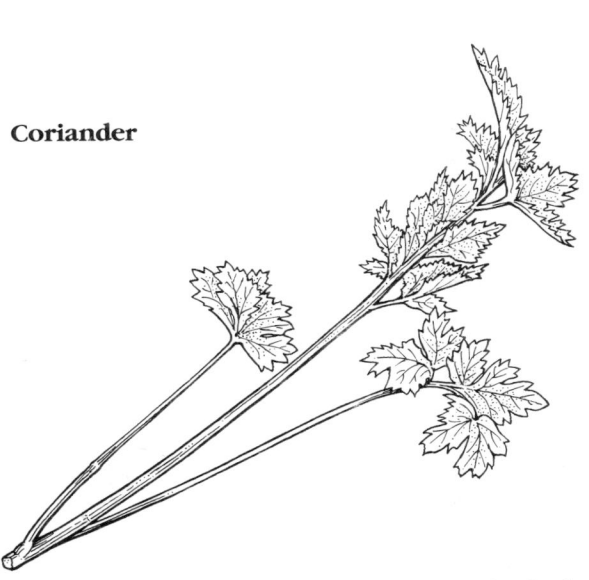

The leaves of the coriander plant are the herb. As a herb, coriander can only be used fresh, but as it is readily and cheaply available from Asian shops and now from many supermarkets, this is not a problem. It also grows well in this country. Fresh, it is used in Greek and Arabic salads, soups and many Middle Eastern dishes as well as in Indian food.

Oregano

To think of oregano is to think of Italy and the Mediterranean, where it is widely used in soups, stews and casseroles to which it imparts its unique flavour and aroma. It is good either fresh or dried but, remember, the dried is more pungent, so go easy. Oregano is the wild relative of the more cultivated marjoram and either may be used as a substitute for the other, although marjoram has a more delicate flavour.

Parsley

There are several types of parsley but, for cooking, the flat-leaved variety is undoubtedly the best, so do try and grow some. Fresh, it can be used generously in sauces, vegetable soups and as a garnish. It loses most of its flavour when dried but can now be purchased frozen, which is better but still no substitute for fresh.

Tarragon

It is vitally important to remember that there are two varieties of tarragon, French and Russian. French tarragon is known as the queen of herbs and is delightfully fragrant, whereas its Russian counterpart is coarse and bitter. Recently, we noticed pots of dried tarragon for sale at a much lower price than normal but a close examination revealed that it was the Russian variety and therefore useless except as an addition to the compost heap, so do watch out. As tarragon loses much of its delicacy when dried, we make our own tarragon vinegar when the fresh is in season. The way to do this is simply to insert a clean, fresh sprig of tarragon into a bottle of good quality wine vinegar. It will take a few weeks to infuse but it will last throughout the winter and can be used in stews, casseroles and sauces, which benefit greatly from the bite of the wine vinegar and the flavour of the tarragon.

Tarragon

Garlic

The one herb which invokes the most emotion is garlic, but strictly speaking it is not a herb at all, it is a vegetable. It is included in most herb books because, like herbs, it is used as an ingredient in dishes rather than served on its own.

Garlic

Garlic is imported in large quantities from the Continent but the finest quality and flavour comes from garlic which is grown in this country.

Garlic has been known for centuries for its medicinal and culinary qualities and is by no means as 'foreign' as some people would have us believe. Although used as the antithesis of everything that is 'not British', the stereotype of the Italian or Frenchman exuding garlic-smelling breath may well have got the wrong nationality. One has only to look at some of the old recipes to be astounded at the quantities of garlic which were used in this country – and not so long ago either. In one of our grandmother's recipes for chutney, one of the ingredients is twelve HEADS of garlic, enough to dismay even the most ardent of continental garlic lovers! Mrs Beaton was also not averse to slipping the odd clove or six of garlic into her dishes, so if any of your customers complain about the inclusion of 'foreign muck' in their food, you may justifiably claim that garlic is part of our national heritage before offering them a sprig of fresh parsley to kill the smell. All herbs have their uses!

Storing and preserving herbs

Fresh herbs do have a rather limited life expectancy once they have been picked, which is a good enough reason in itself for growing some in the garden so that way you can pick only sufficient for your immediate needs. Fresh herbs which have been bought, however, are fairly expensive and so it is worth trying to keep them in prime condition. Wastage costs money. They should be stored in airtight containers in a cool rather than refrigerated place. Even growing herbs are affected by the weather and the leaves which are left on during the winter do not have the same flavour.

You can also freeze herbs and we find that one of the best ways is to chop them up while they are in prime condition, stuff them into the compartments of ice cube trays, top up with water and freeze them. When frozen, turn them out into clearly labelled containers which are stored in the freezer and repeat the process until you have enough stocks to last you until the fresh herbs are in season again. With basil, there is no need even to do that: simply wrap the freshly picked leaves in a little cling film and freeze them as quickly as possible.

The best known way of preserving herbs is to dry them but it does alter their pungency and finesse. Sage and thyme dry particularly well: tied in bunches and hung up or spread on a tray, they can be dried very successfully in a warm, dark and well-ventilated place. However, the wide array of dried herbs available these days eliminates the necessity of having to do this yourself unless you particularly wanted to.

Spices

Just as herbs are the leaves of plants with certain properties, spices are obtained usually from seeds, bark or roots; in the case of saffron, it is the stamens which are the essential bit. A plant such as coriander yields both the herb and the spice: the leaves are the herb and the seeds are the spice. Purists insist that the only really effective way to use spices is to grind your own. These days, it is true that it is a simple task to grind your own spices with the help of an electric grinder, but in a busy kitchen with limited staff, even that small task might be an unwelcome nuisance. It is far easier to use ready-ground spices which are now available in catering-size packs at most good cash and carry warehouses.

Many of the spices which are popular today are, in fact, mixtures or compounds of several spices. Every corner of the world has its own peculiar mixture or blend of spices and this applies not only to the exotic Far East and the Orient but also to the West, where traditional spice mixtures have been popular for centuries. A good example of this is one of the most popular dishes we serve, namely, Beef in a Fine Sauce (see page 170) which was formerly known as Boeuf en

Peverade and has been a great favourite in the North of England since the twelfth century.

The range of spices available is seemingly endless and a good spice merchant's catalogue reads like some wild and exotic incantation.

Below is a list of the spices which we use most frequently.

White peppercorns, Chilli peppers and Black peppercorns

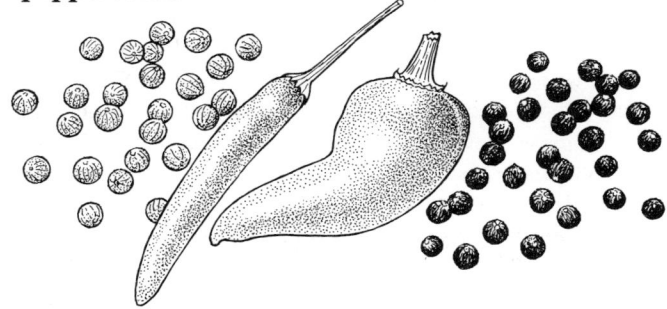

Pepper is, of course, a spice and is universally used by all cooks. What some of those cooks may not know, however, is that both black and white pepper are component parts of the same berry, which has a white interior and a black outer casing. The white interior is the portion of the berry which provides most of the heat, while the black outer casing provides most of the flavour and aroma. Freshly ground whole black peppercorns provide the best of both worlds but some recipes stipulate that only black or white should be used, so it is best to stock both.

As a matter of interest, pepper, in days gone by, was not only highly prized but also highly expensive and that is the reason why today, in poorer countries, chilli peppers are used as a substitute. Pepper is used in every conceivable way: whole or crushed for classic French dishes such as steak au poivre, fresh green peppercorns in sauces for lighter meats, and the newer pink peppercorns to enhance fish dishes. How many of you have realised that pepper is even included in the mixed spice you use in puddings?

Chilli powder consists of dried ground chilli peppers, the hot member of the capsicum (pepper) family. Chilli can add a delicious spiciness to food, though it should be used with caution! Much of the heat of fresh chillies is in the seeds, and to lessen their fire you may want to remove them: cut the chillies open under running water and take out the seeds, being careful not to let the acid juice get into contact with your eyes, or it will sting.

Caraway seeds

Caraway seeds are normally associated with sweets – our village of Goosnargh is the home of the famous Goosnargh cake which contains caraway seeds – but at the Bushell's Arms we also use caraway seeds in goulash and in other stews such as veal or pork. Used sparingly, they produce a beautiful flavour.

Coriander

As a spice, coriander seeds are usually purchased dried and ground and are widely used in Indian, Greek and Middle Eastern cooking. Please do note that the difference in flavours between the fresh (the leaves) and the dried (the seeds) is such that one cannot be substituted for the other. The two are completely different. However, some recipes do call for both the herb and the spice.

Ginger

Fresh root ginger is readily available and is an essential ingredient of many Indian, Chinese and Far Eastern dishes. It does not keep terribly well, so buy it only in small quantities as and when you need it. Ground ginger is said to be an acceptable substitute but in our experience it can be somewhat bitter and because of this we are inclined to use it only in emergencies. Crystallised stem ginger is used to flavour puddings, sweetmeats and ice creams.

Nutmeg and mace

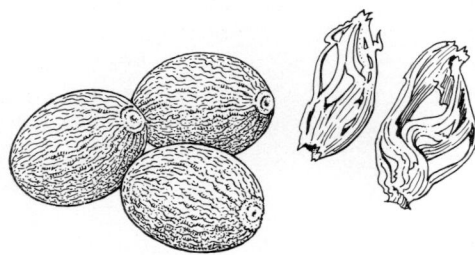

Nutmeg is the seed of the fruit of the nutmeg tree and the reddish waxy outer covering of this seed is mace. The two have a similar flavour but mace is sweeter and stronger and so more suited to stews and casseroles, whereas nutmeg is more at home with soups and various sauces such as béchamel, mornay, onion and bread.

Turmeric root

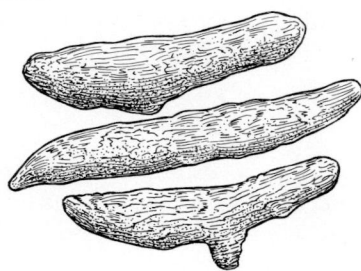

Turmeric is best known for the way it colours a dish bright yellow but as it also has a strong, woody aroma and a distinctive pungent flavour, it should not be used as a cheap substitute for saffron. Fresh turmeric is now readily available and when grated can be added to Indonesian, Indian and Middle Eastern food. Dried turmeric powder, although good, is inclined to be somewhat bitter on the palate, so do be careful to use the flavour and not the colour as your guide. When used correctly, it imparts a delicious and distinctive creamy flavour.

Spice mixtures

Many of the most popular spices seem to be found among the spice mixtures, with Madras Curry Powder – again, you can mix your own if you have the time and inclination – heading the list, 'hotly' followed by mixed spice with Indian garam masala and tandoori mixture in 'hot pursuit'! Garam masala is a curious mixture as it is not often used on its own, most Indian recipes include it as a spice which is added towards the end of the cooking process to revitalise the spices which have been cooking for some time.

Where to buy dried herbs and spices

If you feel inclined to increase your range, stock and knowledge of spices, a visit to one of the ethnic shops, which are to be found in most major towns and cities, is to be recommended. These places are a veritable Aladdin's cave of culinary treasure and you will be made to feel most welcome. We have found the range of herbs, spices, pulses, fruit, vegetables and aromatics which these small shops carry to be truly amazing and the shopkeepers, when approached, are most helpful in explaining the various uses and, as you get to know them better, recipes using them too. Another advantage is the price factor: it is much more economical to buy spices from an ethnic shop than it is to buy the same thing in small jars from a supermarket. It is more practical, too, for the pub caterer as there is a good choice of package size.

Most good cash and carry outlets these days stock spices and dried herbs, usually in either large bags or polypots (Noels) or caterpots (Millstone). They are usually about 0.5 kg (1 lb) in weight, although the quantity can vary according to the type of spice or herb as some are much heavier than others. The main advantages of this type of pot are that they are less expensive by volume than the small supermarket jars, they are sealed with foil to keep the freshness in and the moisture out, and the containers are usually slightly opaque which helps to prevent discoloration from ultra-violet light. We have also found them to be superior in quality to small packets or jars, although these can have a use if you simply wish to do a little experimenting.

Books

The number of books on the market which deal with herbs and spices is legion. One of our favourites, *Herbs with Everything* by Sheila Howarth, is sadly now out of print but the reprinting of Elizabeth David's books will probably include *Spices, Salt and Aromatics in the English Kitchen*. It is an easy read, as Elizabeth David fans will know, and our well-thumbed copy testifies to to the quality and variety of the recipes it contains.

Unless you are particularly interested in the subject, try not to choose a book which contains too much information. Some books on herbs are more like encyclopedias and contain chapter after chapter on the history, cultivation and preservation of herbs. Such works are clearly of no use if you have neither the space nor the inclination to grow and preserve all your own herbs. For the pub caterer who simply wants guidelines on the use of herbs and spices, the leaflets available from suppliers will list all the products available and give information as to their use.

However, at the end of the day, no matter how many books you amass on the subject, there is no substitute for trial and error. Be guided by your own senses of taste and smell and, above all else, do experiment. Set aside a small portion from one of your normal recipes: that way, if things go wrong, the mistake will not be too costly. Alternatively, you could try a special dish for your family and friends. We find that enlisting the opinion of our regular customers is most beneficial as it promotes discussion and the clamour for forks helps to promote the fact not only that we serve food but also that we make it ourselves on the premises. Customers like to feel that their opinion counts and their tastes are being catered for. We are never reluctant to provide recipes or fresh herbs from the garden for any of our customers who want them. It is an inexpensive form of advertising and one which, we feel, links us inextricably with good food and hospitality.

Useful addresses

The British Heart Foundation, 102 Gloucester Place, London W1.

Potato Marketing Board, 50 Hans Crescent, Knightsbridge, London SW1X 0NB.

Flour Advisory Bureau, 21 Arlington Street, London SW1A 1RN.

The Health Education Authority, Hamilton House, Mabledon Place, London WC1 9TX.

4 Catering for vegetarians

What is a vegetarian? The *Oxford English Dictionary* defines a vegetarian as 'one who lives wholly or principally upon vegetable foods; especially one who abstains from animal food obtained by the direct destruction of life'. Vegetarians are not all the same – for example, some will eat eggs and some will not and so on – but basically their principles are identical and it is just that some are stricter than others.

Vegetarians do not eat meat, fish, poultry or any slaughterhouse by-products. Dairy products and free-range eggs may be eaten but cheese offered to a vegetarian should not contain animal-derived rennet. Such cheese is readily available from catering suppliers, supermarkets and wholefood shops. We buy ours direct from the dairy which makes it. Some vegetarians, identified collectively as vegans, will not consume any animal products whatsoever so, in addition to the above, they will also refuse to eat butter, cream, eggs, yogurt, cheese and honey.

Fact: Vegetarianism is growing and shows every sign of continuing to to do so. Today, millions of people have chosen a totally vegetarian way of life and thousands more have drastically cut down their consumption of meat products. Why should people do this? The reasons are varied and powerful and licensees should be aware of them even though they may not subscribe to them themselves.

To vegetarians, probably the most powerful of such reasons is that the killing of living creatures is unacceptable, no matter how humanely it is supposed to be carried out. To their critics they would say 'go to a slaughterhouse and see for yourself'. Vegetarians also argue that meat is not cheap and that, quite apart from considerations of cruelty, the production of meat makes poor economic sense. They back this up by pointing out that over half the world's cereal harvest is fed to livestock being reared for slaughter and that it takes 4.5 kg (10 lb) of grain to yield less than 0.5 kg (1 lb) of intensively reared beef. This, they say, is a shameful waste of resources. A third reason is that the consumption of meat and animal by-products is now suspected to be linked to many of the diseases which plague western society.

Vegetarians are not cranks but deeply caring and thinking people who like to lead full and happy lives. In pursuit of this, they quite naturally like to dine out from time to time, and pubs should be able to provide them with something more interesting than a ploughman's lunch or an omelette. This can be achieved quite easily but before we see exactly how, let's first get clear what vegetarians do not want in their food:

- ☐ NO animal flesh (meat, fowl, fish or shellfish).
- ☐ NO meat or bone stock (in soups, sauces or other dishes)
- ☐ NO animal fats (suet, lard, dripping, ordinary white cooking fat or margarine which contains fish oil) in pastry, frying, greasing tins or other cooking.
- ☐ NO gelatine, aspic, block jelly or jelly crystals for glazing, moulding or other cooking. Agar agar is a suitable alternative.
- ☐ NO other products with ingredients derived from slaughter-house by-products, e.g. cheese made with animal-derived rennet.
- ☐ Vegan food must not be fried in oil that has been used for animal, fish, seafood or eggs and separate serving utensils must be used at all times.

To clarify some uncertainties in vegetarian cookery, the following kinds of food *are* acceptable:

- ☐ **Butter** is made from milk fat and so is acceptable to most vegetarians. However, as it is high in saturated fat, most people would prefer to use a vegetable oil margarine.
- ☐ **Cheese** is acceptable provided that it is not made with animal rennet, an enzyme which is extracted from the stomach of a calf. As stated above, cheese which is free from animal rennet is readily available nowadays.
- ☐ **Cream** is fine but if you are in the habit of buying whey cream, it is important to remember that whey cream is a by-product of cheese; and if that cheese has been made with the help of animal rennet, then the whey cream is not acceptable. We purchase all our cream and cheese from a dairy which does not use animal rennet in its cheese-making process, so both are fine for vegetarians.
- ☐ **Eggs** are acceptable to most vegetarians but, because of the conditions imposed on battery hens, vegetarians will eat only free-range eggs, so when you are out shopping, insist on free-range eggs as a matter of course.
- ☐ **Fats and oils** Solid vegetable fat and vegetable oil are used by vegetarians instead of suet, lard, fish oil or tallow, so why not use them all the time as a matter of course.
- ☐ **Gravies and stock** Proper vegetable stock cubes or yeast extract are acceptable, but cubes

or powders which contain meat, chicken or fish extract are not.

☐ **Milk** Milk is acceptable and may be used freely.

For those who have little or no experience of vegetarians or vegetarian cooking, all this might seem to be too much trouble, but let us assure you right away that it is no trouble at all. The trick is to buy only products which are acceptable to vegetarians and to remember also that vegetarians like to eat healthy food. The two classic examples of this which spring immediately to mind are cheese and eggs: only buy cheese which is free from animal rennet and only buy eggs which are free-range. Another good example is cooking fat: why purchase lard and suet when there are so many vegetable oils and fats available to choose from? Customers who are not vegetarians will not mind in the least and they will be eating healthier food as a result.

By purchasing in this way, it becomes almost effortless to provide food which is acceptable to vegetarians and which could add a new dimension to your menu. Here at the Bushell's Arms we have a special section on the menu for vegetarians but inadvertently, by employing the principles outlined above, we have found that several of the other items on the menu are now suitable for vegetarian consumption. For us, this has been good news as our non-vegetarian customers eat these dishes anyway, simply because they like them, and our vegetarian customers, delighted with the wider choice, are telling their friends.

Perhaps the easiest way to cater for the wide spectrum of vegetarianism is to take special care in describing the flesh-free dishes on the menu, and detailing the ingredients carefully so that the customer can see if it meets their particular dietary requirements. Do not forget to mention if a dish is egg-washed or contains eggs, as vegans will not touch any animal product whatsoever.

Why not ensure that the daily soup is flesh-free? That way, you can offer at least one hot dish suitable for vegetarians. Over the year we offer more than a hundred different varieties of soup, the great majority of which are vegetable soups. This is not because we have tried to make it so, but simply because there are more varieties of vegetables than there are of meat. Add to this the fact that vegetables are a good deal cheaper than meat and the whole thing begins to make sound economic sense. One cautionary note, though: there is no point whatsoever in making a perfectly good vegetable soup with animal stock, so if you are in the habit of making packet soups, check to ensure that they

And of course, all our vegetables are free range....

do not contain any animal stock. Better still, make your own soup, then you will know exactly what's in it and it will work out far cheaper anyway.

Garlic mushrooms and Middle-Eastern dips such as hummus and tzatziki make interesting starters and can be used as accompaniments to vegetable samosas or spring rolls or to fill avocados.

If you serve pizzas, make sure you have one with a vegetable-only topping. If you make a good curry sauce, save a little and add vegetables and pulses to it. There is no need to make a lot. Try a little and see how it sells. Make smaller or individual vegetable flans to cut down on wastage, and remember that all these items will freeze.

So there you have several examples of main courses which can be adapted for consumption by vegetarians without going to a lot of trouble. Of course, if you did wish to cook something especially for vegetarians, the Vegetarian Society (see Useful addresses, below) would be only too pleased to help and advise.

That brings us nicely to puddings, sweets or desserts call them what you will. There are very few things in the sweet line which vegetarians will not eat. Notable exceptions are sweets and puddings which contain animal suet such as mincemeat, steamed puddings and pastries, and sweets containing jelly or gelatine. But, as stated above, it is easy enough to make these things without the use of such products.

Food wholesalers and catering suppliers have also realised that there is a growing market for vegetarian food and are offering an ever-increasing range. Items such as vegetarian schnitzels, spinach and mushroom lasagne and vegetable chilli are now commonplace on their price lists, giving the pub caterer an opportunity to provide authentic vegetarian food without any effort whatsoever (although many of these dishes are not suitable for vegans). Some suppliers have even taken the trouble to submit their products to the Vegetarian Society for their seal of approval so that caterers can be assured that they are totally free of animal products.

One thing that must be said and that cannot be stressed enough is that it is very, very important NOT TO CHEAT. If any item on the menu does not meet vegetarian standards, it must NOT be offered as a vegetarian item. Quite apart from anything else, a vegetarian would be deeply offended if duped into eating something which is patently not acceptable to vegetarians. For a professional caterer, to cheat in such a fashion would be totally unethical and could well contravene the provisions of the Trades Descriptions Act. If you buy proprietary brands, of, say puff pastry and are not sure of the type of fat used, ask your suppliers: they have all the information relating to the products they supply and we have always found them most helpful. If they do not know immediately, they will find out.

Caterers who provide genuine vegetarian food and who have had their menu and food cleared by the Vegetarian Society will be entitled to display the Society's promotional sticker. It is worth contacting them because you may also find yourselves included in their guide to eating places.

Additional help may be obtained from the Vegetarian Society who run residential diploma courses leading up to a Cordon Vert certificate at their headquarters near Manchester. The London centre also runs one-day cookery courses at the Kensington address. The Society is also organising courses with several breweries for their tenants and managers. These courses are well worth attending if you get the opportunity. Also available from the Society are copies of recipes and useful hints for any caterers who wish to include vegetarian items on their menu.

Useful addresses

The Vegetarian Society (UK) Ltd, Parkdale, Dunham Road, Altrincham, Cheshire WA14 4QG.

The Vegetarian Society, The Vegetarian Centre, 53 Marloes Road, Kensington, London W8 6LA.

The Vegan Society, 33–35, George Street, Oxford OX1 2AY.

5 Convenience foods

Convenience food can be defined as food which has been partially or wholly prepared in advance of purchase and which is packagaed ready for use when required. Of all the terms used in the catering industry, few can be less complementary than 'convenience food', unless of course you include phrases such as 'bar snacks', 'pub grub' and 'house wine'. Phrases such as these have become synonymous with poor quality and lack of imagination.

When convenience food as we know it first came on to the market, the quality was poor, to say the least, and it is probably this which has stuck in the minds of the general public. Today, though, the convenience food industry is a multi-billion-pounds-per-year concern, so those same people who wrinkle their noses at the very thought must be buying it in vast quantities. Double standards must be at work. If you were to ask a top-notch restaurateur if he used convenience foods, he would probably turn a delicate shade of purple and say, 'certainly not'. Ask the same person if he used canned tomato purée, self-raising flour, freeze-dried herbs and bottled jams or pickles and the answer would, in all probability, be 'yes'.

The idea and use of convenience foods in any case, are by no means new: drying, salting and pickling are methods of preserving and storing food which have been in use for many hundreds of years. Even the revered Mrs Beaton devoted great sections of her books to salting, pickling and preserving food in a convenient form so that it could be used later.

Let us consider, then, the positive aspects of convenience food:
- ☐ It is available all the year round.
- ☐ Wastage is cut to a minimum: if you don't use the food immediately, it doesn't go off.
- ☐ In the case of ready-prepared meals, portion control and costing are done for you.
- ☐ You save on the cost of preparation time.
- ☐ You do not need the services of an experienced or specialised cook.
- ☐ You can offer a wider choice to your customers. Lines available from suppliers are now so diverse that you can choose almost any dish you like.
- ☐ It can give you the time and opportunity to create new dishes of your own.
- ☐ If you have a children's section on your menu, convenience food is almost a necessity. Children after all, love fish fingers, baked beans and the like, and very nourishing and tasty they are too.
- ☐ Consistent quality.

Obviously, then, these are powerful and realistic points in favour of convenience food. Convenience food has, come on apace in recent years and to a large extent this improvement is due to stores such as Marks & Spencer who pioneered the retail sales of high-quality, ready-prepared food. We use stores like Marks & Spencer and Sainsbury's as a convenient guide to market trends. What they are selling today is a good indication of market tastes and the innovative caterer can use this information to keep one step ahead.

Nowadays, due to modern technology, just about all types of food can be marketed as convenience foods. They can be split into three main categories: frozen, tinned/bottled and packaged. Let us deal with them in turn.

Frozen food

Now very big business, frozen food covers the whole range from chopped herbs to complete meals. There are two basic types of frozen food:

Frozen raw food This category includes foodstuffs such as meat, fish, poultry, vegetables, fruit and pastry, etc., which are ready-prepared and frozen in their raw state. Such foodstuffs are available both in bulk and in ready-portioned-out packages.

Frozen pre-cooked food This category includes complete meals and both multi-portioned and single-portion starters, main courses and puddings. These foodstuffs do not need cooking but merely bringing up to a safe temperature. (See Chapter 11, Public health and hygiene).

With any frozen food it is imperative that you follow the instructions on the packaging and remember that frozen food must never be refrozen after it has thawed.

Canned/bottled food

Once again, just about any kind of food can now be bought in cans or bottles. It is worth remembering that most of it is already cooked so care must be taken not to overcook the contents when reheating. If not all the contents of a tin are only part used, the remainder can be transferred to another container (not left in the can) and kept in the refrigerator, where it will keep for the same length of time as freshly prepared food.

Packaged food

This third category relates really to all the different convenience foodstuffs which do not fall into the two previous categories. They come under a variety of headings:

Dried food This heading includes all powders which are available in sachets, packets, drums, cans and jars. Typical products in this category are powdered milk, mousses, sauces, seasonings, gravies, potatoes, pasta, curry powder and many, many more.

Freeze-dried food This is more properly known as 'accelerated freeze dried' food. Food which has been dried by this method contains no moisture whatsoever and as a result is much lighter in weight. Typical freeze-dried products are potatoes, vegetables, herbs, fruit, soups, curries, stews, paella and so on.

Cooked meats All the different kinds of meat are available ready-cooked. They come in whole joints or in portions and can be sliced or unsliced. They are usually vacuum-packed and chilled. Continental-style sausages come under this heading.

Locally produced food In every area there are local bakeries which specialise in producing fresh sweets, bread and savouries for pubs and other outlets. Most deliver on a daily basis and some will even make up special dishes, for example a vegetarian flan using wholemeal pastry or dishes such as lasagne with your requirements for garlic and herbs. One small point to remember is that such dishes cannot be described as 'home-made'; freshly made, however, is acceptable.

Preparing your own convenience foods

Not all ready prepared foods have to be bought in. There are many that you can prepare yourself by employing cook/freeze, cook/chill or *sous vide* methods. In Chapter 11 and in the section dealing with refrigeration in Chapter 10, we will look at the storage requirements for keeping food at low temperatures. These deal mostly, though, with freezing and chilling comparatively small quantities of prepared food for short periods. Such methods are not to be confused with the cook/freeze, cook/chill operations employed by the larger industrial or commercial caterers. To mount such an operation; you would need specialised equipment such as blast freezers which take no longer than 90 minutes to freeze food to -20°C and blast chillers which cool food down to 3°C or lower in the same time. If you have sufficient turnover and are considering mounting such an operation, specialist advice is available from the Environmental Health Office or the equipment suppliers.

Sous vide, which we mentioned earlier, is a French term which literally means 'under vacuum'. It is a method of vacuum-packing raw food, cooking it in a pressureless steamer and then chilling it down to 3°C or lower within 90 minutes, after which it is then stored at that same low temperature. As it is quite a new concept, there are virtually no guidelines available from agencies such as the Department of Health. One fact which has emerged, though, is that in order, to operate a satisfactory *sous vide* operation, the most stringent standards of hygiene are required. Just imagine what would happen if you were to vacuum-pack bacteria along with the food!

Various equipment dealers offer packages which amount to little more than a vacuum machine, a good fridge and a microwave which would enable you to process certain types of food in this manner with a shelf-life of up to three weeks. To us, these packages seem to be a recipe for disaster. Having said that, it does not mean that the *sous vide* concept is not worth considering, because it is. What we are suggesting is that, before you commit yourself, you should find out as much as you can about the system. There are suppliers who can supply suitable equipment which conforms to the existing hygiene requirements but be wary of those who offer a 'bargain' for the small caterer or you could end up with more than you bargained for.

Convenience foods in the context of pubs

The next question we come to is how convenience food can be applied in a pub catering context. Truth to tell, there is probably a place for convenience food in just about every catering operation, but the extent to which it is used depends entirely on how you see it fitting into your existing operation.

If you reputation, like ours, is for imaginative home-made food, you must choose your convenience foods very carefully as customers become familiar with the smell, taste and style of your cooking and can spot an intruder a mile off! Even so there are applications. Here are some convenience foods which we find particularly useful.

Butter portions We were recently criticised by one of the guide book inspectors who could not understand why, when we went to all that trouble to cook beautiful food, we spoiled the effect by offering butter in foil wrapped portions. The reasons are disarmingly simple. When we served butter in a piece on a saucer or in butter pots, the wastage factor was unacceptable. We also wished to provide our customers with a choice between butter, low fat spread and a spread which was high in polyunsaturates. Portions were the answer to our problems being convenient, space saving and hygienic. We still use them and make no apologies for doing so.

Sugar portions Sugar in a bowl is all very well but again, the wastage factor is high due to extraneous material finding its way into the bowl. Brown sugar also dries out very quickly. Sachets of brown, white and low calorie sugar were the answer for us.

Cream portions Cigarette and cigar ash in cream jugs made us turn to cream pots . Since we have been using them, our profit on coffee has gone up..

Frozen wholemeal puff pastry and filo pastry. Our reasons? We do not have the staff, time, ability or inclination to make them ourselves!

Pitta bread We have tried to make our own pitta bread but we don't have the right sort of oven. As there seems to be little point in buying an oven just to make pitta bread, we buy the ready-made variety.

Frozen individual portion pre-cooked rice A real time-saver and also a space saver on the stove. We use the wholegrain variety as well as saffron and Indian style rices and achieve perfection every time.

Frozen button onions Otherwise known as silverskins. We use these in various stews and daubes. Our reasons for using the frozen variety will be obvious if you have ever spent hours at a sink trying to peel the little blighters!

Freeze-dried herbs When fresh herbs are out of season in this country, imported fresh herbs or glass-house herbs are prohibitively expensive. Rather than do without, we buy freeze-dried herbs which are more reasonably priced but which retain a good flavour.

Ready-prepared stock paste, stock cubes or bouillon We like to make our own when we can, but usually we simply do not have the time.

Chicken kiev! We tried making our own but could never achieve a perfect seal which resulted in all the delicious filling running out during the cooking process. The result was lots of wastage. We now buy frozen luxury chicken kievs which never let us down and which sell very well.

Our reasons for using the above items in a convenient form are pretty sound in that their use has achieved four things:

- ☐ Wastage has been cut down.
- ☐ Time has been saved which leaves us free to get on with more important things.
- ☐ A greater choice of food has been made available to the customer.
- ☐ Correct portions are dispensed which makes costing and therefore profit margins easy to calculate.

Of course, if we had a complete squad of full-time cooks, chefs and porters, and charged a small fortune for our meals, things might well be different. As things stand, however, we have only two full-time cooks, the rest of the staff being part-timers.

Our pub catering operation is unique to us just as yours will be unique to you. It could well be that, at the moment, you do not offer any food apart from the odd sandwich. If that is the case, you may well consider that if you were to mount a catering operation at all, it would have to consist entirely of convenience foods. If you did mount such an operation you would automatically have the following advantages:

Convenience foods

- No wastage.
- Little or no preparation.
- Precise portion control.
- Low staffing levels.
- Precise stock control.
- Easily worked out profit margins.

On the other hand, you may have an established operation which consists of a limited number of home-made dishes which are always on the menu. If those dishes are old favourites and sell well, you are obviously going to keep them there. Even so, you could well be considering whether or not some of your customers might fancy a change. You could provide that change without investing in more equipment and staff by introducing one or two individually portioned frozen main courses. Such a move could be the start of something big.

Here are some final points to bear in mind when buying and using convenience food:

- Do shop around. There are dozens of convenience food manufacturers and, as with anything else, some are better than others.
- It could be a mistake always to go for the cheapest. Remember, you get what you pay for.
- Add you own touches. If you think that a frozen portion of bolognese sauce lacks garlic or oregano, or both, don't mess about complaining, whack them in!

In Chapter 3 we looked at the problems caused by requests for items not on the main menu. If you really don't want to say no, a small stock purchased from a frozen food supplier may be the answer. The major suppliers usually carry mixed cases of lines such as individually portioned vegetarian foods that can be heated to order in the microwave, or batches of sandwiches with different fillings. These allow the small caterer not only the opportunity to try out the different lines but also the means to offer a special item.

6 Functions, theme nights and barbecues

In catering terms, a function is an occasion when a group of people with a shared interest get together to eat, drink and have a good old chin-wag. They can be split into two main categories: externally motivated and internally motivated functions.

Externally motivated functions include the following:
- Weddings, christenings and funerals.
- Anniversaries.
- Eighteenth and twenty-first birthday parties.
- Annual parties organised by people who work together.
- Retirement parties.
- Promotion parties.
- Functions organised by different societies and associations.
- Any other sort of function which is organised or motivated from an outside source.

Internally motivated functions, i.e. those which are organised by the licensee, are usually, but not always, theme-orientated and could include events such as the following, when the food, drink, decor and even dress could be themed to mark the occasion:
- New Year's Eve (Hogmanay in Scotland): 31 December.
- Burns' Night: 25 January.
- St Valentine's Day: 14 February.
- St David's Day: 1 March.
- Commonwealth Day: 13 March.
- St Patrick's Day: 17 March.
- St George's Day: 23 April.
- Midsummer's Day: 21 June.
- Hallowe'en: 31 October.
- Guy Fawkes' Night: 5 November.
- St Andrew's Day: 30th November.
- Winter solstice: 21 December.

Moving away from calendar dates, other theme nights could be based simply on nationality such as Indian, French, Spanish, German, West Indian or American, or any nationality where there is an identifiable culture and cuisine. On the other hand, functions such as a Saturday night dinner dance or a once-a-month gourmet dinner could be organised where the theme aspect would be absent. The extent to which functions of any kind can be organised depends largely on the premises and what sort of facilities are available. Of course, the ideal would be premises where there is a self-contained functions suite with separate toilet facilities, bar and access to the kitchen. Such premises, especially those which can cater for up to 200 covers, are few and far between and are veritable gold mines. The beauty of catering for functions, you see, is that you have a captive audience. They have booked in advance, they often arrive by coach, they all have a meal and, because they are not driving home, they spend freely at the bar. In such circumstances, the caterer can make an excellent profit.

Externally motivated functions

Advance planning

No matter how big or small your capacity for function catering is, the key to success is organisation. Organisation, that is, not only on your part but also on the part of the group of people whose function it is. To this end, it is essential that the details of the booking are recorded in a clear and comprehensive way. Some caterers like to record details of such bookings in a large desk diary; others prefer to have a printed booking form which is simply filled in and ensures that all the essential details are there. Whichever method you prefer, make sure to get the following information:
- Name, address and telephone number of the client or organisation.
- Name, address and telephone number of the person who is organising the function on their behalf.
- Day and date of the function.
- Time of arrival and time of the meal.
- Number of covers, with final number to be confirmed 48 hours prior to the function.
- What sort of function it is.
- The type of food or menu required and the cost per head.
- Whether or not any or all of the drinks are to be added to the account.
- Details of any special requirements such as flowers, cake, music, champagne, etc.
- A deposit on confirmation.

Armed with all that information, you will be in a position to organise the catering and staff requirements, details of which should also be recorded to ensure that nothing is forgotten.

Points to remember

Organisation, then, is the key, but experience has shown that other factors are extremely important too:
- Value for money. Your package need not necessarily be the cheapest around but it must represent good value.

Functions, theme nights and barbecues

- Things have to be as agreed. If, for instance, you have agreed to provide home-made soup, make sure that it is home-made and not packet soup. Similarly, if the main course is 'crispy roast duckling', it should be crispy as stated and not soggy or charred to a cinder.
- Co-ordination and timing are absolutely essential if things are to run smoothly.
- Cutlery, crockery, glasses and table linen must be absolutely clean.
- Presentation should be immaculate. This is, after all, a special occasion, so glasses should sparkle and the lay-out should be attractive.
- Staff should be smart, clean and friendly. Courtesy goes a long way and smiles go even further.
- Greet the organiser on arrival and have a chat before they depart. It would be a nice touch to give them a small present as a thank-you for their custom.

The food

The next point to be considered is the food itself. A good idea is to draw up a selection of different menus which you consider will cover your customers' needs and price range. Here are some suggestions:

Finger buffet The food would be very informal and could include a selection of sandwiches, finger rolls, sausage rolls, canapés, sausage plaits, vol-au-vents and so on.

Buffet – Type A Slices of cold, roasted meat such as pork, beef or turkey. Sliced and de-rinded Continental meats such as mortadella, garlic sausage, salami and schinkenwurst. Egg mayonnaise. Potato salad. Various green salads. Various rice salads. Wholemeal bread rolls or similar.

Buffet – Type B A choice of cold, roasted meats in slices. Sliced and de-rinded continental meats as above. Stuffed potato skins. French-style potato salad. Russian salad. Egg mayonnaise. Various vol-au-vents. A selection of green salads. A selection of rice salads. Chilli con carne. Boston baked beans. Spicy-coated chicken drumsticks. Slices of gala pie. Wholemeal bread rolls.

Buffet – Type C As for Buffet type B, but to include extras such as freshly poached salmon, slices of smoked turkey breast, garlic chicken pieces, Parma ham cornets stuffed with herb cream cheese – in fact anything which you feel will add a touch of luxury.

Functions, theme nights and barbecues

Dinner – Type A

A straightforward dinner menu to suit most tastes. The example below is based on beef, but similar menus could be devised around pork, turkey or ham.

Courgette and fennel soup with
wholemeal bread roll
OR
Prawn Cocktail with homemade
sauce and brown bread and butter OR
Chilled fruit juice

Roast beef and gravy
Yorkshire pudding
Horseradish sauce
Roast or boiled potatoes
Buttered carrots
Brussels sprouts
Boiled and sliced beetroot

Chocolate gâteau
OR
Coffee Renoir
OR
Fresh fruit salad
OR
A selection of cheeses and biscuits

Coffee or tea

Dinner – Type B

A menu designed to cater for a more adventurous type of client who is prepared to pay a little more for something special.

Homemade mulligatawny soup with
wholemeal bread roll
OR
Melon with a raspberry sauce
delicately flavoured with mint
OR
Potted shrimps with salad garnish
and brown bread and butter

Prime sirloin steak
braised in a Marsala sauce
New potatoes
Mushroom beignets
Cauliflower with almonds
Baked cabbage
with garlic and juniper
Aubergine slippers
Gratin of peas

Lemon ice box pudding
OR
Chocolate, pear and ginger trifle
OR
Fresh strawberries with Kirsch

A selection of cheeses and biscuits

Tea or coffee

The above menus are only examples to help you. The final choice, will of course, remain with you, but whichever menus you choose to offer for function bookings, you must bear in mind the following points:

- ☐ You cannot change the menu at the last minute because one or more of the items is either out of season or out of stock. Such failures are obvious and lead to customer dissatisfaction.
- ☐ Items on the menus should be chosen with ease of preparation and service in mind.
- ☐ Catering for functions means, by definition, that you are catering for a substantial number of people, so menus should be designed to be acceptable to the majority.
- ☐ Try not to include items which will deteriorate if kept back for any length of time.
- ☐ Try not to include items which require elaborate last-minute garnishes. Speed of service is of the essence.
- ☐ It is always necessary, when catering for functions, to overstock in case of mishaps or a last minute change in numbers. With this in mind, it is wise to choose items which can be prepared relatively quickly if needed and which can be sold elsewhere on your premises if unused.
- ☐ Keep your costings in mind when you design the menus: asparagus spears, for instance, can be very impressive both on the plate and on the menu, but they can also be very expensive.

If your standard menu has gained a good reputation, there is a distinct possibility that groups of people will approach you with a view to choosing whatever each individual wants. Such approaches are quite flattering really, but if a function organised on that basis is to succeed, your advance organisation is even more critical.

We have found over the years, that the best way to cope with such functions is to take them in a series of steps as follows:

1. Give the organiser a copy of your menu so that copies can be made and distributed among those who wish to attend.
2. Those people then choose what they wish from the menu and pass on that information to the organiser.
3. The organiser then passes that information on to you.
4. You then have a complete list of the guests' names together with their individual choices.
5. Make out tent cards with each guest's name and with details of the meal ordered on the reverse, and place one in front of each place setting. A good organiser will do this for you.

It is then a simple matter to serve the right guest with the food of their choice. This is important for obvious reasons but also because we have found that some people forget what they chose some weeks previously, whereas others change their minds on the day and try to achieve this switch of choice by saying that they ordered something else. The above system prevents any such difficulties.

Wedding receptions

Wedding receptions are unique occasions both for the caterer and for the parties involved. Marriage ceremonies can take place any time from early morning to late afternoon but, whatever time they take place, the meal which follows is more often than not referred to as a wedding breakfast.

Wedding etiquette Nowadays, the meal at a wedding reception can range from the simplest finger buffet to a full-blown seven course meal. It is also true that there is a trend towards the more informal, but even so, old traditions die hard and wedding etiquette, a sort of wedding reception protocol, is something which caterers are expected to be familiar with. Very often, the families concerned will look to the caterer for advice on such matters. Let us take things from the moment the guests arrive:

1. It is the duty of the bride's mother to take up a position at the entrance to the reception room and to greet the guests as they arrive. The bride and groom should be stationed in the centre of the room so that the guests can congratulate them after they have been greeted by the bride's mother. Sometimes, the wedding presents are displayed. As soon as all the guests have been greeted, the meal should be served.
2. If the meal is a sit-down meal, the guests enter the dining room first and are then called to rise and applaud as the bride, bridegroom and bridesmaids are shown in. The seating plan can take any form with the exception of 'the top table', which should be set out as shown in the diagram.
3. When the meal is over, it is time for the cake-cutting ceremony. This over, the cake is removed to the kitchen for the purpose of cutting pieces for the guests. While this is being done, the guests' glasses are charged ready for the toasts and speeches.
4. Order of toasts and speeches. Strictly speaking, this applies only if the meal has been a formal one, but these days people feel cheated if there are no toasts or speeches.
   - ☐ The bride's father should be called to speak as soon as the cake has been served. When he has made his brief speech, he should propose a toast to the bride and groom.
   - ☐ The bridegroom should then make a brief response, after which he should propose a toast to the bridesmaids, expressing his appreciation for their assistance.
   - ☐ The best man then rises and thanks everyone on behalf of the bridesmaids, after which he reads any cards or messages of congratulation.

Photographs Any photographs which are taken at

Plan view of seating arrangements on the top table at a wedding breakfast

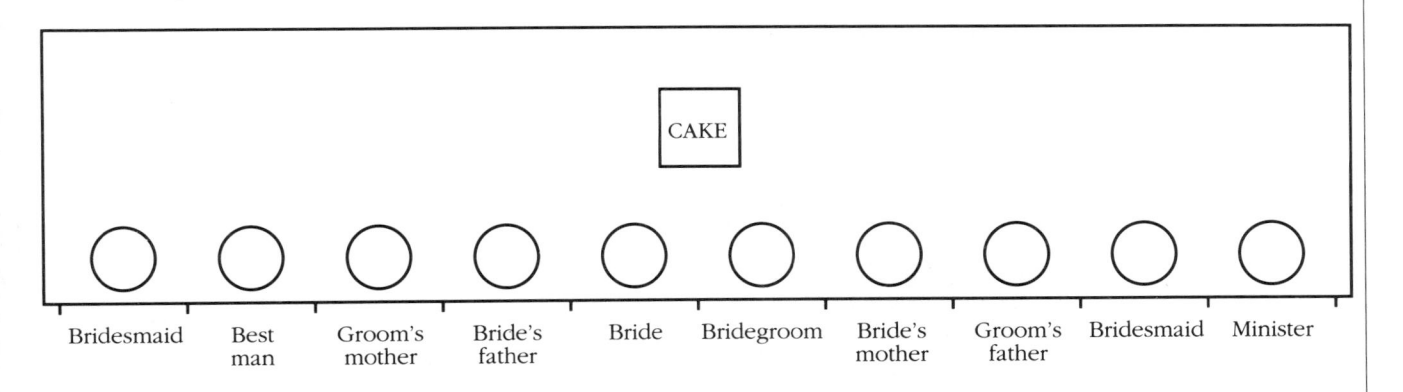

| Bridesmaid | Best man | Groom's mother | Bride's father | Bride | Bridegroom | Bride's mother | Groom's father | Bridesmaid | Minister |

(CAKE positioned centrally behind the table between Bride and Bridegroom)

Functions, theme nights and barbecues

the reception are distributed among family and friends, who then show them off to even more people. Obviously, then, they can be very good publicity for the caterer, so ensure that they are taken in a way which shows off the premises to their best advantage. Why not ask the photographer to supply you with some copies so that you can display them, along with his business card, for your customers to see. More bookings could result.

Changing facilities More often than not, the bride and groom will need somewhere to change. If your premises are residential, this does not present any problem, but if not, another room, possibly in your private quarters, is infinitely more hospitable than forcing them to change in the toilets.

Timing If the wedding breakfast is to be a buffet, timing is not so crucial, but if a hot meal is to be served, it can be critical, especially on a fine day when the photographer gets carried away in a fit of artistic fervour. It is therefore wise then, to discuss this aspect with the parties concerned and come to an agreement beforehand.

Napkins Personalised napkins are available from a number of sources such as catering centres and printers and can add a nice touch with the initials of the bride and groom picked out in silver.

Confetti If you do not want guests to throw confetti or rice on your premises, say so when the arrangements are being made. This is infinitely preferable to forbidding it on the big day.

Internally motivated functions

Internally motivated functions are different in so far as it is the licensee who is the instigator and organiser. They are different, too, in that you can determine the numbers, the food, the style and the cost to suit whatever occasion you have in mind. They are also very useful as a means of generating trade when external bookings are few and far between. Again, though, organisation is of the essence if you wish to build up trade and make a profit.

Theme nights, as mentioned above, can either mark an anniversary of some sort or simply be designed to emulate a national or regional style. Theme nights are becoming increasingly popular but if they are to be successful, there are several things which you need to bear in mind:

- ☐ The food should match the occasion
- ☐ The premises should be trimmed up to match.
- ☐ Staff should dress to match.
- ☐ Customers should be encouraged to dress up too, and to encourage them, why not offer a prize for the best outfit?
- ☐ See to it that admission is by ticket only so that you know in advance exactly how many people will be attending. This will help keep wastage to a minimum and will ensure that the event is not over-subscribed.
- ☐ A half-hearted approach to a theme night will produce a half-hearted response, so do try to be enthusiastic!

Other internally motivated functions, such as a monthly dinner dance or a gourmet evening, do not have a theme as such but can be equally profitable. Again, it is best if they are ticket-only functions for the same reasons as given above.

General tips

- ☐ Do make sure when you are catering for functions or theme nights that you get your costings right. Because of the numbers involved, a small error or omission in the costing can mean a large reduction in profit at the end of the day.
- ☐ When you are arranging tables for a function, remember that an absolute minimum of roughly 2 metres (6 ft) is needed between each table so that guests can sit comfortably and waitresses can pass without difficulty.
- ☐ If the only room available for functions on your premises is normally used as your restaurant, it could be unwise to close it in order to cater for a function unless you could offer a similar standard of food and service elsewhere on the premises. Why? Because you could offend your regular customers and lose the opportunity to turn any passing trade into regular customers.
- ☐ Make sure that you have enough staff to provide a quick and efficient service but remember to include their wages in your costings. It is a good idea to work out how many staff you need for varying numbers of covers and adjust the cost per head accordingly.
- ☐ It is a good idea to take orders for wine before the guests sit down. This way, the wine can be ready and waiting for them on the table and is infinitely better than a wine waiter going through the whole rigmarole when the meal has already started.
- ☐ When planning theme nights which are based on a nationality or region it could be fairly boring if you billed them simply as 'An Australian Night', 'An Indian Night' or 'A Mexican Night'. Try to think of a better theme such as 'Crocodile Dundee', 'Return of the Raj' or 'Tijuana Brass'. All the various embassies have a public relations department or something similar and, as a rule, are only too pleased to send literature and give advice. Directory enquiries will supply the telephone numbers.
- ☐ If people have gone to a lot of trouble with costumes, or even if they have just had a good time, they like to have something to remember the night by. We always ensure that there is someone on the spot to take photographs. Usually one of the customers volunteers to do it. Once developed, we pin the photographs on a board so that those who want a copy can have one and those who did not attend realise what they missed, it's all good publicity!
- ☐ Breweries or drinks' manufacturers will often help with theme nights as part of a promotion for their product, or if you really want to go to town, there are several agencies who organise special nights. Offering a complete tailor-made package with costumes, music and suitable decor, they can transform the pub for the night. Such firms advertise in the trade press.

In a fairly hectic trade, theme nights are one of the few occasions when we have the same opportunity as our customers to let our hair down and the fact that we are all willing to join in goes a long way to making the evening a success. Try one – they are great fun!

Barbecues

Why consider a barbecue?

Throughout the ages, people have been tempted to gather round a camp fire, attracted by the warmth and companionship but perhaps above all by the delicious aroma and taste of food cooked over glowing embers. Nothing changes!

However, it was not long before people realised that some control was needed in order to cook food effectively, rather than simply throwing it on to the fire. In search of a little more sophistication, they began to experiment with tripods, primitive spits and, in Haiti, a framework of sticks and posts which they referred to as a 'barbacoa'. While all that was going on in Haiti, the French too were roasting animals over open fires, roasting them from beard to tail that is. In French, 'barbe' = beard and 'queue' = tail, so put them together and you have the word 'barbequeue', or barbecue.

It does not matter which was first but it was from these simple origins that the present-day barbecues were developed. Today, while barbecues are much more sophisticated and a great deal easier to use, they have lost none of their original appeal. Of course, there are always the purists who insist upon using only wood or charcoal, and in a domestic situation that may be fine, but it does present problems for the commercial caterer.

Many years ago, after a particularly long and pleasant summer, we decided that the way forward for the following year was to take full advantage of the weather and install a barbecue. At that time, commercial barbecues were not available on the market so we had to set about building and designing our own. It was quite a task. We pestered our Greek friends for help and advice and even went to the trouble of manhandling a motorised barbecue on to a flight back from Cyprus. You can imagine how popular we were! But we believed that we could somehow recreate or recapture the magic of Cyprus, Greece and the Levant. Our idea was to use this piece of equipment to supplement the conventional barbecue we intended to build and offer items such as souvla and souvlakia.

Alas, the pace of life here is different, to say nothing of the weather! After some considerable effort and expense, the whole set-up was finally ready. To be brutally frank, it was a flop. In a normal domestic situation it would have been superb, but commercially it was just not viable. Why? Well, to start with, one of the problems with charcoal is that it is really only at its best for an hour or so. Also, if large quantities are being used, it can be difficult to light and can take up to an hour to reach its peak.

Another problem was that we needed a few days of settled weather in order to use our barbecue effectively. Even then, after a successful lunch-time session, the fire would be out before the evening session, which meant that we had to go through the whole rigmarole again. There just wasn't any continuity. We also found was that the slightest breeze would shower hot ash over the customers. Have you seen what sparks from a charcoal fire can do to an Italian knitted white suit?

Despite these problems, one clear fact emerged: the customers really did enjoy it; there really was a demand for barbecues. Although our operation was amateurish, we had, nevertheless, managed to put on several really successful functions, not least of which was a memorable Greek evening with a whole spit-roasted lamb for well over a hundred people, double our normal capacity. It made us realise that the potential for barbecues was, and still is, enormous.

Today, if anything, that potential has increased, but now there is a whole rash of professionally designed, commercial barbecues on the market to help caterers meet the demand. 'Ah,' we can hear you say, 'that may be true, but the weather is still as unpredictable as ever.' True enough, it is; but to run a successful barbecue operation today, you must be prepared, in the same way that your customers are, to take full advantage of any good weather which comes your way. With a modern, commercial barbecue, this is easy to do as they can be set up and ready to use in about 10 minutes. Really!

If you already have a successful catering operation, you may feel that there is simply no need to bother with a barbecue. Similarly, if you are in the process of building up a catering operation, you might consider that you have quite enough on your plate doing just that without adding a new dimension. Sentiments such as those, while understandable, are in all probably ill-considered because it is that very same new dimension which is the important factor. We have already mentioned in earlier chapters, that because of more favourable prices, people often choose to eat out in pubs two or even three times per week rather than just once a month at a restaurant. Even so, the most loyal of customers fancy a change from time to time, and a barbecue can provide such a change without their going elsewhere and without compromising your regular menu.

Staff, too, can get jaded, stuck away in a hot, sweaty kitchen in lovely weather, and a barbecue can fire their enthusiasm by giving them the opportunity to work out

Functions, theme nights and barbecues

of doors. Cooks and chefs seldom have the opportunity to meet their customers in normal circumstances, but with a barbecue, they have an essential role to play, chatting and meeting people. It is a perfect chance for them to do their bit in the sphere of public relations by showing off their skills and even promoting the normal menu as well.

Those who are just starting out with a catering operation may have only a limited amount of capital to spend on decoration and equipment but if they are lucky enough to have a patio area or a beer garden, such areas can easily be made to look attractive without going to great expense. Obviously, it would be wise to make such areas look attractive anyway, but the addition of a barbecue facility makes it possible to capitalise on the effort by making maximum use of the outdoor area.

All licensees know what it feels like to look out into the beer garden on a nice summer's day to see customers making two small drinks last two long hours while they sunbathe and make use of all the facilities. Frustrating, isn't it? A barbecue can change all that by breaking the deadlock. Barbecues are compulsive: the smell of the food and the general activity draws customers and almost compels them to spend.

Having said all that, it is not sufficient simply to buy a barbecue, set it up and hope that customers will appear as if by magic. No, we have to get our marketing right. Barbecues are the fun area of pub catering and in order to make them successful, we need to adopt a certain 'show business' approach. In other words, we need to get our act together and use some common sense. For instance, no matter how nice the weather, it won't do a bit of good to light and set up the barbecue on, say, a Monday lunch-time if you know it is your quietest session of the week. Set up the operation at times which you know are going to provide you with some throughput. Another definite no is to light the barbecue and leave it unattended, sending the cook out if someone looks interested. Barbecues don't work that way.

Here are some useful tips, then, to ensure a successful and professional barbecue operation:
- ☐ Always have someone in attendance at the barbecue.
- ☐ The person who is in attendance should be left to do the cooking and chat with the customers.
- ☐ Someone else should be on hand to take the

- orders, sort out the salads and take the money.
- ☐ At the outset, set up the operation at weekends, lunch-times or evenings or both.
- ☐ Build up the operation from there, making it known that if the weather is good, the barbecue will be lit.

Who knows, once word gets round, you may find that even the quiet Monday lunch-time is a thing of the past

One of the main attractions of a barbecue is its basic informality which has the effect of breaking down the barriers of age and class. Barbecues are so laid back that customers will put up with delays and other inconveniences which they would not tolerate for half a minute in normal circumstances. We have seen people wander round for ages in search of a seat, squeeze on to a tiny table and then finally join a seemingly endless queue for the food, just for the pleasure of participating in a barbecue.

There is also a sort of built-in tolerance regarding the type of food which can be offered. In an indoor setting, a bonfire night party offering beefburgers, sausages, jacket potatoes and beans would require an awful amount of effort to ensure it did not turn into a damp squib, but the very same food, cooked on a barbecue outdoors, will be acceptable to all ages and sections of society.

Speciality nights and certain functions are occasions when barbecues can really come into their own. The capacity or potential output of a commercial barbecue makes it easy for the caterer to cope with literally hundreds of customers.

In recent years, caterers have noticed a growing tendency towards the more informal function. Weddings, twenty-first birthday parties, anniversaries and the like are no longer thought of as essentially formal occasions. Much more emphasis is being placed today on making such events enjoyable get-togethers where guests mingle and chatter in congenial surroundings. A barbecue is the ideal thing for such an event as its very nature renders formality impossible.

Choosing a barbecue

What sort of a barbecue should you consider? To help you decide, we must first look at how barbecues actually cook the food. They cook not by flame or smoke as is popularly believed but by a constant radiant heat.

Charcoal is heated until it glows. If ordinary wood is used, it is burned until all that are left are the glowing embers. Both of these fuel sources leave a steady source of radiant heat which cannot be turned up and down like a conventional cooker.

Gas barbecues heat up lava rock or ceramics or, in the case of the new 'heat-exchange' barbecues, a metal plate, all of which supply the source of radiant heat which actually cooks the food. Gas-fuelled barbecues are obviously much easier to control than those fuelled by charcoal or wood and much quicker too, since there is no waiting for flames to die down and so on.

Purists would argue that these new methods do not impart the same flavour as charcoal. While they are entitled to their point of view, it is, nevertheless, highly debatable, as charcoal itself is both tasteless and odourless. The barbecue flavour we all love is produced by the carbonisation of fats and juices which have dripped on to the heat source. This effect can be heightened by throwing aromatic herbs and twigs on to the heat source.

The actual fuel used to 'fire' the barbecue, then, is of primary importance. Traditional barbecues, as stated above, used charcoal or wood and this is still an available option today. It has to be said, though, that they do create their own problems such as uneven heat, especially in windy conditions, they are messy to fill, they are often difficult to light and they are generally inconvenient.

By far the most popular fuel for commercial barbecues is liquefied petroleum gas, or LPG for short. Calor gas is the best-known form. There are two varieties. The first is propane, which is contained in bulk tanks for heating and cooking and also in smaller portable cylinders (usually red) for larger commercial barbecues. The second sort of LPG is butane, which generally comes in blue cylinders and is used for portable room heaters and smaller commercial and domestic barbecues. The two fuel gases are not interchangeable. A barbecue which has been designed to run on propane should not be coupled to a butane cylinder and vice versa. Quite apart from the safety aspect, the chances are that the barbecue would fail to light and, even if it did, the result would not be satisfactory.

The one major advantage that propane has over butane is its lower freezing temperature. This means that it can be used successfully throughout the winter no matter how cold the weather. Select a barbecue which is fuelled by Calor propane and you can even hold barbecues in the snow! Later in the chapter, when we discuss the possibilities of using a barbecue as part of an outside catering operation, you will learn that all-year usage can be a distinct advantage.

There are also barbecues on the market which are

fuelled by natural gas or even electricity, but, these are generally intended to be installed in a fixed site. This, in turn, causes a loss of mobility which is an integral part of a successful barbecue operation. Theoretically, electric barbecues could be mobile, but free running electricity cables and crowds of people frankly just don't mix.

When actually choosing a barbecue, there are a number of preliminary points to take into account:-
- ☐ Small domestic barbecues are too flimsy for the catering trade.
- ☐ Larger domestic barbecues could conceivably be used for a very small operation but durability might be a problem.
- ☐ Small catering barbecues are available but they are not that much cheaper to buy or to run.
- ☐ Larger catering barbecues give greater capacity and versatility.

Having said all that, some pub caterers run a very successful operation with the use of several smaller barbecues, the customers being allowed to cook the food themselves.

The majority of commercial barbecues use lava rock in a form which is non-combustible, clean and economical. On a good-quality barbecue, the lava rock should reach optimum cooking temperature in about 5 minutes and then maintain an even and controlled heat throughout the session. Lava rock does need to be replaced from time to time, but replacement supplies are easily and inexpensively obtained.

This type of barbecue can be very expensive initially but there are some very sophisticated and stylish models on the market. A glimpse through the catalogues reveals models of all shapes and sizes, even some which incorporate hoods. There are also models which incorporate cupboards, plate racks, holding areas and so on, but such refinements add to the initial cost enormously. It is all too easy to get side-tracked and to lose sight of the fact that the most important aspect is the actual cooking area of the barbecue itself. Some barbecues have a split system which allows two halves to be heated independently. This is a definite advantage, whereas a cooler, holding area is not. All barbecues have their cool spots which can be used as a holding area, but the point is that this is not the way a barbecue operation works. In order to achieve maximum throughput, the food should be cooked and served to order and as quickly as possible.

All the commercial barbecues which incorporate lava rock are fitted with wheels so they can be moved from site to site or wheeled into storage when not in use. Some caterers incorporate the larger models into purpose-built, permanent sites which, with a roof covering, enable them largely to ignore the vagaries of the weather.

Perhaps the most exciting breakthrough in commercial barbecues was the introduction of the heat-exchange concept. Barbecues which make use of this principle are extremely mobile, economical, space-saving when not in use and yet have the capacity to cope with hundreds of orders very quickly. When not in use, these barbecues, being so slim, fold up the same way as an ironing board and so can be stored indoors against a wall, where they will take up no more than a few inches of room space. This also means, of course, that they can be loaded into the back of an estate car with ease.

The heat-exchange system uses Calor propane to heat a metal plate which is shaped like a shallow V. It is this metal plate which supplies the radiant heat to the cooking surface. The cooking surface itself is a slotted, stainless steel plate which allows the fats and juices to drip through on to the heat source to give that full barbecue flavour which is all important. After use, they can be cleaned simply by leaving the gas burners on for a while. A barbecue of this sort is a very professional piece of equipment altogether, especially as the cooking area is split into two halves which can be heated separately. They cost about the same as a small commercial microwave, which means that they are well within the reach of the average pub caterer.

Outside catering operations

The mobility provided by both the heat-exchange and lava rock systems makes them ideal for use at outside catering functions. We have already mentioned weddings and twenty-first birthday parties, but there are other events at which a mobile barbecue could bring in a useful profit. Agricultural shows are a good example, but any event will do where there is a large gathering of people. Even just selling burgers, you can take an awful lot of money in a day.

The manufacturers claim that it is possible to recoup the money laid out for the purchase of a barbecue, in just one season. In order to achieve this, it is necessary to be something of an opportunist. This does not mean that you have to fly around all the agricultural shows and outside catering functions until you are exhausted; it simply means taking advantage of any opportunity that seems cost-effective.

For special occasions, a barbecue can be hired out

either on its own or as a package deal, complete with gas, cook/chef and food. Other pubs could well be interested in such a service, as could your customers for some private function or charity night. Other likely customers are young farmers' associations who have easy access to empty barns, and rotary clubs and tenants' associations. In fact, any group with access to space will hold barbecues throughout the year. Some groups even hold barbecues in the depths of winter where the only source of heat in the freezing cold barn is the barbecue itself. In circumstances such as these it is important to use Calor propane as the fuel rather than butane, but this does not present a problem as most commercial barbecues require the use of Calor propane anyway.

One or two final points in relation to outside catering functions. First, they can be very disjointed affairs, so it is very important to plan ahead in order to define the operation and make it manageable. With a large function such as a wedding, you will obviously want to do the bar as well as the food, but do make sure that the numbers will be sufficient for you to make a profit. With a small function or a night at another pub, make it clear that you will provide the barbecue, the food to be cooked on the barbecue, the chef and the gas and that the organisers should provide all the sundry items such as paper plates, salad stuffs, cutlery and coffee. Those are the items which are messy and time-consuming.

General tips and advice

- ☐ If the weather is fine, or at any other time you know that you could have a reasonable throughput, set up the barbecue. Make sure that there is a sign outside to notify people, and man the barbecue as described earlier so that it looks professional.
- ☐ Keep the barbecue menu simple – no more than two or three items.
- ☐ Make sure that you get your profit margin right – people expect to pay more for a barbecue.
- ☐ Advertise speciality nights in advance by selling tickets, making it known at the time that, if the weather is bad, the food will be available but cooked conventionally. Above all, make the evening fun so that no one will be disappointed if it does end up tipping down with rain.
- ☐ Do not incorporate barbecued items into your normal menu. Split your operations and keep them separate. Offer only simple accompaniments such as various salads, bread and relishes. You cannot have the waitresses dashing into the kitchen every couple of minutes for a portion of chips. Offer only those items which you can cook and keep outside.
- ☐ Remember that food which is not flat, such as chicken pieces, takes much longer to cook than flat-surfaced food such as steaks, cutlets and burgers and should be roasted in the oven or microwaved first. This effectively seals in the flavour which is then released by the barbecue.
- ☐ Avoid food with a high fat content. Burgers which are advertised as 100% meat, are made of 100% of the animal, fat and all, so choose those with some added cereal to reduce flare-ups.
- ☐ Fish cooks beautifully and very quickly on a barbecue but can break up if you are not careful, especially if it is in fillets. It is much better to barbecue the whole fish, as they do in Mediterranean countries. Remember to isolate that part of the barbecue, though: there is nothing worse than a fishy-tasting beef steak.
- ☐ Organise a routine for your barbecue operation – it will certainly prove to be worthwhile. The idea is to ensure that the flow of customers ordering, paying, collecting their food and then moving away is steady and smooth. Make sure, then, that salads are replenished along with cutlery and plates and that the money is taken with the order. Nothing annoys customers more than what they see as an avoidable bottle-neck. Keep salad stuffs, relishes and other accompaniments on a table to one side of the barbecue rather than behind it so that a natural flow is achieved.

If your barbecue operation really takes off, it could be worth considering the provision of a sheltered, permanent site or investing in some form of canopy; these are available from the major barbecue manufacturers.

The really adventurous caterer might like to consider a spit roaster which can take a whole pig or lamb. These are designed by the manufacturers to fit over the top of the barbecue which you have already bought from them. As a rule, they usually make sure that no-one else's spit roaster will fit on to their barbecue, thus ensuring that you have to buy from them again. They are impressive, though, and will cook a whole beast in a matter of a few hours. They might perhaps be out of the reach of the average pub caterer, but for those who are interested in outside catering, they are an exciting concept for a medieval night or a large function.

Possible problem areas

Having extolled the virtues of barbecues, is is only fair to mention that there are some disadvantages and problem areas. Apart from the weather – always the weather! – the most important thing to watch out for is hygiene. The standards of hygiene which apply to a conventional catering operation apply equally outside and must be adhered to. However, in respect of barbecuing, there are practically no guidelines available from the Environmental Health Department, so common sense has to prevail.

Strictly speaking, there should be a wash-basin available for the use of food handlers. Such a facility should be part of the barbecue set-up but in most cases it is absolutely impossible. It is therefore very important to instil into staff who are operating the barbecue that they must wash their hands as frequently as possible. Ensure that all staff use tongs and so on when actually handling the food. Fingers are definitely out. Uncooked food should be kept in covered cool boxes until required.

Food with a high profile such as chicken, if frozen, should be thoroughly defrosted and then fully cooked in the microwave, the oven or on the barbecue. In this respect, it is useful to remember that it takes ages to cook chicken thoroughly on a barbecue, so to be on the safe side it is better to cook it elsewhere first. Any precooked food which is not for immediate use should be properly chilled before reheating. When such food is reheated, it should be brought to cooking temperature throughout. Salads and so on should be covered to protect them from flies, dust etc.

Barbecue and garden furniture manufacturers have a full range of complementary storage units which are designed to be used in conjunction with your barbecue. They not only make a very attractive display but also circumvent the hygiene problems connected with serving food outdoors. One word of warning though, look through the catalogues of various suppliers, as there can be a great disparity in price! Looking through the catalogues ourselves, we came to the conclusion that some manufacturers had simply thought of a fair price and then trebled it, so do shop around!

If you are fortunate enough to be skilled at DIY then you may be able to construct your own servery, but do make sure when you buy cool boxes that they are good quality. Obviously, this means that you will have to pay a little extra, but poor-quality cool boxes are a false economy anyway as they quickly get scratched and chipped and so become a breeding ground for the bacteria which they are designed to keep out.

Safety standards and guidelines for gas barbecues

When choosing a barbecue, it is important to consider the safety aspect. Most commercial models are designed to eliminate as many potential hazards as possible; for instance they have rails to keep the public away from the cooking area and concealed controls to prevent people from tampering with the gas supply. However, as LPG is a flammable gas, potential customers need to be assured that the barbecue which they are purchasing is designed to the highest safety standards and that there are no risks if operated in accordance with the manufacturer's instructions.

In Great Britain, the evaluation and testing of such equipment is carried out by the Calor Appliance Testing Laboratory. Cynics may think that this is little more than a cosmetic exercise and that Calor would obviously pass the equipment to increase their sales of gas. *Nothing could be further from the truth.* Although the Calor Appliance Testing Laboratory is part of the commercial company, it operates as an autonomous unit. The Laboratory is totally independent in its operation as a test house and is divorced from any commercial interest whatsoever. To become (and thereafter maintain) the status of a registered test house, the laboratory must demonstrate to the total satisfaction of external assessors its technical competence and, most importantly, the professional integrity of the staff who run it. Thus, not only is the basic laboratory equipment and instrumentation checked, but also the qualifications of the technicians and the way in which the establishment is run. The external assessors are the National Measurement Accreditation Service (NAMAS) who come under the auspices of the Department of Industry.

Equipment which has been tested by the laboratory and found satisfactory is listed in the Calor Gas *List of Certified Appliances and Components* and may display the red Certified Badge. This is the manufacturer's declaration to the purchaser that the appliance has been designed and independently tested for conformity to relevant standards.

Appliances supplied from Calor's centrally warehoused stock will have been type-tested, and are certified to the latest standards and subject to Calor's rigorous Quality Assurance procedures before being released for sale.

Equipment may also be supplied from the Calor List of Recognised Manufacturers and Suppliers. This lists Manufacturers and Suppliers who have been assessed for their expertise, facilities and procedures in the development and production of LPG appliances, in specific product groups. Such equipment is identified by the brown Recognised Badge.

LPG is quite safe provided that it is handled correctly. However, this chapter would be incomplete if we did not include some points to be aware of when handling and storing LPG cylinders:

- ☐ DO treat a cylinder with care to ensure that the valve is not damaged. A damaged valve might result in a leak which could have serious consequences.
- ☐ DO use a cylinder upright. Horizontally, liquid gas could find its way into the supply pipes which could have serious results.
- ☐ DON'T subject a cylinder to heat, as pressure inside the cylinder could build up to a point beyond the designed safety limit.
- ☐ DON'T store cylinders in cellars or below ground level. LPG is heavier than air so in the event of a leak, the gas would collect at a low level and become dangerous in the presence of a flame or a spark.
- ☐ DON'T store or use propane (red) cylinders indoors in a residence. Propane is contained under high pressure and should only be kept or used outdoors.

If you want any further advice regarding the use or storage of LPG Calor Gas will be only too pleased to supply leaflets or any information if you contact them at the nearest regional office, see opposite.

Useful addresses

Calor equipment, such as cylinders, gas refills and appliances are available from Calor retailers throughout Great Britain – details can be found in the Yellow Pages under 'Bottled Gas'. (Calor central heating services are listed under 'Central Heating'.)

Details of all Calor's services to the catering industry are available from customer services managers at any of the following sales offices:

AREA 1
Calor Gas Ltd
Falkirk Road
Grangemouth
Sterlingshire
FK3 8XS
Tel: 0324 474747

AREA 2
Calor Gas Ltd
171 Elland Road
Leeds
LS11 8BU
Tel: 0532 707193

AREA 3
Calor Gas Ltd
Dock Yard Road
Ellesmere Port
South Wirral
L65 4EG
Tel: 051 355 3700

AREA 4
Calor Gas Ltd
Manor Way
Coryton
Stanford-le-Hope
Essex
SS17 9IW
Tel: 0375 671244

AREA 5
Calor Gas Ltd
Millbrook Trading Estate
Millbrook
Southampton
SO9 1WE
Tel: 0703 777244

AREA 6
Calor Gas Ltd
1-4 Portland Square
Bristol
BS2 8RR
Tel: 0272 232828

Cinders Barbecues, Unit N7, Lune Industrial Estate, Lancaster, Lancashire LA1 5QP. Tel: Lancaster (0524) 66162.
Manufacturers of the portable catering barbecues.

Aeromatic-Barter Ltd, Kynoch Road, Eley's Estate, Edmonton, London N18 3BH. Tel: 01-803 8302.
Manufacturers of lava rock barbecues and spit roasts.

Gas Barbecue Association, 43 Rose Street, London WC2E 9EX.
Basically a trade association aimed at the promotion of gas barbecues.

7 Wine – a brief introduction

The story of wine begins in the mists of prehistory and we will never know who was the first person to sample and linger over that very first fermentation. What we can be sure of, though, is that the discovery of how grapes change into wine was one of the happiest accidents ever to occur. A happy accident but a simple one – grapes only need to be squashed and a little warm sunshine will do the rest.

Although that first vintage was crude and rough by today's educated standards, enough of the magic of the grape would have been extracted and the effect, when consumed, would no doubt have made a welcome change from throwing rocks at dinosaurs! From such an erratic beginning, wine developed to the stage where it became the hallmark of civilisation. Unsurpassed in popularity by any other natural product, wine continues to the present day to epitomise man's relationship with nature's bounty.

The cultivated vine and wine-making originated in the Caucasus, emerging in the Mediterranean area at the dawn of civilisation around 6000 BC. Egyptian wall paintings and papyri show details of workers cultivating the vines and treading the grapes, but it was the Greeks who brought wine to the people. Greek poets waxed lyrical over this 'nectar of the Gods' and scenes of drinking, feasting and other related pursuits were depicted on many a Greek urn. The expansion of the Greek empire resulted in the knowledge and love of wine being extended to many countries around the Mediterranean basin.

Even so, wine at that time was fairly ropey by today's standards and was so rich and concentrated that it was normally drunk greatly diluted with water. It was the Romans who were really the first to crack the art of wine-making. Armed, as always, with superior technology and skill together with all the vital equipment, even glass bottles, it was the Romans who developed the art of storing wine and improving it with age. As the Roman Empire grew, vineyards were established in France, Hungary, Germany and England.

After the collapse of the Roman Empire, the vineyards which had been established were taken over by the Church and so for more than a thousand years, the wine trade in Europe was looked after by the monks, who had the skill to develop and study the science of wine-making. At that time, wine was stored almost excusively in barrels, so when wine was drawn off and air let in, the contents frequently spoiled. Because of this, most wine at that time was intended for consumption the same year.

The spoiling of wine due to contact with air remained a problem until the discovery of the cork stopper which eventually revolutionised wine-making. It was discovered that wine stored in corked bottles which had been redesigned to lie on their sides rather than standing upright not only kept longer but aged in a beautifully subtle way and produced a characteristic aroma or 'bouquet'. This was due entirely to the fact that the cork, being in contact with the wine, remained moist and therefore airtight. This in turn, cleared the way for the development of the superb range and depths of colour, taste and aroma which we find in the best modern wines. Wines which complement our moods, share our celebrations and add new heights to our enjoyment of good food and company.

Today, in the United Kingdom, we have a tremendous range of wines to choose from, a much wider choice of wines in fact than anywhere else in the world. Over the last 15 or 20 years, things have changed so much in the wine-making industry that it is safe to say that 'great' wines are cropping up all over the place. The British are becoming a nation of wine drinkers and are eager to try all these new and delicious varieties which are coming on to the market at prices which are affordable. It would be a very foolish pub caterer indeed who did not take advantage of this fast-growing market.

Why sell wine?

The sale and consumption of wine in the United Kingdom has increased enormously in recent years, so it makes sound commercial sense to take advantage of this. This increased interest and demand is due in no small way to the increase in foreign travel, holidays abroad and so on which has prompted the media to focus on it. The result is that wine is far more readily available today than at any time in its 3,000 years of recorded history.

There are sound reasons why the pub caterer should pay close attention to the sale of wines:
- There is increasing interest in and demand for wine.
- It is the ideal accompaniment to food.
- It has a good profit margin.
- It is easy to keep and serve and is not labour-intensive.
- It completes the picture where pub catering is concerned and creates the right impression.

Wine – a brief introduction

- It is a natural, healthy product if not abused and is also very trendy.

Selling wine

It has never been so easy to sell wine as it is today. In the past, the resistance or reluctance to do so could be attributed to three main areas:
- Wastage.
- Profit margins not fully understood because of the difference of quality and package size.
- Confusion over the lack of a standard measure for a glass of wine.

We can dispose of those three objections right away:

Wastage Since the advent of the wine box, wastage due to unsold wine has been eliminated. Wine in a box remains fresh for 4 months after opening, thereby eliminating any possibility of deterioration before it can be sold.

Profit margins Profit calculators are now an integral part of the price lists which are published by most wine merchants. They are clear, concise and easy to use. Most are based on the use of 125 ml size glasses, eight of which are yielded by 1 litre of wine. The example shown on page 62 even includes VAT on the selling price.

Measures - The use of 125 ml (or 12.5 cl) glasses is strongly recommended. This size of glass, ready lined and stamped, is available from most glassware wholesalers. The use of this size of glass means that you get eight glasses from 1 litre of wine and six glasses from a 75 cl bottle. This is very handy to know when stocktaking and setting profit margins. One word of caution, however: watch out for bottles which contain only 70 cl.

Glasses

For selling wine by the glass, the use of lined and stamped 125 ml glasses makes obvious sense. Of course, when selling wine by the bottle or carafe, the use of a lined and stamped glass is not necessary as the amount of wine is already known. Either way, it is important to remember that glasses, whether lined or unlined, should be big enough and that the best glasses to choose are the simplest. The classic wine glass is really nothing more than a bowl on a stem. Other criteria to watch out for when choosing wine glasses are the following:
- They should be clear so as to show the colour of the wine without any distortion.
- They should narrow towards the lip in order to trap the wonderful aroma or 'bouquet' as it is known.
- They should have a stem so that the temperature of a hand need not affect the temperature of the wine.

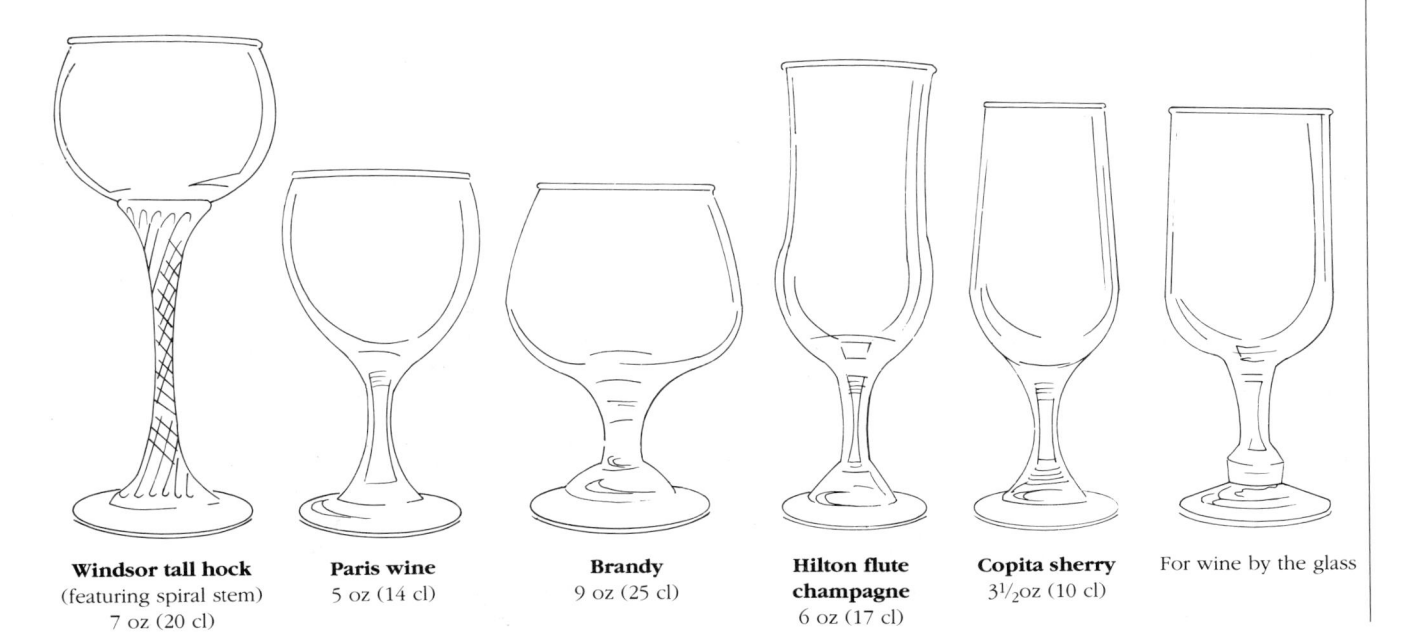

Windsor tall hock
(featuring spiral stem)
7 oz (20 cl)

Paris wine
5 oz (14 cl)

Brandy
9 oz (25 cl)

Hilton flute champagne
6 oz (17 cl)

Copita sherry
3½ oz (10 cl)

For wine by the glass

Wine and spirit retail price calculator

To determine a retail price inclusive of VAT from a cost price *exclusive* of VAT multiply the cost price per unit by the appropriate factor

Margin required	Factor	Margin required	Factor
40%	1.917	51%	2.347
41%	1.950	52%	2.396
42%	1.983	53%	2.447
43%	2.018	54%	2.500
44%	2.054	55%	2.556
45%	2.091	56%	2.675
46%	2.130	57%	2.675
47%	2.170	58%	2.738
48%	2.212	59%	2.805
49%	2.255	60%	2.875
50%	2.300	65%	3.286

The process can also be used to determine a VAT exclusive cost price from a known retail price by reversing the calculation.

Example:

The following example shows how to arrive at a 50% margin (VAT inclusive) retail price:

PRODUCT	Cost price per dozen exc. VAT	Cost price per bottle exc. VAT	Factor	Retail price per bottle inc. VAT
Muscadet de Sèvre et Maine	£33.60	£2.80	× 2.3	=£6.44

Carafes

The most popular sizes of carafe are the half-litre and litre (stamped and lined) which, if using the glass size recommended above, will yield four glasses and eight glasses respectively.

Selling wine by the carafe has distinct advantages, the first and most obvious being that it is labour-saving. Other advantages are that it saves customers' meals from being interrupted, it keeps valuable bar space free for other customers, it improves the appearance of the table, it adds to the general atmosphere and it is profitable. Exactly the same applies to the sale of wine by the bottle.

Dispensers

For draught wines which are offered for sale by the glass, half-litre or litre, the wine box is the obvious first choice because it has tremendous advantages:
- ☐ Elimination of wastage.
- ☐ Convenience.
- ☐ Ease of storage.
- ☐ Pack sizes make profit calculations easy.
- ☐ A variety of wines are now available in boxes.
- ☐ Long life: contents remain fresh for 4 months after opening.
- ☐ Good insulation: contents remain chilled for several hours after removal from the refrigerator.

All the above points are good news for the pub caterer but it does not end there. Better wine and spirit merchants have a variety of dispensing equipment available for use with 3- and 10-litre boxes. Plinths, barrels, hand pumps and free-flow taps are all available and are extremely eye-catching. A far cry from the days of the refrigerated, wall-mounted cabinet, which nowadays would serve a useful purpose housing dry sherry, white vermouth and so on.

Point-of-sale material

The wide variety of eye-catching point-of-sale material now available will bring wine to the notice of the customer if properly displayed.

For an outlet new to wine sales or those outlets which sell only draught wine, a notice informing the customer that wine is available by the glass or carafe is a must. Never assume that customers will know that wine is available; even if they do know, a notice will promote the idea. Such a notice should be written boldly, clear, stylish and placed in a prominent position. Some outlets use blackboards to great advantage. Used in conjunction with other point-of-sale material such as bar towels, paper coasters, stand-up display cards and the like, it is easy to make an impact.

Outlets which also sell wine by the bottle may like to make this known by way of such a noticeboard in addition to a readily available supply of wine lists.

Bottled wine

All public houses have a cellar, or leastways something akin to one, and they are ideal for storing bottled wines, being dark and constantly cool. It would be silly not to take advantage of this.

It would not be practical to discuss at length the virtues and vices of all different kinds of bottled wine, but things are much clearer today than before. Much of the mystique which used to surround the subject has gone and wine merchants today go out of their way to make sure that their customers are not confused. This is clearly demonstrated by the amount of promotional and advertising material which is published, to say nothing of their price lists which these days are full of helpful advice and descriptions. It makes good sense, then, to read these publications, especially as most of them are written by experts.

Also included in most price lists is the 'dry-to-sweet' guide. This has been drawn up by the Wine Development Board. It classifies white and rosé wines only on a scale from 1 to 9. Number 1 signifies the driest of white wines such as Muscadet, Champagne and Chablis, whereas number 9 indicates the very sweetest such as Malmsey, Madeira and Muscat de Beaumes de Venise.

The dry-to-sweet guide has made this particular aspect of choosing a white wine so much easier. It goes without saying that there is more to choosing a wine than merely its dryness or sweetness, but many people find that their enjoyment of white wine is largely dependent on this.

The Red Wine Taste Guide has also been drawn up by the Wine Development Board in conjunction with major retailers. It is not as straightforward as the dry-to-sweet guide for white wines as almost all red wines are dry or medium-dry, and consequently, the guide works in a different way. This Guide uses five categories which are marked from A to E. These categories identify the different styles of red wines in terms of total taste or, in other words, the impression they give to the palate.

The guide starts at A with undemanding wines such as Beaujolais which are easy to drink and intended to be swigged rather than sipped. In category E, at the other end of the scale, are the bigger and more concentrated

Wine – a brief introduction

White wine taste guide

White Wine Guide Codes

1
- Bergerac
- Champagne
- Chablis
- Dry White Bordeaux
- Entre-deux-Mers
- Manzanilla Sherry
- Muscadet
- Pouilly Blanc Fumé
- Sancerre
- Saumur
- Tavel Rosé
- Touraine

2
- Alella
- Chardonnay
  from all countries
- Dry English wine
- Dry Montilla
- Dry Sherry
- Dry Vouvray
- Dry Sparkling wine (Brut)
- Fendant
- Fino Sherry
- Frascati Secco
- German Trocken wine
- Graves
- La Mancha

5
- Austrian Spätlese
- Dry White Port
- EEC Table Wine
- Liebfraumilch
- Medium Cyprus sherry
- Verdelho Madeira
- Vouvray Demi-Sec

6
- Golden Sherry
- Demi-sec Champagne
  and Demi-sec sparkling
- German Spätlese
- Tokay Szamarodni sweet

Red wine taste guide

Red Wine Guide Codes

A
- Bardolino
- Beaujolais
- EEC table wine
- German red wine
- Touraine
- Vin de Table
- Vino da Tavola

B
- Beaujolais -
  Villages & Crus
- Chinon
- Côtes du Roussillon
- Merlot from all countries
- Navarra
- Pinot Noir
  from all countries
- Red Burgundy
- Saumur
- Valdepeñas
- Valencia
- Valpolicella
- Vin de Pays

Wine – a brief introduction

3

vieto Secco
le Dry Cyprus sherry
nédes
esling d'Alsace
ueda
rcial Madeira
anish dry white
ave
lencia
rdicchio
hite Burgundy
hite Rioja
hite Rhône

Brut Sparkling wine
Dry Amontillado Sherry
Dry white Vermouth
Grüner Veltliner, Austria
Halbtroken German wine
Hungarian Olasz Rizling dry
Medium dry English
Medium dry Montilla
Medium dry Vermouth
Moseltaler
Muscat d'Alsace
Pinot Blanc d'Alsace

4

Anjou Rosé
Australian & New Zealand
   Rhine Riesling
Bulgarian Olasz Rizling
Chenin Blanc
Full Amontillado
German Kabinett
German Quality Wine (Qba)
Gewürztraminer d'Alsace
Hungarian Olasz Rizling
   Medium Dry
Medium dry English
Medium dry Montilla
Medium dry Sherry
Medium dry Vermouth
Orvieto Abbocato
Other Gewürztraminer
Portuguese Rosé
Vinho Verde
Yugoslav Laski Rizling

8

ti Spumante
anco, Rosé & Rosso
   Vermouth
ual Madeira
rman Auslese
onbazillac
ontilla cream
le cream Sherry
emières Côtes de Bordeaux
okay Aszu
hite Port

Barsac
Cream Cyprus sherry
Cream sherry
Dark cream and
   rich cream sherry
German/Austrian
   Beerenauslese
German Eiswein
Moscatels/Muscats
Sauternes
Spanish sweet white

9

Brown Sherry
German/Austrian
   Trockenbeerenauslese
Malaga
Malmsey Madeira
Marsala
Muscat de Beaumes
   de Venise

D

ergerac
rdeaux Rouge/Claret
lgarian
   Cabernet Sauvignon
rbières
ôtes-du-Rhône
inervois
orth Africa
oja

Bairrada
Cabernet Sauvignon
   from all countries
   (except Bulgaria)
Châteauneuf-du-Pape
Chianti
Crozes-Hermitage
Dão
Fitou
Hungarian Red
Médoc
Penédes
Ribera del Duero
Rioja Reservas
Ruby & Tawny Port
Syrah

E

Barolo
Cyprus Red
Greek Red
Jumilla
Recioto della Valpolicella
Shiraz from Australia
   & South Africa

Wine – a brief introduction

styles of wine which give a greater sensation of depth and fullness. These wines, of which the Italian Barolo is a good example, are not really intended for drinking on their own and are much more suited to go with food. Wines such as Côtes du Rhône from France and Rioja from Spain are positioned, with others, in the centre of the guide. The guide does not include fine vintage wines which continue to mature in the bottle.

The world of wine is very complex, though, and you may find variations in either of the taste guides' suggested gradings due to differences in wine- making processes. The thing to remember is that they are simply guides, not hard and fast rules. As there are literally hundreds of different wines, it would be impractical to list them all, but as these guides are brought more widely into use, we may expect to see retailers grading wines both in their price lists and on their shelves.

We can sum up our advice in relation to stocking bottled wines as follows:
- ☐ Read the promotional and advertising material.
- ☐ Read the price lists. They are a mine of information and sometimes contain specimen wine lists which are ready-planned for you.
- ☐ Take an interest in the subject, read the articles on wine in your trade papers and if you get the opportunity to go on a tasting, go!
- ☐ Some wines, especially red, mature in the bottle and as they increase in age, they also increase in quality and value. Because of this, some red wines listed in merchants' price lists may not be ready to drink for some time, possibly years.
- ☐ Some years are better than others so make sure that you deal with a reputable merchant and make use of a good pocket wine guide when making your selection (See Recomended reading on page 74).

Wine and the menu

Today, as a general rule, any wine may be served with any course or throughout the meal. If different wines are being served during the course of a meal, though, the lighter ones should precede the heavier ones. Experts and connoisseurs, however, still believe in the sanctity of the correct wine to accompany the food, thereby heightening the enjoyment of both. Here is a simple guide showing which wines are suitable to accompany certain foods:
- ☐ Champagne may be drunk throughout a meal.
- ☐ Dry white goes well with hors d'oeuvre, fish, seafood generally, veal and chicken.
- ☐ Sweet white goes well with puddings, desserts, fruit and nuts.
- ☐ Light red (not colour, refer to Taste Guide) complements lighter meats, grills and some poultry.
- ☐ Heavy red (refer to Taste Guide) for roasts, grills, game birds and casseroles of red meat and game.
- ☐ Rosé – although someone once said that rosé wine is wine for people who do not like wine, it can be good with lamb, chicken and other poultry dishes.

Serving wine

Although personal preferences may vary, there is a recognised optimum serving temperature for every wine. This could be defined as the temperature at which the fullest bouquet and truest taste can be enjoyed. As a general rule, there are three main categories:
- ☐ Wines which are best served at cellar temperature, i.e. 50–60°F or 10–15°C. These include full-bodied white wines, lighter red wines and roses.
- ☐ Wines which need to be chilled to below cellar temperature, i.e. 40–50°F or 4–10°C. These include light white wines and sweet wines, with the exception of vintage ports and Madeiras.
- ☐ Wines which should be served at room temperature, i.e. 60–70°F or 15–21°C. These include full-bodied red wines (i.e. most red wines).

Here are some general rules which relate to the serving of wine:
- ☐ Never apply direct heat to a bottle of wine. If a bottle has to be brought to the table directly from the cellar, the only method that might be acceptable is to decant the wine into a warmed, but not hot, decanter. It is far better, though, to tell the customer to take a smaller quantity in the glass and warm it by hand until the contents of the bottle have come up to room temperature.
- ☐ When chilling wine, make sure the temperature change is gradual. DO NOT put it into the freezer. Instead, use either the fridge, or a wine cooler (often referred to as an ice bucket) which is deep enough to cope with the length of the bottle, half-fill it with cold water, add ice and then insert the bottle of wine for an hour or so. When serving wine in this manner, be sure to use a clean, unperfumed napkin or tea-towel to prevent dripping.

Wine – a brief introduction

- Never add ice to good or fine wine. If water is added to wine at the table, it should be the same temperature as the wine.
- Red wines should be kept upright in a room for 2 or 3 days before serving. Ideally, uncork the bottle 2 hours before serving to allow the wine to breathe, decanting the wine if necessary.
- In the main, young wines (such as Beaujolais Nouveau) may be drunk at a lower temperature than older wines of a similar type.
- It is important to remember that chilled wines warm up in a room very quickly, so do use one of the many varieties of wine coolers to ensure that they are kept at the correct temperature at the table.
- When removing the foil prior to removing the cork, do not cut the foil off level with the bottle opening, instead, remove it from below the bottle flange or remove it completely so as to prevent the wine coming into contact with the metal foil when pouring. Failure to do this has caused people to become ill in instances where lead-based foil was used.
- When removing the cork, first wipe the cork and the mouth of the bottle with a clean, unperfumed cloth. Remove the cork smoothly and, using the clean cloth again, wipe the mouth of the bottle to remove any specks of cork which may have adhered.
- Champagne and sparkling wines should have their corks removed gently and without a minor explosion. Remember, too, that there is considerable pressure in the bottle and a flying metal capped cork could easily blind someone. The correct way is to *grip the cork firmly and turn the bottle*. The cork may then be eased out and the surplus pressure released without the loss of any precious wine. After all, the customer is paying to drink the wine, not to see it flowing away!
- When a bottle of wine has been ordered, it should be shown to the customer before it is opened so that he or she may confirm that it is the wine which they selected. This formality dispensed with, the bottle may then be uncorked in the manner described above and a small amount offered to the host for scrutiny. It is seldom necessary for the host actually to taste the wine to see if it is sound as appearance and smell are enough. These days it is very rare to find a bottle of wine in poor condition and 'corked' wine (dealt with later) is fortunately only discovered once in a lifetime.
- As soon as the above formalities are over with, the wine may be poured into the glasses, remembering that it is still polite practice to serve ladies first. After pouring, there should be sufficient room left in the glass for the wine to be swirled around to enhance the bouquet.

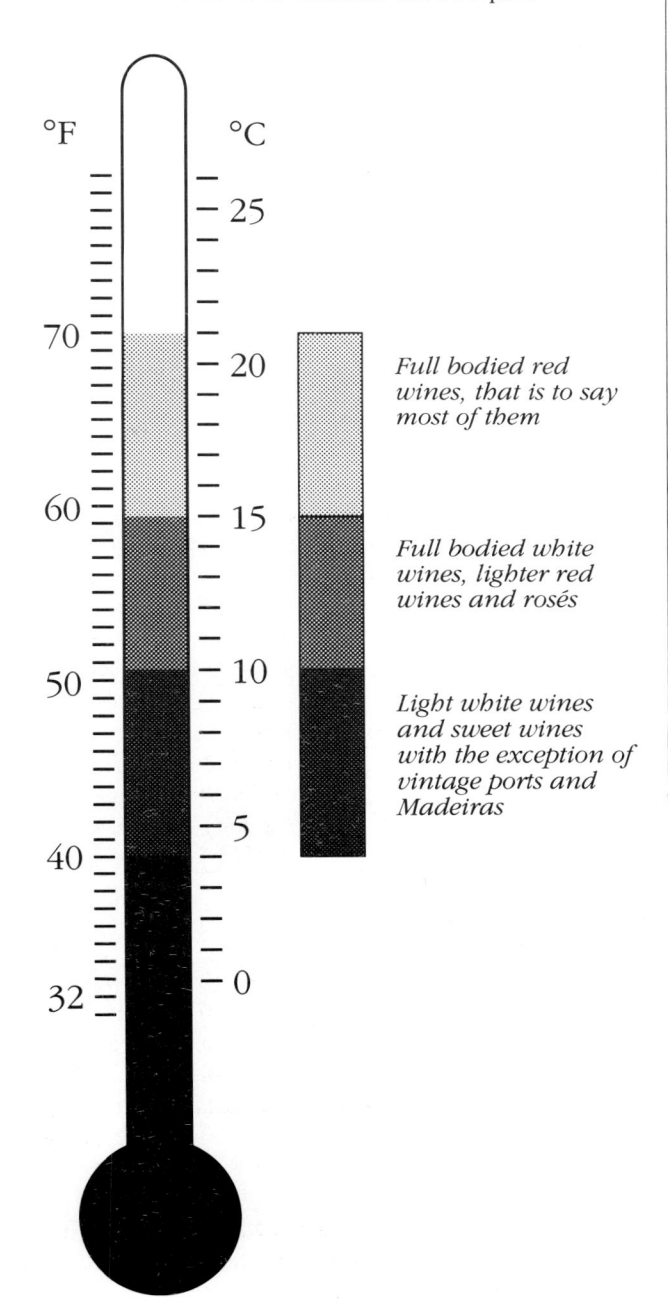

Full bodied red wines, that is to say most of them

Full bodied white wines, lighter red wines and rosés

Light white wines and sweet wines with the exception of vintage ports and Madeiras

Wine classifications

France

Vin de Table Table wine of the lowest classification, made from grapes which may be grown anywhere in France.

Vin de Pays Good, unblended wines produced from certain vines and coming from a registered area.

VDQS (*Vin Delimités de Qualité Superieure*) Wines of superior quality from approved vineyards, most of which are situated in the south of France. With this classification, the French government restricts and controls the type of vine, the method of cultivation, the yield per acre, the vinification and the alcohol content.

AC (*Appellation Contrôlée*) Fine wine of controlled origin, i.e. from a specific vine growing area. The only areas which are allowed to produce AC wines are those with the perfect combination of climate and soil structure. Even then, as with VDQS, the French government regulates every step in the process. AC is the highest and oldest classification of French wine.

Italy

Vino da Tavola This is table wine of the lowest classification and is the Italian equivalent of the French Vin de Table. Most of it is drunk in its country of origin or goes for blending in EEC wines.

DOC (*Denominazione di Origine Controllata*) This equates with the French AC and, similarly, is strictly and rigidly controlled.

DOCG (*Denominazione di Origine Controllata e Garantita*) This is the highest classification of Italian wine. It relates to wines of controlled and guaranteed origin, DOC wines carrying the Italian governmental seal of guarantee. DOCG wine is bottled locally and cannot be sold in containers holding more than 5 litres.

Germany

Deutscher Tafelwein This is the lowest classification of German wine. It is table wine which is the equivalent of French Vin de Table and Italian Vino da Tavola.

QbA (Qualitätswein bestimmter Anbaugebiete) This is quality wine from a defined region. There are eleven of such regions in Germany. Having passed stringent governmental examinations on analysis and taste, they are then given an AP number (*Amtliche Prufungsnummer*).

QmP (*Qualitätswein mit Prädikat*) This signifies official affirmation that the wine in a bottle bearing these letters is of superior quality. QmP wines fall into one of the following six categories or special attributes which are known as *Prädikaten:*

1. *Kabinett* Elegant, mature wine made from selected bunches of grapes which were harvested at the normal time.
2. *Spätlese* Made from grapes which were harvested late. These are full bodied wines.
3. *Auslese* Made from fully ripe and individually selected bunches of grapes, these wines are described as noble and aromatic.
4. *Beerenauslese* Moving yet higher up the QmP ladder, these are wines made from individual grapes which have been affected by noble rot or *Edelfaule* as the Germans call it.
5. *Trockenbeerenauslese* Thought to be the absolute pinnacle of achievement in German wine-making, it is made from grapes which are so shrivelled by noble rot that they look like raisins. It is exquisitely sweet and is comparable with the finest Sauternes. This is reflected in the price which is also phenomenal.
6. *Eiswein* A rare wine made from shrivelled and ice-bound grapes which are harvested in the depths of winter and crushed while still frozen.

Out of these six categories of predicated German wines, it is only the first three which are generally readily available.

Other countries such as Spain and Portugal also classify their wines in similar fashion but with fewer categories. Suffice to say that *Denominación de Origen* or D.O. for short is the Spanish version of Certificate of Origin for wines of specific zones, of which there are nearly thirty; few are exported. The Portuguese *Denominação do Origem* is very similar.

Wine – a brief introduction

Labels

Most of the time, it is not possible for you to taste a wine until you have actually bought a bottle and pulled the cork. This makes the label a very important item when purchasing wine not on taste but on the information given on the label.

Different wine-producing areas have their own idiosyncratic way of expressing the same facts. This is not so much of a problem as it might seem as a basic formula is common to them all. Understand that and you will understand most labels.

The law states that certain facts must be given on any wine label:

- ☐ The country of origin of the wine.
- ☐ The quantity of wine in the bottle or container (expressed in centilitres).
- ☐ The name and address of the responsible bottler or brand owner.
- ☐ In the case of EEC wines, the quality of the wine.

In practice, of course, most labels give much more information such as how sweet or dry the wine is, regional details, the vintage year (where applicable), the alcohol content expressed as a percentage of the whole and the grape variety or blend of grape varieties. Wines from Austalia, New Zealand and the USA usually have lashings of information on the back label in addition to the more formal information on the front.

All information is good news, so do take the trouble to look. The name of the bottler or shipper, for instance, is a good guide to quality and value especially when buying 'table wine', as some of it is the result of over-production in a 'quality' wine area. The licensee who knows his brand names and deals with a trustworthy shipper can purchase some fantastic Vin de Table, so get swotting up on your brand names!

Tips and hints

Crumbling corks

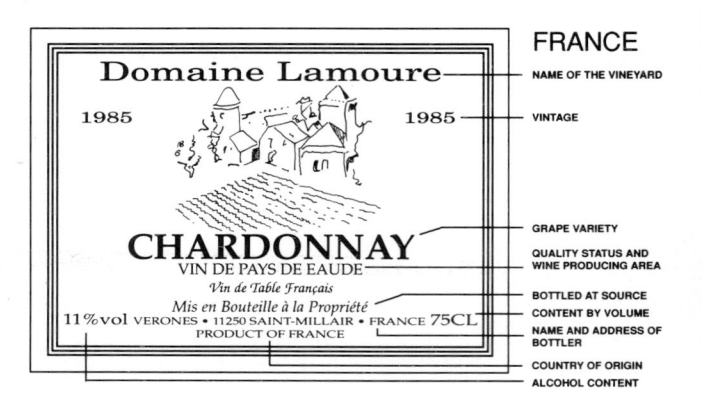

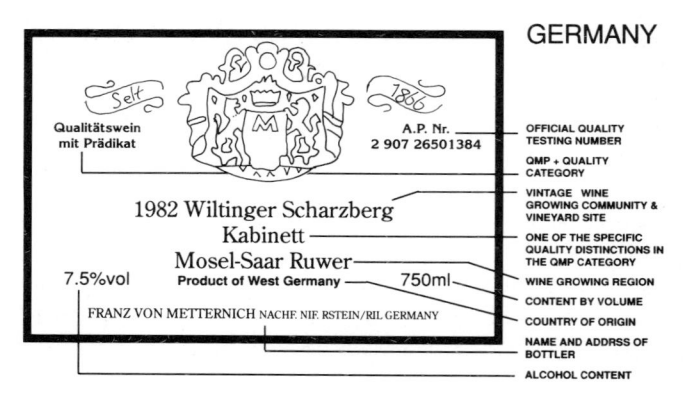

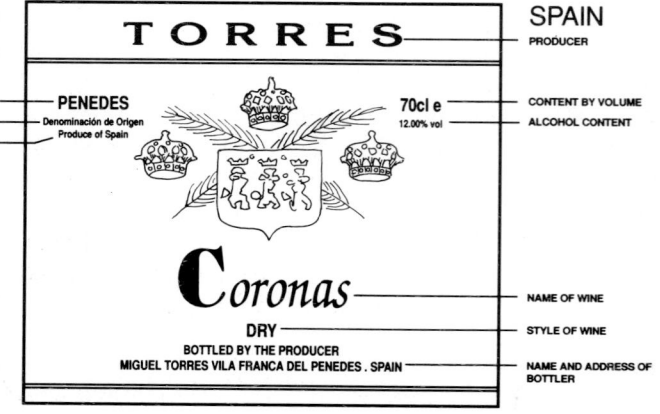

Some bottles of wine, mostly older ones, have crumbly corks which need to be treated with some care or they will disintegrate. Even so, pieces of cork are liable to fall into the wine in the best of regulated circles, but these can be removed from the glass without any harm being done to the wine. There is even a device called a 'butler's friend' which is specifically designed to cope with the removal of pieces of cork from the bottle. It can even remove the whole cork if somehow it has been pushed into the bottle. If such a thing does occur, though, it is probably better if the 'struggle' takes place out of sight of the customer. Just tell them politely that you will remove the offending cork in the kitchen where the lighting is brighter. Exactly the same applies to the next point.

Corks which refuse to come out

Some very young wines, but especially those from Italy, sometimes have corks that simply will not budge, even when using a double-lever type of corkscrew. There is no advantage to be gained from the performance of a feat of strength in front of the customer, especially if you split your breeches in the process. Instead, try warming the neck of the bottle the neck only mind you under a very hot tap. This will soften the wax coating on the cork and also expand the glass which holds it there.

Sediment

There is nothing harmful about sediment its just that it doesn't look that good but it can be kept out of the glass if the bottle is opened and poured with care. Some people like to decant their red wines, and if that is what they want, then they should do it, especially as it is quite a pleasurable occupation. It is not, though, strictly necessary. The only wines which possibly may need decanting in order to exclude the sediment are the very mature red Bordeaux, red Burgundies, northern Rhône reds and crusted or vintage ports. If you do have to decant a bottle of wine, it should have been allowed to stand upright for 2 or 3 days so that the sediment settles in the bottom of the bottle. You then place a light source such as a torch or a candle on a handy working surface and keeping that source of light underneath the neck of the bottle, pour the wine into the decanter in one gentle flowing motion. Do not allow the wine to slosh backwards and forwards or pour so fast that bubbles of air rush to the other end, or the whole purpose is defeated. When the bottle is almost decanted, you will see a thin line of sediment moving up the bottle. When it reaches the mouth of the bottle, stop pouring. If you have done it properly, there should be barely a mouthful of wine left in the bottle.

Corked wine

This has nothing to do with pieces of cork falling into the wine. It is an entirely different thing. 'Corked' wine is caused by an infected cork which gives the wine an unmistakable and foul aroma of decay. Once having had a whiff of 'corked' wine, it is not easily forgotten.

Such bottles, few and far between though they are, should be returned to the place of purchase for a refund or a replacement, which brings us nicely to the next point.

Returns

Bottles which have to be returned because they are faulty or because the contents are 'corked' can sometimes be a problem, especially if you are a tenant and tied to a brewery. The process of recouping the loss can be painfully slow or seemingly hopeless. To those who find themselves in such a position, the advice is to keep pegging away. Make a list of any returns so that you can keep a check on progress, and if you still have no joy, approach your local tenants' association. Those who are free to purchase wherever they wish are in a much stronger position and should establish a returns procedure at the outset of their commitment to a wine merchant. Whichever category you fall into, don't let it drop: your function is to make profit on your purchases and the wine merchant's function is to supply you with wine which is saleable.

Wine merchants' price lists

These are wonderful things to read through and produce lots of ooh's and ah's as you are transported from country to country and from region to region. It is important to remember, then, that these publications have been put together by marketing experts whose intention it is to captivate you totally. As stated above, they can be a mine of information but they can also be a minefield of omissions.

To be specific, almost none of them specifies exactly how much wine a 'bottle' contains. This is very naughty especially, as many bottles, when delivered, are found to contain only 70 cl as opposed to the expected 75 cl. Alright, so it's only 5 cl difference, but multiply that by the hundreds of thousands of bottles sold per annum and the result is a very handsome hidden profit. If you are selling wine by the glass, as many people do, it means that you will not be able to sell your planned six glasses per bottle, which makes an absolute nonsense of your carefully worked out profit-margin. In other words, their hidden profit is coming out of your pocket! So, make sure you *ask before you buy*.

Another facet of wine merchants' price lists which really needs to be watched is the fact that they almost never say whether the wines they list are ready for drinking. This is especially true in relation to red wines. They would probably defend this omission by asserting that people either know or should know what they are looking for. Such an assertion would be nonsense as most people are plainly not that knowledgeable. Considering that most of these price lists are written by experts, it would be a simple matter to include with the description of each wine details such as 'drink now', 'needs keeping' or 'may be drunk now but will continue to improve'. Until such a day dawns, it is necessary to consult an up-to-date pocket wine guide before purchasing any bottled wine or planning a new wine list. It must be said that such recalcitrance on the part of the wine merchants does nothing to improve wine sales and serves only to perpetuate the sort of snobbish mystique which many people associate with the wine trade.

Developments

Although a fairly wide variety of wines are available in boxes these days, trends indicate that an even greater choice may soon be needed. In North America, wine drinkers have shown a preference for fine wine by the glass as opposed to buying the whole bottle. Working on the principle that whatever happens in North America today will happen in the United Kingdom tomorrow, the types of wine which are currently available in boxes could soon be inadequate. This means that in order to provide a wider choice for the 'wine by the glass' trade, bottles must be considered. Selling wine by the glass from bottles, however, presents something of a problem as once a bottle is uncorked and air comes into contact with the contents, the wine begins to deteriorate, albeit slowly at first.

This problem can now be overcome by the use of a device called a Vacuvin. It is relatively inexpensive and is very easy to use. What it does is to extract all the air from a partially used bottle of wine before resealing it. This prevents oxidisation and keeps the contents in good condition. There are other, similar devices available on the market but they have been shown to be less efficient and more expensive. At the top end of the range there is a dispenser which holds up to 10 bottles simultaneously, but at the moment it is too expensive for all but the largest outlets to consider.

English wines

Still on the subject of trends, there has been a recent upsurge of interest in English wines. English wines that is, not British wines. The difference is that English wines are made from grapes grown in English vineyards whereas British wines are made from the concentrated juice of grapes which could have been grown anywhere. There are people who would sneer at the thought of considering English wine seriously and level the accusation that it is merely poor man's Hock. This is not so: English wines have their own characteristics and compare favourably with similarly priced wines from other countries. Grants of St James's have considered it worthwhile to promote English wines, so there is obviously a market. Why not give them a try?

New World wines

The appearance on the market of wines from Australia, New Zealand and the United States of America has created something of a mini-revolution in the wine trade of late. To be honest, wines from these countries, especially Australia, have been available here for some considerable time, so what, you may ask, has changed?

Probably the biggest single change is that these countries take their wine-making much more seriously now than they did before. Couple that with an all-out drive for exports and the result is dynamite. Wines from these countries are now readily available in this country and are well worth trying: they are extremely competitive on price and excellent quality.

The Australians, it has to be said, were winning international trophies for their wines more than 100 years ago, but phylloxera (a serious vine pest) and two world wars more or less put paid to the production of fine table wine. The 1960s, that decade of change, saw a renewal of interest and the outcome has been nothing short of amazing. Hatchard's pocket wine book, for instance, describes the Rosemount Estate's Chardonnay as an 'international smash'. Expressions like that are not used lightly in the wine trade. It does not stop there, however: a quick glance through all the wineries listed under Australia reveals that words such as 'outstanding', 'magnificent', 'extraordinary', 'exciting' and 'legendary' crop up with amazing regularity. They do not exaggerate – the quality can be truly staggering.

New Zealand, too, in recent years, has made a big international impact with table wines, especially whites of amazing quality. Chardonnays, Semillons and Sauvignon Blancs are responsible for New Zealand becoming famous as a wine-producing country and the highly competitive prices dictate that they cannot be ignored.

Since the 1970s, the United States of America, has shown considerable interest in exporting wine and, given American determination, it won't be long before American wines are winning international accolades.

Obviously, wines from these three countries, especially Australia and New Zealand, have reached the stage where they simply cannot be ignored when it comes to planning a wine list, especially when the quality is as good and very often better than their European counterparts.

Setting up wine sales

If you do not sell any wine across the bar at the moment, you have a whole untapped area of the market to exploit and it would be very foolish to suppose that there would not be any call for it. Wine sales are booming, so get with it!

The best way to go about it is to take it in stages:
1. Start off with just two wines such as Liebfraumilch which is medium sweet and a soft red Vin de Table.
2. As your sales of wine get under way, include a medium dry white wine such as a French Vin de Pays or its equivalent.
3. Now is the time to add a crisp, dry white wine such as a Muscadet or a Chablis.
4. To add balance to the range, include a Riesling from Yugoslavia.
5. Now that your sales of white wine are coming along nicely, it is time to introduce a light, fruity red wine such as Beaujolais or a really nice Côtes du Rhône.

It is an easy matter to provide quite a reasonable range of wines by the glass or carafe without stocking any bottles as all the above wines are readily available in wine boxes which are convenient, trouble-free and keep fresh for 4 months after opening. Remember to keep the whites in the fridge between sessions and that's it. What could be simpler?

How to increase your sales of wine

Perhaps the most important thing to be done is to train your staff. You may well be familiar with the wines which you sell and just how they should be served, but your staff might not be so well-versed in the subject. Take them through the different types of wine which you stock. Explain to them which are dry, medium or sweet, or in the case of red wines, what style they are. Explain what temperature the wines should be served at and what sorts of glass you wish them to use. In other words, give them little training sessions. This will give them an interest in the subject and help them to take a pride in what they are doing.

Here is a check-list of ways to encourage your customers to buy wine:

Wine in the bar
- ☐ The wines which you sell should be clearly visible to your customers. Remember, out of sight out of mind.
- ☐ Make use of all the point-of-sale material so that you actively draw attention to the wines which you offer.
- ☐ The dispensing equipment should be the best available for your particular bar and the volume which you sell.
- ☐ Offer a wine of the month on a prominently placed notice.

- ☐ If you serve bar food, suggest a glass of wine to go with it.
- ☐ Try to build up trade even further by offering a special wine of the day or week.

Wine in the restaurant
- ☐ When you lay the dining tables, always include wine glasses. This encourages customers to think of wine.
- ☐ Always offer wine with a meal. If you think that a particular wine goes especially well with one of your dishes, suggest it to your customers when they order.
- ☐ Your wine list should be attractive, interesting and informative. If it is, why hide it on a shelf behind the bar? Have several copies made and place them in strategic positions so that customers will pick them up and read them.
- ☐ When serving parties of four or more, suggest a red wine and a white wine.
- ☐ Don't wait until the main course is served before you take the wine to the table. Get it to the table with the first course or even earlier.
- ☐ Pay attention to your diners during the course of their meal and top up their glasses to two-thirds full.
- ☐ When a bottle of wine has been drunk, offer another one.

Setting up a wine list

There are a few points which need to be considered before you actually begin to select wines:
- ☐ The type or style of food which you serve.
- ☐ The price range of the wines which you intend to offer. This could well be linked with the type of food you serve.
- ☐ How many wines do you wish to offer?

Having sorted those points out, the next thing to decide is how you are going to style the wine list itself. Most people these days find wine lists which are split up into wine-growing regions and countries somewhat esoteric. It is far better to list your wines under types such as Champagne, sparkling wine, red wine, white wine and house wine so that customers who are a little unsure or inexperienced are not embarrassed. An informative description with each wine listed will complete the picture.

A small wine list would probably include the following:
1. Sparkling white wine
2. Medium-dry white wines
2. Dry white wines
2. Light red wines
2. Full-bodied red wines
3. House wines – dry white, medium-dry white and full-bodied red

A medium-sized wine list designed to match a wider range of food would probably look like this:
1. Champagne
1. Sparkling white wine
2 or 3. Medium-dry white wines
4 or 5. Dry white wines
4. Light red wines
4. Full-bodied red wines
3. House wines as above

Obviously, a larger wine list would provide an even wider choice and might include not only a choice of Champagnes but also a much wider choice of dry whites and reds. Whichever wines you choose to stock, do try to ensure that there are wines from different countries in each group. You might even decide to include some of the fabulous Australian and New Zealand wines or something from the land of 'the amazin' raisin', California.

Recommended reading

The New Wine Companion by David Burroughs and Norman Bezzant, published by Heinemann on behalf of the Wine and Spirit Education Trust.

Pocket Wine Book by Hugh Johnson, published by Mitchell Beazley each year.

Sainsbury's Book of Wine by Oz Clarke, published by Webster's Wine Guides.

Profit from Wine, published by the Wine Development Board.

A selection of literature is available free of charge from the Wine Development Board by sending them a large stamped and self-addressed envelope.

Useful addresses

The Wine Development Board, Five Kings House, formerly Thames House North, 1 Queen Street Place, London EC4R 1QS.

8 Promotion and publicity

Working on the assumption that all your market research is completed and that you have formulated a menu to satisfy the wants, needs and spending power of your chosen customers, your next task is to consider all the different ways and means of promoting the menu.

Unless you are in an extremely busy location and intend to cater only for existing customers, you will have to think about just how you are going to attract the customers to come to your pub, buy the food you have on offer and return again and again, hopefully with their friends. If you just hang around waiting to be discovered like a stage-struck teenager, it simply will not happen. You need to make people aware of your operation and motivate them into becoming customers.

The importance of presenting a good image cannot be overstressed. Image is what people see first and remember longest. In modern parlance it is what is known as 'getting your act together'. A good image gives people confidence in you and encourages them to buy the food you have on offer; a poor image will have the opposite effect.

The outside of the pub

If the eyes are the windows of the soul, the exterior of your premises, as we have already discussed in previous chapters, is the outward sign of inward grace, or the opposite if you get it wrong. How can the exterior of the premises promote your menu? Here are some points to consider:

- ☐ How can you reasonably expect people to come in for a meal if your premises look dirty, untidy and neglected from the outside?
- ☐ Have you considered a sign which informs people that food is available? If not, you should do so and ensure that it can be illuminated at night. A dog-eared card in the window with 'Bar Snacks' written on it will not do: hundreds of licensees are already using that method and are still wondering why they don't sell more food.
- ☐ You might also like to take advantage of the 'Pub Facility Symbols Scheme' which is run by The Brewers' Society, 42, Portman Square, London W1H 0BB. The symbols include Family Room, Pub Garden, Acommodation and Disabled Facilities (for the latter the pub has to have been independently assessed by an expert).

For a small fee, they will provide you with the appropriate window stickers and you will be eligible for free inclusion in a regional information brochure.

- ☐ It is a requirement of the Price Marking (Food & Drink on Premises) Order 1979 to have a menu on display, but it is also a great opportunity to advertise and can be very eye-catching. Why not make the most of it? Again, make sure it can be illuminated at night but above all, make it eye-catching and attractive.

Inside the pub

The actual menu

The purpose of a menu is to let your customers (and passers by in the case of the one displayed outside) know what food you offer and the price you are asking. Obviously, then, if it is difficult to read due to poor handwriting, bad layout or because it is falling apart, the object of the exercise is defeated.

Some licensees use blackboards to great advantage: a friend of ours, who has a lovely old pub in the Derbyshire Dales, uses nothing but blackboards. We ourselves use a combination of printed menus in folders and a blackboard which gives details of daily 'specials'. Whichever you choose, the important points to remember are the same:

- ☐ Whether handwritten or printed, it should be easy to read.
- ☐ The presentation and lay-out should be attractive.
- ☐ It should actually create interest.
- ☐ There should be sufficient copies to go round or, in the case of a blackboard, it should be in a prominent position.
- ☐ It should tell the truth or you could contravene the Trades Descriptions Act of 1968. For instance, a vegetarian dish must not be made with beef stock, etc. In this respect, it is also important to ensure that the description fits the item on the menu so that if a customer orders a Chicken Kiev say, he actually gets a Chicken Kiev and not something akin to it. This is not to suggest that you should in any way stifle creativity in the kitchen but if the cook has created a dish which is similar to Chicken Kiev but is stuffed with different ingredients, don't describe it as Chicken Kiev: give it a name of your own and put it on the list of daily specials.

Promotion and publicity

- [ ] You should state whether or not the prices you quote include VAT and service charge. Most outlets these days include VAT and those which do not are losing popularity. Service charge is much better left to the customer's discretion.
- [ ] Tatty or defaced menus should be removed and replaced.
- [ ] Remember that printed menus have to last, so not only should they be sturdy enough to stay the course and remain clean and attractive, but your prices, too, should also be able to sustain any increase in your costs until your next batch of menus are printed.
- [ ] It really does pay to take care with the wording of your menu. Some caterers go for mouth-watering descriptions, some for topical or humorous descriptions, whereas others list all the ingredients and inform the customer how each item is cooked. Your description, whichever style you find that you are best at, should tempt the customer, should be informative and should show that you think and care about the food which you offer.

Front of house

This is a very important area and if chaos is to be avoided, coordination is required:

- [ ] No matter what style of service you are providing, there should always be someone on hand to explain 'the system' to new customers. Customers need to know how and where they order the food, where they can sit, when and where they pay and what sort of service you provide. Leaving customers to wander around wondering what to do is not only counterproductive, it is also bad manners.
- [ ] If you are lucky enough to have a separate restaurant, the whole operation is usually done at the table, except perhaps the ordering, which might be done in the lounge bar and the customers shown to their table when their food is ready to be served. In this situation, the bill is almost always paid when the customers leave.
- [ ] At the other end of the scale, there is counter service which involves customers ordering light meals or snacks from the bar, paying as they order and taking their order to the table themselves.

- Another style of service, and one which is growing in popularity, lies somewhere between the two. This involves the customer selecting a table, perusing the menu and placing an order at an ordering point, after which, the staff do the rest. The question of when they actually pay is an open one but some people dislike paying for a meal before they have eaten it. It is a sad fact of life, though, that some licensees have to insist upon payment when the order is placed because of a high incidence of people leaving without paying.
- Whatever style of service you provide, the front-of-house staff should be familiar with all the items on the menu so that they can answer any queries customers may have. Pleasant, well-informed staff are an absolute must if you want to give satisfaction and see your business grow. Serving and presentation skills need to be taught. Do this yourself and make sure that your staff take a personal interest in your customers. Instil into them the need to be cheerful, helpful and friendly without being pushy and the importance of maintaining these standards all the time.
- Consider uniforms for your staff: it need not cost you a fortune and creates a very good impression. Firms which specialise in providing uniforms for the catering industry advertise regularly in trade journals and offer a wide selection of styles and colour schemes. Why not have a staff meeting so that your staff, under your guidance, can choose a uniform which is appropriate to your style of operation.
- It is a good idea to have a separate food bar so that the main bar does not become congested. A separate food bar is in any case a good idea as it gives you an opportunity to display your food in an attractive manner and provides a focal point for the customer who wishes to dine. We use a refrigerated display unit to show off a selection of starters, cheeses, puddings and fruit. Needless to say, all display material should be spotlessly clean and undamaged, as should all the various serving utensils. Ensure that the display itself really is a display and not simply a jumble. Think of it as a shop window and dress it up so that your customers find it irresistible.
- Crockery, plates, cups and saucers, soup bowls and that sort of thing should also match the style of your operation. When buying your crockery, then, bear this in mind, after all, no matter how much you like willow pattern, say, it would look pretty silly in a bistro operation or a pizza bar.
- Your cutlery should match, too, if you are to avoid place settings which look like they have come from an oddments sale. It actually pays dividends to invest in smart cutlery, cruets and other table appointments.
- Whatever style of operation you run, choose your table mats, napkins and linen with care so that they are distinctive and colourful but in a way that achieves a balance with the rest of the appointments.
- Nothing annoys customers so much as the hard sell where pushy staff are thrusting menus upon them before they have had chance to find their bearings. The soft sell is a much better idea and allows the customer to relax, which is the point of the exercise.

Publicity and advertising

Publicity

Word of mouth is undoubtedly the best and least expensive way of promoting your food. Nothing can equal the selling power of satisfied customers telling their friends, relatives, colleagues and acquaintances about this place which they have discovered where really good food is served in a congenial atmosphere.

Your staff, friends and relatives can also help to spread the word, but you have to make sure that whoever they talk to remembers what they have been told so that the next time they fancy a trip out for a bite to eat, they come to you. To achieve this, have some cards printed, or you could consider having some complementary slips printed which offer, say, a special introductory rate or a free glass of wine. The people who distribute these slips for you would be a good deal more enthusiastic if they had an incentive too. Why not then offer them a free meal for every dozen or so new customers they bring to you?

Once you have the grapevine ticking over nicely, you can get on with the business of organising your publicity campaign. Here are some ideas:

- Mailing shots to local groups, businesses and organisations, i.e. a well-thought-out and informative letter with a copy of your menu attached. If you wished, you could offer them a discount if they patronised you on a regular basis.

Promotion and publicity

We used to be called The White Horse...

- Write to your local press and invite the editor or the features editor over for a free meal in exchange for a write-up.
- Have some interesting and descriptive leaflets printed and negotiate to place them where they will do some good: nearby hotels for inclusion in their room folders, the information desk at the local town hall, tourist board offices, citizens' advice bureaux, taxi firms and the like.
- If your customers tell you that they think your food is superb, ask them to write letters to the different guide books. Guide books rely upon such recommendations and the more they receive about you, the more likely you are to be included.
- Enter the cookery competitions which are regularly featured in *Pubcaterer* and other trade journals. Such competitions are sponsored by big concerns and are always accompanied by a blaze of publicity. If you win, you could even get a television interview – we did! Even if you only get as far as a regional final you will still enjoy a great deal of free publicity.
- Whenever you sit down to do some letterwriting, especially if you are writing to a newspaper or the media, keep your publicity campaign in mind and use the letter to promote your menu. Enclose a copy of your menu and a leaflet.
- Support your local charities. Many licensees get sick and tired of being approached to provide prizes for local worthy causes and charities, but they should work with a long head. Why not supply a meal for two with a glass of wine? Ensure that they publicise your house on the tickets or posters so that everyone can see that you have donated a worthwhile prize and the result is lots of goodwill and publicity at comparatively little cost.

Advertising

Advertising, as opposed to publicity, is something rather different. To start with, it is extremely expensive, and unless skilfully planned, may well not produce results which are commensurate to the outlay. Before you make any decision on advertising, you should consider these points:

- What, exactly, are you advertising? For instance, is it the food, is it some special event or are you simply trying to promote everything you do food, service, facilities and general ambience? If it is the latter, it could mean a long campaign and could cost a fortune.
- You need to identify which sector of the market your advertising is aimed at. Business people, shoppers, young people, tourists or whatever do not read the same papers, so obviously you need to know who you are aiming at before you can decide where to advertise.
- Why, precisely, are you advertising? Is it to boost trade at a slack time? Is it to increase your lunchtime trade? It could be that you simply want to keep your house in the public eye.

All these questions and many more will influence you when you decide when and where you are placing your advertisement.

Here are some suggestions as to where you can advertise:

- Newspapers and magazines: national daily, local evening, local weekly and free newspapers, monthly magazines such as *Lancashire Life*, parish magazines, trade journals.
- Other publications: theatre programmes, town guides, tourist board guides.

- Posters for display in public places such as bingo halls, bus and railway stations, libraries, sports centres and so on.
- Car stickers.
- On public transport.
- Matchboxes, paper napkins, paper coasters, tent cards and other in-house items which customers are likely to take with them.

There is little point in spending good money on an advertisement if the content and layout are amateurish and ill-conceived. Professional help in this area can cost a great deal of money so if you want to avoid this extra cost, you will have to do it yourself.

Look at the advertisements in any newspaper or magazine and you will see that most of them are indistinguishable from each other. That 'sameness' is precisely what you must avoid. Here, then, are some points to watch out for:

- Keep your advertisement simple: too much information only serves to confuse the reader. An advertisement which contains only two or three lines and plenty of space will create a much bigger impact than one of a similar size which is crammed full of information.
- Aim to be unique: your advertisement should stand out above the others; don't let it get lost in a crowd. If you must advertise on a day when all the others are advertising, insist upon the best position, the best page and so on. If all the other advertisements are neatly set up in columns, which they usually are, why not cut them in half with a layout which goes right across the page but is only three or four lines in depth? Aim to get the upper hand.
- Use your imagination to produce an advertisement which will stay in the mind of the reader. If it falls into the 'once read, immediately forgotten' category, you have failed. You might, like, for instance, to consider the use of rhyming jingles, slogans and catchphrases, and why not? Professional advertising agencies do it all the time.
- It is a bad idea to use the same advertisement time and time again. Very few people actually read advertisement pages; they scan them and mentally discard those which they have seen before. If you decide to do a run of advertisements, spend some time on planning and ideas so that you can change your copy and layout each time. That way you can feature a different aspect in each advertisement and keep it simple and uncluttered.
- Brevity, clarity and impact are of even more importance when designing a car sticker or an advertisement to be placed on the exterior of public transport, as people might only have a second or two to take it in.

9 Kitchen layout

Since our first hesitant beginnings in the catering industry, many moons have passed and during that time we have worked in a variety of kitchens. Some were large with a separate scullery and there were others in which you could not swing the proverbial cat. They were all different but they all had one thing in common – problems! The large ones got just as cluttered as the small because free space never remained free for very long.

We used to feel very guilty about the state of our kitchen on busy nights, particularly as customers were picking up the Greek habit of wandering in. One day, we had the opportunity to visit the kitchens of a top-notch hotel and you can imagine how pleased we felt when at first glance they, too, appeared to be in a state of chaos. However, a closer look revealed a smooth and efficient operation and oh, how we envied the equipment! If only we could afford the same, we said to ourselves, our problems would be over.

The real eye-opener, though, came when we visited one of the top Parisian restaurants; of course, the food was superb, but for us, the highlight of the evening was a tour of the kitchen. It was minute. There they were, eight of France's leading chefs, working at stations which barely gave them elbow room with their tall hats continually brushing against the array of bright copper pans which hung from the ceiling. No sophisticated equipment for those boys; simply an oven, four burners, a grill and a small work surface. However, as with the hotel kitchen, it was a smooth and efficient operation and everything they needed was to hand.

What, was the secret? Was it the high staffing levels common to both establishments? No it was not; every single member of staff at both establishments were fully employed coping with the throughput. The secret lay in the kitchen layout. The kitchen was so carefully thought out and designed that the orders simply flowed through.

Having learnt the salutary lesson that it is not so much the amount or range of equipment that matters as much as where it is situated, we sat back and tried to look objectively at our own kitchen operation. In common with most pub caterers, we had acquired our equipment on a piecemeal basis, some inherited from the previous landlord and some bought as the trade started to grow. Eventually, we had the statutory number of preparation tables, the required number of fridges and a great number of ideas, none of which seemed to work. It was time to call in the kitchen design experts.

There are many forms of design service available nowadays. Most of the equipment manufacturers offer such a facility as part of their service although they may charge you for it. Also, if any new equipment is needed, it goes without saying that they will use their own brand, so you must make sure that you are happy with their range of products before you engage them.

CEDA is the logo of the Catering Equipment Distributors' Association of Great Britain and is displayed in the showrooms and on the stationary of its members. One of the stipulations of membership is that a planning and design service should be available. For the smaller caterer, this service has certain advantages as distributors carry a wide range of equipment manufactured by various companies, thus ensuring freedom of choice, rather than being stuck with just one manufacturer. It is advisable to check that a distributor is a member of CEDA for not just anyone can join; membership entails a rigorous examination of the credibility of the applicant.

In addition to the above there are also independent catering consultants who will not only re-design your kitchen but also help with the menu and do a full feasibility study of the whole operation. Needless to say, they are very expensive.

All who offer a design service will discuss with you fully your requirements and draw up a plan for which, if you are purchasing equipment from them, there is usually no charge. Some do charge a basic fee which is refundable if the scheme goes ahead and equipment is purchased. *Before you allow anyone to start work on a scheme, do check just what the charges are.*

All designers worth their salt will incorporate existing equipment into a scheme wherever possible, so a new kitchen need not necessarily cost you an arm and a leg. They will also be aware of Environmental Health requirements thus ensuring that you will not have to make further alterations at a later date to avoid falling foul of the law. Some will even arrange for the design and planning of building alterations, plumbing and electrical installations where necessary. So the advice is, if you are considering a major change in layout or intend to purchase additional new equipment, do take advantage of the many design services available – they could save you time and money.

In spite of all that it is possible to alter the layout yourselves, although if a major alteration involving building work is envisaged, professional advice is a must, as planning applications can present big problems unless you know what you are doing. In addition, tenant licensees will need the permission of the

Kitchen layout

company from whom they rent the premises and, if there is any increase in drinking area involved as a result of such an alteration, the permission of the Licensing Justices will have to be obtained.

However, if all you want to do is to try and improve your operation, there are several pointers that may be of assistance. Very simply, in any catering operation, the orders arrive in the kitchen, meals are prepared and cooked, they are taken out by the serving staff and dirty pots are brought back to be washed. In reality, serving staff come into the kitchen, bump into those going out, there is nowhere to dump the dirty pots and the cook has to trail out in the rain to an outhouse to find the ingredients. This is the time when you wish you had never thought of coming into the catering industry and begin to look at the 'situations vacant' columns in the press. Yes?

So, where do you start? To begin with, there are the hygiene regulations which are covered in Chapter 11. Bearing those in mind then, you must have the following:

- ☐ Separate sinks for the preparation of vegetables and for washing dishes.
- ☐ A separate handbasin for the kitchen staff to wash their hands.
- ☐ Separate preparation tables for raw and cooked food or salads.
- ☐ The equipment and the preparation surfaces planned so that food can progress from raw to cooked in as linear a fashion as possible in the space available.
- ☐ Separate fridges for cooked and uncooked food.
- ☐ Easily cleanable floor and wall coverings. This usually means tiles and stainless steel.
- ☐ Adequate ventilation over cooking ranges and fryers. An extractor fan in the window on its own is not really sufficient.

These hygiene requirements MUST be incorporated into any new scheme, as also must fire regulations. All major alterations must have the approval of the Fire Service, but even if you are just contemplating a simple 'swap around' of equipment, consultation with your local Fire Prevention Officer is well worth considering. His advice is free of charge and could save injury and lives.

The Fire Prevention Officer will insist that no item of equipment is placed in such a position that it blocks or impedes an exit. He will similarly insist that deep-fat fryers should be positioned away from doorways and windows. He will advise on electrical and/or gas installations and all aspects of fire safety. We have always found Fire Prevention Officers to be most helpful and obliging and have no hesitation in contacting them on even the most trivial of points concerning fire prevention and safety. They are only too happy to answer any query, so make use of them, get to know them and, who knows, they may even start to patronise your establishment!

In the next chapter we will look at the range and viability of equipment which is available to anyone who is considering purchasing new, but for the purposes of this exercise we will use the kitchen at the Bushell's Arms as an example to demonstrate how we resolved some of our problems by simply redesigning the kitchen layout.

Another important point to consider before planning the kitchen is the power supply – very important for your cooking needs, but also your heating, too. Is it electricity, natural gas or Calor gas? For us it has always been Calor gas, which we have found more than satisfactory. If you are planning a new kitchen, consider which power form you prefer and plan accordingly. If you prefer gas, but are not connected to a mains supply of natural gas (or are out of reach of one), don't assume you must necessarily stick to electricity – Calor gas is the answer. If you prefer to cook with electricity, take that into consideration, too.

The kitchen at the Bushell's Arms has several inherent disadvantages: it is small, very small; it is the only means of access to our accommodation upstairs; and it acts as the main thoroughfare to the beer storage area, the freezer room and other outhouses. During a busy session, it is rather like Clapham Junction. The problem was that, as with most tenants, our funds were limited, the only way forward was to persuade the brewery to do the job. This they agreed to do but we had to wait until funds were available. Somehow we had to find a temporary solution.

Our first consideration was the menu. We provide an extensive à la carte menu which changes frequently and it is upon this form of menu that we have built our reputation. To alter the menu instead of the kitchen in our case would have meant financial suicide. Another consideration was the fact that we do buy some convenience foods and use short-term freezing of some of the home-made items which appear on the menu, although a large part of the menu consists of meat and fish dishes which are cooked to order. Although we have only a very small kitchen, we do have some advantages: just outside the kitchen, in the pub, we

Kitchen layout

have a sizeable cold display unit underneath which there is a large fridge which houses cooked meats and sweets and still leaves a reasonable holding area for butter and cream, etc. Behind this, on the wall facing the customers as they stand at the display unit, is a very useful row of cupboards on top of which is a nice clean work surface. In the same area but just to one side, we have a small fridge in which we chill bottles of white wine and use the freezer compartment to store ice cream. All sweets and coffee, then, are stored and served front of house. Yet another advantage is that outside, at the back, we have two separate store rooms. One contains three freezers and a large fridge and the other we use for storing cleaning equipment and materials and other possibly noxious substances which should never be kept near food.

You can see from the above that there are some important points to remember:

- ☐ It is important when replanning a kitchen, to consider it as a part of the whole catering operation and not in isolation.
- ☐ If you have the space and the funds, some form of hot or cold display unit is well worth considering. Not only does it relieve some of the strain in the main kitchen area but it also gives customers an opportunity to see for themselves the sort of food which is available. It is a form of advertising, but apart from that, cold puddings and salads gain little from being continually taken in and out of refrigeration in a hot kitchen. Quite apart from the effect it has on the quality, it is most unhygienic.
- ☐ Money, too, has no place in the main kitchen area as coins and notes are notoriously unhygienic and should never come into contact with food. Keep tills out of the kitchen.
- ☐ Dry goods and freezers can be stored in another room provided that it is clean and well ventilated.
- ☐ Crockery and cutlery can also be housed somewhere other than in the kitchen itself. If there is a hot cupboard in the kitchen, this should be stocked up well before the start of each session so as to keep clutter to a minimum.

But to return to the Bushell's, our next consideration was the existing equipment. The kitchen equipment we inherited consisted of a six-ring conventional oven fuelled by Calor, a Calor-fuelled griddle for which we had little or no use, a combination oven, a microwave oven, a small deep-fryer and two fridges, one for

Mind you, it's wonderful training for Rugby League...

Kitchen layout

The original layout of the Bushells Arms' kitchen

1. Wash hand basin
2. Plate rack
3. Double bowl sink
4. Rubbish bin
5. Over shelf
6. Fridge
7. Over shelf
8. Combination oven
9. Calor griddle (unused) with microwave on top
10. Deep fat fryer
11. 6 burner cooking range
12. Preparation tables

uncooked produce and the other for cooked. Our problems were mainly that the kitchen area quickly became congested with dirty dishes and cutlery. Orders were being placed haphazardly on working surfaces and so were either lost or taken out of sequence. Also, at peak periods there were considerable delays. It was obvious that we needed to purchase some new equipment, as plates were being warmed in valuable oven space and the one small deep-fryer was being used for some of the deep-fried starters as well as for chips.

So having already decided that we did not want to alter the menu and that we could not afford to spend a great deal of money, we realised that we would have to streamline the kitchen so that we could cope more easily with our increasing trade. Help was at hand in the form of the Blackburn Catering Centre, members of CEDA from whom we had decided to buy some new equipment. They worked out the whole scheme for us free of charge. The way they went about it is no secret and can easily be used by anyone if they have a mind to do so.

The first requirements are accurate measuring and a scale plan of the kitchen. This applies whether you are trying to redesign your kitchen completely or simply purchasing a new piece of equipment. The easiest way is to take a piece of graph paper, first ensuring that it is large enough for you to work accurately. The purpose of using graph paper is to make it easier to draw to scale and to produce a neat finished drawing. Drawing to scale means that there is a uniform reduction in size, so if, for instance, a window measures 6 feet across and you have decided that each of the small squares on your graph paper represents 6 inches, the window will take up 12 small squares on the drawing. If you wish to know the dimensions of a piece of equipment, say, or the length of a wall, you merely have to count the small squares or use a scale rule to obtain the information.

However, before you dash off to sharpen your pencils, you must decide whether you are going to work in imperial (feet and inches) or metric measurements (metres and millimetres). Metric will probably be easier as graph paper is ruled out in units of ten, but make sure to use a metric tape measure. These days, most people use metric measures so to prepare your drawing in imperial would involve you in lengthy conversions and you would probably find the result inaccurate. An inexpensive scale rule will make life even simpler. If your graph paper is size A4 or twice that size, you will probably be working at a reduction of

Immovable fittings: power and water supply points

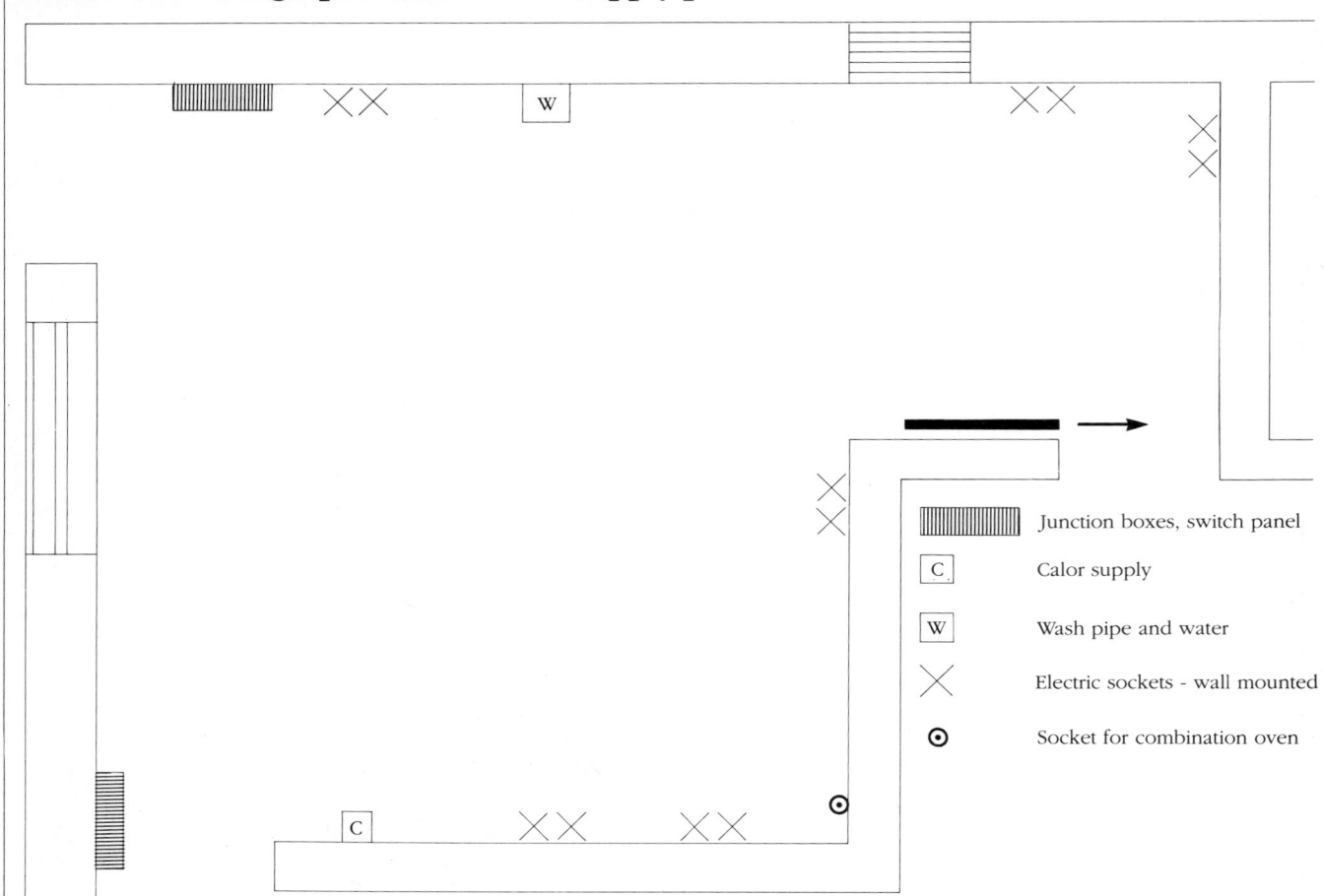

▮▮▮▮	Junction boxes, switch panel
C	Calor supply
W	Wash pipe and water
×	Electric sockets - wall mounted
⊙	Socket for combination oven

1:10 or thereabouts, so be sure to buy a rule which includes that scale. Metric scale rules are sold at most large stationers whereas imperial scale rules are more difficult to find.

The first measurements to take and draw out on your plan are the actual dimensions of the room, remembering that at this stage you are not concerned with the height, but ensuring that any alcoves, doors or windows are marked and placed accurately. You should be able to see at this stage whether or not the scale you have chosen is going to be all right. If for instance 1:10 is too large, reduce it by half to 1:20.

Next, mark in the existing power points – electricity, Calor or natural gas – and the position of any waste pipes. This is very important as these items can prove costly to relocate and their position, to a certain extent, determines where your equipment will be placed. If you are considering purchasing new equipment, it would be wise at this stage to consider whether or not your power supply needs upgrading to cope with the additional demand.

If, as in our case, no structural alterations are to take place, the next stage of your plan is to measure and draw in any fittings and equipment which it is thought will not be moved. For us, this meant sinks, air duct canopy, Calor gas oven and combination oven which has its own power point. Once these are in place on the plan, you can see how much space you have to work with. You will also have the dimensions of any equipment you wish to retain and, by this time, the dimensions of any equipment you wish to purchase. It is a good idea to make a list of all these items of equipment together with their dimensions to make life easier while you are deciding where to put what.

The first problem we encountered at this stage was that the sliding door from the kitchen into the main body of the pub was never closed due to the fact that waitresses were in and out continually. The problem was that this area of the kitchen was in full view of the public, especially those who were placing orders at the food display counter. What the customers could see was a work top upon which the waitresses had dumped dirty dishes. It was unsightly and unhygienic. The problem was resolved by installing a bin liner holder with a lid just inside the kitchen for non-food rubbish such as soiled paper napkins and so on, and next to the sink a scraping ring was inserted into the work surface with a bin below to accommodate food scraps. These two very simple and inexpensive items ensured that incoming dirty dishes could be easily cleared and

Immovable fittings: ovens and sink

[Kitchen layout diagram showing SINK, CANOPY, CALOR OVEN, and COMBINATION OVEN]

stacked neatly and the electric fly killer on the wall just above ensured that there would be no infestation of flies during warm weather.

Our next problem was that the existing sink was not really adequate so we replaced it with a catering sink and a copious draining rack above. As we have no room for a commercial dishwasher, we always employ someone to wash up during busy sessions. This ensures a flow and once the waitresses have deposited the dirty dishes, they simply move across to the centre bench, pick up clean serving cloths and take the prepared food out to the customers. The plan on page 86 shows clearly how our problems were solved and why waitresses no longer bump into the cooks, who are now safely installed in their own little empire! The wash-basin with paper towel dispenser above is situated immediately behind the centre bench, so waitresses and cooks alike can wash their hands frequently and easily. When not in use, it has a stainless steel cover which allows the rest of the bench in which it is situated to be used for salad preparation.

Having eliminated most of the problems we had with dirty dishes and traffic jams, the next thing which needed sorting out was the cooking area. The fridge for uncooked food was outside, so stock had to be brought in and stored in cool boxes for the session. This was very inconvenient because it meant that whenever stock needed replenishing, someone had to go outside, regardless of the weather, and bring it in. What we needed was another fridge inside. This we bought and placed under the preparation table next to the combination oven to be used for uncooked foods only. The fridge for cooked foods was resited next to the back door not an ideal position by any means, but there was nowhere else for it to go.

The main purchase for the cooking area was a grill which, because it was Calor-fuelled, had to be positioned near the Calor supply pipe above the cooker and under the canopy. Also, a second deep fryer was purchased for cooking some of the starters, so we chose the same brand as the existing unit so that they would match and form a compact modular unit, sitting as they do, on top of the hot cupboard. This is the great advantage of modular units which are available from most equipment manufacturers.

To resolve the problem of lost or out of sequence orders, we invested in a 'tab grabber', an inexpensive item which holds orders-in-sequence and in a manner which is clearly visible to the cooks. This was positioned on a new overshelf above the cooks'

The present layout of the Bushells Arms' kitchen

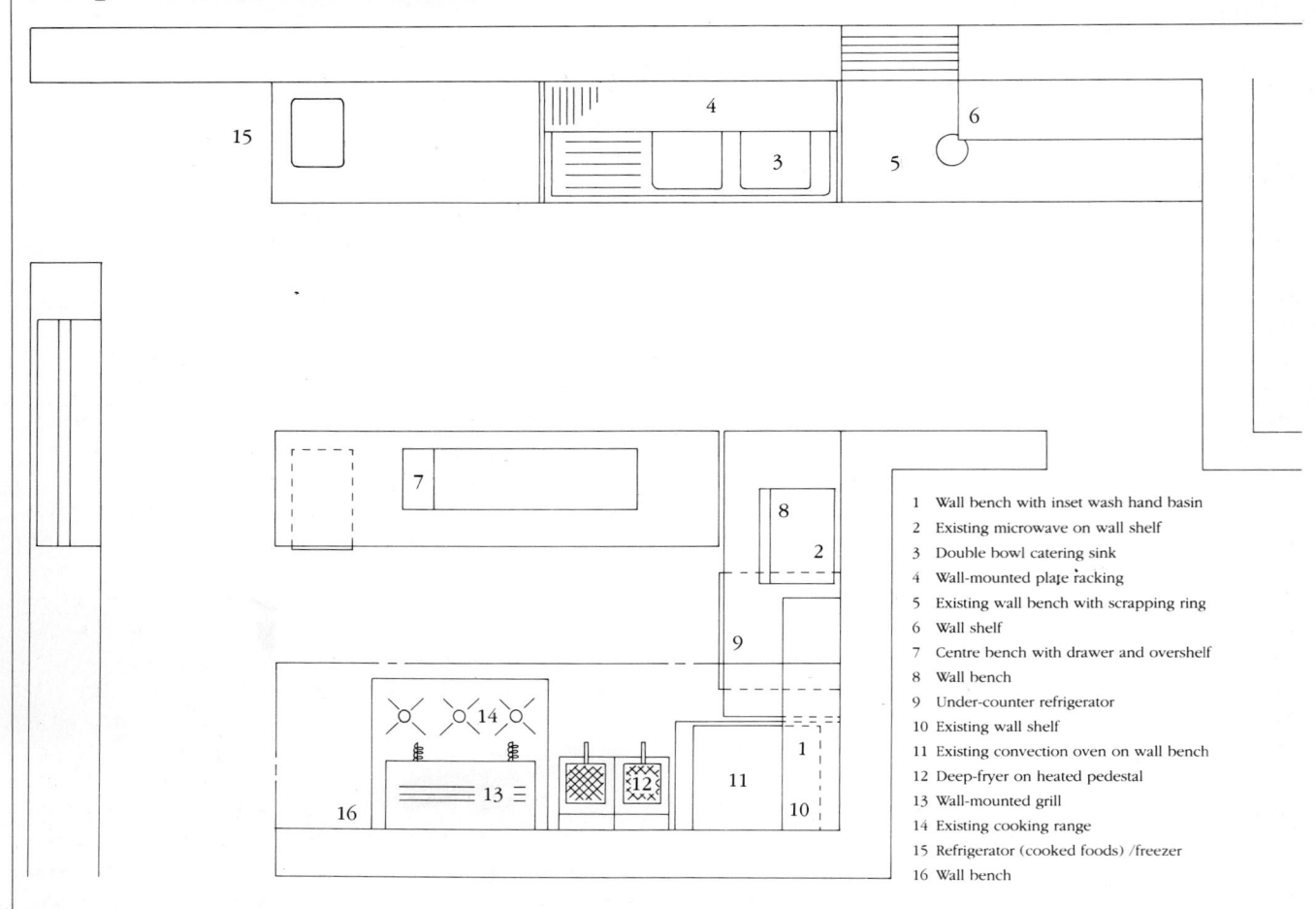

1. Wall bench with inset wash hand basin
2. Existing microwave on wall shelf
3. Double bowl catering sink
4. Wall-mounted plate racking
5. Existing wall bench with scrapping ring
6. Wall shelf
7. Centre bench with drawer and overshelf
8. Wall bench
9. Under-counter refrigerator
10. Existing wall shelf
11. Existing convection oven on wall bench
12. Deep-fryer on heated pedestal
13. Wall-mounted grill
14. Existing cooking range
15. Refrigerator (cooked foods) /freezer
16. Wall bench

preparation table.

The system now, in the cooking area, is that food is cooked on the equipment on the back wall, the cooks then turn round to plate up the meals and, when they are ready, they are put on to the overshelf, from where the waitresses can easily and safely pick them up.

Existing benches were adapted and utilised, reducing the cost so at the end of the day we had a new and much more efficient kitchen for minimum cost. Our only purchases were a grill, a fridge, a deep fryer and a hot cupboard. The revised kitchen is not perfect but it is a great improvement on the old one. It is only an example to illustrate the layman's method of revising a kitchen layout; it is not meant as an example of a perfect kitchen!

A final point to remember is that, although it is possible to simply to swap equipment around using the advice given above, there is so much free professional advice available, it is wise to make use of it for all but the very simplest of alterations.

Useful addresses

Fire Protection Association, Aldermary House, Queen Street, London EC4N 1TJ, OR your local Fire Service in the local telephone directory.

Environmental Health Office – listed in the local telephone directory under the local authority heading.

CEMA (Catering Equipment Manufacturers' Association of Great Britain) 14 Pall Mall, London SW1Y 5LZ. Can provide a list of members who offer a planning and design service.

CEDA (Catering Equipment Distributers' Association), The Secretary, J.N. Humphrey Baker, 16 Merrilyn Close, Claygate, Esher, Surrey KT10 0ED.

All members offer a planning and design service.

10 Equipment

Choosing equipment

Many successful pub caterers, if pressed, will admit that when they first started out, they had to make do with what amounted to nothing more than an ordinary domestic kitchen in which to prepare food on a commercial basis. Through sheer ingenuity and dedication they managed to produce wholesome and attractive food for their customers but before long they were forced into the realisation that equipment designed for a domestic situation is not at all suitable for a commercial catering operation. Quite simply, it just does not stand up to the wear and tear.

In an ideal situation, we would decide what percentage of trade we want from the catering side and allocate that percentage of our funds to setting it up. In reality, what happens is that new equipment is bought on a piecemeal basis due to the fact that not many of us have a large amount of capital to spend at the outset nor are we sure just how trade will develop. When a piece of equipment either 'packs up' or is found to be inadequate, we replace it and as these things never happen at a convenient time, we rush out to the nearest supplier and buy what is readily available with scant thought about planning. Fortunately, most of the time, things turn out alright as most distributors are fairly responsible and nowadays carry quite a wide range.

However, if we took time to shop around, we would probably get a much better deal. One of the points we looked at in the chapter on menu planning is how to arrange the menu so that we were not wholly reliant on just one piece of equipment. Equally, we cannot afford to have costly pieces of equipment just lying around merely as back up as that would take up valuable space and tie up capital which could be put to better use elsewhere.

When we do decide that we really must invest in some new equipment, before we start spending, there are several points which need close consideration:

- ☐ How much money have we got to spend?
- ☐ What do we want the new equipment to do?
- ☐ How much space is available and will it fit into the kitchen layout without disrupting the flow?
- ☐ If purchased for a specific task, will it be adaptable if the menu changes and the original function is no longer required?
- ☐ What is the power source, will it be necessary to have costly alterations to the power supply?
- ☐ What amount of use is anticipated - heavy, medium or light?
- ☐ Is there an adequate service contract available and if anything does go wrong, are spares easily and inexpensively obtained?
- ☐ Do we want to buy or lease?

Once we have satisfied ourselves that we do actually need the equipment, where do we look for it?

Catering distributors do carry a wide range, they will probably stock several makes and will have a comprehensive range of literature. Good distributors [check with CEDA (Catering Equipment Distributors' Association) for your nearest registered supplier] will have trained staff who will be able to listen to your requirements and offer constructive advice on any purchase.

Trade fairs too, are a valuable source of information, if you have the time to attend them that is. However, if you attend a trade fair with the intention of looking at a particular item rather than just going for a day out, do check the list of manufacturers who will be attending otherwise you may find that your journey was wasted. Also, manufacturers who do attend trade fairs are there to promote and sell their products and some are inclined to indulge in the hard sell. Unless you are sure that the equipment which they are offering is exactly what you want, please don't buy just because there is an offer on, you may regret it later. Even if you do not wish to make a purchase, it is well worth the effort to attend one or two trade fairs each year as they are an invaluable source of information as to what is new in the trade.

A casual glance at the morning mail usually reveals a wide variety of trade publications which function mainly as a vehicle for advertising. Their free information service, if you are just starting to shop around, is a good first step to finding out what is on the market and will also give you some idea on prices. Magazines such as *Pubcaterer* are an invaluable source of information on all types of equipment as they are aimed specifically at pubs.

In addition to the usual advertisements, *Pubcaterer* et al also regularly feature articles concerning the purchase and use of all types of catering equipment. Very often, their team of experts will have conducted trials, the results of which are included in the articles. This a great help when trying to establish just what points we need to look out for and in deciding what questions we need to ask ourselves before approaching a salesman. It is wise to remember though, that too much shopping around can lead to 'shopping fatigue' with the result that you buy the next thing you see, which would defeat the object of the exercise.

Equipment

After expressing an interest in a particular piece of equipment, the next stage is to arrange for a demonstration. This may not be possible on your own premises as in the case of dish washers which have to be plumbed in, or it may not be necessary as with refrigerators but with microwaves, combination ovens and the like, it is essential.

When you arrange for a demonstration on your premises, make sure that the salesman does not just cook the food he wants, in the time he wants. Arrange for him to come during say a lunchtime session so that you can try out your own menu items under realistic conditions; better still, see if it is possible to borrow the appliance for a few days. That way, you can try it out in your own time, without any sales pressure and ensure that it is exactly what you want, in your working routine. Wherever possible, try before you buy.

There are some items of equipment which are more or less standard for a pub catering operation:

- ☐ An oven with boiling rings on top.
- ☐ A microwave oven.
- ☐ A deep fryer.
- ☐ Refrigerators.
- ☐ Deep freezers.
- ☐ A grill or griddle.
- ☐ A hot cupboard or plate warmer.
- ☐ A dish washer.

Most pub kitchens will have some of the above equipment, depending on the size of the kitchen and the type of operation. Some will have all of these items. The crucial point to consider though, is not the amount of equipment but that it should be the RIGHT equipment.

Not many pubs need the very heavy range of equipment which is required in hotels and industrial kitchens. Manufacturers have realised this and now produce a medium range which is ideal for smaller outlets. The problem with heavy duty equipment is that because it is designed to cope with a high output, it can create problems in terms of your power supply. Additionally, it is much larger in size so unless you have the space and the throughput, the medium duty range would probably be much more suitable.

When considering the purchase of equipment such as hot cupboards, grills or griddles, bain maries and even deep fryers, it is well worth looking at what is called modular equipment. Modular equipment is equipment which is designed to fit together and provide a neat way of slotting in a variety of items which can be added to at a later stage. Before buying though, you must make certain that you are happy with the entire range in that particular group as items from other groups or ranges will not fit together. For example, the Lincat 'Lynx' range will not fit in with the Lincat 'Silver Link' range. Compact or modular equipment ranges are increasing in popularity with smaller pub caterers which is not surprising as they provide versatility and a reasonable throughput without being too expensive.

By the time we'd paid the designer, it was all we could afford!

Ovens

Static or conventional ovens

The static catering oven with a four or six burner hob, is still a useful piece of equipment. Fuelled by Calor gas, natural gas or electricity, it is the workhorse of many successful kitchens. Even the medium duty range is extremely robust and is well worth considering for those moving up from the domestic models.

In a small operation, it is probably the most adaptable piece of equipment in the kitchen – not only will it bake, braise and boil but it will also act as a holding oven and even a plate warmer if necessary. Its main advantage though, is that it will take the larger trays which are known as gastronorms. Gastronorms make it possible for you to cook up to twenty or so portions of a particular dish all at once and hold them in the oven over a session, thus taking the strain off other equipment.

The burners on top are also extremely useful – soup can be kept hot on one, vegetables on another, a third may be used for sauces and a fourth for pan frying. Even if you drastically change your menu, there are always plenty of uses for a conventional static oven.

The larger caterer, it is true, may find problems with the uneven distribution of heat within a static oven and if you remember your physics from school – warm air rises and cold air descends – this could well be true for those who have to cook large quantities of the same thing. For the smaller caterer who does not have to cook on such a scale, this very same feature could even work to their advantage as pies with a puff pastry topping say, can be cooked on the top shelf, leaving the lower and therefore cooler shelves for slower cooking items such as casseroles. You do have to work harder with this type of oven, though, as you have to remember to move the food around the oven as the cooking progresses.

Convection ovens

Convection ovens cook not only by conduction but also by circulating the hot air within the oven itself so that an even distribution of temperature is achieved. This is done by means of a fan. In effect, this means that food placed on the bottom of the oven will cook just as quickly and evenly as food which is placed at the top. Another advantage is that by not having to continually open and close the oven door to move food around the oven, there is a saving on energy. Quite apart from that, the actual system of circulating hot air within the oven cuts down on the cooking time because it uses energy more efficiently.

Many convection ovens have a cut out device which switches off the fan and the heat when the oven doors are opened, so protecting the operator from being blasted by hot air. Models are also available which incorporate a humidifier to help prevent food from drying out and shrinking.

Convection ovens can be purchased with the hob as an integral part of the design or as a separate unit. You can choose between a gas hob, fuelled by Calor or natural gas or electricity and between four or six burners. The traditional solid steel top which you see chefs using on television programmes are only available with heavy duty equipment. Hob units heated by halogen lamps are also available – the cooking by light concept. Placed beneath a smooth, ceramic glass surface which is very easy to clean, the halogen lamps transmit light directly on to the base of the pan, the rest comes from conducted heat via the ceramic glass. This produces an instant, yet easily controllable heat source. Using electricity, halogen lamps are very economical and effective.

Highly specialised ovens such as pizza ovens usually function on the convection principle. Pizzas need a very high temperature to cook successfully. Pizza ovens achieve this by restricting the height of the oven and extending the base area.

Microwave ovens

Perhaps more than any other piece of equipment, microwaves have been instrumental in bringing about the changes which have occurred in pub catering. It was the advent of the microwave oven which made it possible for all pubs to serve hot food. Alright, at the outset, it may have only been pie and peas but even that small beginning gave many licensees the confidence to develop the concept of pub food further. The result is the burgeoning trade we see today.

At first, microwaves were heralded as the replacement for the static oven, fulfilling all of its functions. This was a trifle over optimistic. Microwaves are smaller and so cannot take the quantity of food which their larger cousins can but this is compensated for by the fact that microwaves can save up to 75% of cooking time.

Today, there are many commercial models to choose from so do not be tempted to buy a domestic model. Domestic microwaves are too slow for even the smallest

Equipment

catering operation, they will certainly not stand up to commercial wear and tear and what is more, if you use a domestic microwave for commercial purposes, the manufacturer's guarantee will be worthless.

So, which type then, do you buy? If you only want to heat up a few pies, then purchase a simple, low cost model but if your menu requires you to provide multi-portions, fast, go for the larger more powerful version. The greater the wattage, the faster the microwave will heat or cook food. Again, do not be tempted to define a commercial microwave simply on wattage as there are high powered domestic models. Manufacturers stress that the main difference is that the commercial model is much more robust. Do try to work out the likely number of door openings/cooking operations per day and the number of meals or dishes required at one time before you actually go to purchase a model. Another good idea is to think about growth in trade. If you want your catering trade to grow, and most of us do, try and work out what that projected growth will be and bear that in mind when you are making your choice of model.

A microwave does not heat food in the same way as a conventional oven. A popular misconception is that a microwave cooks food from the inside, outwards, this is not true. What microwaves actually do, is to penetrate the food for about one inch and cause the water molecules to vibrate, creating friction. It is this friction which provides the heat – rather like rubbing your hands together to warm them.

It is important to remember that it is the water or moisture molecules which are vibrated. If you try to defrost butter in a high powered microwave, you will see sparks flying. This is because butter has a very small water content. A microwave should never be operated without food or liquid in it, this would cause the waves, being deprived of a focal point, to bounce around the machine, resulting in an overheating of the components. It has the same effect as using an electric kettle without water.

There has been an awful lot of scaremongering concerning microwaves, largely due to people not really understanding how they work. The mere mention of radiation was sufficient for people to imagine that their kitchen would be turned into a radioactive wasteland, rather like a culinary Bikini Atoll. The only mushrooming you are likely to see in a microwave is that of a perfect soufflé rising ever upwards or garlic mushrooms sizzling on a plate, so put away your geiger counters and relax!

Microwaves are safe but like any other appliance, they must be handled correctly. The following are safety tips suggested by the Microwave Association:
- ☐ If dropped or damaged in any way, have the microwave checked by a service engineer before using.
- ☐ Ensure that the door seal is undamaged and never operate a microwave oven if the door has obvious damage.
- ☐ Never tinker with a microwave oven yourself.
- ☐ Keep the oven cavity, door and seals clean, use water and a mild detergent.
- ☐ Never use scouring pads, steel wool or other abrasives inside the oven or around the door.

All microwave ovens on sale in the U.K. should conform to British Standards, look for the BEAB label. In order for the oven to operate efficiently and for the safety of users, the microwave energy must be kept inside the oven. This is why considerable research has gone into the design and development of microwave oven doors.

Microwave oven doors are therefore, not ordinary oven doors. They are electrically sealed, precision units, with two or even three interlocking safety switches. These ensure that the energy automatically goes off, the instant the door moves even a fraction, just like switching off a light. When the latch or oven door is opened the microwaves instantly cease. The doors, important as they are, are the most vulnerable part of the machine and whereas a domestic model may stand up to twenty openings per day, it will not be robust enough to stand twenty openings in as many minutes for hours on end which commercial models are required to do. Now you know why it is important to try and estimate how many times you will be likely to open and close the door before you make a purchase.

Many pub caterers under-utilise their microwaves by only using them to reheat food. Housewives are usually far more adept at using a microwave. We were once invited round to a friend's house for dinner and had a superb Chinese meal of seven or eight courses, cooked entirely in a microwave, and yet would be reluctant to try the same thing ourselves. Perhaps we pub caterers are still a little conservative when it comes to making full use of a microwave oven. Microwaves will cook vegetables, fish and lighter meats to perfection. This takes a considerable strain off other equipment. Leaflets are available from the Microwave Association and most microwave manufacturers which give recipes and general cooking hints.

Combination ovens

There are two main types of combination oven – steam convection ovens and microwave convection ovens. They are referred to colloquially as combis. Although these two different types carry out the same sort of tasks, they employ two quite different cooking techniques.

As the name implies, combination ovens offer at least two separate cooking methods within the same oven. For the pub caterer, they are a very attractive package. There are not many of us who have the space, capital or even the need for a full bank of highly specialised equipment. Combination ovens however, offer a variety of cooking methods in the one machine and at a very realistic price. Of course, they vary in size but most of those which are suitable for a pub catering operation, do not take up much more space than a large microwave.

The microwave-convection oven was the first to appear on the market. We have had ours for some years now and have not been disappointed with its performance. The original models were powered by electricity but now there are those available which combine the advantages of gas convection (Calor or natural) with microwave power.

Microwave convection ovens are particularly good if you want to operate a system where the bulk of your menu is freshly cooked to order. This is due to the fact that the microwave combi can be five to ten times faster than a normal convection oven and pastries, en croute dishes and bread rolls can even be cooked from frozen. Such an oven has all the attributes of a standard convection oven and all the advantages of a microwave oven so in effect, you are acquiring three ovens in one. It must be noted however, that apart from the more expensive models, the majority of microwave convection ovens do tend to have a relatively low microwave power output for a commercial piece of equipment.

If you are setting up a pub catering operation from scratch or re-equipping an entire kitchen and want one single piece of equipment to take the place of several, then the steam convection oven has got to be your number one consideration.

Using forced air convection to produce dry heat, the oven will successfully bake pastries, bread, small meat and poultry items which will cook in a very short space of time, in other words, all the functions of a forced air convection oven. Some models have an adjustable fan setting for light-weight items such as vol-au-vents and meringues. One great advantage of the steam-convection combi is that there is no cross flavouring which allows strongly flavoured foods to be cooked at the same time as delicately flavoured food.

On the steam-only function, the oven acts as a perfect prime cooker for dishes which would otherwise have to be boiled, poached or otherwise simmered on a hob – it will even poach eggs. Vegetables cooked in this way are particularly successful, retaining all their colour, flavour and texture. The steam used during this mode of operation is not pressurised so the oven door can be opened at any time without fear of being blasted by a cloud of hot steam. Generally the steam supply is constant but with some models the temperature can be varied to cope with more delicate foods or *sous-vide* cooking techniques.

Hot air and steam injection are used together for roasting meat, cooking fish, poultry and baking bread. For pubs which operate a carvery, the 50% reduction of losses or shrinkages in meat weight which are achieved by this method, can mean a considerable saving on butchers' bills.

Undoubtedly, food wastage, shrinkage and fuel consumption are greatly reduced by the use of a steam convection oven but then, they are more expensive to buy in the first place. Initially, the only models which were available on the market, were designed for large catering establishments and cost many thousands of pounds. Since then, more and more small to medium sized models have become available and at much more realistic prices.

Low priced steamers are available without the convection element and they cook vegetables as near to perfect as you are likely to achieve with any cooking method. Ideal for fish, poultry, lighter meat dishes and *sous vide* dishes, steamers score again by reducing shrinkage and drying out. Additionally, claims by the manufacturers that food cooked in a steamer retains the maximum amount of vitamins, minerals, flavour and texture, are not unfounded.

Deep fryers

With the increased interest in healthy food, a chips with everything policy is no longer economically viable for the caterer and quite apart from that, it is 'old hat' and exceedingly boring. Nevertheless, most kitchens do use at least one deep fryer. There is also still a demand for chips, for as we have said before, people who no longer eat them at home, regard them as a treat when

Equipment

they go out.

You must ask yourself then, how many people am I likely to cook chips for? If the number you arrive at is around 50 people over the day, you will probably get away with a single bowl fryer. If you have to produce chips for 50 people per hour, you will probably need a double bowl fryer. The type of chips you cook will make a great deal of difference to the speed of the operation. For instance, it would be unwise to compare 50 portions of blanched chips with 50 portions of frozen. Small and underpowered fryers can take a long time to recover their optimum frying temperature and if overloaded will produce food which is soggy and saturated. Plunging large quantities of frozen food into hot fat greatly reduces the temperature so it it better to fry smaller quantities rather than fill the basket to capacity.

Remember too, that oil is expensive so you must decide if you are going to filter it yourself or invest in one of the more expensive self-filtering machines. Fish and chip shops usually favour solid fats because they are cheaper but they use extremely large fryers which are easy to clean. The use of solid fat in a small fryer can make cleaning difficult and time consuming.

With the larger machines you must also consider the power source. If there is not an adequate source of three-phase electricity, an appliance powered by Calor or natural gas may be better and cheaper in the long term. Catalytic fryers offer a flame-free system for gas fryers, improving efficiency and producing a soot-free operation with no ignition problems. Such fryers are obviously much easier to clean.

Frying is a messy business at the best of times so any fryer purchased should be easy to clean, easy to maintain and above all, have a good thermostat. By law, when frying with a load of 3kw, you must have an override safety thermostat. On all drums of cooking oil you should see a note about the flash point, this is the temperature at which the oil is capable of igniting. This temperature at which oil will catch fire is usually between 590°F (310°C) and 625°F (330°C).

Cheap cooking oils have an even lower flash point so beware.

However, unless you have the throughput, a single-phase, counter-top fryer may be a better proposition than a larger model. We ourselves use two of these, one for chips and the other for items such as onion rings, crispy coated vegetables and samosas which really do have to be deep fried. Because counter-top models are smaller, they obviously hold less oil which has to be changed more frequently. This is very important for there is nothing worse than the taste and smell of spent oil. Not only does spent oil impair the flavour of the food which is being cooked but the absorption rate is high which leaves the food saturated. The use of two small, separate fryers, rather than one large one, does stop food such as chips from absorbing other flavours or ending up being inadvertently crumb coated.

When purchasing a fryer, look at the shape of the

We couldn't afford fireworks this year, so we bought some cheap cooking oil....

pan – many deep fryers are V-shaped or sloping. This is because the area underneath the element which sits in the bottom of the pan is the coolest part. Particles of food and other debris collect there, and because of the comparatively lower temperature, they do not burn or carbonise and so do not spoil the oil. Generally speaking, the deeper the cool zone, the more effective it is in keeping the oil clean. Shallower, flat-bottomed fryers are usually used for fish or poppadoms and such.

Although the oil in fryers does need to be changed regularly, (the frequency depending on the throughput) filtering the oil and topping it up on a daily basis ensures that the oil is kept free of possible contaminants and ensures maximum use.

Grills and griddles

The purchase of a grill or griddle must be dictated by what is on your menu. If you wish to offer steaks, beefburgers or even fish, then it is probably a good investment provided that is, you can foresee a reasonable throughput. If you only sell a few of these items though, then one of the combination ovens may be a better proposition. There are now some small 'pizza' grills on the market but they are not really suitable for steaks or fish. Grills are produced which can be fixed to floor brackets and come with interchangeable branders. Branders are the things which put lines on to steaks so the use of an interchangeable brander means that different patterns for different types of food is an easy task when all you have to do is change the brander.

Eye level grills are definitely more attractive but if we seem a little less than enthusiastic about grills it is probably because we purchased one some time ago. It is a superb piece of equipment and functions perfectly but unfortunately, we get very little use out of it. Our kitchen is staffed mainly by women, most of whom are not much more than five feet tall and the grill plate, which cooks food perfectly, is just too heavy for them to lift up and down. As it cannot be placed any lower or otherwise re-sited, it is virtually useless and the most annoying part is that it is entirely our own fault, we did not think it through properly before making the purchase.

Another point to remember then, when choosing equipment is to ensure that we are going to be able to actually use it after having taken into account its size, weight and chosen location. Obviously you cannot change or re-site equipment every time you have a staff change.

Most manufacturers of modular equipment offer a griddle as part of the range. Unlike a grill, which cooks with radiant heat from above, the griddle is heated from underneath. Although steak and chops can be satisfactorily cooked on a griddle, this type of cooking method is usually associated with bacon, eggs, beefburgers and crêpes. Griddle cooking surfaces are usually smooth so a ribbed effect is not possible.

Nevertheless, griddles are a very popular piece of pub catering equipment. They are available in a wide variety of sizes and prices and effectively bridge the gap between frying and grilling. In a small catering kitchen, a griddle is a very handy piece of equipment. Those models which are heated by means of Calor or natural gas are extremely energy efficient as they heat up very quickly and cook the food fast, with the minimum of fat. Because of their simple design, griddles are easy to clean and are maintenance-free. Some heavy-duty ovens incorporate a griddle with two adjacent burners as part of the hob unit.

Refrigerators and freezers

In Chapter 11, Public health and hygiene, we will look at the vital role that refrigeration plays in meeting the statutory requirements concerning the storage of food. In such an important area, great care should be taken to ensure that we choose the right piece of equipment.

In order to make the correct choice, we need to understand how refrigerators and freezers work. What is required is the reduction of the ambient temperature inside a sealed box or container which is used for the storage of food. This 'sealed box' can be a small domestic refrigerator, a commercial model or a vast cold store designed to hold large quantities of food at chilled or frozen temperatures. A refrigerator takes heat out rather than puts cold in and in doing so creates considerable heat itself.

This creation of so much heat makes the siting of a refrigerator of utmost importance. Ideally, it should be placed in as cool a position as possible. Because of this, a refrigerator must be able to cope with a hostile environment. In a domestic situation, a refrigerator may be placed some distance away from the oven which will not have a great output anyway. In a commercial kitchen, even with increased ventilation, the temperature gets very, very hot. The continual opening

Equipment

and closing of a fridge door will soon raise the temperature inside under such conditions. It is because of this that models which incorporate fan-assisted cooling to maintain a constancy over a full range of storage temperatures become a must.

As with all equipment, the first point to consider is exactly what we are going to use the refrigerator for. Will it be required for raw meat and fish or do we want to use it for items which have been defrosted after having been cooked and frozen. Remember, different types of food cannot be stored together.

Where space is limited, a combined fridge/freezer may be the answer. For those very lucky people who seem to have unlimited space and capital, a walk-in refrigerator and freezer may be just the thing provided that is, they have the throughput needed to make them economically viable.

When choosing a freezer, even more care must be taken to ensure that you pick the right one for the job in hand. Chest freezers are frowned upon by the environmental health people because there is a very real danger of stock becoming hidden away at the bottom if proper rotation and regular sorting is not carried out.

However, for a small catering operation, chest freezers are useful for bulk storage of frozen food and also for the freezing of fresh foods as the actual construction of chest freezers has resulted in high efficiency.

With regard to freezing capacity, it should be noted that not more than 10% of the total contents of the chest can be frozen in one 24-hour period. The same applies to upright freezers although some models nowadays do offer a range of different temperatures within the one cabinet.

The newer, counter model refrigerators (not to be confused with display units) also offer a choice of temperatures within the one cabinet, including, in some cases, a freezer section. A combination of drawers and cabinets within the unit ensures that food is easy to get in and out. This in turn, makes stock rotation and checking easy and ensures that different types of food are kept quite separate.

Counter models do not offer the same capacity per square foot of floor space as the upright models but they do have the same automatic defrosting and adjustable shelves which make life so much easier when it comes to cleaning and maintenance. Their main advantage is that the cook/chef can have the contents of an entire menu refrigerated or frozen, all in individual compartments and ready to hand. Magic!

Throughout the country, especially in the catering industry, ice cream conservers are often used as freezers. Remember, they are only conservers and they will NOT freeze.

Refrigerated display units are an attractive way of storing point-of-sale food at the correct temperature. They are of course, much more expensive than a standard refrigerator because their main selling point is to be a selling point.

Commercial refrigerators and freezers then, have distinct advantages over their domestic counterparts:

- ☐ They are usually of stainless steel construction which is chip-proof and easy to clean.
- ☐ They have an external thermometer which enables you to check the temperature inside without opening the door.
- ☐ They are assisted by fans which stop when the door is opened.
- ☐ Fridges have glass doors which enable you to see what the contents are without opening the door.
- ☐ They are of robust construction and will stand up to the wear and tear of a busy kitchen.
- ☐ They are purpose designed for commercial use.

Dishwashers

Some years ago, we spent a winter weekend with some friends at a rather posh house in the Lake District. Included in the self-catering facilities was a dishwasher. In those days, that was a real luxury and one that none of the party was privileged to have in their home. We cooked a super meal on the Saturday night, drank lots of wine, coffee and liqueurs and created a mountain of washing up. As there was a dishwasher, that did not matter too much. Being clever clogs from the catering trade, we knew exactly what to do – load it all into the machine and wash them the following morning.

First up on the Sunday morning, we switched on the dishwasher and brewed a pot of tea for when the others came downstairs. Come downstairs they did, with raging thirsts and gasping for a cup of tea. It was then that we realised that all the cups were in the dishwasher which was still going through its cycle. So there we all were, seated in total luxury, gazing out across the lake and drinking tea out of jam jars! The machine meanwhile, kept on going.

Compare that with the 2-minute cycle of today's

commercial dishwashers!

The most popular sort of dishwasher is the single tank type. These are available in two styles, the front-loading, under-counter model which is similar to the domestic model or the larger hooded model which is popular wherever there is a reasonable throughput.

The larger, hooded model is also favoured because of its height, operators do not have to bend down to load the machine which saves on time and back ache. Additionally, they are not that much more expensive and extras such as a pre-wash cycle can be added as and when required.

Both types of machine work on a single tank principle. A pump delivers wash water, under pressure, from the tank to a series of spray nozzles. The jets from these nozzles are arranged in such a way as to strike the dishes from different angles. Some models have rotating spray arms and in others, the basket itself rotates under the power of the jets.

The wash water drains back into the tank and is recirculated until the washing cycle is complete. The wash is carried out at a temperature of 60°C and the final, fresh water rinse at a temperature of 82°C which is sufficiently hot to sterilise and to ensure almost instantaneous air drying.

There is another type of commercial dishwasher on the market which is called the low temperature dishwasher or LTD for short. It differs from the conventional recirculating wash tank machine in that it generally uses domestic hot water which is drained away at the end of each cycle. So far, so good but as domestic hot water usually has a temperature of around 55°C, it is not hot enough to sterilise. This, in turn, necessitates the addition of a chemical to the rinse water to ensure that the pots are sterile. Another point is that because the final rinse is that much cooler, the pots take that much longer to air dry.

Hot cupboards

The term hot cupboards is somewhat misleading, apart from the display type of hot cupboard which is designed to hold food on show, most are used as plate warmers. Except in the case of salads and so on, customers do not like food to be served on a cold plate. We have to find some means then, of heating crockery effectively. You can of course, use the bottom of a static oven, space permitting but if the temperature rises, you are in effect, re-firing the pots. Another point, and we have no scientific evidence to back this up, is that crockery which has been heated up quickly, appears also to cool down quickly.

Adequately heated crockery is a must for any catering establishment and must be warm enough to ensure that the food is kept hot but not so hot that the waitresses cannot carry it. A small hot cupboard will do this adequately but it must be said that they do take quite a while to heat up. If space is a problem, there are models available as part of a modular range which can act as a base unit for fryers or bain-maries.

Bain-maries

Originally, bain-maries were a very gentle method of cooking which involved standing the cooking vessel which contained the food into a bath of water. This same method is often used in a static oven for cooking delicate egg custards, pâtés and the like. Commercial models come in two main types:

The first type and the one which is favoured by large industrial caterers, is literally a tank of heated water into which containers of soup or vegetables are placed.

The second type comes in a variety of shapes and

Equipment

sizes and is really a means of holding hot food, very similar to placing a pan on a burner but at a much lower temperature. There was a time when this type of bain-marie was popular for holding cooked vegetables but after an hour or so, all the goodness had gone out of them or with cauliflower say, you were left with a pan of mush.

Bain-maries nowadays are not used in enlightened circles for holding vegetables and so on as most people like their vegetables crisp and freshly cooked, 'al dente' as the Italians would say. You are much more likely to see bain-maries nowadays as part of a modular set-up, containing items such as baked beans, chilli con carne, soup or hot fillings for jacket potatoes. Used in this way a bain-marie can leave the burners on top of your static oven free to perform more important functions.

Finally, a totally useless piece of information but nonetheless interesting, bain-maries were named after Mary, an alleged alchemist and sister of Moses. How about that?

Additional equipment

Setting up a first home is always great fun, especially shopping for all the bits and pieces for use in the kitchen and dining room. Setting up a first catering operation can be somewhat different. Usually, by the time you get to the pots and pans stage, limited funds have started to diminish and the original intention to have matching sets of copper pans starts to look a bit sick. The danger is that, as funds begin to diminish, so does your enthusiasm, at which point it is all too easy to go to the nearest supplier and buy the cheapest on offer. Please don't do that, however tempted you are.

Standard oven pans and dishes

As with the larger equipment which we discussed in the previous chapter, you do need something which will stand up to the wear and tear. Spend some time and a little extra money and discuss the purchase as carefully as you would if you were buying an oven. After all, you are going to have to work with the pans and dishes you choose so do make sure and get the right thing. Tell the supplier what sort of range you have, Calor gas, natural gas or electricity, whether or not you are starting from scratch, the type of food you intend to cook and the number of covers you expect to cater for. Of course, you do not have to buy the full range immediately, so choose a range which you can add to as and when required. Keep your menu in mind so that the pans and dishes which you purchase will be suitable for the type of food which you prepare. Above all, buy the best that you can reasonably afford.

In addition to the larger oven pans and dishes, most catering kitchens will need a good selection of saucepans and skillets, whereas other items such as double saucepans and fish kettles could be dispensed with unless they were absolutely necessary. Fish kettles, it is true, are the right kit for the job but if you only cook a whole salmon once in a blue moon, why not wrap it in foil and bake it in the oven? The result can be just as good. Similarly, a basin or bowl fitted on to a pan of boiling water will act as a double saucepan and the same basin or bowl, placed inside a larger pan of boiling water, would be acceptable as a steamer. It is not necessary to buy everything all at once; give yourself sufficient time to find out if you really need a specialised piece of equipment before buying it.

What most caterers do need, though, are two or three gastronorms. These are large, deep, metal containers which are capable of cooking and holding a large amount. However, not everything is cooked in large quantities so these have to be supplemented by a selection of the larger domestic casserole and oven dishes.

Microwave dishes

Some firms produce a range of receptacles and dishes which are designed specially for use in microwave ovens. Some of such firms are linked to the manufacturers of the microwave ovens themselves so obviously the suggestion will be that, to get the best out of your microwave, you should purchase the range of dishes which are specially manufactured for this purpose.

In a busy catering kitchen the idea of having a separate set of dishes for use in the microwave is not really practical. It is important though, to remember that most microwave ovens will not tolerate metal dishes or utensils; even gold lines or patterns on a china plate can cause sparks to fly. Any other type of container which is metal-free and which will stand the heat of the cooking process is safe and will produce satisfactory results.

Clockwise, from left to right: Samosas (page 159), Smoked mackerel pâté (page 162), Falafel (page 161), Prawn cocktail (page 162)

From left to right: Cheese and ale soup (page 163), with puff pastry lid and without, Lovage soup (page 164), Chunky mushroom soup (page 163), Courgette and fennel soup (page 163)

Mediterranean-style fish steaks (page 166), Fish pies (page 165), Gravlax (page 166)

Chicken Olympus (page 167), Ferique (page 167), Hindle wakes (page 167)

Stifado (page 169), Malayan pork curry (page 175), Exmoor lamb casserole (page 173)

Clockwise from top left: Yigantes (page 177), Aubergine slippers (page 177), Hummus (page 179), Yogurt and cucumber dip (Tzatziki) (page 180)

Coffee creams (page 188), Westmorland tart (187), Pavlova (page 186), Danish spice cake (page 186)

Tartare sauce (page 180) in preparation

Left: A six-grid combi steamer; *right:* a hot cupboard and (behind) table

A smaller hot cupboard

A four-compartment bain-marie

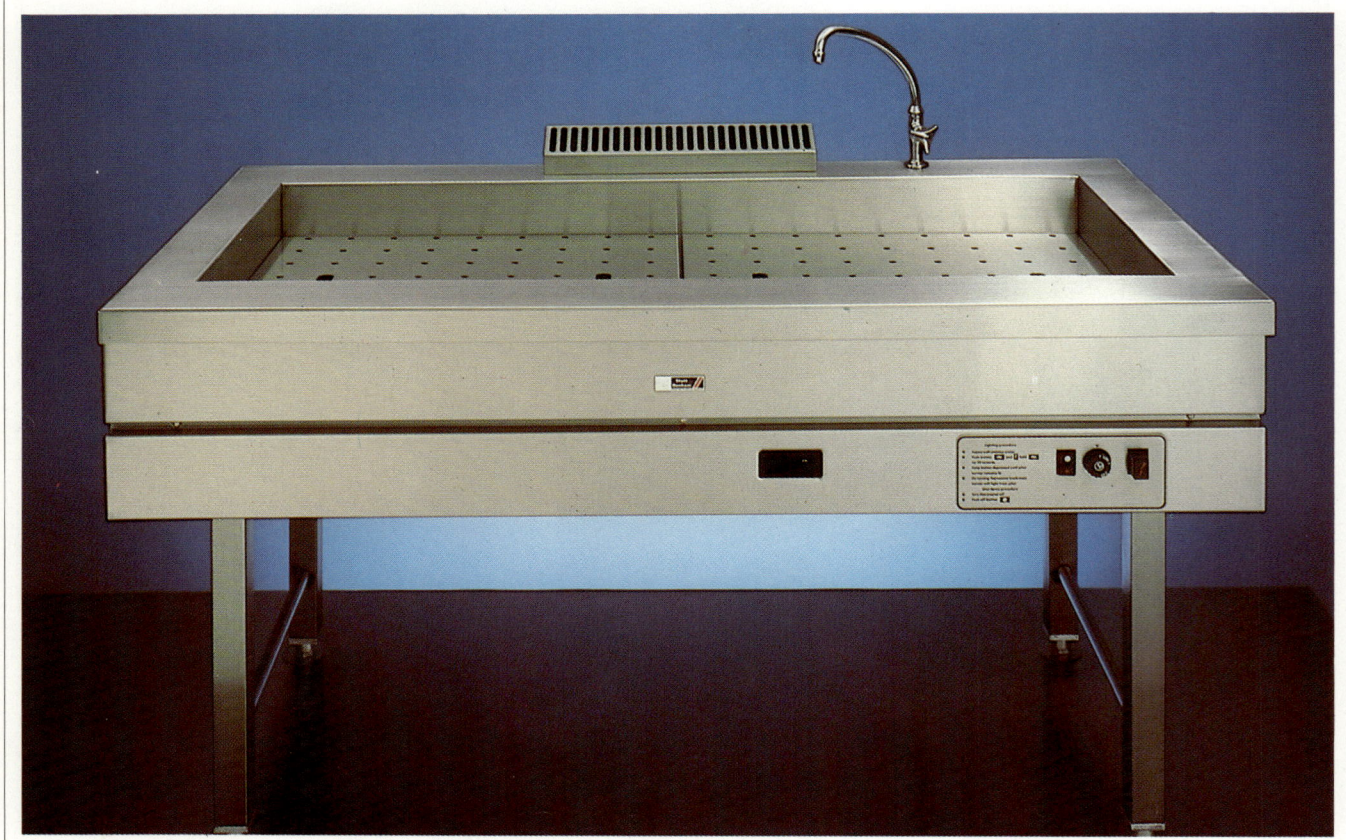

A heavy-duty bain-marie

Left: A forced convection oven; *right:* An autofry deep fryer

A gas forced convection oven range

A grill

A catering microwave combination oven

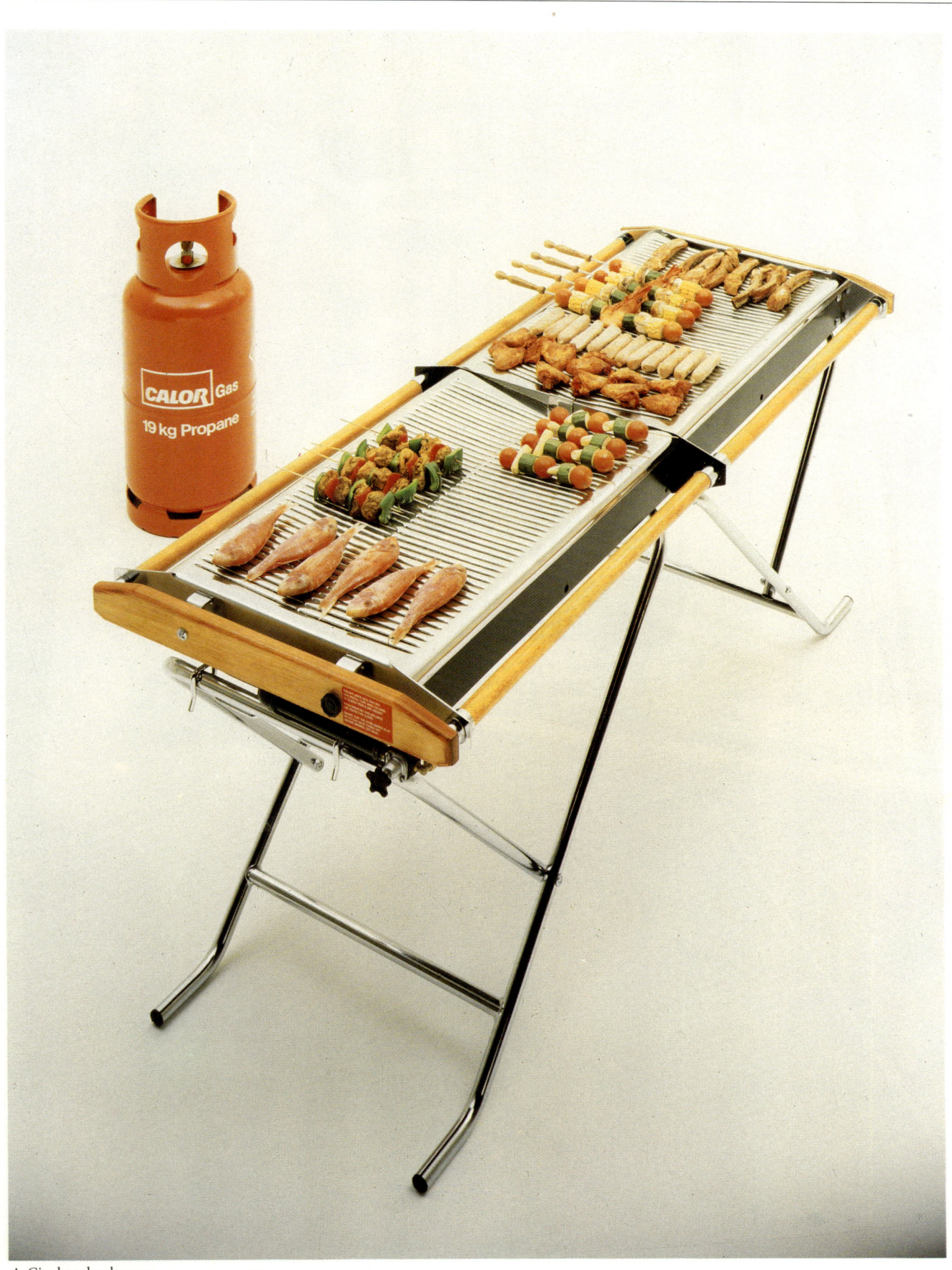

A Cinders barbecue

x

A barbecue can be the ideal way of attracting customers

Left: Space well-used in a small kitchen – The Volunteer; *right:* Preparing fresh fish at The Cavalier, Colley Weston

Tile-lined walls are essential for kitchen hygiene

A blackboard menu is simple but effective

Customers relax in the attractive surroundings of The Royal Oak

If you can provide a children's play area in your garden, you will cater for all the family

Space between the tables is important for creating a comfortable eating area

A rural thatched pub can attract people from miles around

An urban pub in a busy town centre

Equipment

Liquidisers and food processors

As the use of ready-prepared fresh vegetables increases, the use of mechanical preparation aids such as peelers, chippers, dicers and so on is diminishing, even in very large establishments. Liquidisers and food processors are still essential labour-saving devices, though, and nowadays they are extremely versatile. We ourselves use two such machines, a food processor and a mixing machine. The food processor we find is an absolute boon: it helps us make perfect taramasalata in just 2 or 3 minutes, hummus is also made in a trice, breadcrumbs can be prepared in seconds and home-made mayonnaise is simplicity itself. Its uses are simply legion and life without it would be impossible. The mixing machine, too, is an absolute essential as it is really several machines in one. Obviously, it will mix all sorts of things, but the liquidiser and mincer attachments in particular, are indispensable for soups and home-made pâté.

To be honest, there are lots of different mixing machines and food processors on the market and they are frequently advertised in the various trade journals. Performing a myriad of functions, it is just a question of choosing the one to suit your needs. Having said that, once you have purchased such a machine, you will probably find a lot of uses for it.

Slicing machines

We invested in a slicing machine some years ago and found that our profit margin went up immediately. On reflection, it is hardly surprising as prior to this we had been slicing roast beef and ham by hand.

We consider that a slicing machine is an essential piece of equipment and, although a new machine can be very expensive, many catering equipment suppliers will supply reconditioned models at very reasonable prices. Our own slicer is a reconditioned machine and suits our purpose perfectly adequately.

Slicing machines, whether manual or powered, are extremely dangerous and must not, on any account, be used by persons under 18 years of age. Anyone operating a slicing machine must be fully instructed in how to use it safely (see Chapter 11).

Knives and chopping boards

The reason why we mention these two together is not simply because they are used in conjunction with each other but because both should be colour-coded to prevent the occurrence of cross-infection (see Chapter 11). Colour-coded boards and knives are now freely available from all catering equipment suppliers and make life much easier for the caterer. Simply buy a selection of each colour, decide which colour you intend to use for each different type of produce and then, when you come to use them, simply match the colour of the knife handle to the colour of the board.

More often than not, qualified cooks and chefs prefer to use their own set of knives. This is fine because, as qualified people, they will be aware of the risk of cross-contamination anyway. Even so, they should still be required to observe the colour-coding in relation to the chopping boards.

Recommendations as to which colour should be used for the various purposes are usually contained in a leaflet which is included as part of the purchase, but you can devise your own colour-coding system if you wish, so long as everyone is aware of it and the system is rigidly adhered to. We use red for raw meat, blue for raw fish, yellow for chicken and white for salads and fruit.

It goes without saying that all knives should be sharp. Blunt knives are dangerous, so the regular use of a good 35 cm (14 inch) steel is a must.

Special knives and implements which you might like

Equipment

to consider are as follows:
- ☐ A bread knife.
- ☐ A grapefruit knife.
- ☐ A garnishing knife.
- ☐ A zester.
- ☐ A cheeseboard knife.
- ☐ A scorer for decorating lemons, oranges, cucumber, etc.
- ☐ A pair of really good kitchen scissors.
- ☐ A garlic crusher – choose the sort which is cylindrical, they work much better.
- ☐ Two cooks forks. Why two? Think of those heavy joints of meat!
- ☐ Two or three vegetable/paring knives.

Casserole dishes

A good selection and quantity of casserole dishes is a must but remember for your own sake, whether they are multi-portion size or individual portion size, that they should be microwave- and dishwasher-friendly. The cast-iron type of casserole and serving dishes may look great but they weigh a ton, they are very expensive, they are quite brittle and if you put one into the microwave by mistake you could easily find yourself shopping for a new microwave.

When selecting individual portion size dishes which are intended for oven-to-table use, you must remember that they should look attractive as well as being the right size for the portion. If they are too large, your carefully planned portion control system will soon be a thing of the past and your profit margins will suffer.

These days, there is a tremendous selection of glazed earthenware dishes and casseroles. They are both attractive and inexpensive as well as being versatile.

Crockery

Moving out of the kitchen to the front-of-house operation, you have to consider what sort of crockery is most suitable for your needs. The question is, though, what are your needs in this respect? Here are some guidelines:
- ☐ It should be robust enough to stand up to continuous and repeated use.
- ☐ It should be part of a range which can be added to as and when required. Accidents will happen in even the best of regulated circles, so replacements should be easy and quick to obtain.
- ☐ It should be an attractive design. Simple, unfussy lines are undoubtedly the best.
- ☐ It should be easy to stack, store and carry. Oval plates can be very attractive but our staff tell us that they cannot carry as many oval plates out to tables as they can round ones. So there is another point: consider your staff because they would probably like to have a say in the matter anyway.
- ☐ It should be oven-, microwave- and dishwasher-friendly.
- ☐ Bear in mind that you probably do not need to buy the whole range – look for dual functions.
- ☐ Think about your menu and the sort of food that you offer. You would not, after all, like to see ice cream served in soup bowls because you had forgotten to buy ice cream coupes.
- ☐ Salt and pepper pots should be easy to fill.
- ☐ Whichever way you serve butter, either loose (as it were) or in foil-wrapped portions, you will need an appropriate dish. Nothing looks worse that butter, wrapped or unwrapped, just bunged on the plate. If served on a small plate, chill it first and use a butter curler.
- ☐ If you serve tea as well as coffee, you will need tea pots for one, two and four people.

Cutlery

Cutlery should be matching but easy to sort out. What we mean by this is that, while table knives, forks and spoons should match dessert knives, forks and spoons, the difference between them should be obvious so that staff can see at a glance which is which. This not only saves time when putting cutlery away at the end of a busy session but also helps to ensure that the customers get the correct cutlery.

It pays, with cutlery, to buy the best you can afford. Cheap cutlery looks cheap and customers do notice.

If you serve steaks, do invest in proper steak knives and save them for use only with steaks.

If you serve fish, consider buying fish knives and forks. It is true that many places nowadays do not bother to invest in separate cutlery for fish dishes, but we think that this is a great pity. Apart from the fact that they are the correct cutlery to use with fish, they do look well on a table and can add that extra touch which sets you apart from other outlets.

One final point: whatever type or style of cutlery you buy, do make sure that you have enough. Experience has taught us that it is far better to have too much cutlery than to have just enough.

Coffee machines

The main thing to remember about coffee (and tea for that matter) is that if, the fullest flavour and aroma are to be achieved, it should be made more or less on demand and served immediately.

Having said that, by far the most popular method of serving coffee in pubs and restaurants is the 'pour-and-serve' method. This is the type of system which produces jugs of freshly filtered coffee and keeps them hot until required for use. This system works quite well if the demand for coffee is brisk, but even so the wastage factor is high and, with the price of coffee as it is, the system leaves something to be desired if you have not got the throughput.

One way to overcome this persistent problem is to invest in an espresso coffee machine. And invest is the word! They are rather expensive but they will provide a perfect cup of coffee every time, they will increase your profit on coffee, they will increase your sale of coffee and they are versatile. These machines will produce perfect cappuccino and espresso coffee every single time. Nowadays they are available with integral coffee grinders and automatic dosage control in addition to water and steam arms, and all at the touch of a button. All you have to do is buy the beans and the machine will do the rest – no mess, no fuss, no complications, no wastage and a good profit margin. But they are more expensive.

If you do not sell a lot of coffee or if your clientele is a little conservative, the 'Cafetier' system could be just what you are looking for. This type of system relies upon the use of various sized glass jugs (two-cup, six-cup or eight-cup) and the boiling water is filtered through the coffee grounds by means of a central plunger which eventually holds the coffee grounds in place at the bottom of the jug. True, the initial outlay is not insignificant but, once purchased, the system is trouble-free and lasts for years. The idea is that if, for instance, coffee for two is ordered, you prepare a two-person sized jug in the prescribed manner, take it to the table, press down the plunger and leave it with the customers who help themselves.

Sundries

Catering equipment catalogues are rather like a glimpse into Aladdin's cave – all that lovely equipment, utensils and gadgets. It really does need a superhuman effort sometimes to resist buying the lot. For most of us, limited financial resources and the need to watch outgoings help us to resist such temptations but even so the average catering kitchen will contain much more equipment and many more utensils than mentioned above.

- ☐ **Wooden spoons** A selection of these is essential, but remember to keep them scrupulously clean and replace them often. Exactly the same applies to **pastry brushes**.
- ☐ **Serving spoons and ladles** Stainless steel ladles come in various sizes from 75 g to 300 g (3 oz to 10 oz) and, as a minimum, two of each size are needed. A 200 g (7 oz) perforated ladle and a pea ladle are also useful. If correct costings and portion control are to be achieved, the use of known capacity ladles is vital. Buy several serving spoons, both plain and perforated.
- ☐ **Scoops and slices** Chip scoops, fish slices and pie lifters are all very useful and will get continuous use.
- ☐ **Tongs** There are many types on the market including serving tongs, catering tongs and sandwich tongs. Buy several of each type.
- ☐ **Chefs bowls** These are a must. They are stainless steel and come in four sizes from 20 cm to 40 cm (8 inch to 16 inch). Buy one of each as an absolute minimum.
- ☐ **Colanders and bowl strainers** These are always useful, so make sure to have several of varying sizes.

The list could be endless but the above are some of the more or less essential sundry items of equipment. A quick look round our own kitchen reveals other items such as whisks, potato mashers, measuring jugs, weighing scales, tin openers, skewers, kebab swords, graters, pastry cutters, olive stoners, baking sheets and trays of various sizes, roasting tins various, a centrifuge for drying salad stuffs, a toaster and a mortar and pestle.

Obviously, all this equipment represents a substantial outlay, especially if you buy everything at one go, but fortunately for most of us, we usually inherit a large portion of the equipment in the kitchen from the previous licensee. Even so, just buying additions and replacements can prove to be enormously expensive unless you shop around. So before you go dashing off to your catering equipment supplier, do have a look round the cash and carry first. It could save you an awful lot of money!

Useful addresses

Microwave Association, West End House, 11, Hills Place, London W1R 1AG

CEMA (Catering Equipment Manufacturers' Association of Great Britain), 14 Pall Mall, London SW1Y 5LZ
   Can provide a list of members who offer a planning and design service.

CEDA (Catering Equipment Distributers' Association), The Secretary, J.N. Humphrey Baker, 16 Merrilyn Close, Claygate, Esher, Surrey KT10 0ED.
   All members offer a planning and design service.

11 Public health and hygiene

In the annals of catering mythology no area has been the subject of so many tales as Public Health. 'Did you hear about the place in Burnley, Perth, Sidmouth or Maidstone – the places may differ but the story stays the same – 'well, the Public Health went round and closed them down because they were serving rats as chicken; cockroaches were dropping into the soup; there was so much grease about that the pans were stuck to the tables.' You have heard all the endings and can no doubt recognise the element of exaggeration as opposed to truth which comes with the need to tell a good tale. If the stories are true, closure is richly deserved anyway.

It is small wonder, then, that the name was changed to 'Environmental Health' which does not roll off the tongue as easily. Even so, the change of title has done little to end the myths; quite the reverse, it has added a linguistic value to a range of new stories which are even more insidious than the old as no one is too sure just where the boundaries of truth lie. The new crop of 'fairy tales' includes accounts of premises being closed by the Environmental Health Department for not having a separate sink in which to wash the salad stuffs or for not having stainless steel cladding on the walls from floor to ceiling. What a load of codswallop!

Probably all of us have had a little shudder over those tales and may even have added to the myth by relating, for instance, the story about the kitchen which was closed down because the women working there were instructed by the Environmental Health to remove their wedding rings and refused.

Silly, is it not, but how much more silly is some of the catering trade's attitude towards the Environmental Health? To see them as fickle bureaucrats whose sole aim in life is to close your kitchen down or at the least ensure that you have to spend a great deal of money that you cannot afford is to do the trade and the Environmental Health Officers an injustice. The main problem is that, all too often, small caterers know too little about the aims of the Environmental Health Department to be able to define just where the truth lies. This is the fault of caterers themselves: as professionals, they *should* know.

The main aim of the Environmental Health Department is to protect public health. Their contact with caterers is to ensure that all food served to the public is of such a standard that it will not make the customers ill through various types of food poisoning and further to protect the public and employees through the Health and Safety at Work legislation. Whatever can be wrong or unreasonable about those aims?

In order to help the Environmental Health Inspectors carry out their work effectively they have been given certain statutory powers, without which they would have an impossible task. They have the right to inspect premises that serve food and if necessary, they have the right to apply for those premises to be closed.

So let us dispel the myths and look at the means and procedures for closing down a premises. The Food Act 1984 sets out the conditions under which a local authority or an inspector acting on behalf of the local authority can close food premises.

When an inspector finds a very serious condition in any food premises such as sewage flooding into the property, or a serious infestation of rodents or insect pests, or grossly insanitary conditions, or where a food poisoning outbreak has occurred and he considers that it would be dangerous for the premises to remain open, he can apply for an Emergency Closure. In order to do this, a charge or complaint, called at law an 'information', is laid before a magistrate. This can only be done after 3 days' notice has been given to the owner of the business. The magistrate can then make a closing order if he is satisfied that the continued use of the premises involves imminent risk to health. The Act also allows for Ordinary Closure and this can occur when an inspector finds a breach of the Food Hygiene Regulations. It must be said that not many closing orders are made. Indeed, the most important factor in its use is the *threat* of action under the Act rather than its application. Usually, when an inspector tells the occupier of the food premises that he intends to apply for an order, the occupier closes the premises himself, thus preempting any court decision.

If this does not happen and an information or complaint is laid before a magistrate, the local authority must give 14 days' notice to the occupiers stating that it intends to apply for a closing order. The court may make the closing order where it is satisfied that continued use of the food premises would be dangerous to health. After such an order is made, the local authority must specify, in writing, to the occupier of the food premises the measures to be taken before the business can be reopened. When those conditions have been met, the occupier can then apply to the local authority for the order to be lifted.

This is all a far cry from a total stranger simply walking into a working kitchen, unannounced, and saying 'as there is no sink for salad preparation, we are closing down the kitchen.'

Public health and hygiene

Having decided then that your premises are not 'so filthy and/or verminous that the food handled there is at risk of being grossly and dangerously contaminated' and as such are unlikely to be closed down, what do you need to know and do to ensure that all the food you produce is of the highest professional standards?

It can be said that when it comes to hygiene, 40 per cent is common sense, 40 per cent elbow grease and 20 per cent awareness. Common sense should tell you that food left out in a hot kitchen will go off, and similarly that pots washed in dirty water are full of germs. A rota is needed to ensure a regular and systematic cleaning not only of the pots, pans and cutlery but the kitchen itself. However, this is not enough. You need also to be aware of cross-contamination from one type of food to another. The dangers of defrosting poultry and other points require a more specialist knowledge.

Food poisoning is very serious. It can kill and, what is more, it is on the increase, as the recent publicity over the scares about salmonella and listeria have shown. Clearly, not enough common sense, elbow grease or awareness is being used; nor has it been in the past, hence the necessity for legislation and a 'policeman' to enforce it. Unlike trying to dodge a speed trap, dodgy practices when it comes to hygiene regulations will put your business at great risk. If food poisoning does occur, it will have a devastating effect on your trade, so it is in all our best interests to ensure that all preventative measures are taken. After all, customers come to eat, not commit gastronomic *harakiri*.

This chapter will cover all the points in general terms, but if there is any point you are not sure of or you want further details regarding types of wall covering, floor coverings, sink sizes and so on, in fact anything you are not sure of, *do contact the Environmental Health Department* of your local authority. They will be only too pleased to help.

The law

In order to outline the standards required, the Act we should look at is the Food Hygiene (General) Regulations 1970. This sets out the requirements and rules covering all the hygiene aspects of a catering operation and so is a good place to start.

First, we should look at the actual premises. Food that is being offered to customers should *not* be prepared in a domestic kitchen, as you may wash clothes in there, feed the dog/cat or leave nappies soaking in a corner. Commercial kitchens are subjected to far more wear and tear than domestic ones, so lightweight equipment soon gets chipped and paintwork soon starts to flake with the increased moisture and the kitchen quickly becomes unhygienic. What may be may be all right for the family is not suitable for your customers. In any case the purchase of cheaper, lightweight equipment is false economy.

If the food operation consists only of sandwiches or rolls and hot pies, these may be prepared in the bar provided that a separate area is set aside for that purpose. The regulations regarding knives, chopping boards, etc, outlined later in the chapter, have still to be adhered to. Ceilings, walls, floors, counter tops, tables and working surfaces should be smooth, impervious to moisture and capable of being effectively cleaned. If part of the bar area is used the same wash-basin may be used, but if you are serving salad as an accompaniment, this must be washed in a sink set aside for the purpose.

In this type of operation, hot display cupboards are sometimes used for pies and flans, *they must only be used to keep food hot, not to heat it up, and such food must be disposed of at the end of each session*. Remember also that sandwiches or rolls on display need to be adequately covered, and if they are held at room temperature, thrown out at the end of the session.

Most pubs these days provide what is colloquially called a 'knife and fork' service. This is food that cannot be eaten just with the fingers. For this type of operation you do need a separate kitchen. It should be large enough for the food handlers to work in safety. The layout of the kitchen should be arranged such that there is a regular progression from raw food to cooked or prepared food like a conveyor belt, i.e. raw food at one end and the finished product leaving from the other. There should be no back-tracking in the system as this can lead to cross-contamination.

The walls, ceilings and floors of all 'food' areas must be kept in good condition, free from rotting woodwork or flaking paintwork and must be impervious to moisture. In effect, this means they must be easy to clean. The kitchen and food areas must be well ventilated; a simple extractor fan is often not enough. One way to test the ventilation to give some indication as to its effectiveness is to close all the doors and windows on a busy session and see if the fan will clear the air. Fifteen air changes per hour is the recommendation – you might like to ask the Environmental Health Officer how to work this out!

Public health and hygiene

The premises must be well lit. This is essential to ensure that the food handlers can work safely and to make sure that any cleaning is effective.

A separate wash-basin with a nail brush and soap or other suitable detergent and clean dry towels or disposable paper towels, for the sole use of food handlers, should be conveniently situated so that they can easily and frequently wash their hands. A notice extolling foods handlers to do so, must be prominently displayed.

There must be adequate sinks for washing food and utensils. If you have not got a dishwasher, you need two sinks for the pots – one for washing, one for rinsing – and a further sink for washing food, e.g. salad or vegetables. Plates can be dried on a plate rack provided it is not placed over a food preparation area and it is clean and unchipped. Dishwashers are recommended, provided that the manufacturer's instructions regarding the right amount of detergent to use and regular cleaning are followed.

The law also requires that there is a constant supply of hot and cold water sufficient for the needs of the operation. You must therefore have enough to ensure that you do not run out of hot water in the middle of a busy session and have to resort to boiling pans of water to do the washing up. However, you may just have cold water in a sink which is reserved solely for washing fish, vegetables or salads, but, as we have said, that sink must be used for nothing else.

Bacteria

These are some of the the basic requirements so now we can look at what all the fuss is about. This can be summed up in one word – bacteria. Bacteria are living organisms which unfortunately like the same sort of things that we do, including us. They need food and warmth and given favourable conditions, they multiply at an alarming rate, doubling their numbers every 20 minutes.

Certain foods are particularly hazardous because they are bacterial favourites; meat, milk, fish and eggs and all products using them are most at risk. This is why you must be extra careful when dealing with them. Although these proteins are major sources of food poisoning, vegetarians cannot be too smug as all food contains bacteria, even cereals. So the following guidelines should be used for all food:

- ☐ Raw and cooked food *must always* be kept separate from each other.
- ☐ Ideally, raw food should be kept in one fridge and cooked food in another. If you use the same fridge for both, put raw food on the bottom, cooked food on top. The law does allow for mixed fridges but for your own peace of mind do have separate ones.
- ☐ Use separate work stations for raw and cooked food.
- ☐ When preparing raw food, clean and sterilise between types of food, e.g. meat and poultry.
- ☐ Use separate knives and boards for raw and cooked food. Colour-code all your boards and knives, by either using the plastic ones or marking the wooden ones. A tip: in our kitchen, only the cooks are allowed to use certain colours and work areas because they are the only ones allowed to handle raw food. It cuts down on error.
- ☐ Wash your hands thoroughly after handling raw food and again in between different types of raw food.

Thorough cooking will destroy bacteria, so make sure that all raw food, including cereals, is thoroughly cooked. This is not always possible, as with the case of rare or blue steaks or vegetables. However, if you start off with

Oh, well – looks like Fritto misto di funghi again!

Public health and hygiene

as hygienic a situation as possible, you cut down on the risk.

- ☐ Don't leave raw food hanging around in a warm kitchen. Refrigerate it as soon as it arrives. We know this is not always possible as deliveries never arrive when you want them to, but try to provide a holding fridge and tell your suppliers that, if you are not around, this is where raw food must be left, not dumped in a warm kitchen.
- ☐ Thoroughly wash all vegetables, salad stuffs and cereals that may only be lightly cooked or not at all. Cover and refrigerate.

One of the major causes of food poisoning in the catering industry is not defrosting food properly. Deep-frozen poultry is particularly hazardous: a large bird can take days to defrost and, if the inside is still frozen, the outside will cook, leaving the interior a maternity ward for bacteria.

- ☐ Ideally, defrost in a refrigerator. If you have not got the space, then defrost in as cool a place as possible, but don't forget about the food. Once the food is defrosted, bacteria will continue to double every 20 minutes at room temperature, so refrigerate it.
- ☐ Check that frozen food is thoroughly defrosted. If possible, use a thermometer.
- ☐ Always read the instructions on frozen foods re ideal storage temperatures and defrosting times.
- ☐ Plan your defrosting ahead. Never try a short-cut by immersing in a bath of cold water.

Freezing or refrigerating will not kill bacteria. It will stop them multiplying, but only proper cooking kills them.

- ☐ Once raw food is properly cooked the bacteria on it will be killed.
- ☐ If you keep food very hot (above 63°C), any bacteria which get on to it later will also be destroyed.
- ☐ Once cooked food is cooled, additional bacteria will soon start the cycle again, thriving at kitchen temperatures. So after cooking, cool the food as quickly as possible and then refrigerate it.
- ☐ Aim to keep food out in the kitchen for as short a time as possible. If it is not actually being prepared, it should be in the fridge or the cooker, not lying around in the kitchen.
- ☐ A permanent stock pot is acceptable only if it is kept hot at all times. If it cools down, use it at once or throw it out. *Keep it hot or don't keep it at all.*

Reheating food can also be dangerous. Unless you reheat food to cooking temperature, all you are doing is providing an incubator for the new bacteria which have arrived since the initial cooking.

- ☐ Make sure that any reheating is thorough and that the cooking temperature is reached throughout. Food reheated in a microwave is particularly vulnerable as microwaves can reheat unevenly, so make sure that it is stirred or rested during the heating process and then serve it immediately.
- ☐ Never reheat more than once. Leftovers which have been suitably refrigerated may be used the following day but never after that.
- ☐ Gravies and soups are always at risk, being an ideal breeding ground for bacteria, so if they have been kept warm in a bain-marie or boiling on the stove, at the end of every session throw them out.
- ☐ In the chapter on healthy food, we looked at cooling down meat stock in order to skim off excess fat. We make no apology for stating once again that such stocks which have been skimmed of fat must be reheated to cooking temperature, after which they must not be allowed to be reheated once again. In other words, after cooling, only one reheating is allowed.
- ☐ Food which has been kept warm in bain-maries or hot cupboards must be thrown away after each session. Most at risk are items such as meat pies and gravies.
- ☐ Another area to watch out for is composite soups and the like. That is, if you make a soup with, say, a base of pulses which take a long time to cook and then add vegetables, you must ensure that the vegetables are thoroughly cooked. This is not as straightforward as it sounds: with large pans the addition of another ingredient cools the liquor down, so allow enough time for them to cook through. If you don't, you will see a fermenting mess in some 10–20 minutes and the soup will take on a bitter taste. No matter how many gallons you have made, it must be thrown out.
- ☐ Eggs have recently been found to contain salmonella, so the advice is not to use raw or partially cooked eggs, and always store them under refrigeration as you would raw meat.

The temperature range at which bacteria will multiply most successfully and rapidly is just about that found in an average working kitchen. Since it is a fact that at high temperatures (over 100°C) bacteria are killed, and at low temperatures (below 2°C) they become inactive, it is obviously common sense to maintain these temperatures whenever possible. But what does this mean in practice? All raw meats/poultry, etc., must be refrigerated until required for cooking. After cooking, any food not intended for *immediate* consumption must be rapidly cooled and refrigerated. It is not sufficient merely to take them off the stove. Remember with large pans that there is a lot to cool down, so put it in as cool a place as possible. Warm food should not be placed in a refrigerator as it will only increase the temperature and put all the other food in there at risk. All food should only be moved out of the refrigerator for preparation or cooking and, unless it is needed for *immediate* consumption, it should be replaced in refrigeration. Food displayed for sale should remain on display at room temperature for the shortest possible time. Do not overstock display cabinets, etc. Display the minimum quantity possible and keep the stock for replenishment at controlled temperature (hot: over 63°C; cold: below 2°C). Keep a constant check on the temperature of refrigerators if there is not a built-in thermometer. Fridge thermometers are easily and inexpensively purchased. We keep one in each fridge. It is important that fridges are kept at the correct temperatures to prevent bacteria from multiplying. Cold display cabinets should be serviced regularly, but do watch out for a build-up of dust in the air vent, the usual cause of the temperature rising. We give ours a good sweeping with a stiff hand brush about once a month.

Always remember the adage *when in doubt, throw it out*.

Staff and personal hygiene

All food handlers have not only a moral obligation to maintain high standards of personal hygiene but a legal responsibility to protect food from the risk of contamination as well.

All clean cuts or uninfected abrasions of the skin must be covered with a coloured waterproof dressing. Any septic wounds can easily contaminate food, so any food handler with any such sores must be excluded from the food area.

Any food handler suffering from vomiting or diarrhoea or any 'tummy bug' must not work with food. This is not always easy in a small establishment with few staff, but it must be done. One very busy weekend, the 'tummy bug' that had been going around the village hit three key members of our staff, including one of us. Three down on a busy Saturday night did not please the customers who had to wait for their food and it did our trade a lot of harm. It is a great pity that customers cannot realise that it is better to wait for an hour than risk either carrying a virus or being ill themselves, but this is the sort of thing you cannot tell them. One thing is for sure, if they do pick up a bug at your place they *will* complain, so take heed.

Tobacco of any description (including snuff and chewing tobacco) is prohibited in food and bar areas, not just because of the risk of ash getting into the food but because smokers are more inclined to cough and splutter, notwithstanding the fact that smoke creates an unsatisfactory working atmosphere. There is also a risk of contaminating food from saliva getting on to the fingers whilst smoking.

Although all our staff are prohibited from smoking, we experienced problems with smokers (pipe, cigarettes and cigars) leaning over the cold display unit to look at the sweets. We were also troubled by the smell of pungent tobacco wafting into the kitchen from smokers who sat at tables closest to it. Our way around this was to declare the whole of the area nearest the kitchen a NO SMOKING zone. It has not hurt the trade at all; quite the reverse: non-smokers welcome the opportunity to sit in a smoke-free area and we can ensure that our displayed food is free from one possible hazard at least.

But we digress; back to the food handlers.

One requirement that cannot be overstressed is the frequent and careful washing of hands, particularly after visiting the lavatory. As stated earlier, caterers have a statutory obligation to provide adequate hand-washing facilities. They must also ensure that they are used. The compulsory notices are not really enough; we somehow have to 'drum' into staff that they must continually wash their hands. We have found that the best way is to make our own notices and continually change them, make them as eye-catching as possible and, above all, nag!

All kitchen and catering staff should wear clean and washable protective clothing and emphasis should be placed on the fact that the clothing is for the protection of the food not for the protection of the food handlers clothing. Hair should be covered or, in the case of waitresses neatly tied back so there is no danger of it trailing into food. All outer clothing should be placed in a locker or outside the kitchen or food areas.

One annoying and most unhygienic habit a lot of food handlers get into is picking at food. Apart from the fact that it is illegal to eat in a working kitchen, continually stuffing bits and pieces into the mouth is a sure way to transfer bacteria. Stop it before it starts.

Also to be discouraged are nail-biting, nose-picking, finger-sucking and scratching. If anyone is caught doing any of these, they must wash their hands immediately before handling food.

Jewellery is another possible source of contamination, so it should be removed before handling food.

Try and arrange it so that waitresses handle the actual food as little as possible and if, say, they serve sweets, make sure that they wash their hands, use tongs or slices and make sure that the utensils are frequently washed.

It is important to stress that servery areas must be kept clean, and all spillages wiped up immediately, though not with the same old dish-cloth. Use sterile paper towels, disposable cleaning cloths or cloths soaked in a sanitising agent. Enforce a 'clean-as-you-go' regime to cut down on the risk of cross-contamination.

There are many instructive courses on food hygiene run by the local authorities and the Royal Institute of Public Health and Hygiene and it is advisable to attend at least one. The problem is that, in an industry which uses a lot of part-time and transient staff, it is very difficult to get them to attend courses. Try to develop your own training sessions. At staff meetings, set time aside to cover some topic of hygiene. Don't try to bombard them with too much information at once though: young staff soon get bored and the older ones think that they have heard it all before. The Environmental Health Department will be only too pleased to help with information.

Even with staff who have attended courses, it requires constant vigilance to make them practice what they have been taught. One problem we have found with catering college trained staff is that they can quote all the different types of bacteria and so forth, but trying to equate their knowledge with getting down on their hands and knees to clean is another matter. If not carefully watched, it is all too easy for some staff to develop a 'this is what we do at college and this is what we do at work' approach.

Cleaning and disinfection

All kitchens become dirty in a very short space of time. You only need to look at the state of the cooker at the end of a session to see how much can accumulate in the space of a couple of hours. It is therefore essential to use a cleaning procedure that is both highly organised and efficient.

Cleaning can be split into two categories: visible dirt that can be removed by cleaning and invisible (i.e. bacteria) that requires disinfecting and sanitising. It is essential to adopt a procedure which is sufficient to both clean and sanitise surfaces and equipment which come into contact with food.

In a food premises there are areas and equipment which require weekly cleaning, daily cleaning and cleaning as they are used. Equipment generally will require cleaning as it is used. A routine should adopt a formal plan with everyone knowing, what has to be cleaned, and when and who is responsible for doing it. The premises or equipment, etc., will only remain clean (as required by law) if the cleaning routine is strictly observed at all times. It is important not to allow the standards to fall.

There are items of equipment which will need to be cleaned at the end of every session, some which are cleaned once a day and parts of the kitchen itself that have a once weekly 'scrub down'. Cleaning is a 'chore' but there are ways to make it more pleasant. We have Monday as our cleaning day and three of our 'more mature' ladies strip the kitchen down to the accompaniment of lots of village gossip and numerous pots of tea.

There are several commercial firms who will provide a 'blanket' cleaning facility, but they are very expensive and they talk in terms of a six-monthly or annual clean. We cannot think of anything in a kitchen that could be safely left for months without a thorough clean. To be fair, they do deep-steam all equipment, but the temptation must be there to leave things for the industrial cleaners rather than do them yourselves.

Such things as filters for the air ducting are difficult to clean and, again, you can find commercial firms who will undertake their cleaning. We use a strong solution of pump cleaner to soak them in, followed by a good rinse and it brings them up like new.

Today, there are many efficient detergents on the market but none of them dispense with the need for hot water and elbow grease. In spite of what the manufacturers may say, there is no easy way to clean a kitchen. Equipment must be taken to pieces and scrubbed. Similarly, no amount of gentle spraying will effectively clean an awkward corner. To clean a kitchen properly involves careful planning and a lot of hard work – there are no short cuts.

Unfortunately, it is not enough even to give a thorough clean with an effective detergent. You need also to disinfect and sanitise after such a cleaning, but do be careful to carry out the manufacturer's instructions carefully. Even today, hot water at 80°C or above is still one of the most effective disinfectants.

Keep your cleaning materials out of the food areas when not in use, remember, they are usually toxic. Use the disposable type of cleaning cloths for both wiping up spillages and general cleaning. Remove all brushes and mops from the kitchen area and don't forget that they also need regular cleaning, or else you are merely smearing the previous session's dirt on to the floor or walls. Just wiping only spreads germs and bacteria. Don't forget: they must be killed.

Washing up

If you wash up manually, you do need two sinks, one for washing and one for rinsing. There are mixtures of detergents and disinfectants produced commercially that both remove dirt and kill micro-organisms. They are useful preparations, but in practice it is necessary to make two applications, the first when the solution acts mainly as a detergent and the second, following a water rinse, when the solution acts as a disinfectant. If you are using a manual system of washing up, air-drying is better than wiping, particularly if it is speeded up by a hot rinse.

All chopping boards, be they plastic or wood, need a good scrubbing prior to sanitising. Pastry brushes which have been used with egg wash or milk need boiling and/or soaking in a sterilising solution.

Commercial dishwashers are effective, but the manufacturer's instructions must be followed. Thermometers must be provided and maintained, together with regular servicing and water softening, to ensure proper working order.

After washing and drying, articles should appear bright and clean and free from grease smears. They should then be handled as little as possible and stored in protected storage areas.

It is important not to forget tea-towels, which should be boil-washed with a good commercial cleaner. Have an adequate supply and, as soon as they are damp, replace them with clean ones. Do not dry and reuse just because they look clean.

Storage

Dry goods, freezers and other ancillary items can be stored in a separate room, provided that it is clean, well ventilated and vermin-proof. Toxic cleaning materials must be stored away from any food.

Vermin and pest control

Pests are those unwanted creatures (other than awkward customers!) which infest our houses and premises, attracted by the shelter and the food we provide for them. Some of these pests are actually harmful to us:
- ☐ Rats and cockroaches may be carriers of salmonella.
- ☐ Rats and mice cause physical damage to buildings by gnawing electric cables, water pipes, etc.
- ☐ Rats, mice, cockroaches and flies defecate and micturate randomly on food, work surfaces, etc.
- ☐ Flies' feeding habits involve vomiting digestive juices on to their and our food.

Keep these pests out or kill them.

Preventative measures and warning signs

The risk of infestation can be reduced if you maintain regular inspection of the premises looking for warning signs. At the same time, look for holes in windows, doors and brickwork and, if you find them, fill them in. Make sure that all doors fit properly.

- ☐ Don't leave food lying around in the kitchen.
- ☐ Maintain a high standard of hygiene – most pests prefer dirt.
- ☐ Keep stock turning over in the store room. Stock control means that pests don't get a chance to establish themselves.
- ☐ To keep flies out, fit fine mesh over opening windows and put fly curtains over doors.

There are several signs of infestation to watch out for:

- ☐ Seeing the rodent or insect itself.
- ☐ Droppings.
- ☐ Gnawing damage to food or buildings.
- ☐ Spillages and damaged packs of food, etc.
- ☐ Rodent smears, i.e. the marks they leave as they brush against skirtings, etc.

Treatment

If you find evidence of infestation report it to either a commercial pest control company or the Environmental Health Officer. Don't try to treat the problem yourself. Treating infestation requires specialist knowledge of the food preferences, suitable poisons, baits, traps and the life-cycle of the pests concerned. Any treatment short of this is useless.

Flies *can* be dealt with safely by yourselves by electrocution (the 'blue light' machine) or the use of sticky fly paper.

Never use fly sprays in food premises: regardless of what the manufacturers say, they are still a poison.

Waste disposal

Waste from customers' plates and general waste from food preparation is always a health risk. It will always have been left out a room temperature for some time, and remember every 20 minutes …..

In the kitchen, waste should be stored in plastic or metal bins, (preferably with a liner) which must be in good condition and stored as far away from the food preparation areas as possible. Such bins must have tight-fitting lids and must be emptied after each session or *at least* once a day. After emptying, they should be cleaned thoroughly.

Outside, you need sufficient metal or plastic bins, preferably with a plastic liner, to store *all* your waste. As in the kitchen, they need tight-fitting lids and should be cleaned regularly. Outside though, bins do need to be protected from the weather, animals and other pests. It is in your own interest, however, to make sure that they are protected because pests outside the premises can easily move indoors.

Health and safety at work

The recent health and safety legislation is extremely complicated because it covers not just small catering-style businesses but large manufacturing industries as well. So we will look at the safety requirements for all working kitchens, regardless of which legislation it comes under. The main object of all the health and safety legislation is to ensure that employees, visitors and customers are provided with a healthy and safe environment when on your premises. The inspection of catering establishments is at the moment under the jurisdiction of the Environmental Health Department; manufacturing industry comes under the auspices of HM Factory Inspector.

Perhaps the best place to start, and a requirement, is to carry out an inspection of the premises yourselves. It is important to remember that an inspection is not just a quick look around but a detailed and comprehensive survey of the property.

So, what are we looking for? Well, there are things like worn carpets which can be tripped over, jagged edges to doors, badly worn stools with nails protruding – many things that are not obvious at a cursory glance. Electrical equipment needs to be checked for dangerous wiring to plugs. Floors need special attention: for example, does the kitchen floor turn into an ice-rink when wet? Are all the toilet areas hygienic with constant hot water, is there always soap and are there hand-drying facilities? Is the kitchen too small for the number of people working in there, so that they bump into one another with hot food?

Has all equipment that needs a guard got one? Are knives and other sharp kitchen implements stored safely? Is the ventilation sufficient for employees to work in a comfortable atmosphere? Is the lighting bright enough for people to work safely with dangerous equipment? Pay particular attention to passageways in work areas and outside: are they well lit and free from obstructions? All these items require regular scrutiny.

Itemise all the points you find room by room and replace or repair where necessary.

Public health and hygiene

There is dangerous equipment in a working kitchen and the Offices, Shops and Railways Premises Act sets out the procedures for minimising the risk.

No persons under the age of 18 may under any circumstances use dangerous machinery such as slicers, whether they are manual or powered. All persons over the age of 18 who use equipment such as slicing, mincing, chopping, chipping or mixing machines must be fully instructed in their use and cleaning. Until that person is deemed to have sufficient knowledge, they may use the equipment only under supervision.

One interesting point of the Health and Safety at Work legislation is that, once an employee has been fully instructed in the use of equipment or has been expressly forbidden to use a particular item, if an accident occurs through misuse, they as well as the employers may be prosecuted.

General points on safety include the following:

- Containers of hot liquids or fats should be secure, so that they cannot be tipped over.
- In the event of a fat fire, extinguish all air by the use of a fire blanket or tight-fitting lid. *Never use water:* it could cause an explosion.
- Make sure that all staff are trained in fire drill, and that they know where the extinguishers are and how to use them. Only powder extinguishers should be kept for use in a kitchen.
- Be extra careful when lighting gas stoves: never put your head inside (although you may sometimes feel like doing so!) or leave the gas escaping unlit. In the event of a leak, open all the doors and windows and switch off the gas at the source. Call a fitter. Never go looking for a gas leak with a naked flame.
- ALWAYS use the last slice device on a slicer and ALWAYS switch off before cleaning. Purchase a device for holding the blade while you remove it.
- DON'T press food into a slicer or mincer with your fingers: always use the proper utensil.
- NEVER place sharp knives in a sink full of water hidden by soap suds: they can inflict a serious injury to anyone who does not know they are there. Always wash and dry knives with the sharp end away from the palm of the hand.
- Check the safety valves and seals on pressure cookers prior to use.
- In the event of electrical equipment failing, switch off at the mains and call an electrician. Do not tamper with electricity yourselves unless you know what you are doing.

The provision of a first aid kit is a legal requirement and, ideally, it should contain only those items designated under the Health and Safety (First Aid) Regulations 1981 and nothing more.

For a small business with 6 to 10 employees, your first aid box should contain the following:
- A guidance card or leaflet
- 20 individually wrapped sterile adhesive dressings. For kitchens they should also be coloured and waterproof
- 2 sterile eye pads, with attachments
- 2 triangular bandages (if possible, sterile)
- 2 sterile bandages for serious wounds (if the triangular ones are not sterile)
- 6 safety pins
- 6 medium sterile unmedicated dressings 10 cm × 8 cm
- 2 large sterile unmedicated dressings 13 cm × 9 cm
- 2 extra large sterile unmedicated dressings 28 cm × 17.5 cm
- 1 bottle of sterile water if tap water is not available

If you are in any doubt, your local pharmacist or supplier will be able to advise you.

If you employ 10 or more persons who are on or about the premises at the same time, to comply with the Social Security Act 1975, you must keep an accident book. These are easily obtained from the larger booksellers or from HM Stationery Office. Although we ourselves do not employ anywhere near that number of people all at one time, we keep an accident book anyway. Making an entry in the book does not relieve you of any other statutory obligations, but if there is any 'come-back' you have an accurate record of what happened and have shown that you take your responsibilities seriously.

We cannot emphasise too strongly that, if you are in any doubt about any point or need further information, you should contact your local Environmental Health Office. They *will* be helpful and understanding. If you have any qualms, just think of the damage a prosecution could do to your business.

Useful addresses

Environmental Health Office c/o the local authority in the telephone book.

The Royal Institute of Public Health and Hygiene, 28 Portland Place, London W1N 4DE.

12 Bookkeeping and account management

Payment

Pubs are by definition a 'cash' business: apart from one or two exceptions, customers pay for pub products on the spot; licensees do not invoice them allowing a month for payment. So as a start, you have to ensure that your procedures for taking cash are correct – a tin box under the counter is definitely out. You need an efficient till.

Till

There are many sorts of electronic tills on the market. Some very sophisticated ones are linked in to a computer system and these we will look at later on in the chapter. Some pub caterers choose the pre-programmed till which has menu items rather than numbers. With these, the actual order is 'tilled' in, and the till then adds up and gives a receipt, so saving time and error by the waiting-on staff having to look up prices; these are more expensive.

With the more usual tills, the amounts have to be punched in, the till will then add up and, like their larger cousins, give a print-out of the money taken during the session and at the end of the day. You do a cash reconciliation at the end of each session, i.e. you add up all the cash in the till, deduct the float (the change you have put into the till at the start) and the amount should be the same as that registered by the till. Our waiting-on staff do this and it takes about 5 minutes.

If there is a discrepancy, it is easier to find it sooner rather than later. The main causes of a deficiency are – when the wine and food accounts are kept separate – the wine money not being transferred to the final bill, incorrect 'tilling in' or a mistake in the addition. If there is an error, you then have to look further. We use triple numbered sheets for food orders – one for the customers, two for the kitchen. This means that we can have a three-way check: the actual cash = the till roll = the food receipts, and all three should balance. The numbers on the sheets mean that we can check if one is missing.

It really does not matter which system you use, only that you have a system that works and works for you. If the cash is not correct at this stage, there is no point in inaugurating an intricate method of accounting because it will mean nothing. Checking the cash will also stop the staff being careless and may prevent 'fiddling'. In a trade where customers are hard fought for and profit margins are comparatively low, you must ensure that as much as possible is done to reduce the margins of error and risk.

Acceptable currency

One of the areas which has often puzzled us is just which currencies we can or cannot accept, so while we are dealing with 'cash', we thought a few pointers on currency, cheque and credit cards would not come amiss. As we have said, because cash is crucial, you have to ensure that any money taken is guaranteed and this means that it is acceptable by the banks.

Strictly speaking, Scottish, Manx, Channel Island and Northern Ireland bank notes are issued for use in the country of origin. That is, retailers outside that country are not legally required to accept them in payment for bills. However, this does not apply in practice and banks will usually accept these notes from their retailing customers. The main question is whether the notes are of the same monetary value as our own currency or subject to a fluctuating exchange rate. In particular, bank notes issued in Northern Ireland are value-for-value the same as pounds sterling, but bank notes issued in the Republic (Eire) are Irish punts and are in effect foreign currency. There are a few, very high-value Northern Irish and Scottish notes, which licensees in Wales and England may not have seen before. Although the risk of forgery is slight, if you are uneasy, you can decline to accept them, but if the customer has had a meal and the banks are closed, what else can you do?

Cheque cards

Don't accept personal cheques without a cheque guarantee card – unless you know the person very well!

Cheque cards are issued by the major banks and building societies as a means of guaranteeing cheques up to a fixed amount, subject to the proviso that they are accepted in accordance with the standing instructions. Although the logos shown on the cards will vary from bank to bank, they all contain set pointers for the payee to check. These instructions are usually sent out by either the agencies themselves or the Association for Payment Clearing Services, whose address can be found at the end of the chapter.

Within the spirit of the scheme, only one cheque per transaction is allowed. Therefore a total bill of £75 cannot be met by a cardholder with a limit of £50 offering one cheque for £50 and another for £25. The bank or building society is within its rights to refuse one or both of the cheques.

Nor should cheques be accepted from limited companies. Below is a facsimile of a cheque cards which explain the layouts and show you what to look for.

Bookkeeping and account management

Front of standard cheque card

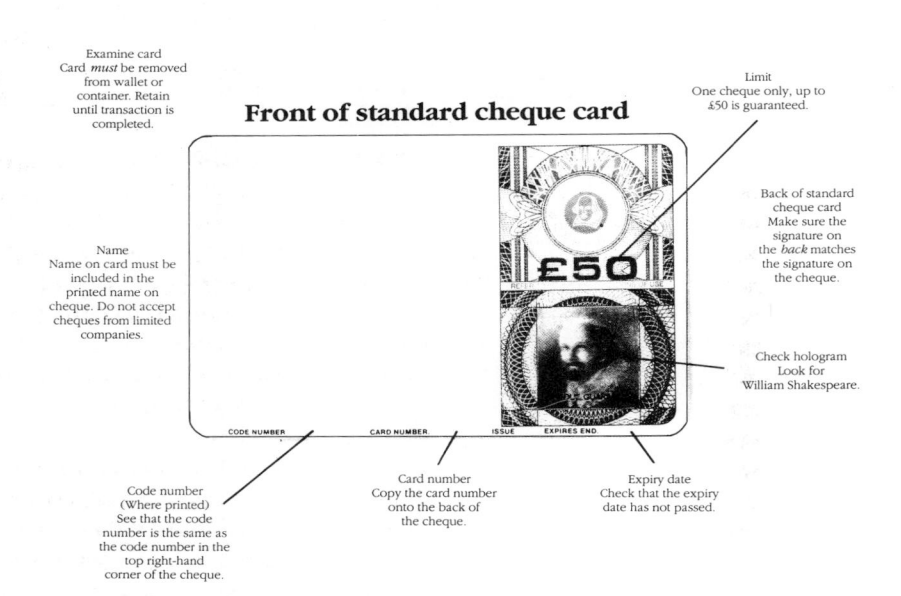

- **Examine card** — Card *must* be removed from wallet or container. Retain until transaction is completed.
- **Name** — Name on card must be included in the printed name on cheque. Do not accept cheques from limited companies.
- **Limit** — One cheque only, up to £50 is guaranteed.
- **Back of standard cheque card** — Make sure the signature on the *back* matches the signature on the cheque.
- **Check hologram** — Look for William Shakespeare.
- **Code number** (Where printed) — See that the code number is the same as the code number in the top right-hand corner of the cheque.
- **Card number** — Copy the card number onto the back of the cheque.
- **Expiry date** — Check that the expiry date has not passed.

Eurocheque

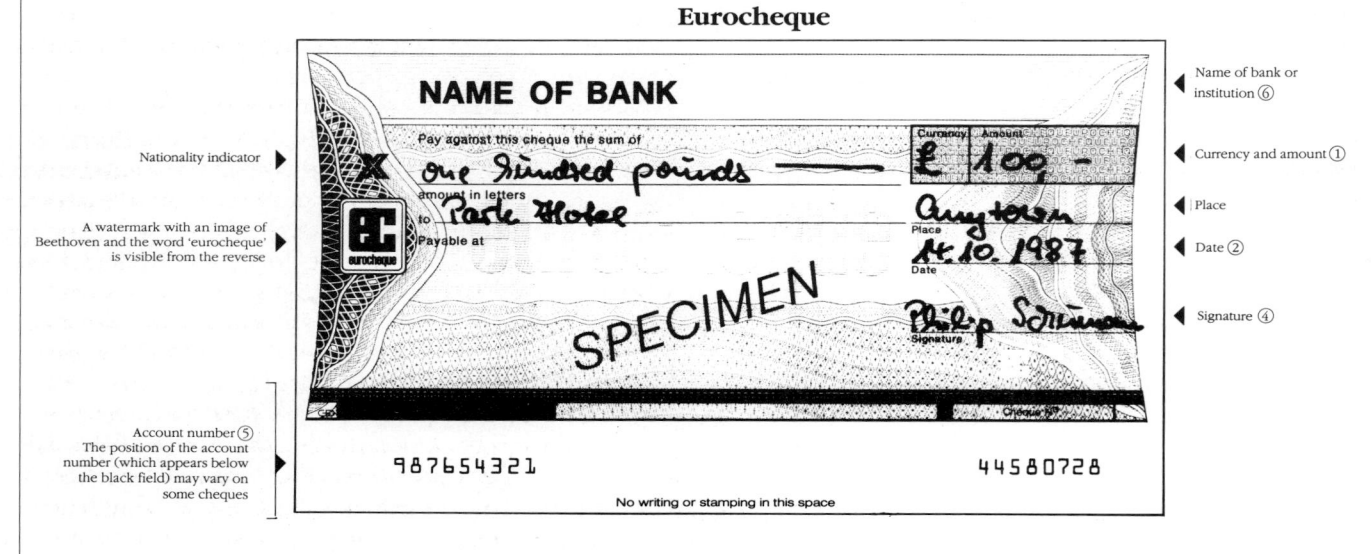

- Nationality indicator
- A watermark with an image of Beethoven and the word 'eurocheque' is visible from the reverse
- Account number ⑤ — The position of the account number (which appears below the black field) may vary on some cheques
- Name of bank or institution ⑥
- Currency and amount ①
- Place
- Date ②
- Signature ④

Eurocheque card

- Nationality indicator
- Valid until end of year shown ③
- Hologram with image of Beethoven, ec symbol and year
- Name of bank or institution ⑥
- Signature ④
- Account number ⑤
- Card number ⑦

Credit cards

Unlike a cheque with a cheque card, which can be accepted by anyone, to operate a credit card facility, the retailer must join a scheme. All credit card operators charge a once-and-for all joining fee and then take a percentage fee on all transactions. Members of certain trade associations such as the NLVA may well qualify for reduced rates. The main benefits are that there is no possibility of not being paid and that customers may spend more on a credit system than by cash. The paperwork is relatively simple but you do have to wait for your money.

EFTPOS or SWITCH

These systems are not yet available to pubs, but are likely to be so in the future. EFTPOS or Electronic Funds Transfer at Point of Sale is more commonly known as SWITCH. This is not a credit facility, as customers use their autocheque cards but do not need a cheque book. All the customer has to do is sign a piece of paper, then the card will be 'swiped' – yes that is the correct term! – through a computer terminal and the amount of the purchase will be transferred from his or her current account to that of the retailer, all within a few days.

Sterling travellers' cheques

These involve very little risk; provided that the cheques are countersigned in the presence of the retailer who can then compare this with the signature already on the cheque. For large amounts, you can ask for some identification but bear in mind that trying to get a refund could prove expensive or well nigh impossible. However, it is unusual for travellers' cheques to be dishonoured and for the amounts involved in pubs they are a reasonable risk.

Eurocheques

This is a cheque guarantee scheme run by most big banks on the continent of Europe and around the Mediterranean. Customers of participating banks are able to pay for goods and services in the country they are visiting, using Eurocheque cards and Eurocheques. The acceptance of Eurocheques is very much on the same basis as bank cheque cards and provided the cheques are drawn in sterling, they are guaranteed up to a fixed amount, always provided they are taken in accordance with the scheme with the usual safeguards being observed: the routine is shown left, 1 – 6.

Foreign currency

Visitors to the UK from abroad sometimes bring travellers' cheques in their own currencies such as French Francs or German Marks. They usually change these travellers cheques into sterling at banks or Bureaux de Change and do not try to spend them in pubs or restaurants. However, occasionally such foreign currency travellers' cheques may well be all they have to pay with.

All banks will purchase foreign currency and foreign currency travellers' cheques from customers (including retailers such as licensees) at published rates, but if you decide to accept such cheques or if you have no option but to do so, there are certain pointers to watch out for. The main snags in accepting such notes are as follows:
- ☐ Forged notes/travellers' cheques.
- ☐ Incorrect recognition of notes/travellers' cheques.
- ☐ Exchange rate fluctuations between acceptance and sale to a bank.

Accepting such travellers' cheques usually 'guarantees' payment, but there is still the problem of working out the sterling equivalent, less charges, plus the lesser risk of adverse exchange rate fluctuation.

You could always telephone the bank for advice and obtain a rate of exchange and the sterling equivalent (less charges) which would, of course, solve the problem. That is provided that the bank will cooperate and the request is made during normal business hours.

However, if you wanted to accept non-sterling travellers' cheques and the bank is closed or will not assist, the way forward is as follows: most daily papers quote currency exchange rates. If the paper quotes a 'spread' i.e. a higher and a lower one, then use the higher rate. If the paper quotes a tourist rate, then use that one. The procedure is to divide the currency amount by the rate of exchange and deduct, say 10%, to allow for exchange rate fluctuations and a handling charge.

Let us take a practical example: some American customer offer US dollars travellers' cheques to the extent of $50 in payment for a meal: today's paper quotes a tourist rate of 1.6750 dollars to the pound, so US$50 divided by 1.6750 is £29.85; 10% would be roughly £3.00, thereby a net value could be placed on the travellers' cheque towards payment of the bill of £26.85:

$$\frac{US\$50}{1.6750} = 29.85 - £3.00 = £26.85.$$

Once you have sorted out a system to ensure that the procedures for collecting cash are satisfactory you have to move the money from front of house and into the business itself.

Business management

Regardless of size or turnover, a pub business has to operate and cover exactly the same functions as a large manufacturing organisation. You purchase raw materials which then have to be converted into a marketable commodity, all within the parameters of acceptable expense.

It may be that you have a pub purely as a form of self-indulgence; you like the way of life and, provided that the business ticks over, that is all you require. Or you may aim to make a certain amount of profit over a fixed number of years. Either way, if you do not 'balance your books' correctly none of your ambitions will be realised.

Although the quote from Mr Micawber is somewhat clichéd, nevertheless it is still true:

'Annual income twenty pounds, annual expenditure nineteen nineteen and six, result happiness. Annual income twenty pounds, annual expenditure twenty pounds ought and six, result misery.'

The premise remains the same, although the procedure you have to adopt to achieve 'happiness' is rather more complex than that envisaged by our Dickensian friend.

Establishment charges – or the cost to open the doors

This is the expenditure which is incurred before you start to do any trading, the costs involved within the building itself:

- ☐ Rent or mortgage/bank loan repayments.
- ☐ Rates.
- ☐ Cost of refuse collection.
- ☐ Cleaning costs.
- ☐ Water charges.
- ☐ Insurance premiums.
- ☐ Heating and lighting costs.
- ☐ Hire purchase payments.
- ☐ And others.

Although the amounts can be challenged from time to time – for instance, as licensed property rates are based partially on turnover, any change in trading could result in a reduction – they still have to be paid. Costs which you have more control over are the following.

Other fixed charges

Items such as motor expenditure, stocktaking, accountancy, gardening, telephone and postage you do have a little more control over: you can decide if you want to spend on them and to a certain extent how much.

Variable costs

These are the items of expenditure that are subject to fluctuation. In our case, the main area of variable costs is wages. However, whether fixed or variable, these charges have to be equalled by sales before you can even think about taking any money for yourselves.

Spreading your expenditure

Until you have been trading for at least a year, it is very difficult to assess your expenditure and even after that the figures have constantly to be revised. There is expenditure that has to be paid for in advance, such as rates, but the majority is paid for in arrears, such as telephone, electricity bills, etc. Then there are the costs for insurance or accountancy that usually come in one large bill once a year.

The salvation of our own business has been to move as many items of expenditure as possible over to fixed charges. We realise that this will not work for everyone as different pubs have different trading patterns. Ours is one where the trade is fairly constant all year round, with only marginal seasonal variations.

Although we have a reasonably high turnover, we found that any increase in expenditure did not really show itself for 2 or 3 months. Add a few large bills on top of that and the coffers were empty. We somehow had to rationalise the expenditure. One thing that really surprised us was how little variation there was over the year; another was how helpful organisations such as the Electricity Boards *et al* (who can use their sophisticated computers to predict future usage) could be.

We choose to pay most of our bills on a monthly basis by either direct debit or banker's order. It would be more prudent having worked out our expenditure by the month to set the money aside until it was needed in some form of savings account and that way it would gain interest. That's one of the jobs we have been meaning to get around to!

An initial step in budgeting is to list the figures for establishment and other fixed charges (see Table below). If you have been trading for over a year, these can be taken from last year's accounts, revised to include inflation or increased trading.

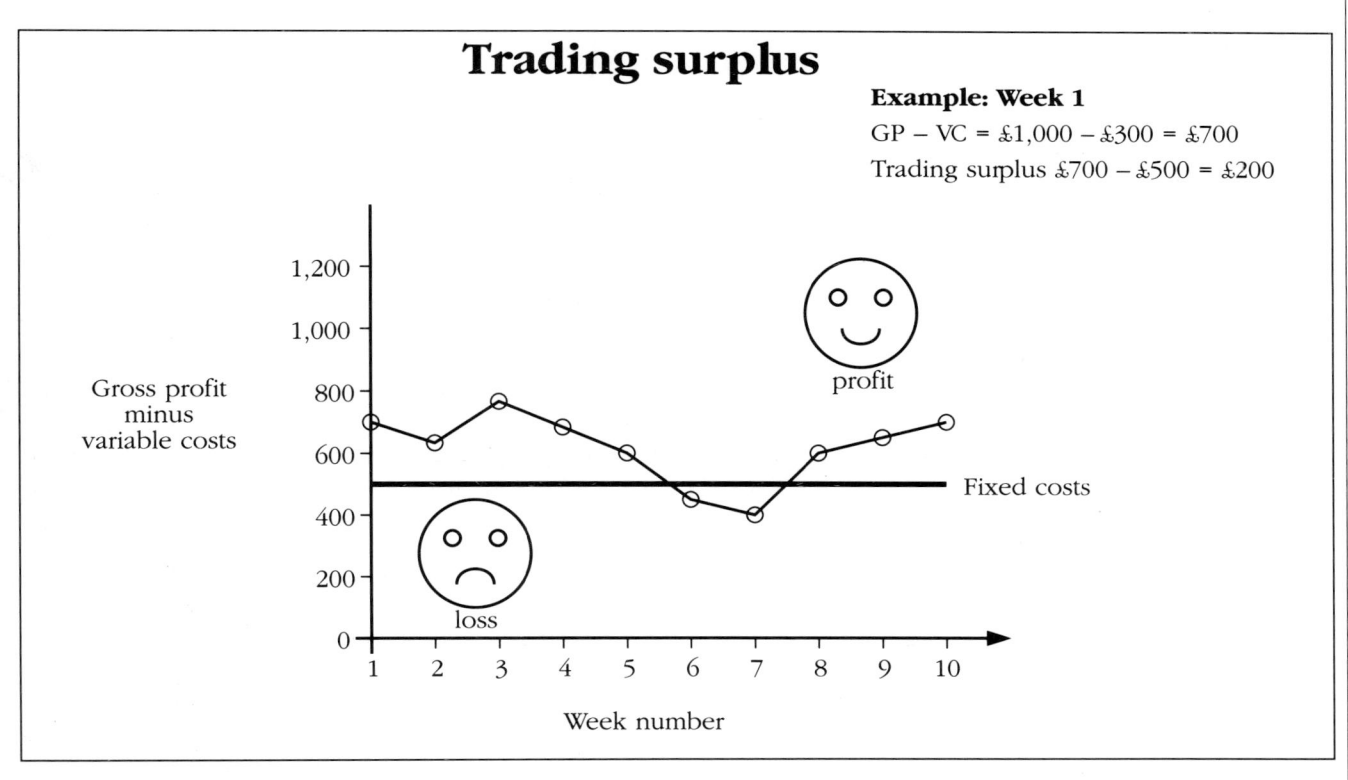

Trading surplus

Example: Week 1
GP − VC = £1,000 − £300 = £700
Trading surplus £700 − £500 = £200

Graph: Gross profit minus variable costs plotted against Week number (1–10), with a horizontal line at £500 labelled "Fixed costs". Points above the line indicate profit; points below indicate loss.

Item	Cost per annum (£)	How paid
Establishment charges:		
Rent	13,000	D/D weekly
Rates	2,500	D/D monthly
Insurance	250	annual account
Cleaning	1,200	weekly + invoices
Repairs	1,500	invoices
Heating/lighting	5,000	D/D monthly
Total	23,450	
Other fixed charges:		
Telephone	780	D/D monthly
Accountant	1,200	D/D monthly
Stocktaker	480	invoice
Staff pension	300	D/D monthly
Postage	100	cash
Sundries	250	cash
Total	3,110	

Divided by 12 or 52 these figures will give a monthly or weekly amount respectively for the fixed charges appertaining to the business. (We have not listed all the outgoings, just a selection to illustrate the method.)

Using the gross profit figures we detail in Chapter 13 on stocktaking, and taking a week as an example, we have:

Gross profit − Bar	£500
Gross profit − Food	£500
	£1000
Fixed costs − Estab.	£300
Fixed costs − Other	£200
	£500
Variable costs − Wages	£300
Deduct total costs:	£800
Trading surplus for period	£200

The figure for total costs is what is referred to as the break-even point, the point at which sales match outgoings. It means we have not made any money for ourselves but we should not go bust either. As we are firm devotees of graphs, we put the information in this form.

Bushells Arms weekly sheet

INCOME

FOOD	MON	TUES	WED	THURS	FRI	SAT	SUN	TOTAL	VAT	NET	Code
Lunch	131.05	91.95	75.05	17.40	137.60	68.40	241.47	762.92	99.45	663.47	7
Eve	116.40	186.75	274.85	208.80	159.75	464.30	272.88	1683.73	219.60	1464.13	8
TOTAL	247.45	278.70	349.90	226.20	297.35	532.70	514.35	2446.65	319.05	2127.60	
LIQUOR											
Lunch	41.39	23.75	20.44	14.08	58.25	39.66	86.10	283.67	37.05	246.62	2
Eve	96.48	107.55	206.43	176.63	230.06	382.76	174.41	1374.32	179.25	1195.07	3
TOTAL	137.87	131.30	226.87	190.71	288.31	422.42	260.51	1657.99	216.30	1441.69	
OTHER											
Telephone				16.00				16.00	2.10	13.90	
G.M/C		46.00						46.00	6.00	40.00	
TOTAL		46.00		16.00				62.00	8.10	53.90	
TOTAL	385.32	456.00	576.77	432.91	585.66	955.12	774.86	4166.64	543.45	3623.19	

FUNDS SUMMARY AND RECONCILIATION

	CASH	BANK	DEPOSIT
Balance brought forward	2500.00	2750.00	4000.00
Total business takings	4166.64		
Cash from bank			
	6666.64		
Expenditure totals	508.80	1693.65	
	6157.84	1056.35	4000.00
Bankings: current	2500.00		
deposit	500.00		500.00
other (specify)		3000.00	2500.00
	3157.84	3556.35	4500.00
Cash introduced: selves			
other (specify)			
Balance carried forward	3157.84	3556.35	4500.00

EXPENDITURE

DATE	REF	DETAILS	TOTAL	VAT	Code	NET
23/11	436	Brewery	638.65	83.25	01	555.40
23/11	436/1	Brewery Rent	250.00	—	11	250.00
26/11	D/D	Electricity Board	230.00	—	15	230.00
26/11	D/D	Telephone	65.00	8.55	17	56.45
27/11	437	Butcher	150.00	—	02	150.00
27/11	438	Greengrocer	130.00	—	02	130.00
		TOTAL BANK PAYMENTS	1693.65	91.80		1601.85
22/11		Wages — net	376.30	—	26/27	376.30
22/11	440	Dairy	22.50	—	02	22.50
23/11	441	Petty Cash — from book	50.00	—	02	50.00
24/11	442	Window Cleaner	10.00	—	24	10.00
24/11		Personal Drawings	50.00	—	34	50.00
		TOTAL CASH PAYMENTS	508.80			508.80

WAGES SUMMARY

Gross pay:	
Bar —	140.00
Food —	250.00
Cleaning —	40.00
	430.00
Deductions: PAYE	40.20
NIC	8.50
OTHER	5.00
	53.70
Net pay	£376.30
Employers NIC	

If you wish to keep the catering side of the business completely separate from the bar, the fixed costs can be apportioned between the two. If the foods sales are 60 per cent of the business, then they will be responsible for 60 per cent of the fixed charges. Variables such as wages can be easily apportioned anyway. In all these calculations the end result will not be wholly accurate until the end of your financial year, and even then they may be subject to an adjustment by your accountant. Even so, they are sufficiently accurate to give an indication of any trading levels and you should be able to see if you are making a profit at the end of the day.

Basic bookkeeping

Before embarking on any system to produce a break-even point, you must establish a basic method of bookkeeping.

Company and partnership accounts are required by law to be audited by an authorised accountant and all businesses have legal obligations to keep records which show the following information:

☐ The amounts of sales and expenditure.
☐ VAT payable and claimable.
☐ Employees' income tax and National Insurance contributions.

As we have stated before, the legal requirements are minimal in comparison to the information you require for yourselves.

Most businesses collate information in units of a day, a week, a month and a year. On a daily basis, we record the amount of sales, these are usually split between the bar and food and lunchtime and evening sessions. A separate record should be made of any extraneous items such as gaming machines, pay phones, etc. Splitting the information allows for more effective planning. Expenditure can also be entered daily or, as in most cases, weekly.

The sample weekly sheet contains the sales split, the amount of VAT payable, details of expenditure and cash and bank reconciliations. The cash and bank must balance at the end of the week. If it does not, there is something wrong, although having said that, there is usually a discrepancy of some sort.

One of the main reasons why there is a cash discrepancy is the failure to keep an adequate record of petty cash. It is very important that you do, so either a separate petty cash book or a cash box, complete with float, that can be balanced in the same way as the tills is advised.

A monthly analysis sheet can be dealt with in one of two ways. The first is by just using the weekly analysis sheet as a record and only extracting the information from it once a month to determine profitability. Alternatively, you can work on weekly calculations and average them out at monthly intervals. If the figures are correct, there should be very little difference between the two sets. One factor that could influence the findings is how you define a month. If you use calendar months, some will have five weeks in them, and they are also inclined to start and finish in the middle of a week. Fiscal months, i.e. those determined by the start and finish of a financial week, will have the same problem insofar as some will be five-week, but at least with a fiscal month you can ensure that they start and finish at the right time.

Armed with monthly figures, it is easier to extract additional information. For example, you may like to know the ratio of staff wages to sales:

$$\frac{\text{Total wage costs} \times 100}{\text{Total sales}}$$

Profit percentages are worked out in exactly the same way.

Of course you do not have to stick rigidly to weekly or monthly analysis: you can choose any period. Frequent analysis is important to ensure that if anything is wrong, it can be spotted before becoming critical. Longer periods are useful for establishing a more accurate overall trading picture.

Planning

In some ways, what we have written so far is defeatist in attitude: you are trying to ascertain if you are making a profit or not. There is another form of approach, namely to twist the whole thing around and use as a starting point the profit you actually want to make.

To achieve a pre-tax profit of £10,000 per year, you need a trading surplus of, say, £200 per week.

The gross profit in our example is 50% so to use very convenient figures:

Gross profit – Bar	£500	
Gross profit – Food	£500	£1,000
Fixed costs – Estab.	£300	
Fixed costs – Other	£200	£500
Variable costs – Average	£300	£300
GP minus all costs = Trading surplus		£200

To achieve a gross profit of 50%

$$\frac{1,000 \times 100}{50} = £2,000 \text{ net of VAT}$$

VAT is 15%. 15% of 2,000 is 300. So to make a profit of £10,000 per year you must take £2,300 per week inclusive of VAT.

If the takings are below target, you have to think of ways of improving trade – perhaps a special promotion or some form of advertising may help. Another possibility is to look at some of your costs and check that we have not set the target too high. All businesses have an optimum trading level. This is the trading peak, above which you cannot go no matter how hard you try. There are all sorts of factors which affect this, including location, size of premises, type of operation etc. There are many pubs with a high turnover that make very little profit, mainly because the figure for overheads is just too high.

Earlier in the chapter we looked at fixed charges and those that we had a little more control over. All charges can be challenged. Rates, as we have said, are based on turnover, so if that goes down, you have a case for review. We have managed to halve our electricity bills over the last 2 years, not by cutting down on consumption but by ensuring that we were on the correct tariff for our type of operation. Our first step was to have an energy survey done. The Electricity Board will conduct a survey or you can call in an independent surveyor, your local branch of the NLVA or your brewery who will also be able to advise on tariffs.

Unfortunately, it is all too easy for the business to become an entity in its own right, whereby we work to service the business needs, not our own. So, whether it is electricity, wages, postage or petrol, spend some time and effort to watch your costs so that a suitable balance can be maintained and so that there is some money left at the end of the day for you.

Value added tax

You must be wondering by now when we were finally going to mention value added tax, or VAT for short. Well, here goes!

Value added tax is a tax on most business transactions that take place in the United Kingdom and the Isle of Man. In order to qualify for paying VAT, a person has to have an annual turnover (not profit) above the VAT threshold. The threshold can be changed at any time. It is the *person* who is registered for VAT not the business. Each registration covers *all* the business activities of the registered person.

The *person* can be defined as a sole proprietor, a partnership (including husband and wife), a limited company, club, association or charity. You should register for VAT if at any time there are reasonable grounds for believing that your taxable turnover will exceed the threshold in the coming year, or if, at the end of any calender quarter, your taxable turnover has exceeded the threshold in that quarter and/or preceding ones. Failure to register can result in a hefty fine.

Self aggregation

Most pubs are run by couples, and in the great majority, the turnover on food is less than that on the bar. If the annual turnover on food is below or, if you are just starting out, is anticipated to be below the VAT threshold you may not have to register for VAT. As you can imagine, this is not popular with Customs and Excise who administer VAT and they are inclined to challenge any move to separate any activities if it appears to them that, in reality, they are dealing with a single business and the separation is wholly or mainly for VAT avoidance purposes.

There are, however, many reasons why it may be beneficial to separate the bar and catering activities, but you must satisfy Customs and Excise on certain criteria. So let's assume that, in a husband and wife partnership, the wife is running the catering operation and the turnover is below the VAT threshold. For a myriad of reasons they decide to split the business, but to satisfy Customs and Excise she must ensure the following:

- ☐ The catering operation is run as an entirely separate business.
- ☐ Day-to-day records which relate only to the food must be kept and appropriate annual accounts must be prepared. The records should be sufficiently detailed to prove that her activities are below the threshold.
- ☐ For income tax purposes, the business should be assessed separately.
- ☐ 'The wife' should open a separate bank account, perhaps called 'food account' or simply 'catering', for which she is sole signatory. It is into this account that all proceeds from the catering operation should be paid and from which all payments must be made.
- ☐ Staff wages, PAYE and national insurance contributions should be paid for from the food account.
- ☐ Invoices and purchases should be in 'the wife's' name.
- ☐ She must also be legally responsible for all trading activities, i.e. responsible for payments, insurance, etc., and the proceeds of sales should be at her sole disposal. In other words, she administers the money.
- ☐ A proper site rental agreement should be drawn up whereby the wife pays a small rental for the area of the bar or pub specifically used for food sales, and including the kitchen, etc.

Even after satisfying these criteria, Customs and

Excise may still dispute the arrangement. If you are thinking of inaugurating this system, do discuss it fully with your accountant. After reading this book, we hope your catering operation will exceed the threshold anyway!

Registering for VAT

You register for VAT by completing a form which is available from your local office. The Customs and Excise will then issue you with a registration certificate within a few weeks. However, you must start charging VAT and keeping VAT records from the date you were first required to be registered for VAT. Tax periods can normally be arranged to fit in with your financial year. If you would like this to be done, say so when you register.

After registration you will be sent the main handbook and a selection of leaflets pertinent to your business. Unlike the other government agencies, Customs and Excise do not automatically notify businesses of changes in VAT requirements: you are expected to look out in the press, radio, television, or enclosures with the tax return for any alterations.

Once you have received your pack, you then have to decide if you wish to pay VAT in the normal way or whether or not you are going to use a special retailer scheme.

Special retailer schemes

VAT is split into two main areas:
- [ ] there are two rates of tax, standard and zero (which is nil). The government can move supplies from zero-rated to standard at any time.
- [ ] There are also exempt supplies. These have no tax on them at all and it would take an Act of Parliament to make them taxable.

In the normal way of paying VAT, a tax invoice should be prepared for every sale. It should contain an identifying number, name, address and VAT number of the business, the date, and the total amount if inclusive of VAT. As this is not always possible in a cash business like ours, an alternative is to use one of the special retailer schemes.

As a caterer, there are only schemes A or F which are suitable. In scheme A, all sales are standard-rated, whereas scheme F covers both standard and zero-rated. If you use such a scheme, you are only required to make a note of the gross daily takings, which simplifies the procedure considerably. Customs and Excise have leaflets explaining the schemes, or your accountant will be able to help.

VAT records and returns

The information contained in the weekly analysis sheet is sufficient for VAT purchases, provided that it contains details of all sales and purchases. VAT cannot be reclaimed unless you have a receipt which contains the supplier's VAT number, a point to watch out for with items obtained from petty cash.

VAT is usually paid once a quarter, the information is collated from your records. The returns are not difficult to compile: basically, you add up all the tax payable from sales, known as output tax, and deduct the tax due from purchases, called input tax, record the information in the respective boxes and take one away from the other. This is an over-simplification, we know, but completing the actual return is probably the easiest part of VAT as the forms are self-explanatory.

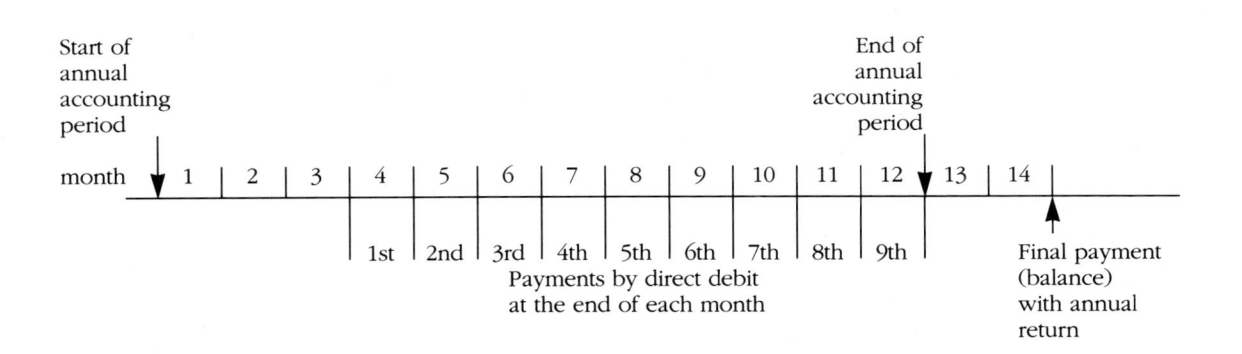

Start of annual accounting period — month 1 | 2 | 3 | 4 | 5 | 6 | 7 | 8 | 9 | 10 | 11 | 12 | End of annual accounting period | 13 | 14 | Final payment (balance) with annual return

1st | 2nd | 3rd | 4th | 5th | 6th | 7th | 8th | 9th
Payments by direct debit at the end of each month

All businesses have a legal requirement to keep business records for 6 years. Business records include the following:
- ☐ Records of daily takings such as till rolls.
- ☐ Cash books and other accounts books.
- ☐ Bank statements and paying-in slips.
- ☐ VAT account (though they don't give you a copy).
- ☐ All VAT invoices and credit notes, systematically filed.
- ☐ Relevant business correspondence.

On quarterly returns the money has to be paid to Customs and Excise within 1 month. In a business like ours, this usually amounts to quite a large sum, as all our sales are taxed at standard rate whereas most of our food purchases are zero-rated. Many caterers hive off the VAT due into a deposit account until it is required.

If a return and tax payment is filed late, i.e. more than 30 days after the end of the return period a fine is payable. Not having the ready cash to pay the tax is *not* a mitigating excuse.

Annual accounting

There is no doubt that a lot of small businesses have run into difficulties by not budgeting properly for VAT and have found themselves liable for monthly instead of quarterly returns. This may help their cash flow but it does mean extra paperwork. As a means of helping small businesses, Customs and Excise introduced the Annual Accounting Scheme.

In order to qualify for the scheme, you must satisfy the following requirements:
- ☐ You must have been registered for at least 1 year.
- ☐ Your turnover must be less than the requisite ceiling.
- ☐ Your returns and payments must be up-to-date at the time you apply to join.

According to the Customs and Excise information leaflet 'VAT and small businesses – Annual Accounting Scheme', the scheme operates as follows. An estimate of the amount of VAT due for the next 12 months is made, based on last year's figures. The amount is then divided into 10 to work out your monthly payments. You would then have to make 9 monthly payments by direct debit, starting at the end of the fourth month of your financial year. You would have 2 months after the end of the year to put in your annual return and make the tenth payment, adjusted to balance your account. The main advantages of the scheme are as follows:
- ☐ By paying a set amount each month, the amount of VAT is certain and spread over a whole year to help your cashflow.
- ☐ There is only one VAT return to fill in each year instead of four.
- ☐ You have an extra month to fill in and send in the annual return and any balancing payment due.

Details of all the various schemes are available from Customs and Excise through a full range of leaflets. You will find their address in your local telephone directory.

Self and staff usage

In the chapter on stocktaking, we will look at the importance of keeping a record of staff food, wastage, food taken out for own use, etc., in fact the need to be able to show the difference between food used and sold. At first glance, this would seem to have nothing to do with VAT, but it is an area in which the VAT authorities show more than a little interest. For one thing, they can easily assess how much money you should be making on the amount of goods you have purchased and if it is below their estimate, they want to know why. It is not enough to say that any discrepancy is due to wastage: you must be able to show some record.

The rules on self and staff usage are clearly defined: if you own a catering establishment and you provide yourself and your family with meals, you need not account for VAT on them, but you must pay the tax on the full cost of any standard-rated items such as ice cream, sweets, soft and alcoholic drinks that you take out of the business. However, you can give your staff free food and drink without paying VAT, but if they pay for it in any way either by cash or deductions from wages, then it becomes VATable.

Giving your friends or *customers* free meals and drinks is regarded as business entertainment and you must pay or not claim back the amount of input tax incurred in the provision of the meal or the drinks provided.

However, if you give meals or drinks in exchange for an identifiable benefit to the business – for example, to coach drivers or party organisers, or as a raffle prize – you can deduct any VAT incurred but you must account for output tax at cost price. In more simple terms: you give a meal with wine as a raffle prize; all the food was purchased at zero rate, the bottle of wine at standard rate. You can claim back the input tax on the wine but you must pay output tax on the cost price of the entire meal.

Service charges and tips

If you make a service charge of, say, 10%, it is standard-rated. Any tips, freely given by the customers to the staff over and above the total charge are not eligible for VAT; no VAT is due on the tip.

Private motoring

If you use your car for both business and private motoring, you must keep a detailed record of the mileage and apportion the cost accordingly, and records to show that the cost of private mileage has not been included in the business expenses. However, if you use a special retailer scheme, you have to treat all road fuel purchases as input tax and then apply a scale determined by Customs and Excise to apportion the usage between business and personal. Details of the scales are available from either your accountant or the local VAT office.

Computers

Until quite recently, most small businesses regarded a computer as beyond their reach, assuming not only that the initial cost would be prohibitive, but that quite specialised knowledge was required to operate one. The advent of the personal computer has changed all that. Even so, many caterers are still reluctant to use such a machine.

There are many models of computer on the market and trying to select a suitable one can be both time-consuming and confusing. Basically, you buy your computer, called the hardware, and then you purchase suitable programs, called software. It is the software programs that perform the specific task; the hardware is the means by which they do it, visually on the screen, or in the form of a printout or of graphics. So the first point to consider when purchasing a computer is whether there is suitable software available for the model you are looking at.

All computers have a disc drive, where you insert either a hard or floppy disc, and it is upon this disc that you work. The smaller computers have a single disc drive, so when you copy your disc, which you must, you have continuously to interchange discs which takes a little time. The more expensive models have a double disc drive and are much faster.

Perhaps the simplest means of choosing a suitable computer or computer system is to ask other people in the trade their advice. Find out what type of computer they use and its advantages and disadvantages. Your local specialist shop should also be able to help – after all, they are the experts – or you may consider a visit to a computer exhibition. Another avenue worth looking at is the various courses run by the local polytechnic or night school: a basic computer course will at least give you a feel for computers. Details of courses available in your area can be found at the local library.

Because there are so many types of computer available and the technology is moving so quickly, today's state-of-the-art model may be old-fashioned tomorrow. If you are purchasing a small personal computer, this is not too important, but if you are looking at one of the more complex systems, it is a point you should be aware of. One solution to this problem is to rent instead of buying, an option that is becoming more and more popular. But whatever method you choose to acquire a computer, as with any other major acquisition, find out as much as you can before committing yourself. If purchasing, wherever possible, do arrange to try before you buy!

What sort of machine can you expect? Well, at the top end of the range are computer systems incorporating tills which automatically record the

...or this model, which cleans the pipes twice a week as well...

BREWMASTER II

takings, can give detailed analysis of the menu items sold, work out gross profit margins and even sort out re-ordering. Of course, these are expensive, but they have the facility virtually to run the business side of the operation to a very sophisticated level.

There is no need to spend an awful lot of money, though, if you want to computerise your records. At the bottom end of the scale, we have an Amstrad word processor, purchased initially to write this book! However, we decided that the machine was under-used and, as the facilities were there anyway, we now use it for our business accounts.

The only problem with using a very basic computer and a simple program is that you very soon get 'hooked' and you want more information. There are lots of software packages to fit even a basic word processor, ones that deal with wages, tax and insurance, spreadsheets that allow you to predict growth, profit margins, etc., and many, many more. Even the most simple program can produce a degree of analysis that is far superior to anything you can provide yourself.

As we have stated continually the more information you have on your business, the more likely it is to succeed. Computers are a way of keeping detailed information and analysis in an easy and compact form. Do at least consider one.

Today there is a lot of help for small businesses. The Small Firms Advisory Service can help with structuring a business and obtaining loans. Most of the larger banks can help if you wish to secure a loan from them or get information about their services. Universities, polytechnics and night schools run part-time courses on business management and computer studies – the local library has details. The Open College and the Open University have a variety of courses available at all levels that can benefit a small concern. So don't flounder: there is a lot of free help and advice around.

Useful addresses

Association for Payment Clearing Services, Mercury House, Triton Court, 14 Finsbury Square, London EC2A 1BR.

Customs and Excise (VAT) address in local telephone directory.

The extracts from the Customs & Excise leaflet *VAT and Small Businesses* – Annual Accounting Scheme were reproduced with the permission of the Controller of Her Majesty's Stationery Office.

13 Menu costing, stock-taking and suppliers

Menu costing

In the preceding chapter, we briefly talked about gross profit margins. Gross profit is the amount of profit made after deducting the cost of the product only. It does not take into account the figure for overheads. Expressed another way, it is the balance left from the sale price of an item on the menu after the cost of the ingredients alone has been deducted.

Gross profit margins might sound boring but it cannot be stressed too much how vital it is to get them right. If we get the amount of 'mark-up' (the figure you add to the cost) wrong at this stage, there is nothing that can be done to rectify losses at a later stage. For instance, you cannot approach customers a few months after they have had a meal and ask them for an additional couple of quid because you have since discovered that you made little or no profit on the transaction. You must get your calculations right at the outset to ensure making a profit rather than a loss.

Any gross profit figure can be aimed at, but the norm appears to be between 50 per cent and 60 per cent, although if you are operating a separate restaurant, you could expect to increase that. Some caterers opt for a smaller gross profit margin so as to generate a greater turnover. This, in effect, means selling more meals at a lower price and in order to do this successfully, the higher turnover really is vital. For such an operation, it is essential to have the right location in order to ensure a steady supply of customers.

In an area where there is plenty of competition, you may think it prudent to undercut the opposition on price, but in doing this you can easily make a rod for your own back. Experience has shown that improved quality and service are far more likely to increase trade than knocking a few pence off the price of a steak and kidney pie.

A disturbing trend which has developed over the past few years, and one which shows no sign of abating, is that the figure for overheads or operating costs is greater than the cost of the product. For example, over a 12-month period it may cost £100,000 to buy the products you sell such as food, wine, beer and so on but over the same period it could well have cost £125,000 in heating, lighting, rates, wages and so on. It is precisely this which makes it so important to calculate the correct gross profit margin and why you need accurate menu costing. There is absolutely no point in running a catering operation if, at the end of the day, the money you have taken is insufficient to cover all your overheads *and* to make a profit which is commensurate to the effort and hours involved.

It is probably because of this rather than the possibility that they may not be able to cook too well that so many caterers are attracted to convenience foods. Convenience foods arrive fully costed out. With for instance, a 'boil-in-the-bag' dish, the cost per portion would be known exactly, whereas items on the menu which you prepare and cook on the premises have to be costed out and, what is more, a constant check has to be maintained on such costings.

Begin, then, by looking at such an item which you intended to prepare and cook yourselves:

Mediterranean Chicken (six portions)

6 chicken legs	37p each	£2.22
1/2 onion, chopped	20p lb	£0.10
250 g (8 oz) diced mixed peppers	34p lb	£0.17
250 g (8 oz) mushrooms	92p lb	£0.46
2 teaspoons fresh tarragon	70p punnet	£0.25
600 ml (1 pint) chicken stock	£7.20 tub	£0.10
1 glass white wine	£1.80 bottle	£0.30
500 g (1 lb) tomatoes, chopped	£6.20 case	£0.51
		£4.11

£4.11 divided by six gives the price per portion = £0.69 per portion.

That all looks fairly straightforward and provided you measure out the ingredients properly, it is. The reality, though, can sometimes be different. For instance, the price quoted above for diced mixed peppers is for the frozen variety but, in practice, these would be supplemented by dicing up the thick ends and slices left over from salad preparation. This might seem like a bonus at first sight but when you consider that fresh peppers cost 70p per lb, it makes a difference to the costing. Even so, it is better than putting them down to wastage which would be a complete loss.

Other things which can alter the initial costing and which are easy to overlook should be identified. Suppose you run out of your cheap cooking wine and have to buy a glass of wine from the bar: in order to keep the bar profit margins at their correct level, you will have to pay the full retail price instead of the 30p quoted. The tomatoes which you intended to use are not suitable for cooking, being the pale, hard, salad type, so you replace them with a 450 g (15 oz) can of tomatoes which costs only 30p.

Menu costing, stock-taking and suppliers

Where do all these things leave your basic costing? In actual fact, there is a difference of 4p which in itself is not a lot, but multiplied a few times, it is something you need to be aware of. How much more would it have cost, though, if someone had gone out specially to get the exact ingredients? The best thing to do in cases like this is to compromise and cost the dish out at 71p per portion. Small adjustments do tend to average out so long as you are not making them throughout the menu all of the time.

The price of fresh vegetables, meats and fish can vary from week to week, forcing you to work out an average price anyway. Some textbooks would not approve of this but, as we all know, catering for real can be anything but a textbook operation.

Averaging out and compromising *does not* mean relying on guess work. There are simple ways to make an assessment of the price fluctuations of variable items. Fresh meats can vary in price over the year so, before you price up a particular dish, talk to your butcher, as he will be able to advise you on seasonal variations. The same applies equally to fresh vegetables although, with these, there is usually a seasonal alternative.

Fresh fish is much more of a problem. A popular fish such as fresh haddock can vary by as much as £1.00 per lb in the space of a week if conditions at sea have been rough. We overcome this problem by putting fresh fish on the daily specials board, having already explained on the main menu that if fresh fish is available, that is where it will appear. Another way to overcome this, perhaps, is to include fish dishes on the main menu anyway but write 'Market price' or MP for short instead of quoting a price. If you choose to use this method though, you must tell the customer what the cost is at the time the order is placed. We don't think that this method is a very satisfactory solution to the problem as it tends to inhibit the customers and discourage them from ordering those items.

Portion control

One aspect related to costing which really must be closely watched is portion control. An ugly sounding phrase, isn't it? Unfortunately, though, the general public have taken it to their hearts and use it in a scathing fashion to describe catering establishments which serve convenience foods to the exclusion of all else. Portion control is, nevertheless, of vital importance to a profitable catering operation.

A good place to start is with the plate size. A plate which is too small tends to cause food to be heaped on to it rather than arranged. This can be offputting for the customer and possibly embarrassing when half the meal finishes up on the table. At the other extreme, a plate which is too large causes the food to look somewhat lost and gives customers the idea that they are not getting value for money. Some of the food you serve will probably be in dishes, so make sure to get the right size at the outset, even if it means buying a few different sizes to experiment with.

You are now ready to start. Plate up a typical meal and then remove each item from the plate in turn and weigh them individually, making a note of the weight of each item. Exactly the same should be done with individual pies and crumbles and the like, remembering not to overfill them, as enough space must be left under the topping or crust for the filling to expand when heated. In any case, pies which bubble out in this fashion not only make a mess of the oven but also end up dry and tasteless. Casseroles and stews cannot be ignored as you will need to know how many portions you will get out of each batch.

So far so good, but how do you put this into practice on a busy session? While you are weighing out your portions, it is the ideal time to look around for suitable serving utensils. During a busy session, you can hardly start weighing out all the portions, but on the other hand nor can you leave it to guess work. What you need is a scoop which holds, say, just one portion of chips or a slotted spoon which holds exactly the right amount of broccoli and so on. This way, you achieve your aim to control the portions you serve, quickly and with minimum effort. It is important to ensure that your procedure for the control of portions and the use of the different utensils is second nature to your staff.

Some years ago, our staff got into the habit of treating what they referred to as 'nice' customers by piling up their plates and, for a while, no amount of 'war dances' on our part seemed to break the habit. The ludicrous part was that the customers they had been so keen to impress complained about their plates being piled high and sent their plates back with half the food still left on them. Do keep an eye on your staff, then, and ensure that they know exactly what portions they are required to serve. It does well to remember that customers who have been overfed with starters and main courses are hardly likely to order a pudding. That would be the catering equivalent of an own goal!

Having worked out the sizes of your portions, the next step is to cost them up. The Mediterranean Chicken we looked at above was simple – six chicken legs = six portions but not all dishes work out so conveniently. To cost a Steak and Kidney Pie for instance, you would need the costs of the raw meat, the onions, any herbs you wish to use, the stock, any additional ingredients and the pastry. In order to allow for shrinkage, you need to cook the mixture before weighing it, to ensure accuracy. What is more, if you are not using ready-made pastry lids, you must also work out how many lids you get to a mixing of pastry. Next, divide the weight of the filling by the portion size and you will see how many portions you get out of the batch.

A useful tip is to start a card index system for all the different items on your menu, using a different card for each item. Each card should show all the ingredients of the dish concerned together with the cost of each ingredient. The cost can be entered in pencil, which makes it easier to alter if the price of a particular ingredient changes. If you also include on each card the cooking method, the system then doubles as a very useful and complete guide to your cooking operation. It is important to stress that the price of the various commodities should be checked from time to time and if an increase in price is revealed, an adjustment should be made to either the selling price or the size of the portion.

Other points to remember
Still on the subject of costing up, remember to include not only a figure for vegetables but also for any garnish which may be used. As a general rule, a portion of chips is usually 175–250 g (6–8 oz), whereas a portion of vegetables is usually around 50 g (2 oz) but remember, whatever size of portion you use you have to know exactly what that size is or the whole exercise is pointless. These days, suppliers provide potatoes of a uniform size for jacket potatoes (usually 250 g/8 oz) and price them up at so much per potato so they, too, are easily costed.

It is worthwhile mentioning at this point that some menu items are consistently difficult to cost. One of the main ones is soup. Most places offer a 'soup of the day' and with good reason. If, say, the chicken and mushroom pies are not selling as quickly as they normally do, you could well find that you have an abundance of fresh mushrooms and chervil. You would hardly consider marking them down as wastage but instead, make a mushroom and chervil soup. This way you can continually ring the changes with your soup and add interest to your menu.

Unless you are in the habit of using packet or frozen soup, it is most unlikely that you will always make 10 litres (2 gallons) of soup! Sometimes you may make only a few pints, whereas at other times you make make many times that amount. The point of all this is that the cost of the ingredients will vary considerably. For instance, our Old English Cheese and Ale Soup costs a good deal more to make than does our Lovage Soup, which is virtually free to us (see Chapter 16). The thing to do with items such as soup which are difficult to cost up is to adopt a swings and roundabouts policy and try to average out the cost over, say, a period of a month. In practice, this means that if you made an expensive soup one day, you would try to offset that with a cheaper one the next and so on.

Once you have worked out what the food costs, you have to decide how much to charge for it. The formula is simple:

$$\text{Selling price} = \frac{\text{Cost price} \times 100}{100 - \%GP \text{ required}} + VAT$$

Expressed in words, that comes out as 'the cost price multiplied by one hundred, divided by one hundred minus the percentage of gross profit required, plus value added tax'.

Therefore, if you want a mark-up of 60 per cent on a dish which costs you £1.00 to make, it works out like this:

$$\frac{£1.00 \times 100}{40} = £2.50 \times 1.15 \text{ (VAT at 15\%)} = £2.88$$

To help you with your costing, we have worked out a ready-reckoner which covers cost prices from 25p to £2.75 and gross profit margins from 40 per cent to 70 per cent with and without VAT. It is easy to use and should make life easier for you. Taking the example above, if you want 60 per cent gross profit on an item with a cost price of £1.00, simply look up the correct column and you will find £2.88.

Many marketing pundits assert that certain figures are psychologically more acceptable than others and as £2.88 is rather an awkward figure to work with anyway, it would be better if it were rounded up or down. The figures which are felt to be more acceptable are those ending with 0 or 5 or 9, so £2.88 could be rounded off to £2.85, £2.99 or even £3.00. We are inclined to stick to 5 or 0 as these are much easier for the waitresses to add up, making errors less likely.

If you wish to make life even simpler, you may like to operate a fixed profit margin on all your menu items, although there is a school of thought which advocates a slightly higher profit margin on dishes which sell well in order to compensate for the poorer sellers. Back to the swings and roundabouts!

Unfortunately, it does not end there as there are several other factors which will affect the gross profit margin. In order to eliminate as many of these as possible, it is wise to keep a record of any problem areas. All these records to be kept!

Wastage

You will no doubt have heard quite a bit about wastage and no, it is not that which comes back on customers' plates! That is simply waste or swill or whatever you choose to call it and, in any case, has already been purchased. What you have to concern yourselves with is quite another thing. Wastage can be defined as food which could have been sold but, for one reason or another, was not. The importance of keeping a record of wastage cannot be overstressed. The main causes of wastage are as follows:

- ☐ Age – the food is too old or is suspect in some way. Remember the adage 'when in doubt, throw it out'.
- ☐ Not cooked correctly – burned pie crusts, etc.
- ☐ Cooked vegetables left over at the end of a session.
- ☐ Accidents – food dropped on the floor or spilt.
- ☐ Incorrect order – the waitress has misheard.
- ☐ The contents of bain-maries and hot cupboards such as pies, etc., after a session keeping warm, or any food left unrefrigerated for a session (see Chapter 11, Public health and hygiene).
- ☐ Refund given to customer following a complaint. It is not sufficient simply to make a note of the amount refunded; the food must also be entered on the wastage sheet.

It is also very important to keep a record, yes – another record – of stock which you have taken for your own consumption and stock which goes towards staff meals. To be frank, we reached the stage at one time, where we found that the number of staff meals which were being taken from the menu was so high that it had seriously affected our profit margins. Having learned our lesson the hard way, we now purchase produce for staff meals separately and count them as part of the overheads. It may seem somewhat mean but even a small number of staff can get through a heck of a lot of food if given free range of the menu. Whatever you do, don't let it happen to you: Staff meals, in any case, are supposed to be 'reasonable sustenance', not a three-course dinner such as people would buy on a night out.

Although there are only the two of us, we find that it works better to buy our own food separately. If you decide to do this, you must remember not only to keep the receipts but also to record them as personal consumption, otherwise it will be assumed that they are receipts for the catering operation and an adjustment will be made automatically. It is a common misconception that caterers eat nothing but the most expensive items on the menu, so you must be able to show that you do not. We also allow members of staff to purchase food at cost price and again, there is nothing wrong with this provided that it is accounted for and a record is kept.

Unfortunately, from time to time, some customers leave without paying. It would be nice to think that they would come back and rectify matters but, sadly, 99% of them do not. The only thing you can do is to keep a record of such occurrences and mark it down on your wastage sheet. Try and impress on your staff the need for vigilance in this area and, if you are fortunate enough to have any means of tracing such people, do get in touch with them and ask them politely if they wouldn't mind settling their bill.

Most business people – and publicans and restaurateurs are no exception – are frequently asked to provide prizes for raffles, charities and the like. Sometimes, we even run our own promotions where the prize is a meal with a

Menu costing, stock-taking and suppliers

127

bottle of wine. If you do any of these things, be sure to keep a record for stock-taking and other purposes.

This might all seem to be a great deal more trouble than it is worth but, as you will see later on in the chapter, these few items can seriously affect your gross profit margins. Another point to bear in mind is that, unless you have a precise record of these 'allowances', the Customs and Excise will assess the VAT content on the cost of all food consumed or used and not on the cost only of the food sold.

Stock-taking

It is safe to say that stock-taking is one of the most tedious chores imaginable and it is doubtful whether even professional stock-takers enjoy it. The fact that it is such a bind does not make it any the less important, but often it is left to a junior member of staff or just skimped through. You need to take stock to ensure that the profit margins you have so carefully worked out are actually being achieved, so don't let it slide: do it properly.

Basically, put in a nutshell, stock-taking amounts to this:

Goods in stock + Goods sold = Goods purchased.

The formula is simple but to arrive at an accurate result takes planning and a deal of tenacity, especially as it needs to be carried out at regular intervals. Another irksome point about stock-taking is that it has to be done all at one time. You cannot space your stock-take over a week or even a few days and because of this, most catering operations take stock perhaps once a month or even once a quarter. Others take stock only

Ready reckoner

Cost Price	% 40	SP ex VAT	SP +VAT	% 45	SP ex VAT	SP +VAT	% 48	SP ex VAT	SP +VAT	% 50	SP ex VAT	SP +VAT	% 53	SP ex VAT	SP +VAT	% 55	SP ex VAT	SP +VAT	% 58	SP ex VAT	SP +VAT	% 60	SP ex VAT	SP +VAT	% 63	SP ex VAT	SP +VAT	% 65	SP ex VAT	SP +VAT	% 70	SP ex VAT	SP +VAT
0.25	40	0.42	0.48	45	0.45	0.52	48	0.48	0.55	50	0.50	0.58	53	0.53	0.57	55	0.56	0.64	58	0.60	0.64	60	0.63	0.67	63	0.68	0.78	65	0.71	0.82	70	0.83	0.95
0.30	40	0.50	0.58	45	0.54	0.63	48	0.58	0.66	50	0.60	0.65	53	0.64	0.74	55	0.67	0.77	58	0.71	0.82	60	0.75	0.86	63	0.81	0.93	65	0.86	0.99	70	1.00	1.15
0.35	40	0.58	0.67	45	0.64	0.73	48	0.67	0.77	50	0.70	0.75	53	0.74	0.85	55	0.78	0.83	58	0.83	0.95	60	0.88	1.01	63	0.95	1.09	65	1.00	1.15	70	1.17	1.35
0.40	40	0.67	0.77	45	0.73	0.83	48	0.77	0.89	50	0.80	0.92	53	0.85	0.98	55	0.88	1.01	58	0.95	1.09	60	1.00	1.15	63	1.08	1.24	65	1.14	1.31	70	1.33	1.53
0.45	40	0.75	0.86	45	0.82	0.94	48	0.87	1.00	50	0.90	1.04	53	0.95	1.09	55	1.00	1.07	58	1.07	1.23	60	1.13	1.30	63	1.22	1.40	65	1.29	1.48	70	1.50	1.73
0.50	40	0.83	0.96	45	0.91	1.04	48	0.96	1.11	50	1.00	1.06	53	1.06	1.22	55	1.11	1.28	58	1.19	1.37	60	1.25	1.44	63	1.35	1.55	65	1.43	1.64	70	1.67	1.92
0.55	40	0.92	1.05	45	1.00	1.15	48	1.06	1.22	50	1.10	1.18	53	1.17	1.33	55	1.22	1.40	58	1.31	1.51	60	1.38	1.59	63	1.49	1.71	65	1.58	1.82	70	1.83	2.10
0.60	40	1.00	1.15	45	1.09	1.25	48	1.16	1.33	50	1.20	1.29	53	1.27	1.46	55	1.33	1.53	58	1.43	1.64	60	1.50	1.73	63	1.62	1.86	65	1.71	1.97	70	2.00	2.30
0.65	40	1.08	1.25	45	1.18	1.36	48	1.25	1.44	50	1.30	1.40	53	1.38	1.59	55	1.44	1.66	58	1.55	1.78	60	1.63	1.87	63	1.76	2.02	65	1.86	2.14	70	2.17	2.50
0.70	40	1.17	1.34	45	1.27	1.46	48	1.34	1.45	50	1.40	1.50	53	1.49	1.71	55	1.56	1.79	58	1.67	1.92	60	1.75	2.01	63	1.89	2.17	65	2.00	2.30	70	2.33	2.68
0.75	40	1.25	1.44	45	1.36	1.57	48	1.44	1.55	50	1.50	1.61	53	1.60	1.84	55	1.67	1.92	58	1.79	2.06	60	1.88	2.16	63	2.03	2.33	65	2.14	2.46	70	2.50	2.86
0.80	40	1.33	1.53	45	1.45	1.67	48	1.54	1.66	50	1.60	1.72	53	1.70	1.96	55	1.78	2.05	58	1.90	2.19	60	2.00	2.30	63	2.16	2.48	65	2.29	2.63	70	2.67	3.07
0.85	40	1.41	1.63	45	1.54	1.77	48	1.63	1.76	50	1.70	1.83	53	1.81	2.08	55	1.89	2.17	58	2.02	2.32	60	2.13	2.45	63	2.30	2.65	65	2.43	2.79	70	2.83	3.25
0.90	40	1.50	1.73	45	1.63	1.88	48	1.73	1.87	50	1.80	1.94	53	1.92	2.21	55	2.00	2.30	58	2.14	2.46	60	2.25	2.59	63	2.43	2.79	65	2.57	2.96	70	3.00	3.45
0.95	40	1.58	1.82	45	1.72	1.98	48	1.83	1.98	50	1.90	2.04	53	2.02	2.32	55	2.11	2.43	58	2.26	2.60	60	2.38	2.74	63	2.57	2.96	65	2.71	3.12	70	3.17	3.65
1.00	40	1.67	1.92	45	1.81	2.09	48	1.92	1.94	50	2.00	2.30	53	2.13	2.45	55	2.22	2.56	58	2.38	2.74	60	2.50	2.88	63	2.70	3.11	65	2.86	3.29	70	3.33	3.83
1.05	40	1.75	2.01	45	1.91	2.19	48	2.02	2.04	50	2.10	2.42	53	2.23	2.56	55	2.33	2.68	58	2.50	2.88	60	2.63	3.02	63	2.84	3.27	65	3.00	3.45	70	3.50	4.03
1.10	40	1.83	2.11	45	2.00	2.30	48	2.16	2.18	50	2.20	2.53	53	2.34	2.69	55	2.44	2.81	58	2.62	3.01	60	2.75	3.16	63	2.97	3.42	65	3.14	3.61	70	3.67	4.22
1.15	40	1.92	2.20	45	2.09	2.40	48	2.21	2.14	50	2.30	2.65	53	2.45	2.82	55	2.56	2.94	58	2.74	3.15	60	2.88	3.31	63	3.11	3.58	65	3.29	3.78	70	3.83	4.40
1.20	40	2.00	2.30	45	2.18	2.50	48	2.31	2.33	50	2.40	2.76	53	2.55	2.93	55	2.67	3.07	58	2.86	3.29	60	3.00	3.45	63	3.24	3.73	65	3.43	3.94	70	4.00	4.60
1.25	40	2.08	2.40	45	2.27	2.61	48	2.40	2.42	50	2.50	2.88	53	2.66	2.69	55	2.78	3.20	58	2.98	3.43	60	3.13	3.60	63	3.38	3.89	65	3.57	4.11	70	4.17	4.79
1.30	40	2.17	2.49	45	2.36	2.71	48	2.50	2.54	50	2.60	2.99	53	2.77	3.19	55	2.89	3.32	58	3.10	3.57	60	3.25	3.74	63	3.51	4.03	65	3.71	4.27	70	4.33	4.98
1.35	40	2.25	2.59	45	2.45	2.82	48	2.60	2.99	50	2.70	3.11	53	2.87	3.30	55	3.00	3.45	58	3.21	3.70	60	3.38	3.89	63	3.65	4.20	65	3.85	4.44	70	4.50	5.18
1.40	40	2.33	2.68	45	2.55	2.92	48	2.69	3.10	50	2.80	3.22	53	2.97	3.43	55	3.11	3.58	58	3.33	3.83	60	3.50	4.03	63	3.78	4.35	65	4.00	4.60	70	4.67	5.37
1.45	40	2.42	2.78	45	2.64	3.03	48	2.79	3.21	50	2.90	3.34	53	3.09	3.55	55	3.22	3.70	58	3.45	3.97	60	3.63	4.17	63	3.92	4.51	65	4.14	4.76	70	4.83	5.55
1.50	40	2.50	2.88	45	2.73	3.14	48	2.88	3.32	50	3.00	3.45	53	3.19	3.67	55	3.33	3.83	58	3.57	4.11	60	3.75	4.31	63	4.05	4.66	65	4.29	4.93	70	5.00	5.75
1.55	40	2.58	2.97	45	2.82	3.24	48	2.98	3.43	50	3.10	3.57	53	3.30	3.79	55	3.44	3.96	58	3.69	4.24	60	3.88	4.46	63	4.19	4.82	65	4.43	5.09	70	5.17	5.95
1.60	40	2.67	3.07	45	2.91	3.35	48	3.08	3.54	50	3.20	3.68	53	3.40	3.91	55	3.56	4.09	58	3.81	4.38	60	4.00	4.60	63	4.32	4.97	65	4.57	5.26	70	5.33	6.13
1.65	40	2.75	3.16	45	3.00	3.45	48	3.17	3.65	50	3.30	3.80	53	3.51	4.04	55	3.67	4.22	58	3.93	4.52	60	4.13	4.75	63	4.46	5.13	65	4.71	5.42	70	5.50	6.32
1.70	40	2.83	3.26	45	3.09	3.55	48	3.27	3.76	50	3.40	4.26	53	3.62	4.16	55	3.78	4.34	58	4.05	4.65	60	4.25	4.89	63	4.59	5.28	65	4.85	5.59	70	5.67	6.52
1.75	40	2.92	3.35	45	3.18	3.66	48	3.37	3.87	50	3.50	4.03	53	3.72	4.28	55	3.89	4.47	58	4.17	4.79	60	4.38	5.04	63	4.73	5.44	65	5.00	5.75	70	5.88	6.76
1.80	40	3.00	3.45	45	3.27	3.76	48	3.46	3.98	50	3.60	4.14	53	3.83	4.40	55	4.00	4.60	58	4.29	4.93	60	4.50	5.18	63	4.86	5.59	65	5.14	5.91	70	6.00	6.90
1.85	40	3.08	3.55	45	3.36	3.87	48	3.56	4.09	50	3.70	4.26	53	3.94	4.53	55	4.11	4.73	58	4.40	5.07	60	4.63	5.32	63	5.00	5.75	65	5.29	6.08	70	6.17	7.10
1.90	40	3.17	3.64	45	3.45	3.97	48	3.65	4.20	50	3.80	4.37	53	4.04	4.65	55	4.22	4.86	58	4.52	5.20	60	4.75	5.46	63	5.14	5.91	65	5.43	6.24	70	6.33	7.28
1.95	40	3.25	3.74	45	3.55	4.08	48	3.75	4.31	50	3.90	4.49	53	4.15	4.77	55	4.33	4.98	58	4.64	5.34	60	4.88	5.61	63	5.27	6.06	65	5.57	6.40	70	6.50	7.48
2.00	40	3.33	3.83	45	3.64	4.18	48	3.85	4.42	50	4.00	4.60	53	4.26	4.89	55	4.44	5.11	58	4.76	5.48	60	5.00	5.75	63	5.41	6.22	65	5.71	6.57	70	6.67	7.67
2.05	40	3.42	3.93	45	3.73	4.29	48	3.94	4.53	50	4.10	4.72	53	4.36	5.02	55	4.56	5.24	58	4.88	5.61	60	5.13	5.90	63	5.54	6.37	65	5.85	6.73	70	6.83	7.85
2.10	40	3.50	4.03	45	3.82	4.39	48	4.04	4.64	50	4.20	4.83	53	4.47	5.14	55	4.67	5.37	58	5.00	5.75	60	5.25	6.04	63	5.68	6.53	65	6.00	6.90	70	7.00	8.05
2.15	40	3.58	4.12	45	3.91	4.50	48	4.13	4.75	50	4.30	4.95	53	4.57	5.26	55	4.77	5.49	58	5.12	5.89	60	5.38	6.19	63	5.81	6.68	65	6.14	7.06	70	7.17	8.25
2.20	40	3.67	4.22	45	4.00	4.60	48	4.23	4.87	50	4.40	5.06	53	4.68	5.38	55	4.89	5.62	58	5.23	6.02	60	5.50	6.33	63	5.95	6.84	65	6.28	7.23	70	7.33	8.43
2.25	40	3.75	4.31	45	4.09	4.70	48	4.33	4.98	50	4.50	5.18	53	4.79	5.51	55	5.00	5.75	58	5.36	6.16	60	5.63	6.16	63	6.08	6.99	65	6.43	7.39	70	7.50	8.63
2.30	40	3.83	4.41	45	4.18	4.81	48	4.42	5.09	50	4.60	5.29	53	4.89	5.63	55	5.11	5.88	58	5.48	6.30	60	5.48	6.30	63	6.22	7.15	65	6.57	7.55	70	7.67	8.82
2.35	40	3.92	4.50	45	4.27	4.91	48	4.52	5.20	50	4.70	5.41	53	5.00	5.75	55	5.22	6.00	58	5.60	6.43	60	5.60	6.43	63	6.35	7.30	65	6.71	7.72	70	7.83	9.00
2.40	40	4.00	4.60	45	4.36	5.02	48	4.62	5.31	50	4.80	5.52	53	5.11	5.87	55	5.33	6.13	58	5.71	6.57	60	5.71	6.57	63	6.49	7.46	65	6.88	7.88	70	8.00	9.20
2.45	40	4.08	4.70	45	4.45	5.12	48	4.71	5.42	50	4.90	5.64	53	5.21	5.99	55	5.44	6.26	58	5.83	6.71	60	5.83	6.71	63	6.62	7.61	65	7.00	8.05	70	8.17	9.40
2.50	40	4.17	4.79	45	4.55	5.23	48	4.81	5.53	50	5.00	5.75	53	5.32	6.12	55	5.56	6.39	58	5.95	6.85	60	5.95	6.85	63	6.76	7.71	65	7.14	8.21	70	8.33	9.58
2.55	40	4.25	4.89	45	4.64	5.33	48	4.90	5.64	50	5.10	5.87	53	5.43	6.24	55	5.67	6.52	58	6.07	6.98	60	6.07	6.98	63	6.89	7.92	65	7.29	8.38	70	8.50	9.78
2.60	40	4.33	4.98	45	4.73	5.44	48	5.00	5.75	50	5.20	5.98	53	5.53	6.36	55	5.78	6.64	58	6.19	7.12	60	6.19	7.12	63	7.03	8.08	65	7.43	8.54	70	8.67	9.97
2.65	40	4.42	5.08	45	4.82	5.54	48	5.10	5.86	50	5.30	6.10	53	5.64	6.48	55	5.89	6.77	58	6.31	7.26	60	6.31	7.26	63	7.16	8.23	65	7.57	8.71	70	8.83	10.15
2.70	40	4.50	5.18	45	4.91	5.65	48	5.19	5.93	50	5.40	6.21	53	5.74	6.61	55	6.00	6.90	58	6.43	7.39	60	6.43	7.39	63	7.30	8.40	65	7.71	8.87	70	9.00	10.35
2.75	40	4.58	5.27	45	5.00	5.75	48	5.29	6.08	50	5.50	6.33	53	5.85	6.73	55	6.11	7.03	58	6.55	7.53	60	6.55	7.53	63	7.43	8.54	65	7.86	9.04	70	9.17	10.55

SP= Selling Price

once a year and only then because they are compelled to.

Stock-taking must coincide with the end of a trading week or month so as to coincide also with the end of a similar period on your accounts. It has to be said that, although all stock-takes are important, the most essential and accurate stock-take should be that which occurs at the financial year-end. Any mistake or inaccuracy then cannot be easily adjusted and will usually end up coming out of your own pocket. It is plain to see then just how important it is to take stock regularly and how foolish it would be to do it only once a year.

The normal or usual method of stock-taking

If the food operation is quite small and has a limited number of items on the menu, simply go round all the fridges, freezers and cupboards and write down all food stocks. Do not include items such as napkins or cleaning materials but do include dry goods such as flour, pulses, sauces and the like. The thing to remember is *if you can't eat it, don't cost it*.

This is usually the time when you decide to be ruthless and clear out a jar of something which has been at the back of the cupboard for ages. Fine, clear it out, but remember to mark it on your wastage sheet.

Having completed your list – and here comes the main drawback with this system – you then have to cost it up. This means that you have to go through all the invoices since the last stock-take and price every item. Try doing that when your last stock-take was 12 months ago! Some of the more obscure or infrequently used products may still be on the shelf since your last stock-take; if so, that is where you will find the cost.

You can see, then, that this method is extremely time-consuming and laborious especially if you have a year when each month-end seems to fall on a weekend or to coincide with a pastime. Such patterns do occur and, when they do, the last thing you want is to be bogged down with lengthy calculations.

A simpler and more accurate method is to use a stock-book. When stock arrives, it is checked to ensure that it is all present and correct and then entered into the stock-book. Stock-books are available from most stationers, although it is a simple matter to make your own from either an exercise book or a loose leaf folder with each sheet or page representing one product.

Once the stock-take has been completed and costed up, adjustments have to be made for wastage, staff and self usage, etc., as such food has been bought but not sold and a cash deficiency will show. You need to find out what has happened to such food and your aim is to cover as many eventualities as possible. To achieve this, you need to total up the various amounts for wastage, staff and self usage, etc., and then make an adjustment in order to calculate an accurate gross profit. There are two ways of doing this:

- ☐ Cost up all these items which have been used but not sold. Cost them at selling price but remember to deduct the cost of vegetables where appropriate and VAT. The resulting amount is the amount you allow for. *Add this amount to your sales*. The problem with this system is that if you are not careful you could end up paying VAT on the so-called 'allowances', so this method is not recommended.
- ☐ This a much simpler method and makes use of the card index system mentioned earlier in the chapter. Take the cost price from the appropriate recipe/cost card and *Deduct this amount from your purchases*.

It is therefore a good idea *not* to let the lists of wastage, staff and self usage get too long. We cost ours up every week. Not only does this save us making lengthy calculations but also any excesses can be spotted immediately and, if necessary, action can be taken to rectify the situation. For example, if an unusual amount of, say, battered haddock is being thrown away, it could be due to one of the following reasons:

- ☐ For some strange reason, a usually popular item is not selling well that week. It does sometimes happen.
- ☐ The quality of the product is not as good as usual. Contact the supplier. Was there any sign of deterioration when the product arrived? Did it show signs of starting to defrost?
- ☐ Too much is being taken out of the freezer at one time. The potential sales are being wrongly assessed if this is the case, so work out a maximum holding amount.

If one item continually shows up on the wastage sheet, it may be that it is simply a poor seller. If that is the case, don't mess about: take it off the menu. Similarly, if you are not happy with the quality of the product, change your supplier or manufacturer.

Yet another list we use to help us spot any potential problem areas is a customer complaints sheet (see right). We find it really useful to make a note of the time, date and exact nature of any complaint when it occurs and also to make a record of any action we have

Complaints sheet

Time and date	Table number	Nature of complaint	Action taken
1.30 1 April '89	7	Customer complained the Gazpacho Soup was cold.	Explained it was supposed to be. Customer satisfied.

taken as a result. To start with, most customers who complain do so in good faith and for what they consider to be a genuine reason, so by taking their complaint seriously and listening to what they have to say, you will not be giving them grounds to complain even further.

On the whole, we are fortunate in that we receive very few complaints, so when a spate of complaints did occur, a closer analysis was clearly needed. It transpired that most of the dissatisfaction concerned two particular items on the menu.

We discovered with one that the wording on the menu was wrong. The way we had described the dish could be interpreted two ways and when the customer received something slightly different from what they had anticipated, they complained. We altered the description and the complaints ceased. The other series of complaints concerned the product itself. It was a convenience food. Prior to including it on the menu, we had tried it and thought that it was satisfactory. The customers did not. We removed the product from the menu and, again, the complaints ceased.

If we had not kept a complaints sheet, it could well have taken longer to discover the reasons behind the above complaints. True, where there was a refund, it would have shown up on the wastage sheet and there is a certain amount of feed-back from the staff, but sometimes it takes a complaints sheet to show a pattern.

Some dissatisfied customers do not always reveal precisely what the problem is, while others are not always as articulate as they might be. Keep a complaints sheet, then, and link it with your wastage sheet.

To return to the main theme, however: the method of stock-taking you use really does depend on the type of operation you run and it will take a certain amount of trial and error before you find the one most suited to your needs.

Our system

The system we have devised for our own set-up seems to work quite smoothly, with the minimum of effort, giving us accurate results and a constant check on the gross profit margins.

As we have already stated, we provide an extensive à la carte menu which makes use of both fresh and convenience food. For convenience foods, we use a loose-leaf folder allowing a page for each item. Stock is booked into it at the time of delivery and a note made of any price changes at the same time, before the invoice has gone to file. The next stage is that it is booked out by the case. This means, in effect, that when a particular case is opened is when it is booked out, irrespective of whether it is a slow-selling item which could remain in the freezer for weeks. It is booked out just that once.

Exactly the same applies to cases of canned tomatoes

Stock sheet

PRODUCT: Chicken Kiev
SUPPLIER: A.K. Kitchens/Hedge
10 per case

1	2	3	4	5	6	7	8
Date week no.	Order no.	Quantity received	Price per case	Stock used	Stock remaining	Maximum stock held	Comments
					3	3	opening stock as counted 31st April
4th May A	N224709	2	£12	3	2	3	£24 stock left

and the like. They are booked out of stock just the once. We do this in an exercise book. You could just use a piece of paper, but loose paper easily gets mislaid. For each day of the week, we just jot down the cases that have been opened.

No fresh produce, such as meat and vegetables, is booked in at all as we assume that it will be used within the week. The same applies even if the produce has been 'made up' and then frozen, for example steak and kidney pie filling: it is still ignored as it will be used in a very short time anyway.

To get the closing stock figure, at the end of each week we transfer the items marked down in the exercise book to column 5 on the relevant page of the main stock-book. If you look at the sample stock page above, you will see that during week A, two cases of kievs were delivered (columns 1–3), three cases were used (column 5), three were already in stock (column 6, previous week), so there are two remaining. *This is the amount we cost up.*

Total *all* the remaining stock up and do not forget those sheets which have not had any entries either for deliveries or stock used.

We then do a random check on one or two items to ensure that the freezer does contain just two boxes of kievs and that the system is working. Most weeks there is some fresh produce left, so we complete a quick physical stock-take, cost up what is remaining and add this figure to the one obtained from the stock-book.

The only area we have left out is dry goods, i.e. pulses, flour, sauces, etc. The strange thing about this area is that, over the years, the figure for dry goods has varied very little, so we have a standard amount that is added to the stock each week. During the full stock-take once a quarter, of course we include dry goods and check that the amount we are allowing is correct. However, please do not assume that this will work for every catering operation – you may find that you have to include dry goods in your booking-out operation if the amounts vary from week to week.

We now have sufficient information to work out the gross profit margins. As you will see from the example of the weekly stock-take and reconciliation sheet above, we get two main figures, the cost of food used or consumed and the cost of food sold. The figure we are most concerned with is the the gross profit on the cost of food sold.

When the gross profit is worked out on a weekly basis, to be fair, it is not meticulously accurate, but it does balance out over a period of a few weeks and it does cause problem areas to show up. At first sight, it may seem rather complicated but once you get into the system and really get used to it, you will be rewarded by the fact that it will take only approximately 1 hour of your time per week.

Menu costing, stock-taking and suppliers

When you first start to use our system, you may prefer to do a full physical stock-take once a month so that you can spot any hiccups such as stock not being booked out. Once the system is running smoothly, though, once a quarter should be adequate.

Once you have these basic figures, it is a simple matter to check on any of the listed items as a percentage, provided you remember the following rule. *You can only make comparisons on a LIKE WITH LIKE basis.* For example, wastage and staff food may be expressed as a percentage of the purchases as they are both at *cost* price but they cannot be expressed as a percentage of sales. The reason for this is that sales are at *retail* price.

So, to express wastage, say, as a percentage, you must make the following calculation:

$$\frac{\text{Wastage} \times 100}{\text{Cost of food used}} = \ldots\ldots\%$$

The same formula can, of course, be used, for any of the 'allowances'.

If you have decided to operate a fixed gross profit margin and keep a record of the factors which can affect that margin, it stands to reason that the two should balance.

As we have said, a weekly reconciliation is not absolutely accurate but it should average out. If there is a persistent imbalance, perhaps it may be due to a clerical error, in which case it can easily be checked. If no such error can be found, the imbalance could be due to other reasons, such as one of the staff pilfering stock or poor security generally. If such is the case, the only remedy is to increase the physical stock-takes and increase vigilance generally.

We are aware, as we stated earlier, that stock-taking can be a bind, but as it is so important, you might as well take an interest in it and pride yourself in achieving accurate results. After all, it does pay dividends – straight into your bank account!

Rotation of stock

For some reason or other, commercial supplies of perishable goods, unlike their domestic counterparts, do not have a 'sell by' date displayed on the packaging. What is more, most frozen goods for commercial use do not display any coding whatsoever. You have no means, then, of knowing just how long the supplier has had them in stock. At best, some give information as to the optimum temperature at which the product should be stored and others list the ingredients but as a rule, that is all. You have no option, then, but to rely on the integrity of the supplier and to ensure that, once such goods come into your possession, they are not only stored at the correct temperature but also used in strict rotation.

Experience shows that it is not sufficient simply to put new stock at the bottom of, say, the freezer and assume that staff will only take from the top. Gracious no! That's far too simple! During a busy session when you are far too busy to get more stock from a freezer yourself and you detail a part-time member of staff to get it for you, you can be sure that they will wreak havoc among your carefully stacked produce. Even then, it is odds-on that they will not remove stock in sequence.

The simplest way round this is to mark the stock yourself in the first place, but not with a date as even dates, amazingly, can cause confusion. It is fairly safe to assume that most people know their alphabet, so it is best to use that. Using one letter per week, the alphabet will cover six months, at which point you start at A again. When you have completed two alphabets, you have covered one year. Now you know what the A stands for in column 1 of the stock sheet! Use a felt-tipped pen, similar to those which are used in supermarkets and which are safe with food. Make your letters bold and large, marking each side of a package if you feel it necessary.

Stock control

Stock control means making sure that you do not carry too much stock. It is vital if you wish to ensure that your hard-earned capital is not tied up in unnecessary stock when it could be elsewhere, gaining interest. Those of you who are already licensees will no doubt know of the importance of stock control in relation to the bar, and in this respect, you possibly operate a stock-book which shows the maximum level of stock to be held. Exactly the same applies to your catering operation. Column 7 on the example stock sheet shows the maximum stock which you have decided should be held.

In order to work out accurately how much you will need to hold, you will have to keep a list of the quantities of each of the items you have sold. When you have done this for a few weeks, a pattern will emerge. Of course, if you are fortunate enough to have

Bushells Arms, Goosnargh
Weekly Stock-take and Reconciliation

Week Number ....
Date ....

Opening Stock ....
Add Purchases at Cost Price (excl. VAT) ....

Total ....

Less Closing Stock ....

Equals Cost of Food **USED/CONSUMED** ....

Less Staff Food at Cost Price ....
Less Wastage Food at Cost Price ....
Less Goods taken for own use ....
Less Customers left without paying ....
Less Entertaining/Promotions etc. ....
Less Goods Sold to Staff ....

Equals Cost of Food **SOLD** ....

WEEKLY SALES OF FOOD (EXCL. VAT) ....

Weekly Sales of Food ....
Minus Cost of Food Sold ....

Equals Gross Profit on Food Sold ....

Gross Profit as a percentage:

$$\frac{G.P. \times 100}{Sales} = \ldots\ldots\ldots\%$$

G.P. Before Allowances = Weekly Sales of Food **MINUS** Cost of Food **USED/CONSUMED** = Gross Profit on Food **USED/CONSUMED**

As a percentage:

$$\frac{G.P. \times 100}{Sales} = \ldots\ldots\ldots\%$$

computerised tills or software that automatically records stock, all this will be done for you. If you have not, the idea is to hold sufficient stock to ensure that you do not run out between deliveries, plus a little bit extra to cover you for any emergency such as a delayed delivery, but not so much that it will last you for weeks and weeks.

From time to time, suppliers come up with special offers which seem very tempting, but it is wise to remember to buy them only if you know that you can sell them within a reasonably short space of time.

Finally, please do not be tempted to think that the various areas discussed in this chapter are more trouble than they are worth. Quite the reverse: our experience has shown that they are crucial in the calculation and maintenance of a healthy gross profit margin. Do try and work out a system to suit your own needs and which will provide you with all the information you need and more. One thing is for sure, if you do not get your gross profit margins right at the outset, you could very easily make a loss instead of a profit. In this respect, it is prudent to remember that after gross profit come overheads and that, at the end of the day, there should be something left for *you*. You are professional people after all, so treat it as a professional discipline and ensure that a potentially difficult area runs smoothly, efficiently and profitably.

Suppliers – how and where to buy

Once you have embarked upon a catering operation, you will quickly discover that leisurely shopping trips to Sainsbury's or Asda are a thing of the past. Buying for a catering operation requires consummate skill in order to conserve valuable time and energy and you need to look at the alternatives which are available.

Probably the main factor which will influence your choice of supplier will be location. We ourselves are fortunate in that our business is situated on the outskirts of a large town where there are several cash and carry outlets, all within easy reach, and all the major suppliers deliver to the area several times each week. The plethora of eating houses in and around the Ribble Valley has resulted in a sizeable infrastructure of catering suppliers who will deliver everything from freshly caught fish, game and vegetables to specialised ethnic foods and all on a daily basis. We really are spoiled for choice.

Local shops and suppliers

No matter where you are located, the major suppliers will be able to reach you but before we consider them, it is perhaps a good idea to look at local shops first. If you are located in a small or similarly close-knit community, there are distinct advantages in supporting local tradesmen and provision merchants. Quite apart from any other consideration, they will often become loyal customers, but we have felt for some time now that we get better value as large customers of a small concern than we do as small customers of a nationwide distributor.

The local butcher, for instance, if he is a good one, will often provide an excellent service and is hardly likely to supply you with inferior meat when everyone in the district knows that he supplied it. It is also likely that he will value your trade because of the recommendations you are able to give your customers. In other words, you can be a good advertisement for his business. Using your local butcher has other advantages, too: he can give you good advice as to which is a good buy and he will be able to supply you with the smaller quantities which you will sometimes need. Local butchers can also prove to be a boon when it comes to providing specialised cuts of meat for regional dishes and many of them make their own sausages and the like. In short, your local butcher will usually go out of his way to make life easy for you.

The local greengrocer can also be a great help, as not many licensees have the time to go to the wholesale vegetable market at the crack of dawn, which is usually when all the best produce is sold. However, if you can find a local supplier who does take the trouble to do just that and who can supply you with the range and quality which you require, all at the right price, well so much the better.

Recently, many greengrocers have set their stall out to supply ready prepared, fresh vegetables to the catering industry. They usually deliver their produce in vacuum packs, which means that, if the seal is unbroken and the packs are kept in refrigeration, the contents will keep for a couple of days. Greengrocers which specialise in providing such a service will cut the vegetables up in any way you wish, which means, of course, that you can buy chipped potatoes from them. It has to be said that they are not as good as those which are freshly peeled and chipped on the premises but they do save on preparation time. They also compare very favourably in price and quality with their extruded, frozen counterparts. Suppliers such as these are a godsend for the caterer because they dispense with the need to resort to the use of frozen or canned vegetables which, in any case, can be expensive as well as unpleasant. The small firm which supplies us with this type of produce even delivers on a Sunday!

In many rural areas, there should be an abundance of fresh eggs and poultry and a recent resurgence of cottage industries means that produce such as local farmhouse cheese, preserves, honey, yogurt, ice cream and so on are once more readily available. Long may this situation last – a mature locally made farmhouse cheese will knock the spots off the sort of cheese which comes in a plastic pack! Rural produce is also a winner with customers, who love the honest flavour of real country produce. If you are located in a town or city, don't despair: many of these cottage industries will be pleased to deliver.

Still on the subject of small suppliers, we must not forget housewives. Yes, housewives! That vast, untapped labour force of women who are either stuck at home with a young family or who, for one reason or another, do not work. Some of them can cook superbly. Many housewives develop particular skills over the years and can often provide specialised pies, puddings, sweets and so on which can liven up an existing menu. An important point to remember, though, is that if they are producing food for resale, their kitchen should conform to Environmental Health standards. If this is not possible, it can always be arranged for them to use your kitchen for an hour or two and produce their specialities there.

Frozen food suppliers

Most caterers use some frozen goods, even if it is only ice cream or the odd item of convenience food to supplement the menu. At the other extreme, some catering outlets have menus which consist of nothing but frozen convenience food. The point in mentioning this is that most of the major suppliers of such produce publish super glossy brochures with an interesting and, in many cases, high-quality range. Some of them can make a really interesting read, but more than that, if you are stuck for fresh ideas – it happens from time to time – you can always pinch a few of theirs. If, after reading these brochures, you are tempted to buy, make sure that you are not tempted to buy more than you need as good-quality convenience foods are not cheap. If it comes to that, no convenience foods are cheap. Ask yourself who pays for their manufacture, packaging, promotion and delivery!

The 'reps' from such firms visit regularly and can be very helpful in answering questions or sorting out any problems you may have. Most frozen food suppliers offer a telesales service where they telephone you at a prearranged time to take your order. Usually, they will insist on a minimum order, although as a general rule, it is not usually excessive.

In addition, most of these large suppliers offer a discount system which usually takes the form of a sliding scale depending on how much you spend per order. These things are not hard and fast by any means and you may, for instance, be able to negotiate an overall discount on all your purchases. On a similar tack, perhaps the supplier will offer you a straight discount on an item for which you have a particularly heavy demand. Sometimes, even breweries have been known to negotiate standard discounts on behalf of their tenants and other licensees who are connected with them. When a 'rep' calls, then, don't blow him out in rapid fashion. Take time out and *talk to him* and find out what benefits, if any, there are in buying from his firm.

Having said all that, it must also be said that most of the discounts mentioned above will be available only if you pay cash on delivery as they are hardly likely to give you a discount and credit as well. If you want a monthly account (usually the maximum), you will usually have to forgo some of the discount advantages in exchange for the facility of paying monthly.

Cash and carry outlets

For many small caterers, however, a weekly expedition to the cash and carry will provide the bulk of their requirements. In fact, most cash and carry outlets, realising the potential market, have extended their range of catering products although the range does vary from region to region.

Some cash and carry merchants provide an excellent butchery department and will even arrange for fresh meat to be delivered. Some are experimenting with the supply of fresh fish – always a winner – and nearly all have a separate section for the supply of fresh vegetables and fruit.

Many cash and carrys have deliberately sought specifically to attract pub caterers. To help them achieve this, they provide information sheets and in-house brochures which list the products on offer in a manner which is aimed at that market. Nowadays, whole sections of their warehouses are set aside for the sole convenience of caterers and they not only provide their 'own brand' products at attractive prices but also put on tastings and demonstrations. Some of them even go so far as to sponsor national pub catering competitions and so on. Obviously, they consider the catering industry to be a major portion of their business. At a good cash and carry of this sort, you will be able to find everything you are likely to need such as uniforms, knives, chopping boards, notices, cleaning materials, dairy produce, fresh meat, fresh vegetables and, if you are not tied to a brewery, a full range of wines, spirits and soft drinks.

Most cash and carrys will allow payment by cash or by cheque, although with the latter method, you need to have cleared this facility with them when you become a member. One group has even introduced a charge card which allows a monthly account facility.

Specialist catering suppliers

One of the most successful suppliers to the catering industry now provides a very sophisticated service, delivering a full range of goods – everything you would expect to find in a well-stocked cash and carry, with the exception of fresh foods – right to your door. Their service is nationwide and boasts an extensive back-up of advisers, very comprehensive price lists and, of course, a telesales service. They obviously intend to take some trade away from the cash and carry outlets. Their minimum order is, of necessity, higher than that of the frozen food supplier, but not excessively so, and they pride themselves on the standard of their drivers and the fact that their invoicing system cuts down on paperwork.

Choosing your supplier

Now that we have looked at the main sources of supply which are available, how do you choose?

To begin with, much depends on your location and the type of operation you are running. All sources of supply are like the proverbial curate's egg, i.e. good in parts. If, for instance, you wish to use your local butcher, greengrocer or farm dairy, it is vital that they are able to supply you with the quality and range of produce which you require. That might seem obvious at first, but let us examine it more closely. Take the local poultry farmer: he may well be able to provide you with superb free-range turkeys, but are they the right size? Are they available all the year round? Does he draw the tendons and sinews out of the legs properly? What are you going to do with the parts of the bird which are not as popular as the breast meat? Can he guarantee price and quality? All these questions need thought before a commitment is made.

One of the really irritating things about small producers is that most of them fail to provide proper invoices, preferring instead to give scruffy bits of paper which are impossible to decipher at a later date. Having said all that, we are firm devotees of local produce and are able to purchase cheeses, yogurts (both normal and Greek-style), poultry, free-range eggs, well-hung beef – and that means matured, not the other – and local lamb which is second to none in quality. We find that the enthusiasm and care shown by our small, local suppliers is well worth the extra couple of pence per pound. Another useful advantage is that most of them are only too happy to supply you with goods in an emergency, even though they may have closed.

If you do decide to opt for just one supplier, it is prudent to be aware that, even with the biggest of them, things can and do go wrong from time to time. We were badly let down on two occasions when one of our major suppliers failed to deliver. It goes without saying that both of these occasions were busy, bank holiday weekends and that there was no way of contacting them – firms like that do not work over any weekend, let alone a bank holiday. We were absolutely stuck and lost a great deal of trade and goodwill. Never again!

Conversely, if you opt for several suppliers, you do need to ensure that you are organised so that you remember on which days they will telephone for the order and on which days they will deliver. These are details which you can negotiate, but remember that if you have too many suppliers, you will find that far too much time is being spent messing around with orders and waiting for deliveries. Large suppliers though, do, provide comprehensive invoices which are easy to process.

The ironic part in writing about these things is that, in practice, you will very often stick to one supplier because of something really simple. For example, suppose there are two suppliers with almost identical ranges, prices and discounts: one arrives at a time

Menu costing, stock-taking and suppliers

Sorry, Fred – did you say Swede or Turnip?

which is convenient to you, the driver is cheerful and he puts the order in the right place; the other will arrive at any time from 7.30 a.m. onwards, moans all the time about his workload and will not deliver the produce if you are not in. There really is no contest between the two!

Of course, there is always the cash and carry, but that too can have its problems. To begin with, it usually means making a journey, which in itself means time and expense. Add to that the fact that more often than not you can get stuck at the payout behind someone who appears to be purchasing the entire stock for a sweet shop and you will realise that it can be more trouble than it is worth. This is especially true when you can see time moving inexorably towards lunch-time. At times like that, you will vow never to set foot in a cash and carry again.

Basically, what we are saying is that you will have to shop around, so to speak, until you find a supplier who fits in with your requirements. Moreover, you will probably continue to chop and change as your business develops. When 'reps' call, it may seem like a chore at the time, but do take time out to talk to them: they are there to help you if they can and, at the end of the day, you do not have to buy from them. Read your trade magazines, too: they are an invaluable source of information regarding services and new products. Also, talk to your fellow caterers if you get the opportunity, and find out where they buy their produce and what sort of a deal they get. All these points boil down to one piece of advice: it is all too easy to become lodged in your own little groove, but don't let that happen! Look around you and take an interest in your purchasing because it can pay real dividends.

14 Staff

Time and time again you will hear licensees and small restaurateurs bemoaning the quality and quantity of their staff, but how many times do they stop and think how much of the problem is due to themselves? Catering jobs, and in particular pub catering jobs, are among the lowest paid there are and yet we expect so much for our money. All right, we know that staff bills more than anything can make or break the business so wages have to be watched very carefully, but how many times have we forked out hundreds of pounds for fancy menus yet balked at the idea of spending £100 on staff uniforms? No, the staff are expected to provide their own out of the couple of quid or so an hour they are paid. So in order to examine the staff 'problem' objectively, we need to look at two points: namely, what is expected from staff and what the staff can expect in return.

Most pub catering operations operate around the 'family' unit with husband and wife forming the base, older children helping out and staff filling in where needed. There is really nothing wrong with this as it can create a friendly and intimate atmosphere, but it can also create problems. In this type of set-up, the licensees are inclined to do the cooking and administration themselves, leaving the front of house, public relations side to staff who work on a casual basis. They are not given adequate training and yet they are expected to perform a myriad of tasks.

Front-of-house staff play a vital role, no matter how good the food or drink is or what the place looks like, if customers are not treated correctly by the staff, they will not return. We know of very successful places who serve what can only be described as mediocre food and yet are full every session; the atmosphere is friendly and relaxed and the staff superb and that is what draws people in. If the wrong staff are employed, they will cost not only time and money but lost profits as well.

As a small employer, pubs can have a number of 'natural' advantages:

- ☐ Close personal relationships between the employer and employee. Staff will work with you rather than for you.
- ☐ An understanding of individual employees' problems from face-to-face contact. You can discuss problems as and when they arise and defuse any potential trouble more amicably.
- ☐ As part of the leisure industry, customers come to pubs on the whole to enjoy themselves and this can make for a pleasant and enjoyable occupation which gives staff the opportunity to meet a wide variety of people in congenial and relaxed circumstances. In other words, it can give tremendous job satisfaction.
- ☐ 'Peculiar' pub hours may be ideal for housewives or students who have other commitments.

Those are points which may help offset the disadvantages of working in the pub trade. Later on in the chapter, we will be looking at other ways in which you can make our staff feel more comfortable.

Identifying your staffing needs

The first hurdle you must get over is deciding when you need staff and what you we want them to do. As with most other things in this trade, staff are acquired on a piecemeal basis: a Wednesday night gets busy, so you get someone in to wait on; the part-time cellarman was inherited from the previous landlord and when you find ourselves bogged down with paperwork you get someone in to do the VAT. Without careful planning the whole set-up becomes a hotch-potch which is not good for you and not good for the staff.

Perhaps the simplest way to start is to sit down with a piece of paper and list all the jobs that need doing: cleaning, bar, paperwork, cooking, bottling-up, etc. Then you must decide which jobs you yourselves are going to do. You may be rotten cooks and hopeless at paperwork but superb front of house; if this is the case, it is foolish to employ waitresses when what is needed is a cook. Many places employ a cleaner out of habit, but in a small pub it may be worth considering if most of the cleaning cannot be done at the end of a session by the waiting on and bar staff. So it is important to have a clear job definition before any interviews take place.

Once you have defined staff duties, you then have to decide when you need them. Some sessions are busier than others: in our case, we need only one waitress on a Monday lunch-time, but we need three on a Sunday. This is perhaps the most difficult area because the trade can fluctuate so much, and that causes problems: too many staff on at a quiet time and the overheads spiral, too few and customers complain about being kept waiting and poor service. Even in the course of one session you can do all your trade in the space of an hour and yet you have to employ staff for three.

After you have looked at when you need staff, you may find that you need a cook for 5 days per week. Of course, you can employ two or three 'casuals' to cover the sessions, but consideration should be given to employing someone full-time. There are undoubted benefits: a person who is employed full-time has much more commitment, they can get to know the business more thoroughly and cover if you want to go on holiday, etc.

Because of the unsociable hours and your location you may want someone who will 'live in'.

Another aspect you need to consider is the amount of 'experience' required. Do you need a fully trained cook/chef? A person with experience and training may be required if you do not have the expertise to build or develop a catering operation. The local catering college or the City and Guilds Institute will be able to help in defining qualifications so that you can look for a person who has been trained to cover your type of operation.

If you feel confident enough to give the training yourselves, then one of the government training schemes or YTS may be able to provide a suitable applicant. However, these are not just a source of cheap labour: you have to ensure that adequate training is given, and arrange for the person to attend a course at a local catering college as part of their employment. In the end, you will be the ones who benefit.

All these factors must be decided before you embark on any advertising.

Finding staff

Advertising for staff

It may be that you do not need any new employees and that existing employees can do the job or be trained for it. If this is not the case, the next stage is to advertise. This can be done in numerous ways:
- ☐ By word of mouth from existing employees.
- ☐ A card advertisement placed in local shops.
- ☐ Jobcentres. These provide a free service for both full- and part-time staff. You will need to sort out the rate of pay before contacting them.
- ☐ Advertisement in local papers.
- ☐ Local catering colleges often have a notice board or an information service for jobs available in the area.
- ☐ A notice in the pub itself.

Before placing an advertisement, it is important not only to define the job but to sort out terms and conditions, and to give the applicant an easy way to contact, with perhaps a closing date. Spend some time wording the advert: a 'waiting on staff wanted' on a scruffy piece of paper pinned up in the ladies is hardly likely to encourage anyone, nor is listing so many demands that it reduces the possibilities to one in a million. Make sure that, if an applicant does telephone everyone knows the procedure: it may be their first contact with you and first impressions count. We usually have a few forms ready that can be filled in by us or, if we are not available, by one of the staff. So a Telephone Screening Form for waiting on staff would be something like that shown below.

Name ....

Address ....

Telephone ....

Age ....

Experience (if any) ....

Transport ....

Any sessions that they cannot or do not want to work

....

When available for interview...................................

After the closing date, the forms can be sifted through and unsuitable candidates can be eliminated, not on grounds of sex or colour, but perhaps because they live several miles away and have no transport, or because they do not want to work weekends or pastimes (late hours). Telephone all suitable applicants and arrange for an interview. Unsuccesful applicants should also be informed as not only is it common courtesy but bad manners are a bad advert for the business.

Interviews

Before the interview, you must have it clear in your own minds what you are looking for. Taking the example of waiting on staff, some of the qualities you should consider are as follows:
- ☐ A pleasant, friendly and comfortable manner, neat and tidy appearance, not scruffy (after all, they will be handling food).
- ☐ If they are to be handling cash absolute honesty and, if possible, the ability to add up quickly and work the tills.

- ☐ Pub catering can be quite fractious, so staff need to be able to think on their feet and answer or deal with any queries from the customers.
- ☐ To know and explain the menu and take orders.
- ☐ To know the correct accompaniments and be able to serve food quickly and efficiently; i.e. carry more than two plates.
- ☐ Serve wine - correctly.
- ☐ Have the ability to deflate any possible problem areas before they develop into complaints.
- ☐ Be prepared to work weekends and pastimes if required and be on call if possible.

Of course you may be lucky and find someone with all the attributes. Most of the time you will more be than happy to find someone with some of them, but with adequate training you can develop their skills to your satisfaction.

Every effort should be made to make the interview as comfortable as possible. As a start show the applicants around the place so they can see where they will be working, ask if they know the place and the type of food served, ask if they have they eaten here themselves? Show them the menu and give them time to look at it and comment about it. Most interviewers like to make notes. Try and keep them in the form of a checklist using ticks or numbers (see below): there is nothing more offputting than seeing someone write copious notes about you, and it's not a police interview after all.

Try and arrange comfortable and relaxed seating, a cup of tea or coffee also helps, and if possible, try and ensure that there are no interruptions – even the telephone can make an applicant uneasy. Above all, arrange the interview at a quiet time, because the last thing anyone wants is existing staff or customers gawping around doors staring at them. The initial impression will set the tenor of the whole interview, so don't start off with difficult questions: choose the sort that allow the interviewee to open up, such as 'what do you think about...?' or 'have you any ideas about...?' and allow plenty of time at the end of the session for the applicant to ask any questions they like. They should also be told when they should know the outcome – as soon as possible. Be as professional as possible from the outset because this is the way you will want your staff to behave.

Arrange a suitable gap between interviews so that applicants do not meet each other coming out. It also gives you enough time to evaluate and note your impressions. Some employers like references, but contact with the applicant's former or current employer should not be made without permission, and don't be too tempted to rely solely on another person's judgement.

Remember that good staff can increase your business and as such, interviewing is a worthwhile investment of your time. Prepare your questions in advance – it is all too easy to omit vital questions especially if the interview is going well.

Try hard to be objective when interviewing; you can easily be misled by gut reactions which sometimes can be inaccurate. Even if you feel that you have found the ideal person for the job, make sure that you complete the interview and check their references.

When preparing your questions, remember to keep in mind the following points:
- ☐ Questions should be open – in other words, they should not invite a straight 'yes' or 'no' answer. Open questions usually begin with how, what, when, where, who or why.
- ☐ Questions should not be ambiguous.
- ☐ Questions should be asked one at a time.

- ☐ Questions need not necessarily relate specifically to the job vacancy. You will probably wish to find out what the candidate is like as a person.
- ☐ Questions should not indicate the answer you would like to get.
- ☐ Questions should encourage the applicant to show some emotion or feeling – you don't want a zombie working for you.

Having prepared your questions, you must decide which are the three main types of answers which you are likely to get and categorise them into (1) Above average, (2) Standard, (3) Poor, so that you can mark 1, 2 or 3 on the sheet next to each question as the candidate answers.

Training

Perhaps one of the areas that sets aside a small catering operation from the larger, more sophisticated ones is the attitude adopted towards staff training. All too often we employ someone, give them a menu, tell them to wear black and white and call them a waiter or waitress and, when things go wrong, we get angry. It really isn't fair.

No matter what the size of the operation, you need to think carefully about the image you wish to project to the customer, and to do this satisfactorily, you need to define your customer service standards from the outset. This does not mean a universal acceptance of the 'have a nice day' syndrome, which sits uncomfortably in a British pub anyway. It means setting a standard for each particular operation and giving the staff sufficient training so that they feel comfortable and confident about their job.

Imagine that each customer has never been in the place before, they come in for a meal, maybe a little apprehensive and hungry. Those first impressions will set the tenor for the whole meal. The menu is completely new to them, so it may require a little explanation, they are not sure of the procedure for ordering food, so someone should be on hand to help them. The idea is to create as comfortable an atmosphere as possible and so deflate any possible problems from the outset.

It is up to you to decide how you want your staff to deal with customers and, in order to do this effectively, you need to formulate your service standards. Once again, you need a professional approach and the first step along the way is some form of consultation, with the staff, with the customers, with other people in the trade. One avenue worth looking at is the questionnaire asking customers to comment on the service, food, etc. You will get some silly answers but they are usually only a small percentage and a careful examination of the completed forms will show up any problem areas you may have.

Once the standards have been discussed and agreed, they then have to be put into practice. One of the ways is to write the various points down and either give each member of staff a copy at the outset of their employment or pin them on to the notice board. One way we have found most successful is to pick a different point each week, print it out and place the card or sheet in a prominent position. Below are some of the standards that may apply to front-of-house staff:

- ☐ Always greet the customer with a smile and direct eye-to-eye contact.
- ☐ If you are chatting or involved in something else, always stop what you are doing and go forward to meet them.
- ☐ If you cannot deal with a customer immediately, explain and get back to them as soon as possible.
- ☐ Get to know the menu and which dishes need accompaniments and what they are, e.g. tartare sauce with fish.
- ☐ At the start of each session, check the specials board (if there is one) and check the number of portions available so if you are likely to run out of anything you know before people order.
- ☐ Familiarise yourself with the sweets.

No doubt you can think of other service standards that may be more applicable to your own operation, but the main point is that you devise a formula as a start. Don't forget that standards are needed for the kitchen staff as well.

Perhaps the best way to communicate your service standards is at a staff meeting. Staff meetings are an essential part of staff management and training. They provide the opportunity for both staff and management to bounce ideas off each other. That way, you get to know each other's problems and perhaps more importantly each other's aims. Whereas you want to ensure that your customers' wishes are adhered to, the staff may be looking for ways of making their job a little easier; usually a compromise can be reached.

Some pubs actually pay their staff to come to staff meetings, but we usually provide food and drink and turn the meeting into a social get-together. The importance of the feedback we get from our staff cannot be overstated: often they are full of ideas and, quite honestly, can sometimes know more about particular aspects of the job than we do.

Perhaps one of the most important ways to apply your service standards is looking at the role you have as models. A 'do as I say, not as I do' mentality is totally destructive.

It is important not just to consider 'in-house' training. Today there are many courses available (although unfortunately not one on pub catering as such) to help a small catering operation. Catering colleges run full- and part-time courses in all aspects of the trade, not just cooking, and a full range of the courses is available either from the colleges themselves or from the City and Guilds of London Institute (see Useful addresses at the end of the chapter). The Institute also runs a specific skills scheme whereby students can gain a qualification by being assessed in a realistic work environment. These schemes are usually operated not by individuals but by a large organisation such as a brewery as part of their 'in-house' training.

So, once you have decided to employ someone, your first consideration should be to give them what is known as 'induction training'. Induction training has several main purposes, all of which are important:

- ☐ It welcomes new staff.
- ☐ It fulfils your responsibilities as an employer.
- ☐ It is the start of the team-building process.
- ☐ It helps to promote self-confidence which may be lacking initially.
- ☐ It makes the new employee aware of his or her responsibilities.
- ☐ It gives basic job knowledge.
- ☐ It clarifies basic points such as rate of pay, normal finishing time and so on.

Induction training should not be left to chance or just skimped through in a haphazard or half-hearted fashion. What is needed is a checklist for each new employee which, when completed, should be kept on file for future reference. It should look something like the one shown opposite.

After induction training, you will almost certainly find it necessary to instruct staff how to perform different tasks such as how to arrange a salad, how to change a till roll, how to lay a table properly and so on. Whatever the task, it is important that the training involved is carried out properly so that everyone – you, the trainee, other staff and the customer – are satisfied with the end result. Opposite is the way to go about it:

INDUCTION TRAINING CHECKLIST

Name:
Job title:
Date of commencement:
1. Meet other staff/instructor
2. Tour of pub
3. Place of work/main duties
4. Work rota/pay arrangements
5. Sick notification
6. Care of personal property such as uniform
7. Fire drill
8. Personal hygiene
9. Security
10. Hazards at work
11. House rules
12. Contract
EMPLOYEE'S SIGNATURE:
LICENSEE'S SIGNATURE:

- ☐ **Preparation** Make sure that you have everything you need before you start and that everything is in good working order.
- ☐ **Put the trainee at ease** Relax your trainee with a little chit chat before you get down to the actual training.
- ☐ **Check existing knowledge** The trainee may already know what you are about to teach.
- ☐ **Context** Explain what you are about to teach and how that particular task fits into the trainee's job as a whole.
- ☐ **Incentive** Encourage some enthusiasm by giving the trainee a good reason for learning what you are about to teach.
- ☐ **Explanation** Explain to the trainee that the session will fall into several stages and that he or she will be involved in each stage.
- ☐ **Stage-by-stage** Don't give it to the trainee all at once in a huge indigestible chunk. Break the task down into stages and let the trainee do it before moving on to the next stage. While training, ask as many open questions as you can to ensure that the trainee knows not only what to do but why.
- ☐ **Practice** Get the trainee to do the whole task unaided. Correct any mistakes in a manner which is encouraging.
- ☐ **Congratulate** When the trainee has mastered the task, make sure that he or she feels a sense of achievement.

- ☐ **Full circle** Refer back to the context and incentive and remind the trainee where this new task will fit into the job from now on.

Employment law

Employment law is complex and involved, requiring a book on its own, so we have tried to cover only the points which relate directly to a pub catering operation. The rule is, if you are in any doubt at all, contact your local Department of Employment or ACAS (which is an independent Government-funded body) office or, if you are a member of the National Licensed Victuallers' Association, their nearest office. The NLVA has experts in this field, and if you are a member, the advice is free.

One of the points to remember is that under employment law there are no such things as full-time or part-time employees. The main categories are:
- ☐ Persons employed for more than 16 hours per week.
- ☐ Persons employed for more than 8 hours per week for 5 years or more.

Contracts of employment

All employees have a contract of employment which forms the basis of the employment relationship. In simple terms, an employee agrees to work for an employer in return for wages. A contract is made, which is enforceable through the courts, when the offer of employment is accepted. Most employment contracts need not be in writing to be legally valid; a verbal agreement can be sufficient. However, employees who work more than 16 hours per week have, within 13 weeks of starting work, a statutory right to a written statement, as have employees who have worked more than 8 hours per week for over 5 years.

One of the anomalies of this legislation is that there is no one to enforce it, but industrial tribunals have the power to say what a written statement should contain. In the event of a dispute, failure to provide such a statement would not be viewed favourably.

Writing down the contract can minimise later disagreements. The details of the contract should include the following:
- ☐ The employer's name.
- ☐ The employee's name.
- ☐ The date the employment began (see section on continuous employment, page 144).
- ☐ Job title and duties.
- ☐ Hours of work and other related conditions.
- ☐ Holidays and holiday pay if applicable.
- ☐ Incapacity for work: terms and conditions relating to sickness and sickness pay. If none, say so.
- ☐ Pensions and pension schemes: if none, say so.
- ☐ Amount of notice of termination to be given.
  (a) by employer (insert period),
  (b) by employee (insert period).
  Fixed-term contracts should state date of expiry instead.
- ☐ Person(s) employee should contact if he or she has any grievance.
- ☐ The disciplinary rules which apply to the employment: state them or where they can be found (they must be easily accessible).
- ☐ Whether a contracting-out certificate under the Social Security Pensions Act 1975 is/is not in force for the employment in respect of which this written statement is being issued.

Although you are not obliged to provide a written contract of employment for all the staff you employ, it is worth while considering providing one, so that both parties are aware of what is expected of them. It can be in the form of individual drawn-up contracts or just one pro-forma, individually addressed and signed. As stated previously, verbal agreements are just as binding, so a staff meeting at which all staff are informed of the code of practice will suffice for employees outside the scope of the above legislation. All staff should be aware of disciplinary procedures.

If your pub has a mainly seasonal trade, you may have thought about a fixed-term contract, which is when a person is employed for a set period of, say, 6 or 12 months. What a lot of people do not realise, however, is that if you provide an employee with a fixed-term contract it obliges the employer to pay the person for the *complete period specified*. This can be unfortunate, to say the least, if you find that you no longer need them half-way through! Fixed-term contracts need a lot of thought before being offered because they guarantee employment and pay and, in addition, if the contract is continually renewed, the employee can accumulate rights under existing law. ACAS are the people to advise on this point.

Disciplinary procedures or house rules

There are two main areas of disciplinary concerns: the first and really the most important is to ensure that the highest standards of service are adhered to. The second relates to circumstances which may lead to the dismissal of a member of staff.

Most areas that need to be covered by house rules are common sense: we do not want employees to turn up late continually, waste time, neglect their duties or offer poor customer service, by just hanging about and chatting or appearing for work looking like something the cat dragged in. These can be considered to be minor misconducts.

A little more serious are not turning up for work without an explanation, offensive language or unsatisfactory behaviour towards customers, colleagues or people left in charge. Also discrepancies in cash or stock attributable to the employees' area of duty, behaviour which can affect the reputation of the business, smoking in non-smoking areas, and non-compliance with public health regulations, not washing hands, etc.

Gross misconduct includes theft, knowingly undercharging or overcharging customers, wilful damage, any act or threat of physical violence, deliberately serving under-age drinkers, etc.

A disciplinary procedure will normally operate as follows:

1. **A formal verbal warning** – in the case of a minor offence.
2. **A written warning** – for subsequent minor offences or a more serious offence.
3. **A final written warning** – for further misconduct. The warning should make it clear that dismissal may follow failure to improve.
4. **Dismissal** – may be carried out without the previous steps in the case of serious misconduct.

It is important to keep a record of *all* warnings. Persons dismissed will be eligible for pay as set out in their contract of employment.

Dismissal procedures The law does provide for an employer to dismiss an employee provided that there is sufficient reason for the dismissal and that the employer has acted reasonably in doing so. Among the commonest reasons for dismissal are misconduct, inability to do the job, ill-health and redundancy. The employee has the right to receive the reason for the dismissal in writing if he or she requests it. The request itself need not be in writing.

Staff who have worked for an employer for 16 hours per week for more than 2 years or who have worked for 8 hours per week for more than 5 years have the right to make a complaint to an industrial tribunal if they feel that they have been unfairly dismissed.

I wanted to get rid of him, but he threatened to come back – as a customer!

Continuous employment

When a business or undertaking is transferred, the contracts of employment of the staff employed at the time of the transfer are transferred with the business to the new owner. It is as if their contracts of employment had originally been with the new owner and if they are subsequently made redundant, they are eligible for redundancy pay covering *all* their employment period.

It must be stressed that the legislation relates only to businesses or undertakings not bricks and mortar. What is becoming more and more common these days is if a business has several long-term staff and is subsequently sold, the liability to be assumed by the new employers is subject to the negotiations of the purchase price, so if any redundancies have to be made, the cost has already been allowed for.

This area of law is very complex and subject to change in interpretation. You should therefore seek advice as soon as you believe that you may become involved in a business transfer.

Employees over retirement age are not entitled to redundancy pay.

Wages – rates of pay

The *minimum* rates of pay for all persons *over the age of 21* employed in the licensed trade (hotel, restaurant or pub) are fixed by the Wages Council. This is a body of representatives of employers' and employees' associations which meets on a regular basis to fix a basic rate of pay.

Once the rate has been decided, the information is passed to the Wages Inspectorate, a branch of the Department of Employment, to enforce. Most pubs will be covered by the rate set for the Licensed Non-residential Establishment but if most of their trade is on the food side, they should adhere to the rates set out for Licensed Residential Establishments and Licensed Restaurants. The Wages Inspectorate has the right to determine which section a particular establishment comes under, based on the type of trade not the name.

Under the 1986 Wages Act, a minimum basic rate per hour is fixed up to a maximum of 39 hours in any week and an overtime rate for all time worked in excess of 39 hours in any week. Workers must be paid at least these basic rates for all time during which they are required to be, and are, available for work at their place of work. So, if an employee turns up for work at an agreed time and there is no one in the place, they must be paid. You cannot say that an employee must turn up for work at 10 a.m. but that his or her pay will only start when the first customer arrives.

Also fixed under the schedule is the limit for deductions (or payments made by a worker) for living accommodation, if an employee lives in. But this is something of an anomaly because a higher amount for living accommodation may be agreed provided that it does not result in the employee being paid less than the minimum due under the Wages Order. The effect of this requirement is that a worker's gross pay must be at least the *total* of (a) the minimum due at the hourly rates stated above *and* (b) the *extra* amount agreed for accommodation.

Confused? If you are, it is hardly surprising, but basically what it means is that, if more is charged for accommodation, then the hourly rate must be increased accordingly to compensate for the deficiency so that the totals remain the same as if the accommodation charge had not been increased.

If staff are charged for food and drink they must not be charged more than the cost to the employer. For more on this subject, see the section on VAT in Chapter 12.

Areas such as holiday pay, sickness pay, pensions and extra payments for days such as bank holidays and the like are the subject of individual negotiations between each employer and employee.

Failure to pay the minimum rate can result in a hefty fine, so it is important to ensure that you are aware of the rates. It is no excuse to say that you have negotiated a lower rate with an employee and they are happy with it. The first step is to 'register' with the Wages Inspectorate. If you live in a large city, you will find them in the telephone directory; if not, the local Jobcentre or the brewery will be able to provide their address. Once you are on their 'mailing list', the Wages Inspectorate will notify you automatically of any changes in the minimum rates. The notice setting out the minimum rates must be displayed where staff can easily read it.

Records to show whether or not employees have been paid at least the statutory minimum for each week must be kept and be available for inspection by the Wages Inspectorate if required, and all records must be kept for a minimum of three years. The simplest way is to incorporate the information in the wages book which we will look at later in the chapter in the sections on tax and National Insurance. The information the Wages Inspectorate needs is as follows:

- ☐ The number of hours worked – including overtime.
- ☐ The rate of pay.
- ☐ Details of all deductions (as detailed above) including charges for accommodation.
- ☐ The net amount paid for the time worked.

The Wages Inspectorate has the authority to visit premises to inspect the records and talk to the employees. Usually, a visit takes place after a complaint has been made by an employee, but this is not always the case. They may just call in or they may telephone beforehand to arrange an appointment, but Inspectors do have a statutory right to examine your records.

One minor point to watch out for is that many employers and employees like to keep below the National Insurance and tax thresholds. This is fine provided that it is the number of hours worked that is reduced not the rate of pay.

Having due regard to all that has been said so far about wages, it is as well to remember that the statutory minimum wage is no more than rock bottom. If you expect your staff to generate more trade by being enthusiastic, efficient and cheerful, they are hardly likely to come up with the goods if they know that you are paying them the absolute minimum rate for the job. Perhaps a good idea is to start them off on the minimum rate – but preferably a little more – and increase the rate after 1 year of service and again after 2 years of service. This will provide an incentive for staff to stay with you. A high turnover of staff, after all, is the last thing you want.

Age restrictions on employees

Children over the age of 13 years but under 16 years may be employed in a limited way. As the restrictions apply even if the work is carried out without pay or if the child or young person is the son or daughter of the proprietor, it would be prudent to check with the local Education Authority just what restrictions apply. In addition to the main Act, most areas have by-laws which govern the employment of very young people. For instance, they may not be allowed to work in a kitchen or on a Sunday, or the Authority may insist on a medical examination or written permission from the parents which must go through them. So do check first. If you are not sure if a person is over the age of 16, ask to see their National Insurance card.

The employment of young people between the ages of 16 and 18 years is subject to either the Shops Act 1950 or the Young Persons (Employment) Act 1938. As it is the nature of the job that defines which Act applies, one establishment may be subject to them both depending on job definition. Both are extremely complicated Acts covering Sunday work, the permitted number of hours to be worked, time off, rest periods, etc. This legislation comes under the jurisdiction of the local Environment Health Office, so check with them as to the current position, as at the time of writing amendments to the Acts are proposed.

Statutory rights

Over the years, employees have become entitled to a wide range of statutory rights, derived from parliamentary acts or regulations which affect the employment relationship. In general, despite any express term to the contrary, they cannot be waived. They include the following rights:

- ☐ **not to be discriminated against** – on grounds of race (if a work-force is predominantly black or white and the labour market is multi-racial, word-of-mouth recruitment may be considered discriminatory if it reduces the opportunity for all races and both sexes to apply.)
- ☐ **not to be discriminated against** – on grounds of sex or marital status.
- ☐ **to equal pay** – with members of the opposite sex if it can be shown that they are doing equal work or work of equal value.
- ☐ **to an itemised pay statement** – which should show hours worked/rate/overtime and all deductions.
- ☐ **to maternity benefit**s – all pregnant women have the right to paid time off for antenatal care. Most pregnant women with 2 years' or more service or who have worked for more than 8 hours for 5 years or more are entitled to return to work after giving birth. But if the firm employs five or less and it is not practical to take her back, any application made in respect of unfair dismissal may not succeed.
- ☐ **to minimum pay and employment conditions** – see section on wages.
- ☐ **to notice of termination of employment** – most staff are entitled to receive at least 1 week's notice after one month's service, 2 weeks after two years' and so on up to 12 weeks for 12 years.

- ☐ **to payment in cash** – some workers are entitled to receive their wages in cash, so to change to a banking system without their approval could be breach of contract.
- ☐ **deductions from pay** – unless they are PAYE or NI, deductions should not be made without the knowledge and written consent of the employee.
- ☐ **to pay when laid off** – if this is likely to apply, provision should be made in the contract of employment. Even so, statutory guarantee payments may well apply even if the contract does not provide for them.
- ☐ **to redundancy pay** – if applicable.
- ☐ **to a safe system of work** – see the section on health and safety at work in Chapter 11.
- ☐ **to statutory sick pay** – paid by the employer but reimbursed (see section on National Insurance).
- ☐ **to time off** – (a) for public duties (civic, magistrate, jury service, etc.), (b) to look for work if made redundant with at least 2 years' service, and (c) for trade union activities.
- ☐ **to belong or not to belong to a trade union.**
- ☐ **to be transferred automatically if the business changes hands** – see section on continuous employment.
- ☐ **not to be unfairly dismissed** – see above.
- ☐ **to written reasons for dismissal** – see above.
- ☐ **to a written statement** – see section on contracts of employment.
- ☐ **to the rights under the Rehabilitation of Offenders Act** which gives certain convicted persons the rights: (a) to answer 'no' to the question 'have you ever been convicted of a criminal act?', (b) not to be refused employment because of a 'spent' conviction, and (c) references must not mention any 'spent' conviction.

Most of the above points relating to statutory rights and contracts of employment have been taken from an excellent handbook published by ACAS called *Employing People*. We have been able to cover only a very small part of the employment laws. For any additional information, please contact the Department of Employment, ACAS or the Wages Inspectorate: not only do they have a wide range of leaflets – far too many to list here – but they can answer any questions relating to specific points.

Income tax – PAYE

To use a literary analogy, if VAT can be compared to Dickens's Circumlocution Office, then the Inland Revenue is positively Kafkaesque – a large and unwieldy bureaucracy established to collect income tax through a series of confusing and constantly changing legislation. No wonder some people find it menacing.

The Inland Revenue is split into two main sections:
- ☐ Inspector of Taxes, who deals with the assessment of personal and company taxation, Pay As You Earn, etc. These are the local offices to contact for any help or information.
- ☐ Collector of Taxes, to whom all the money is sent. Although the main Accounts Office is at Cumbernauld in Scotland, most local offices have a small section who can deal with queries.

It is to the latter that an employer pays the PAYE and National Insurance deducted from employees' pay. Payment is made each month from the paying-in book provided.

Unfortunately, the service and help that you are able to get from the Inland Revenue varies considerably throughout the country. If you are fortunate, as we are, to have a local tax office that incorporates an Enquiry Section, your entry into and dealings with the Revenue are comparatively smooth.

As soon as you start employing someone, even if it is only for a few hours per week and they are below the tax threshold, you should notify the Inland Revenue. Why? Because when you submit the accounts at the end of the year and include an amount for wages, it may be assumed that it is some sort of fiddle if the Inland Revenue has no record of you as an employer. After registration, you will receive a 'starter pack' which contains all the relevant guides, tax tables and forms you are likely to need. Included in the pack are details of National Insurance requirements.

Although the literature produced by the Inland Revenue and Department of Social Security contains detailed and straightforward information on how to operate PAYE, your PAYE tax office will be pleased to help in case of difficulty. You can telephone, write, or call in at your tax office for free advice. If it is not nearby, there are PAYE Enquiry Offices throughout the UK, who will be able to give you general advice. All PAYE tax offices are listed in the telephone directory under 'Inland Revenue'.

Some people get themselves into an awful muddle about their responsibilities concerning PAYE and NI and there is really no need. You purchase staff's services and process their wages through your wages book, deducting tax and National Insurance in the same way as VAT but following a different set of guidelines.

The legal obligations of an employer are set out in the Income Tax (Employments) Regulations, 1973, Statutory Instrument No. 334, which can be obtained from HMSO (see Useful addresses at the end of the chapter). All employees come under the auspices of PAYE, regardless of how much they earn. The procedure to adopt at the start of employment is contained in P7, which is a booklet entitled *Employers' Guide to Pay As You Earn*, and on P8, which is roughly the same information in sheet form. You use whichever you feel most comfortable with.

A new employee will fall roughly into one of three categories:

1. An employee who has been working for another employer within the *same* tax year in which he/she starts working with you, (tax year is 6 April until following 5 April) and who has an up-to-date P45 from the previous employer or the Unemployment Benefits Office. Continue their PAYE deductions.
2. (a) An employee without a P45 who signs certificate A of the P46 form – a school-leaver. Operate emergency cumulative code.
   (b) An employee without a P45 who signs certificate B of the P46 – only or main employment. Operate emergency code.
   (c) An employee without a P45 who does not sign either A or B of P46. Deduct tax at basic rate.
3. Existing employee previously paid below the tax threshold and now paid above it.

If a category 1 employee has a P45, start deducting tax in accordance with the tax tables; if not, follow the procedures set out in the P7 guide.

Employees under categories 2 and 3 should be asked to complete form P46. The action you then have to take is governed by the information they provide and the amount of wages they receive.

In Table A from the PAYE booklet you will see the procedure for dealing with an employee who is going to work for you for more than 1 week and who is not in receipt of a P45. For those of you who are not familiar with tax instructions, it will give you some indication of what they look like. Basically, in understanding all tax and National Insurance requirements, you have to view it a step at a time. The answer to the first question will lead on to the next and so forth.

Unfortunately, many of us in the catering trade employ people who do not easily fall within the standard categories and this is the area which creates the most problems.

- ☐ Employees who have a main job and work for you for only a couple of hours per week. These are the ones who do not sign either certificate A or B on the P46 and pay tax at basic rate. See table A on page 148.
- ☐ Employees whose main job is part of the Youth Training Scheme. Get them to complete form P46, then submit it to the tax office with a note giving details of their YTS employment. Under the YTS scheme, young people can be taken on as either 'trainees' or 'employees' and their status can be changed at any time. Do check with your local tax office as to the status of any such employee. With 'trainee' status, they are usually treated as though their 'part-time' job is their main one.
- ☐ If a young person is taken on with a YTS with you, the same conditions apply.
- ☐ Students employed during the vacations and earning below the tax threshold for the year may

You haven't met our new Tax Inspector, have you?

Table A

For an employee who is going to work for you for more than one week

➤ prepare form P46

➤ find out the employee's NI number – leaflet NP15 tells you how to do this

➤ ask the employee to consider either Certificate A or B on the front of form P46 and sign one of the certificates if appropriate

➤ issue coding claim form P15 (where the chart below tells you to) and a reply envelope. Fill in the employee's NI number in the box provided in Section A of the form and also complete the tax reference box. Employers dealt with at Centre 1 can ignore the tax reference box.

➤ follow the chart below

QUESTION

Has the employee signed either Certificate A or B on the front of form P46?

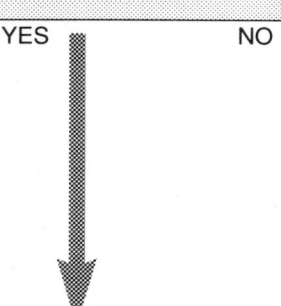

YES ↓   NO →

ACTION NEEDED

If the pay is over £1 a week (£4 a month)
- send form P46 to the Tax Office straight away
- issue P15
- prepare a deductions working sheet
- deduct tax using code BR

QUESTION

Is the total pay in the week more than the PAYE threshold?

YES ↓   NO →

ACTION NEEDED

Certificate A signed	**Certificate B signed**
• send form P46 to the Tax Office straight away	• send form P46 to the Tax Office straight away
• issue P15	• issue P15
• prepare a deductions working sheet	• prepare a deductions working sheet
• deduct tax on a normal basis using the present emergency code. This is shown in the introduction to the Guide and described in paragraph B15. Treat previous pay and tax as NIL	• deduct tax on week 1/ Month 1 basis using the present Emergency code. This is shown in the introduction to the Guide and described in paragraph B15

QUESTION

Is the total pay in the week equal to or more than the NIC lower earnings limit?

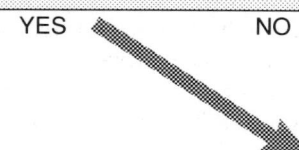

YES ↓   NO ↘

ACTION NEEDED

- keep the form P46
- prepare a deductions working sheet
- enter 'NI' in the code space and the record NIC
- record the employee's name, address and the amount of pay

ACTION NEEDED

- keep the form P46
- do not prepare a deductions working sheet
- record the employee's name, address and the amount of pay

fill in form P38(S). However, you must discuss the matter with the tax office before you accept such a form from a student. Students employed throughout the year or during term-time only complete form P46. There is more information about students in paragraph E50 of the booklet P7, *Employers' Guide to PAYE*.

The onus is on employers to ensure that the tax requirements relating to *their* business are adhered to, so once an employee has provided a P45 or completed a P46 or P38(S) and you have followed the instructions given by the Inland Revenue, your obligation ends. It is up to the employee to notify the tax office of any additional income for such as pensions or extra jobs. In fact, tax codes are used so that the employer does not know the personal details of his/her employee.

Income tax is based on the gross pay and this includes basic wages, overtime, holiday pay, sick pay, payments from a service charge, payments for travelling to work and payments for travelling time – in fact, all the monies given by you the employer. It does not include rent-free accommodation in which an employee is obliged to reside by nature of his/her duties, or free board and lodgings given by the employer or tips received by the employees directly from customers.

'Benefits in kind', i.e. items provided by an employer in other than money such as company car, telephone, goods or services, etc, may result in an additional tax liability for the employee. However, these would not usually apply to a small catering operation which has no directors or 'higher paid' employees, but a manager or chef could easily come within the thresholds. Ask the tax office for a leaflet.

If you operate a private pension scheme that has been accepted by the DHSS as a 'contracted-out' scheme, the amount payable by the employee can be deducted from the gross pay before tax.

National Insurance

There is no need to register as an employer for National Insurance. This is done automatically when you register with the Inland Revenue and you get your starter pack which includes information on National Insurance.

The NI contributions which you pay for an employee are called Class 1 contributions. They are worked out as a percentage of the employee's earnings and are paid to the Collector of Taxes (Accounts Office) each month along with PAYE tax. They comprise two parts, the employee's share and the employer's share. As an employer, you have to pay both of these deductions but you deduct the employee's share from their pay.

Class 1 contributions are payable as follows:
- By employees who are between 16 years and retirement age (normal retirement age is 65 for men, 60 for women). Those over retirement age must present a certificate of age exemption (form CF384) or a certificate of earner's non-liability (form CF381) as proof. You can accept other proof of age such as a birth certificate.
- By those whose weekly earnings are above the lower earnings limit. The limit is usually revised each year.
- Some married women and widows have the right to pay NI contributions at a reduced rate, but they must give a valid certificate. There are several forms of certificate which are acceptable, so if in doubt clear it with your local DHSS office. If a married woman or widow has not worked for 2 years, the certificate lapses automatically.

In all the above exemptions, the employer continues to pay his share of the contributions at standard rate. The onus is on the employee to provide proof of exemption. If you are in any doubt whatsoever, deduct contributions at standard rate until you have clearance from DHSS. If you do not, you may have to pay any discrepancies yourself.

If an employer sets up an occupational pension scheme, then both employer and employee will pay contributions at a lower rate on part of their pay. This is called 'contracting-out'. Any scheme must satisfy the conditions set by the Occupational Pensions Board who will then issue a certificate, giving an employer the right to pay and deduct contracted-out contributions from those employees covered by the scheme. Although the employee is entitled to tax relief on these schemes (that is, gross pay minus the pension contributions), NI contributions are worked out on the gross pay. A private pension scheme is an added incentive for staff to stay with you and has benefits for you both.

Employees' National Insurance numbers are the basic reference for both the Inland Revenue and the DHSS. Today, persons reaching their sixteenth birthday are automatically issued with their National Insurance number in readiness for when they start to pay contributions. However, some older employees may not know theirs. Instructions on how to obtain a National Insurance number are contained in both tax and NI brochures.

Employers are responsible for paying Statutory Sick Pay (SSP) and Statutory Maternity Pay (SMP) to their employees who are eligible. DHSS has comprehensive documents setting out the methods and rates of payment and these are available from local offices. SSP and SMP are treated as gross earnings and should be included in gross pay when working out PAYE and NI. Any SSP/SMP paid can be recovered by deducting it from the payments of NI contributions made to the Collector of Taxes.

Employers have a statutory obligation not only to deduct PAYE and NI but also to keep records which show details of such payments and any monies earned. For certain employees, a deductions working sheet (P11) is used to record all pay. In the starter pack is a form on which details of other employees' earnings may be entered. However, we suggest that you keep a 'proper' wages book. Then not only will you be able to keep the records required by the Inland Revenue and DHSS but you can incorporate the information needed by the Wages Inspectorate on the same sheet. Before you purchase such a book, check that it can record all the information all departments require.

It may seem like a lot of unnecessary paperwork but it does not take up too much time per week and will ensure that, if there are any queries the answers are readily at hand. It will also help to keep an easy check on the true amount of money you are paying out in wages. In weekly accounts, it is only the net amount of pay that is recorded and it is all too easy to lose sight of the hidden expenditure of PAYE and NI that has to be paid out.

If you have employees who pay PAYE and NI, at the end of the fiscal (financial) year you will have to complete an end-of-year return. It looks daunting at first sight, but if you have kept your wages book up to date it is only a matter of adding up and hoping (fingers crossed) that the whole thing balances.

There are software packages to fit most personal computers for employees' wage records, which work out the tax and insurance due, and these take all the sweat out of having to work the figures out by hand. But if you intend to send in end-of-year information on magnetic tape or floppy disc, you must have the permission of both the DHSS and Inland Revenue. Your local computer shop will be able to advise you on the packages that have been approved.

Officers of the Inland Revenue and DHSS have the legal right to inspect records to make sure that the correct amounts of tax and National Insurance contributions have been deducted and paid over to the Inland Revenue. These are quite painless and are aimed at trying to ensure that you know the system rather than trying to catch you out, provided that you keep adequate records, of course, and are not operating any fiddles.

If you are in any doubt about any of the procedures relating to tax, National Insurance or employment law and wages legislation, do contact your local department; they will help. All produce numerous leaflets explaining all the legislation and they are getting increasingly easy to read. Most queries, however, can be answered on the telephone. The main point to remember is to try and get it right from the outset and then any problems you have will only be minor ones.

Useful addresses

Department of Employment, ACAS, Wages Inspectorate – see local telephone directory.

Inspector of Taxes – see local telephone directory.

Department of Health and Social Security – see local telephone book.

City and Guilds of London Institute, 76 Portland Place, London W1N 4AA.

The National Licensed Victuallers' Association, Boardman House, 2 Downing Street, Farnham, Surrey GU9 7NX.

Elizabeth Johnson BA (Hons), Training Consultant, 4 Colders Green, Meltham, Huddersfield HD7 3JH. Tel: Huddersfield (0484) 851336.

Her Majesty's Stationery Office Publications Centre, PO Box 276, London SW8 5DT.

The extracts from ACAS – *Employing People* was reproduced with the permission of the Controller of Her Majesty's Stationery Office.

15 Licensing law

Make no mistake about it, the law as it relates to licensing in the United Kingdom is extremely complex. Couple that with the fact that the law in Scotland and Northern Ireland, although amounting to much the same thing, is different to the law which applies in England and the result is a bewildering mass of legislation.

It would be a Herculean task to memorise all of it, so the best way to tackle the subject is to go for key areas and break them down so that they become less like gobbledegook and more like a set of rules which have a certain order to them. A sort of 'divide and conquer' technique.

The main areas, then, are as follows:
- ☐ The different types of licences which are available.
- ☐ Extensions to those licences.
- ☐ Permitted hours.
- ☐ Children.
- ☐ Drunkenness.
- ☐ The conduct of licensed premises.
- ☐ Entertainment.
- ☐ Weights and measures.
- ☐ Gaming.
- ☐ The police.

First, we will deal with those areas as they apply in England, after which we will point out any differences which are peculiar to Scotland and Northern Ireland.

In England, many Acts of Parliament touch upon the sale and consumption of intoxicating liquor, but the main and most important one for our purposes is The Licensing Act 1964 which regulates the sale of alcoholic beverages in licensed premises. In other words, premises must be licensed before they may sell alcohol. In England, all such licences are granted by the local Magistrates and are known as 'Justices' Licences'.

Licences – different types

In respect of any of the licences listed below, it is a legal requirement for a notice giving the name of the licensee and the nature of the licence to be affixed to the premises. Failure to do so is an offence.

Full Justices On and Off Licence

Most public houses have this sort of licence which permits the sale and consumption of intoxicating liquors of all descriptions both on and off the premises.

Full Justices On Licence

This is exactly the same except that off sales are not allowed. This type of licence is usually granted to snooker clubs, dancing clubs, sports centres and the like but with various 'conditions' which are attached by the Magistrates. A 'club' which is licensed in this way, then, has a Full Justices On Licence with Club Conditions and should not be confused with a Registered – i.e. Members – Club.

Wine and Beer Licence

These are rare now but those which still remain are usually pubs. They are Full Justices On and Off Licences but permit the sale and consumption, on and off the premises, of beer and wine only. The sale of fortified wines such as sherry and port is permitted but the sale of spirits is not. In the West Country, such licences also permit the sale of cider. In theory, a Wine Bar could be licensed in this way, but in practice, a Full Justices On and Off Licence would be much more likely.

Restaurant Licence

Permits the sale of all types of alcohol but only to diners. Off sales are not usually permitted and persons who are not dining may not purchase alcohol. Diners who are under 18 years but over 16 years may consume but not purchase beer, porter, cider or perry and only in that part of the premises which is set aside for meals.

Residential Licence

This authorises sales of intoxicants to residents and their guests only. Private hotels usually have this sort of licence which may be combined with a Restaurant Licence as well. A 'dry lounge' must also be available for use by the residents and the provision of a 'main meal' is also a prerequisite. Such a licence would not be granted to an establishment which provided bed and breakfast only.

Licensing law

The licences detailed above provide a basic framework, so to speak, for various extensions which may be granted at the discretion of the Licensing Justices. All applications for extensions are scrutinised very carefully and it is by no means a forgone conclusion that an extension will be granted simply because it has been applied for.

Extensions

Extensions to Justices' Licences can be divided into two categories – those which are temporary and those which are of a more permanent nature.

Temporary extensions

There are two kinds of temporary extensions.

Special Order of Exemption This is an extension to normal 'permitted hours' and is sought by licensees for special occasions such as twenty-first birthday parties, weddings, anniversaries, charity nights and so on. Applications for Special Orders of Exemption should be made in duplicate – one copy for the Clerk to the Justices and the other for the local police office.

Applicants will be required to show that the event for which the extension is sought is a genuine special occasion, that is to say, a 'one off' and not simply an excuse for yet another late-night booze up.

Before such an application is heard in court, the police make enquiries and report to the magistrates who, if they think it necessary, will require the applicant to appear before them. If the application is allowed, a fee is charged and the order issued. The written order will specify the hours of the extension and, when in use, must be made available for inspection by any authorised person.

Occasional Licence This is the licence which is needed if a licensee wishes to set up a bar somewhere other than on his normal licensed premises. Wedding parties on non-licensed premises, agricultural shows and the like, are typical occasions when such a licence would be required.

The procedure when making an application is precisely the same as for a Special Order of Exemption.

If an Occasional Licence is granted, the licensee has an added responsibility in that he is required to ensure the smooth running not only of his normal licensed

Honest – when the extension began, he was twenty-one!

Licensing law

premises but also of the premises to which the Occasional Licence applies.

More permanent extensions

There are three kinds of extensions which are of a more permanent nature.

Supper Hour Certificate This operates for 1 hour after the end of normal 'permitted hours'. It applies only to those customers who have had a table meal in a part of the licensed premises which is set aside exclusively for dining. In other words, customers who wish to take advantage of a Supper Hour Certificate must have had a meal and must remain in the dining room area.

That same dining room, having been legally 'set aside' for dining, may not be used for any other purpose. In practice, this means that if the bar is busy but the dining area is not, the dining area may not be used as an overflow area for customers from the bar who are not having a meal.

What, then, is a meal? The rule is that the food must be prepared on the premises in some way and not merely sold as supplied, like a packet of crisps or nuts. A sandwich has been held to be substantial enough to be a meal when served at a table, on a plate, accompanied by garnish, cutlery and a napkin.

Drinking-up time in respect of a Supper Hour Certificate is half an hour, but only in the designated dining area. Normal permitted hours apply in the rest of the premises.

As with a Restaurant Licence, persons who are under 18 years but over 16 years may consume but not purchase what are termed 'long drinks', i.e. beer, porter, cider or perry, as an accompaniment to their meal but only in that part of the premises which is set apart for meals. The term 'long drinks' does not include a slug of whisky topped up with water or lemonade or indeed spirits of any sort.

A Supper Hour Certificate may also be added to a Restaurant Licence.

Extended Hours Order These are something of a rarity nowadays but where they do exist, they are added to a Supper Hour Certificate which must have previously been granted.

An Extended Hours Order permits the sale of intoxicating liquor until 1 a.m. but the holder of such an order is required to 'habitually provide musical and/or other entertainment as well as "substantial" refreshment'.

In plain language, an Extended Hours Order applies to restaurants which provide entertainment in addition to meals. The entertainment has to be live entertainment where the performers are actually there on the premises. Television, piped background music or a juke box would not be considered to be entertainment for the purposes of this order.

An Extended Hours Order, when granted, is generally accompanied by certain conditions. It may be seasonal, it may be restricted to certain days of the week or both. Once granted, it must be used but never on Sundays.

Special Hours Certificate This is the one which covers 'night clubs' and is usually added to a Full Justices On and Off Licence (a pub licence). Much less frequently it is added to a Restaurant Licence. The following conditions and prerequisites apply:

- Maximum to 2 a.m. (3 a.m. in London). Minimum 12 midnight.
- May be restricted to particular days of the week.
- May be seasonal.
- May be both.
- Once granted, must be used – 90 per cent use minimum as a rough guide.
- May be revoked if not 'habitually' used – unlike Supper Hour Certificate which may be used or not, at will.
- Music, dancing and/or other entertainment, food (substantial refreshment prepared on the premises) and drink must be provided at all times. If one of these facilities finishes, all must finish.
- If added to a Restaurant Licence, all persons must have a meal and the sale of intoxicants is 'ancillary' to the other facilities.
- A Music and Dancing Licence is a prerequisite, to ensure among other things that the required safety standards are achieved and maintained. This involves a very thorough annual inspection.

It can be seen, then, that a 'night club' is simply a pub with music, singing, dancing and food.

Permitted hours

The Licensing Act 1988, as most licensees will no doubt be aware, made certain radical changes. Undoubtedly, the largest and most significant change was the modification of permitted hours.

Permitted hours in all licensed premises are from 11 a.m. to 11 p.m., Monday to Saturday inclusive. On Sundays, Christmas Day and Good Friday, permitted hours are from 12 noon to 3 p.m. and from 7 p.m. to

10.30 p.m. but premises which have a Supper Hour Certificate may serve intoxicants with meals between the hours of 3 p.m. and 7 p.m. but only in the designated area set aside exclusively for diners.

Drinking-up time, the time allowed for customers to finish the drinks which they have purchased up to the end of permitted hours, is 20 minutes. In premises which have any sort of late licence, drinking-up time is 30 minutes, but in the case of a Supper Hour Certificate, only in that area which is set aside exclusively for diners.

Obviously, those who do not adhere to permitted hours run the risk of prosecution. The licensee would be prosecuted for selling or supplying intoxicants outside permitted hours and the customer would be prosecuted for drinking outside permitted hours. Where an extension is in force, it is an offence to fail to display the notice.

Children

One day, while we were serving lunches, a middle aged chap came in, walked up to the bar and after a quick, furtive look round, said in a conspiratorial way, 'Do you allow children in?' The answer was, 'Yes, if you are having lunch, just go straight through into the dining room.' Out he went to the car park and came back in holding the hand of a young lady who must have been at least 17 years old.

In the licensed trade, there is almost universal confusion regarding children and young persons. Are they allowed in? What can they drink and where are they allowed to sit? There is so much confusion that it makes Fred Carno's Circus look well ordered and disciplined.

The key ages to remember are 5 years, 7 years, 14 years and 18 years.

The first one is plain and simple: it is an offence to give alcohol to a child under 5 years of age.

Moving on to the next category: it is an offence to be drunk in charge of a child apparently under the age of 7 years in a highway or other public place. This would obviously include a family room or a beer garden.

Children under 14 years of age are not allowed in the bar of licensed premises during permitted hours. The only exceptions to this are children who are resident or who are passing through, say, to the dining room. A 'bar' is defined as that part of the premises which is used solely or mainly for the sale and consumption of intoxicants. A dining room or a family room which does not have a bar and is completely separate, obviously falls outside this definition of a bar, as, indeed, does a beer garden. A beer garden, in fact, being outside, is not even part of the licensed premises.

What about young people who are over 14 but under 18? Well, to start with, they are allowed to be in a bar during permitted hours and may purchase non-alcoholic drinks and make use of whatever facilities are available. They may not purchase or consume alcohol in a bar. In this respect, offences can be committed by all concerned: the licensee for selling, the person who made the purchase for buying and the person who is under age for consuming.

Many licensees feel that allowing persons who are under 18 but over 14 to frequent their premises carries with it too much of a risk unless they are accompanied by a parent or other responsible adult, and they could well be right. Section 16 of the Licensing Act 1988 deleted the word 'knowingly' from the offence of selling alcohol to persons under 18 choosing instead to provide a defence of 'exercising all due diligence to avoid the commission of such an offence'.

Finally, persons who are under 18 are not permitted to be employed in the bar of licensed premises.

Drunkenness

There can surely be nothing more damaging to the licensed trade than drunkenness. It is by no means a new problem, but in recent years, the media have homed in on alcohol abuse in all its nasty and antisocial forms to such an extent that it is now well and truly under the spotlight.

Quite apart from all that, though, it is illegal. Probably most people know that it is an offence to be drunk and disorderly or drunk and incapable in a public place, but for our purposes, the law does not stop there. Right at the outset, the licensee has a responsibility and can be prosecuted for selling alcohol to a person who has already had more than enough to drink. People who aid a drunken person to obtain alcohol or who actually procure alcohol for a drunken person also commit offences.

A drunken person who refuses to quit (leave) licensed premises when requested to do so also commits an offence and a licensee has a right to ask the police to assist him to eject such a person.

Obviously, for the caterer, drunkenness or any other

Licensing law

sort of excessive behaviour is bad news and can do untold damage to trade, so quite apart from the legal responsibility, it is in your own interest to see that such behaviour is not permitted.

Conduct of licensed premises

Of course, we have already dealt with drunkenness as a separate issue, but to be more specific, the Licensing Act 1964 clearly states that a licensee commits an offence if he allows 'violent, quarrelsome, drunken or disorderly' conduct on his premises. If a licensee were convicted of permitting such conduct on his premises, the fine of up to £100 would be the least of his worries as the Licensing Justices could well consider that he was unfit to run licensed premises and revoke his licence.

It is also highly illegal to run a brothel on licensed premises no matter how profitable it may be.

It is illegal to sell alcohol on credit, customers are not allowed to run up a 'slate'. Obviously, the use of credit cards or payment by cheque is permitted, but in view of the increase in frauds in this area, it is wise for licensees to be vigilant.

Entertainment

The Local Authority is responsible for the issuing of Public Entertainment Licences which permit Music and Dancing or Music Only in licensed premises and regulate the hours allowed.

A Music and Dancing Licence is a prerequisite for a Special Hours Certificate and involves a rigorous annual inspection to ensure that safety standards are kept up to requirements. Fire exits, emergency lighting, wiring, fire extinguishers, entrances and exits all come under close scrutiny. Needless to say, such requirements can prove to be very costly.

As the name implies, a Music Only Licence is like a Music and Dancing Licence but without the dancing. It is the sort of licence which is required for licensees who wish to provide live entertainment involving three or more performers. Three or more means three or more on any one occasion, so if there are three or four solo artists or two duets which appear separately but on the same night, this licence would still be needed.

Video shows on licensed premises which are put on as a means to attract customers require a Cinema Licence, irrespective of whether an admission fee is charged or not. Even a video linked to a television set in the bar requires such a licence, whereas a normal straightforward television does not.

Televisions, record players, juke boxes, tapes, cassettes, radios, compact disc players and any other means which are used to provide entertainment which your customers can hear, including live music and video shows, require a licence from the Performing Rights Society which covers copyright on the music for and on behalf of the composers and arrangers.

While the Performing Rights Society's licence covers the actual music, organisations such as Phonographic Performance Ltd and Video Performance Ltd collect royalties for the record, tape and video companies whose products are being used in public as it were. They also have a right to charge an annual licence fee and to prosecute those who infringe their copyright.

Weights and measures

Whisky, gin, vodka and rum must be served in quantities of one- sixth, one- fifth or one-quarter of a gill or multiples thereof and licensees are required by law to display a notice which states which particular fraction of a gill such spirits are dispensed in on their premises. Other spirits such as brandy and liqueurs are not covered by these regulations and may be dispensed from any measure or even poured freehand. However, where an optic is used, it must be approved and stamped to show that it does, in fact, deliver the correct amount.

An additional word of caution: if you advertise, publish or otherwise imply that a measure is involved in some way, you are obliged to use the correct equipment to ensure that the measure is exact.

See Chapter 7 for advice on wine by the glass or the carafe.

Weights and measures are covered by the Trading Standards Officer who is employed by your local authority. These are the same people to whom you pay your rates, so, in theory, if you are in need of any advice in this area they should be only too pleased to help, but don't bank on it!

Gaming

This means the playing of games of chance for money. There are only two such games which are allowed on licensed premises. They are cribbage and dominoes and even they must be played for small stakes only. Any other games of chance require permission from the Magistrates before they may be played on licensed premises, but even then, any game which involved a bank or a banker would not be allowed.

On the other hand, any game which is not 'gaming' in the legal sense and which relies upon the skill of the individual such as skittles, snooker, darts or pool may be played at will and if the contestants wish to put money on their ability to win, they may do so.

The police

The police have power to enter licensed premises at any time during permitted hours and half an hour following. They also have power to enter licensed premises at any time if they suspect that offences are being committed or are about to be committed.

It hardly needs saying that a licensee who refuses to admit the police commits an offence and, once again, the resulting fine would be the least of his worries as the Magistrates would probably consider that such a person was unsuitable to hold a Justices Licence and revoke it.

It is also an offence for a licensee to entertain a police officer whilst he is on duty. This offence is rather quaintly known as 'harbouring' and is probably intended to discourage licensees from attempting to procure favours from the police and for the police not to frequent licensed premises when they should be attending to other, more pressing matters. Obviously, plain clothes officers could come and go without the licensee knowing, so it would appear that this offence relates mainly to uniformed officers.

Scottish licensing law

The Licensing (Scotland) Act 1976 is the act which regulates the sale and consumption of intoxicating liquor on licensed premises in Scotland. It has to be said that the law in Scotland as it relates to licensing amounts to much the same thing as it does in England except that the administration and some of the phraseology are slightly different.

The Scottish equivalent of Licensing Justices are Licensing Boards which are a sub-committee of a District Council. Their statutory meetings are held in

Licensing law

January, March, June and October.

Permitted hours are rather like they used to be in England before the 1988 Licensing Act and are from 11 a.m. until 2.30 p.m. and from 5.0 p.m. until 11 p.m., Monday to Saturday inclusive. Sunday hours do not exist as such, but if an application is made to the Licensing Board and the application is granted, the hours are from 12.30 p.m. until 2.30 p.m. and from 6.30 p.m. until 11 p.m. Objections can be raised, however, and if upheld, the board will not entertain another application for 2 years.

The so-called 'all-day opening' in Scotland is something of a misnomer in that any extensions to the above permitted hours have to be applied for. The Licensing Board can grant an extension of hours to cover a period of 12 months if they feel that all the relevant circumstances are right.

A 'regular extension' to Sunday hours in pubs (where granted) is not permissible except where the pub has a restaurant and, even then, only in the restaurant area.

Types of licence

Public House Licence This is the same as a Full Justices On and Off Licence in England and Wales.

Off-Sale Licence Off sales only.

Hotel Licence The same as a Full Justices On and Off Licence.

Restricted Hotel Licence Must serve main meals for residents and non- residents in an area where there is no bar counter. Alcohol may be served to residents and their non-paying guests and to diners as an ancillary to a main meal. Can supply alcohol without a meal to residents and their private friends provided that those friends are paid for by the resident.

Restaurant Licence Exactly the same as in England but there must not be a bar counter.

Refreshment Licence Must provide refreshments including food and non alcoholic beverages for consumption on the premises. Bar counter not allowed. Off sales not allowed.

Entertainment Licence Granted to establishments

such as dance halls, theatres, cinemas and proprietory clubs. They may sell alcohol for consumption on the premises as an ancillary to the entertainment provided. The licensing board may impose conditions to ensure that this is adhered to.

Northern Ireland licensing law

Once again, the law as it relates to licensing in Northern Ireland is very similar to English and Scottish law.
Permitted hours are as follows:
- ☐ Monday to Saturday inclusive – 11.30 a.m. to 11 p.m.
- ☐ Sundays – 12.30 p.m. to 2.30 p.m. and 7 p.m. to 10 p.m.
- ☐ Christmas Day – 12.30 p.m. to 10 p.m.
- ☐ Good Friday – 5.0 p.m. to 11 p.m.
- ☐ Drinking-up time is 30 minutes at the end of each session.
- ☐ Off licences which are not licensed for Sundays or Christmas Day are allowed to open from 9.30 a.m to 9 p.m.

Public houses, hotels and restaurants which comply with certain standards such as a function room and adequate kitchen facilities, may apply to the Magistrates for late-night opening until 1 a.m. on up to 6 days per week, Sunday excluded.

All licences in Northern Ireland must be renewed annually in September in the local Magistrates Court.

In Northern Ireland, persons under the age of 18 years are only permitted in those parts of licensed premises which do not contain what is termed an 'open bar', i.e. a family room or a restaurant. Restaurants do not have an open bar in Northern Ireland. Additionally, persons under 18 years are not allowed to purchase alcohol and are not permitted to consume it on licensed premises and, what is more, are only permitted to be in an off licence when they are accompanied by a parent.

Spirit measures in Northern Ireland are one-quarter of a gill.

Useful Addresses

The National LVA, 2 Downing Street, Farnham, Surrey GU9 7NX. Tel: Farnham (0252) 714448.

The Scottish Licensed Trade Association, 10 Walker Street, Edinburgh EH3 7LA. Tel: 031-225 5169/7287.

Federation of the Retail Licensed Trade Northern Ireland, 91 University Street, Belfast BT7 1HP. Tel: Belfast (0232) 327578.

Useful reading

An ABC of Licensing Law, Published by the National LVA and available from John King, Manager, Member Services, National LVA, 2, Downing Street, Farnham, Surrey GU9 7NX.

16 Recipes

STARTERS

Starters are gaining in popularity, particularly at lunchtime, when people often want something light to eat. On our menu, the starters double up as snacks.

The recipes for Samosas and Cheese and Bacon Triangles are two very different starters using filo pastry. Filo is an almost transparent, tissue-like pastry which can be baked in the oven or deep-fried. It is very difficult to make yourself but is readily available frozen. Easy to use if you follow the instructions on the packet, filo is a very adaptable crispy, light pastry. Perhaps the main point to remember is that, if you are going to deep-fry the filo, you should use water to seal it; if it is to be baked, use a melted fat such as butter, ghee, margarine or similar.

Triangles for filopastry Samosas

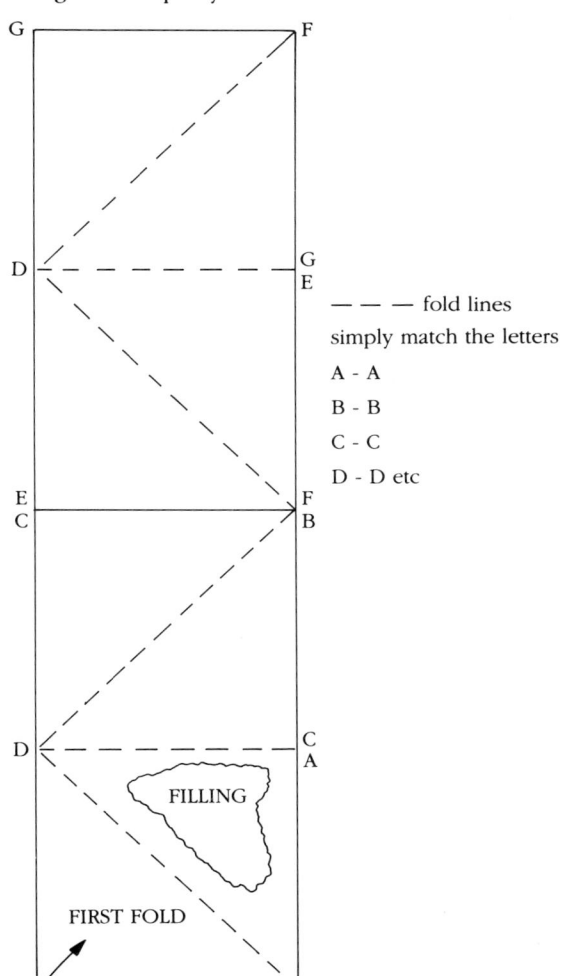

– – – fold lines
simply match the letters
A - A
B - B
C - C
D - D etc

Samosas

Makes 48 (serves 24)
Cooked samosas will freeze well and can be reheated in the microwave, combi or oven. Do not re-fry them or they will become saturated with fat.

- 1 kg (2 lb) potatoes, peeled and cut into small dice
- 175 g (6 oz) carrots, peeled and cut into small dice
- 2 garlic cloves
- 1 fresh green chilli, de-seeded
- 50 g (2 oz) fresh ginger
- 25 g (1 oz) fresh coriander
- 4 tbsp ghee or vegetable oil
- 1 large onion, chopped finely
- 1 tsp ground cumin
- 1 tsp garam masala
- 1/2 tsp chilli powder
- 175 g (6 oz) garden peas, fresh or frozen
- 4 tbsp water
- 2 tbsp lemon juice
- salt to taste
- 24 sheets of filo pastry

Plunge the diced potatoes and carrots into boiling, salted water for about 3 minutes. Drain and dry well. In a food processor, or by hand, finely chop the garlic, green chilli, ginger and coriander. Melt the ghee or oil in a large frying pan and sauté the onion until golden. Stir in the cumin, garam masala and chilli powder and mix for a few seconds. Frying off the spices helps to bring out the flavour. Add all the remaining ingredients except the pastry, including a little salt to flavour. Continue stirring over a low heat for about 5 minutes until the vegetables are just soft. When this is done, check the seasoning and add a little more salt and lemon juice if necessary. Leave to cool a little.

To assemble the samosas, cut the sheets of filo pastry lengthwise, and place about a teaspoon of the mixture on the pastry as shown in the diagram. Take care not to overfill them. Using water to seal the pastry, fold up the samosa as shown until you have a triangle with no open edges. Deep-fry the samosas until golden.

Two samosas make a good portion and can be served with a small salad, fresh lemon, thick yogurt and a Raita (page 180).

Variation

For an alternative filling, replace the potatoes and carrots with ground or finely minced beef (see recipe for Keema Curry, page 172).

Cheese and Bacon Triangles

Makes 12 (serves 6)
These are very simple and quick to make and are very popular with our customers.

> 6 rashers of lean, smoked bacon, de-rinded
> 12 triangles of processed cheese such as Dairylea
> 6 sheets of filo pastry

Cut each of the bacon rashers in half, then stretch each one over the back of a knife until it forms a long strip. Wrap the bacon evenly around a triangle of cheese and enclose it in filo pastry in the same way as for the samosas. Deep-fry until golden and serve with a small salad.

Garlic Mushrooms

Makes 20 (serves 4)
We find that these are a very popular starter, especially with young people. There are many different recipes but we have chosen this one not only for its simplicity but because this dish can be cooked in a variety of ways, either in the microwave, combi or static oven or even under the grill. The mushrooms can be prepared in advance and cooked to order.

Note that because parmesan cheese contains animal rennet, this dish is not suitable for vegetarians. To make it so, replace the parmesan with a vegetarian cheese and use vegetable stock instead of chicken.

> 20 medium-size mushrooms
> a little oil or melted butter of margarine
> 1 tbsp butter or margarine
> 50 g (2 oz) onions, chopped finely
> 4 garlic cloves, crushed
> 75 g (3 oz) breadcrumbs
> sherry to moisten
> 25 g (1 oz) grated parmesan cheese, plus extra for finishing
> vegetable or chicken stock
> watercress to garnish

Wash and de-stalk the mushrooms and dry them all thoroughly. Brush the caps with a little oil, melted butter or margarine and set aside. Melt the butter or margarine in a skillet, add the chopped onion, mushroom stalks and crushed garlic and fry until soft. Mix in the breadcrumbs and moisten with the sherry. Cook until the breadcrumbs swell, adding more sherry if necessary. Finally, stir in the parmesan. Spoon the mixture into the mushroom caps and sprinkle a little extra parmesan on top.

These can now be cooked to order. In a suitable dish, place a little stock, add the required number of mushrooms (5 should make a portion) and cook in a microwave on High for about 3 minutes, a static oven at Gas Mark 7/220°C/425°F for 7 minutes, under the grill for 4 minutes or in a combi at medium power, maximum temperature, for about 2 minutes. Keep the garnish simple: a little watercress (or a similar green leaf) is ideal. The main thing to ensure is that garlic mushrooms are served piping hot, perhaps with a crisp granary roll.

Tangy Chicken Livers

Serves 10
When using chicken livers it is vital to ensure that they are really fresh. The best way to tell is by look and smell. If any of the livers are discoloured, discard them. Chicken livers sometimes have the bile sacs attached. These are small, green parcels which, if not removed, will give the livers a very bitter taste.

> 1.25 kg (3 lb) chicken livers
> butter or oil for frying
> 1 large onion, chopped finely
> 2 garlic cloves (optional)
> 50 g (2 oz) can tomato purée
> 300 ml (1/2 pt) chicken stock
> 150 g (5 oz) thick yogurt
> salt and freshly ground black pepper
> toast to serve

Wash and dry the livers and slice into bite-size pieces. For the best results, cook one portion at a time. In a small frying pan, melt a little butter. Add about 1 teaspoon of chopped onions and a crushing of garlic, stir in approx. 175 g (6 oz) of chicken livers and sauté until the colour changes. Mix in 1/2 tsp of tomato puree and sufficient chicken stock to moisten and cook for about 1 minute, stirring constantly. Season with a little salt (if necessary) and freshly ground black pepper. Finally, add a blob (about 1 tablespoon) of yogurt, heat through and serve on triangles of toast.

Variations

To make the dish less fattening and more healthy, leave out the butter and start off with the stock. To make a change, replace the stock with sherry, add more garlic and leave out the yogurt to make Spanish-style Chicken Livers.

Stilton and Broccoli Pancakes

Makes 16 (serves 16 as a starter or 8 as a main course)

Pancake:
250 g (8 oz) fine ground wholemeal flour
a pinch of salt
2 eggs
600 ml (1 pint) skimmed milk
oil for frying

Filling:
1.2 litres (2 pints) white roux or similar sauce (page 183)
250 g (8 oz) Stilton, grated
500 g (1 lb) broccoli spears

Sieve the flour and salt into a baking bowl and make a well in the centre. Break the eggs on to a saucer to ensure that they are fresh and then drop them into the well. Using a wooden spoon, start to beat the eggs and, as they break up, drizzle in a little of the milk. The idea is to beat just the liquid, allowing the flour to fall in bit by bit. Once all the flour has been incorporated, beat the mixture as vigorously as possible until a thick smooth batter has formed. Carry on beating as you add the remaining milk, taking care that no lumps form. A simpler way to do the beating is to use an electric whisk or, if you are feeling particularly lazy, an electric blender.

Heat a little oil in a frying pan (or use a non-stick pan) and when it is very hot, pour in a little of the batter. Quickly swirl the batter around until it covers the bottom of the pan. Cook on a high heat until the underside is golden, then turn the pancake over with a fish slice or palette knife. Leave tossing for Shrove Tuesday! Once the second side is cooked, remove the pancake from the pan and cover with greaseproof paper. Repeat until all the batter is used up. Pancakes can be made in advance and saved, suitably chilled, until needed.

To make the filling, prepare the white sauce and while it is still hot, add the Stilton and allow it to melt. Line each pancake with broccoli spears and pour over a little sauce. Roll up the filled pancake, pour over a little more sauce and serve immediately.

If the pancakes are not to be used straight away or if they are to be served throughout a session, make the stilton sauce in advance and allow it to cool. Once all the ingredients are cooled, the pancakes can be assembled in advance and reheated to order either by covering with foil and heating at Gas Mark 4/180°C/350°F for 20 minutes in the static oven or in a microwave or combi oven for 3 minutes.

Variations

Pancakes can be filled with a wide variety of mixtures: ham and cheese, sweetcorn and crab, cheese and tomato, spicy minced beef or a seafood mixture. As a starter, one pancake should be sufficient; as a main course, serve two.

Falafel

Makes 60 cakes (serves 30)

Falafel or Egyptian Pepper Cakes may at first look very fiddly to make as the beans have to be skinned, but we have found this to be an almost addictive task. Leave a bowl of soaked beans in the kitchen and just about everyone who passes has to have a go. The beans are skinned in no time!

In the authentic recipe, the beans used are ful nabed which are available from Greek delicatessens and can be bought ready-skinned, but Falafel can also be made with either dried broad or lima beans. We prefer lima. Although this is not an authentic recipe, the flavour of these Falafel closely resembles the original.

1.25 kg (3 lb) lima beans
50 g (2 oz) fresh coriander
50 g (2 oz) fresh parsley (preferably common or broad-leafed)
1 tbsp ground cumin
1 tbsp ground coriander
1/2 tsp chilli powder
1 tsp freshly ground black pepper
1 large onion, chopped
6 garlic cloves
25 g (1 oz) baking powder
500 g (1 lb) plain flour, sifted
oil for frying

Soak the beans for at least 24 hours.

Skin the beans if necessary and cook them in boiling, salted water for about 20 minutes (depending on the beans used) until they are soft but not sloppy. Drain them really well. If they are still a little wet, dry them over a little heat or even in the microwave.

In a food processor, mix together all the herbs, spices, onion and garlic until really smooth. Place the cooked beans in a large bowl, add the spicy mixture and baking powder, and add the sifted flour a little at a time. Mix well together and make the mixture as smooth as possible. The finished mixture should be firm enough to handle.

Form the mixture into small, flat cakes about 5 cm (2 inch) in diameter and deep-fry in very hot oil. Try one at first: if it breaks up, add a little more flour. Alternatively, the cakes can be baked in a preheated oven for about 15 minutes or they may be frozen and deep-fried, without defrosting, to order. Two Falafel are a portion and are delicious served with a chunk of fresh lemon, yogurt or hummus.

Variation

For a change, leave out the coriander, cumin and chilli powder and add 2 tablespoons of tomato purée and 1 tablespoon of oregano for Pizza Pepper Cakes.

Smoked Mackerel Pâté

Serves 12

This is a very quick and tasty starter, and served with hot toast, it makes a delicious lunch-time snack.

> 6 smoked mackerel fillets
> 125 g (4 oz) cream cheese
> 1 tbsp fresh dill (optional)
> 1 tbsp creamed horseradish
> 2 tbsp mayonnaise
> 1 tbsp lemon juice
> freshly ground black pepper

Skin and bone the mackerel and place it together with all the other ingredients in a blender or food processor until smooth. Spoon into ramekins and serve chilled.

Variation

To make the pâté less fattening, use 'light' cream cheese and low-calorie mayonnaise.

Prawn Starters

The ubiquitous prawn cocktail has had a very bad press recently but you cannot get away from the fact that prawns are still an extremely popular starter. Most caterers buy frozen prawns and not all are as careful about defrosting them as they should be. Prawns should be defrosted in a colander placed over a bowl in a refrigerator. Do not be tempted to defrost them quickly by running them under the tap or leaving them out in a hot kitchen, and never leave them in the water left from defrosting.

A simple starter is a portion of prawns served in a scallop shell, accompanied by an attractive salad, freshly baked petit pain or brown bread and butter and a seafood sauce or Andalusian Mayonnaise (page 180). If you want to serve a prawn cocktail, make sure that it looks attractive: choose a glass large enough to eat out of and line it with finely shredded, crisp lettuce. Place a little seafood sauce on top, add the portion of prawns, coat with sauce and decorate according to taste with a couple of prawns with their shells on perched over the rim of the glass. Serve with thinly sliced brown bread and butter. (As a change, you could use crab meat instead of the prawns).

Another traditional way of serving prawns is inside an avocado. Avocado pears should always be served ripe. You can test them quite easily by gently pressing them: if the flesh gives slightly, the pear is ready. If the pears are hard, leave them overnight next to a few unpeeled bananas and in the morning they will be soft. To serve, slice the avocado lengthwise and remove the stone, place a portion of prawns in the well and serve with seafood sauce. If you use the larger avocados with the smooth skins, half is a sufficient portion; if you use the smaller avocados with the darker bobbly skins, you need to serve the whole pear for an adequate portion.

SOUPS

One of the things that has always amazed us is that the ratio of hot to cold food sales in hot weather goes up. No-one feels like cooking on a hot summer's day and yet they want a change from salads and feel the need for something hot: soup sells really well. So whether you are planning a winter menu or a summer one, do take some care over the soup. Not only is it a convenient starter but it will double up as a substantial snack, and nothing could be easier to serve.

We serve a wide variety of soups (more than 100 over a period of time) but space dictates that we can include recipes for only four here: a simple mushroom soup that is always popular; courgette and fennel, a firm favourite with our customers; lovage for when you get your herb garden going; and a cheese and ale soup served with a pastry topping, for something just a bit special.

Chunky Mushroom Soup

Serves 20

    1 kg (2 lb) mushrooms
    50 g (2 oz) butter or margarine
    1 large onion, chopped finely
    1/2 tsp grated nutmeg
    2.25 litres (4 pints) vegetable stock or water
    a sprig of fresh thyme
    50 g (2 oz) white breadcrumbs
    600 ml (1 pint) milk
    chopped fresh parsley or thyme to garnish

Wash and dry the mushrooms and chop them very finely. In a large pan, melt the butter or margarine, add the onion, mushrooms and nutmeg and gently sweat. Cover with the stock, add the thyme and bring to the boil, removing any scum that may form. Simmer for 15 minutes. Slowly sprinkle in the breadcrumbs - a few at a time or they will go lumpy - and cook for a further 5 minutes. Add the milk, and reheat but do not boil. Garnish with a little chopped parsley or fresh thyme on top before serving.

Courgette and Fennel Soup

Serves 20

    1.25 kg (3 lb) courgettes
    1 kg (2 lb) fennel bulbs
    1 large onion, chopped finely
    3 garlic cloves, chopped finely
    a knob of butter or margarine
    1 wine glass of sweet sherry
    2.75 litres (5 pints) vegetable stock or water
    salt and pepper
    Garnish:
    cream or natural yogurt
    fresh parsley or spring onion tops, chopped

Trim the courgettes and fennel and remove any discoloured bits but do not peel them, then chop them into small pieces. In a large pan, melt enough butter or margarine just to coat the bottom and add all the vegetables. Sauté them until they change colour but do not allow them to brown. Add the sherry and sweat the vegetables for a further minute to bring out the flavour. Add the stock or water, bring to the boil and simmer until the vegetables are soft (about 20 minutes). Do not overcook them. If using water, add a little salt and pepper. Liquidize the soup until smooth and adjust the seasoning if necessary. Serve garnished with a drizzle of cream or a small blob of natural yogurt topped with chopped fresh parsley or spring onion tops.

Cheese and Ale Soup

Serves 20

With its puff pastry lid, this soup is not at all suitable for a busy session, but it is a very impressive soup for a quiet lunch-time.

    75 g (3 oz) butter or margarine
    3 large onions, chopped finely
    175 g (6 oz) cornflour
    600 ml (1 pint) water
    1.2 litres (2 pints) bitter beer
    1.25 kg (3 lb) Lancashire or Cheddar cheese, grated
    15 g (1/2 oz) parsley, chopped
    600 ml (1 pint) milk
    To serve:
    croûtons, chopped parsley and Wholemeal Scones (page 182) or lids each made from about 50 g (2 oz) puff pastry

Recipes

Melt the butter or margarine in a large saucepan, add the onions and sauté them until transparent. Add the cornflour, stirring all the time, and allow it to brown a little. Pour in the water, little by little to prevent lumps forming, then add the beer. When the mixture has stopped foaming, it should resemble a thick pouring sauce. Sprinkle in the grated cheese and the parsley and stir until the cheese has melted. If the mixture starts to curdle or separate, mix a little cornflour with the milk before adding it slowly.

If liked, decorate with croûtons and a little parsley and serve with a wholemeal scone. If you are going to top the soup with pastry, leave it to cool and then three-quarters fill individual ovenproof soup bowls. Roll out the pastry and make lids for the soup, sealing the edges well. Bake in a combi oven at full power, maximum temperature, for 2 minutes or a very hot (Gas Mark 8/230°C/450°F) static oven for 7 minutes until the pastry has risen like a golden dome. When the lid is broken, the lovely aroma of the soup is released.

Lovage Soup

Serves 20
- a knob of butter or margarine
- 2 large onions, chopped finely
- 4 garlic cloves, chopped finely
- 1 head of celery (with leaves), chopped
- 1 kg (2 lb) potatoes, diced
- 375 g (12 oz) fresh lovage leaves (not stems), chopped
- 1.75 litres (3 pints) vegetable stock or water
- 1.2 litres (2 pints) milk
- salt and pepper

Garnish:
- lovage or celery leaves, chopped
- cream

Melt the butter or margarine in a pan and fry the onion and garlic until they start to lose their colour. Add the chopped celery. After about a minute, add the potatoes, but be careful that they do not stick. Sprinkle in the lovage and fry for about 1 minute. The smell is absolutely wonderful! Add the stock or water (and season if using water), bring to the boil and simmer until the potatoes are cooked (about 20 minutes). Finally, add the milk. Liquidise the soup and serve it with chopped lovage and celery leaves on top of a drizzle of cream.

FISH

Fresh fish is a delicious addition to any menu but, unlike meat, its life expectancy is very short: it quickly become stale and should therefore be cooked as soon as possible after it is bought. When it is really fresh, fish has quite a pleasant smell; a strong odour means it is past its best. If possible, try to see the whole fish and check that the eyes are bright, the gills dark pink and the scales glossy and firmly attached, all pointers to the fish's freshness. When choosing fillets, press your finger into the flesh: if it is fresh, it will spring back without leaving an imprint.

Fishmongers will deliver fish on a daily basis, but if your turnover is only small, why not select just one day to start with. Friday is a traditional fish day, so start serving fresh fish on Fridays until it is possible to judge the demand.

Frozen fish is readily available and is of good quality if you buy from a reputable supplier. Avoid the cheaper products such as fish fingers and seafood snacks which use minced or reconstituted fish.

Russian Fish Pies (Koubiliac)

Makes 12
This is an ideal way to use left overs and convenience foods to produce a quick and very appetising dish.

- 1 kg (2 lb) cooked salmon
- 50 g (2 oz) butter or margarine
- 1 onion, chopped finely
- 375 g (12 oz) mushrooms, chopped
- 500 g (1 lb) frozen wholegrain rice, thawed
- 1 heaped tbsp chopped fresh dill
- 1 heaped tsp chopped fresh parsley
- 600 ml (1 pint) soured cream (smetana) or natural yogurt
- 2.75 g (6 lb) frozen puff pastry, thawed
- 3 hard-boiled eggs, sliced
- egg wash

Bone the salmon and flake it into reasonable chunks. In a skillet, melt the butter or margarine and fry the onion until soft. Add the mushrooms and fry lightly for a minute or two. In a large bowl, mix the rice, mushrooms, onions, dill and parsley with enough soured cream or yogurt just to bind the mixture.

Roll out the pastry and cut into 12 25 cm (10-inch) squares. Place about 3 tablespoons of the rice mixture in the centre of each square of pastry. (Remember that the frozen rice will swell when cooking.) Top the rice with a good helping of salmon and a few slices of hard-boiled egg. Cover with a little soured cream.

Egg-wash the edges of the pastry and bring the corners up into the centre to form a smaller square. Crimp the edges together, egg-wash the top and bake in a preheated oven at Gas Mark 7/220°C/425°F for 15-20 minutes or in a combi on high power, maximum temperature, for 3-4 minutes. Serve with a salad.

Fish Steak with Scallions and Ginger

Serves 6

Allow one fish steak per person. Suitable fish include halibut, tuna, shark, cod or haddock.

>12 scallions or spring onions, cut into very fine slivers
>75 g (3 oz) fresh ginger, cut into very fine slivers
>6 fish steaks (weighing 175-250 g/6-8 oz each)
>3 tbsp sesame seed oil or other similar oil mixed with 3 tbsp light soy sauce

In a shallow dish large enough to hold the steaks side by side, scatter the scallions and ginger slivers. Arrange the fish steaks on top and pour over the mixed oil and soy sauce. Marinate the steaks for about an hour, turning them occasionally but making sure that the onions and ginger remain on the bottom.

The steaks can be cooked one at a time to order in a hot static oven, Gas Mark 8/230°C/450°F for 20 minutes, or in a combi at maximum power, high temperature for 3-4 minutes, or under a hot grill for 7 minutes, or in a microwave at medium power for 5 minutes. Simply take out a steak, place in a dish with a few of the scallions and ginger on the bottom, spoon over some of the liquor and cook.

Serve with a salad or wholegrain rice.

Fish Pies

Makes 16

These are probably our best seller. When we are making Fish Pies, we often buy a little extra fish and experiment with it for dishes on the 'Specials' board.

Almost any white fish is suitable provided that it can be skinned and boned easily. This is particularly important for a dish in which the fish is masked by a sauce and hidden under a pastry crust. We try to keep the fish pieces in bite-size chunks: it looks good and people can then see what they are eating. If you are using frozen fish, defrost it completely before you start cooking.

>1.75 litres (3 pints) roux sauce (page 183) made with fish stock
>250 g (8 oz) scampi
>1 tbsp chopped fresh chervil
>1 kg (2 lb) haddock or cod, cooked, boned and skinned
>500 g (1 lb) halibut, cooked, boned and skinned
>500 g (1 lb) salmon, cooked, boned and skinned
>250 g (8 oz) prawns
>1.75 kg (4 lb) frozen puff pastry, thawed, for lids

Make up the roux sauce and while it is still cooking, add the scampi and chervil. Break up the cooked white fish and salmon into bite-size pieces and add it to the sauce. Mix in the prawns and divide the mixture between 16 individual pie dishes.

Roll out the pastry and use it to make a lid for each of the pies. Bake at Gas Mark 8/230°C/450°F for 10 minutes until the pastry has risen and is light, crispy and golden-brown. Alternatively, cook in a combi oven at full power, maximum temperature for 3 minutes.

The mixture can be made in advance, but remember only to add hot fish to hot sauce or cold fish to cold sauce. Pies made in advance must be kept under refrigeration and can be baked to order.

Gravlax - Scandinavian Pickled Salmon

Serves 6 as a main course or 12 as a starter

Strictly speaking, this has no place in the fish section as it is usually served as a starter, but with a tossed salad and rye bread and butter it makes a delicious light main course - well worth the effort involved in its preparation. Gravlax is usually made with the tail end of the salmon, so when a whole fish is purchased the main body can be cut into darnes (fish steaks), leaving the tail section for this dish.

1½ lb salmon (tail section)
12 black peppercorns, crushed
1 tbsp sea salt
1 tbsp granulated sugar
1 tbsp chopped fresh dill
1 tbsp brandy (optional)
For the mayonnaise:
2 tbsp Dijon mustard
2 tbsp chopped fresh dill
300 ml (1.2 pint) ready-made mayonnaise
½ tsp lemon juice
1 tsp brandy (optional)

Fillet the fish into two triangles or ask the fishmonger to do it for you. Mix the crushed peppercorns with the salt, sugar, dill and brandy, if used. Spread a quarter of this mixture over the bottom of a flat dish.

Lay one piece of salmon, skin side down, on top of this and spread two-thirds of the remaining mixture over the fish. Place the second piece of salmon, skin side up, over the first and coat it with the last quarter of mixture, rubbing it well into the skin. Cover with foil and a well fitting plate with some weights on top, and refrigerate for 3-5 days, turning the fish occasionally.

To serve, slice thinly with a very sharp knife, parallel to the skin, as you would for smoked salmon.

The ideal accompaniment to Gravlax is a mustard and dill mayonnaise. To make this, simply mix the Dijon mustard, chopped dill, the lemon juice and brandy into the ready-made mayonnaise.

We usually serve 50 g (2 oz) of wafer-thin slices as a starter, and 125 g (4 oz) as a main course.

Mediterranean-style Fish Steaks

Serves 12

This is a very simple dish, full of colour, but in order to gain the full flavour, only very fresh ingredients should be used. Frozen peppers or tinned tomatoes will not give the same result.

12 fish steaks weighing 175–250 g (6–8 oz) each
500 g (1 lb) mixed peppers, chopped roughly
1 kg (2 lb) tomatoes, chopped roughly
1 large onion, chopped roughly
4 garlic cloves, crushed
600 ml (1 pint) fish stock
300 ml (½ pint) white wine
2 tbsp olive oil
juice of 2 lemons
1 tsp chopped fresh tarragon, or marjoram or parsley
24 black olives (optional)
salt and pepper

Place the fish steaks in an oven-proof dish large enough to hold them side by side.

In a large bowl, mix together all the other ingredients and pour the mixture over the fish. It may seem a little dry, but a lot of liquid will be released during cooking. Bake in a preheated oven at Gas Mark 6/200°C/400°F for 30–40 minutes and serve with wholegrain rice and a green salad.

CHICKEN

The increasing popularity of chicken is good news for the caterer because it is so easy to cook. Pan-fried or microwaved chicken dishes can be produced in a matter of minutes. Without a doubt, the best type of chicken to buy is corn-fed, but this is not always easily available and can be rather expensive.

Chicken pies are always a firm favourite, but to ring the changes, try including leeks and ham flavoured with a touch of fresh sage, or add corn, tomatoes, bacon and a spot of nutmeg to the chicken filling. Wherever possible, buy the whole bird and prepare it yourself: not only will the price be lower but you can then prepare your own stock and use any leftovers for soup. We have not included any turkey recipes in the book, but turkey could be substituted for chicken in all the following recipes except Ferique.

Ferique

Serves 12

Ferique is a Middle-Eastern dish made from wholewheat. It is very nourishing and tasty although rather filling. In the original recipe, the eggs are boiled with the wholewheat, but this is not advisable as there are bacteria in egg shells.

- 1 kg (2 lb) wholewheat
- 2 tbsp olive oil
- 2 onions, chopped
- 4 garlic cloves
- 1 tsp tumeric
- 1.2 litres (2 pints) chicken stock or water
- 12 chicken legs
- 12 eggs, lightly boiled
- 2 tbsp chopped fresh or dried fenugreek leaves
- salt and pepper

Clean the wholewheat thoroughly and leave it to soak in cold water overnight.

In a saucepan large enough to hold the chicken legs side by side, heat the oil and fry the onion and garlic until transparent. Add the tumeric and drained wholewheat, cover with the stock or water and simmer until soft, adding more liquid if necessary. This can take 2–3 hours, so a pressure cooker can greatly reduce the cooking time. While the wheat is cooking, cut all the surplus skin and fat from the chicken and score each leg twice with a sharp knife.

Once the wholewheat is soft, add the chicken, shelled eggs and fenugreek and simmer until the chicken is cooked. This will take about 20–30 minutes. Check the seasoning and add salt and pepper if necessary.

Serve in a deep bowl, allowing one piece of chicken and one egg per portion'.

Hindle Wakes

Serves 12

This very old dish was brought over to Lancashire by the Flemish weavers and was formerly known as 'Hen a la Wake'. The wakes were the annual holidays and it is thought that this dish was used to celebrate them. The original recipe uses a whole chicken or hen, but this makes it rather difficult to portion and serve. Our adaptation uses chicken fillets but we think the flavour is the same.

- 300 ml ($^1/_2$ pint) chicken stock or water
- 300 ml ($^1/_2$ pint) white wine
- grated zest and juice of 2 lemons
- 175 g (6 oz) no-soak prunes
- 1 tbsp fresh honey
- a sprig of fresh thyme
- 12 chicken fillets (weighing 175–250 g/6–8 oz each)
- 300 ml ($^1/_2$ pint) single cream
- salt and pepper

In a shallow skillet, heat the stock, white wine and zest and juice of the lemons with the prunes, honey and thyme. Once it is simmering, add the chicken fillets and cook them, turning them over in the liquid. This will take about 5 minutes. Lift out the chicken pieces and keep them warm.

Sieve the cooking liquor and return it to the pan. Add the cream and reduce the liquor (by rapid boiling) until a coating sauce is produced. Check the seasoning and serve the fillets coated in the sauce.

Chicken Olympus

Serves 12

If you do not want to make your own Hollandaise the ready-made variety is suitable but do not use the packets that you have to mix yourself.

    300 ml (1/2 pint) Hollandaise sauce (page 185)
    1 tsp fresh chervil or parsley, chopped finely
    4 rashers of lean smoked bacon, chopped finely
    75 g (3 oz) grated cheese
    12 chicken fillets (weighing 175–250 g (6–8 oz) each)
    12 asparagus spears, blanched if fresh
    about 1.25 kg (3 lb) puff pastry

Mix together the Hollandaise sauce, chervil or parsley, bacon and cheese.

Ensure that the chicken fillets are free from particles of bone and cartilage them, then place them, smooth side down, on a board. Spread each one with about 2 teaspoons of the mixture and top with an asparagus spear cut into 1 cm (1/2- inch) pieces. Close the chicken around the filling. Roll out the puff pastry and wrap each chicken filet in pastry. Bake in a preheated oven at Gas Mark 7/220°C/425°F for 15–20 minutes or in a combi for 4–5 minutes depending on the size of the fillets.

Variations

Almost any filling is suitable for this type of dish and the puff pastry will ensure that the flavour and moisture are kept in. Make sure, though, that the filling is not too wet or it will make the puff pastry soggy.

Cream cheese with chutney and apple slices make a tasty Ploughman's Chicken. For something more exotic, spread a thin coating of curry mayonnaise, cover with slices of fresh mango and, instead of the puff pastry, make a crumb coating with dried banana chips and plain digestive biscuits.

Chicken and Apricot Tiffin

Serves 12

This is a delicious creamy dish. Although it is quite highly spiced, it is not hot.

    50 g (2 oz) ghee or 6 tbsp oil
    2 large onions, chopped
    4 garlic cloves, crushed
    1 tbsp curry powder
    2 tsp ground cumin
    3 tbsp garam masala
    1 tsp ground coriander
    2.25 kg (5 lb) chicken, diced
    50 g (2 oz) wholemeal flour
    2 x 450 g (15 oz) cans of apricots
    125 ml (4 fl oz) lime juice
    water or chicken stock to cover
    50 g (2 oz) creamed coconut
    3 tbsp finely chopped fresh coriander (optional)
    Garnish:
    thick natural yogurt
    fresh coriander, chopped if liked

Heat the ghee or oil in a large saucepan. Add the onions, garlic and all the spices, and fry until the onions are transparent. Add the chicken and sauté it until golden-brown. Sprinkle with the flour. Pour over the juice from the apricots and the lime juice and sufficient water or stock to cover. Simmer for about 30 minutes or until the chicken is cooked.

Add the coconut, apricots and fresh coriander and cook for a further few minutes. Garnish with a blob of thick yogurt and fresh coriander and serve with wholegrain rice.

BEEF

Beef has traditionally had a place in the food provided by British inns: in England, roast beef and Yorkshire pudding are still a popular Sunday lunch, and the quality of Scottish beef is legendary.

Many caterers like to include at least one steak on their menu, but unless you intend to develop a separate steak section, it is probably best to choose a plain grilled sirloin, as this is the cut that most people associate with steak. Even these can be varied by the use of different sauces and now there are even frozen individually portioned sauces readily available.

Austrian-style Steak

Serves 12
- a knob of butter
- 1 large onion, cut into small dice
- 175 g (6 oz) carrots, cut into small dice
- 175 g (6 oz) celery, cut into small dice
- 2 garlic cloves, crushed
- 2.25 kg (5 lb) rump steak, trimmed of fat and sliced thinly
- plain flour for coating
- 1.2 litres (2 pints) beef stock
- 150 ml ($1/4$ pint) Marsala
- 2 tbsp red wine vinegar
- $1/2$ tsp mace or nutmeg
- 4 bay leaves
- 150 ml ($1/4$ pint) single cream

Melt the butter in a pan and sauté the diced vegetables with the garlic until they soften. Divide the steak into 12 portions. Place a generous spoonful of vegetable mixture on each slice and roll it up. Secure each of the parcels with a cocktail stick and roll them in flour. Brown in a sauté pan to seal them, then place them in an ovenproof dish that is large enough to hold the steak parcels side by side.

Add the stock, Marsala, wine vinegar, mace and bay leaves to the residue in the pan. Bring to the boil and pour over the steaks. Bake in a preheated oven at Gas Mark 5/190°C/375°F for about 1 hour.

When the steak is cooked, stir in the cream, remove the cocktail stick and serve.

Boeuf en Daube

Serves 12
- 2.25 kg (5 lb) braising steak
- about 50 g (2 oz) plain flour or cornflour to thicken
- 2 or 3 rashers of streaky bacon
- 1 large onion, chopped
- 4 garlic cloves, crushed
- 2 tsp beef bouillon paste dissolved in a little boiling water
- 1 litre ($1^3/4$ pints) red wine
- a large sprig of fresh thyme or 1 tbsp dried thyme
- 1 tsp cinnamon
- salt and freshly ground black pepper

Cut the beef into 2 cm (1-inch) cubes and roll in seasoned flour. In a heavy-bottomed saucepan, fry off the bacon until crispy. Lift out the bacon with a slatted spoon leaving the fat. Sauté the onion and garlic and transfer to a casserole dish. Lightly brown the beef in the remaining fat and add it to the casserole dish.

Add the dissolved beef bouillon and all the remaining ingredients to the pan. Bring gently to the boil and pour over the meat. Cover the casserole with a lid and braise in a moderate oven (Gas Mark 4/180°C/350°F) for about 2 hours. The meat should cook through but retain its shape.

Stifado

Serves 12
- 2.25 kg (5 lb) rump or chuck steak
- 500 g (1 lb) button onions
- 1 large onion, chopped
- 600 ml (1 pint) beef stock
- 1 wine glass of oil
- 3 wine glasses of red wine
- 2 tbsp double concentrate tomato purée
- 6 garlic cloves, crushed
- 5 bay leaves
- 12 allspice berries
- 1 tsp ground cumin
- salt and pepper

There is no need to sauté the meat and onions for this recipe. Simply mix all the ingredients together, cover and cook in a hot oven at Gas Mark 4/180°C/350°F for about 40 minutes then at Gas Mark 4/180°C/350°F for a further hour until the meat is firm yet tender. The tomato purée should be sufficient to thicken the dish, but if it is not, add a little flour or cornflour.

Beef in a Fine Sauce

Serves 12

This rich and spicy dish has been popular in the North of England since the twelfth century.

   1/2 tsp ground cloves
   1 tsp freshly ground black pepper
   1 tsp ground cinnamon
   1/2 tsp tumeric
   salt to taste
   50 g (2 oz) plain flour for coating
   2.25 kg (5 lb) point steak, cut into bite-size pieces
   50 g (2 oz) butter
   24 small onions or shallots
   4 garlic cloves, crushed (optional)
   2 glasses of red wine
   2 tbsp wine vinegar
   1.2 litres (2 pints) beef stock

Mix the spices and a little salt with the flour and coat the meat. Melt the butter in a pan and lightly sauté the onions and garlic if used. Transfer to a casserole dish. Next, seal the meat in the hot fat, remove it from the pan and mix it with the onions.

Add the remaining flour to the pan, and carefully stir in the wine, wine vinegar and stock. Bring to the boil and pour over the meat and onions. Mix well, cover the casserole dish and place in a preheated oven at Gas Mark 4/180°C/350°F for about 2 hours.

Serve with plain boiled or mashed potatoes and lightly cooked green vegetables.

Beef Stroganoff

Serves 12

   2.25 kg (5 lb) rump steak
   1 tbsp fresh thyme
   flour for coating
   25 g (1 oz) butter
   2 onions, sliced thinly
   2 garlic cloves
   1 kg (2 lb) mushrooms, sliced thinly
   1 tbsp French mustard
   300 ml (1/2 pint) medium-sweet sherry
   1.2 litres (2 pints) soured cream (smetana)
   salt and freshly ground black pepper

Trim the beef of all fat and cut it into thin strips about 5 cm (2 inches) long. Strip the thyme leaves from the stalks. Coat the meat in a little seasoned flour. Melt a little of the butter in a pan and fry the meat until it is golden-brown (about 5–7 minutes). Remove the meat from the pan and set aside.

Add a little extra butter and sauté the onions, garlic, thyme and sliced mushrooms. Return the meat to the pan and add the mustard, diluted with a little sherry. Slowly add the remaining sherry, heat to simmering point and allow to cook for a further couple of minutes. Add the cream and heat to serving temperature. Serve with rice or pasta such as tagliatelli.

MINCED BEEF

One of the problems when people start cooking is that they are inclined to be a little blinkered: they look through the cookery books, see something that they like and then go out and buy the ingredients. This is the way that most of us start to cook, but as caterers, we have to watch our profit margins and take advantage of seasonal offers. So, if the butcher says that lamb is good quality and cheap, we take advantage of it.

We have decided to include four recipes for minced beef to give you some idea of the diversity that can be obtained from one basic ingredient. They are all very different in taste, texture and appearance, but they should all cost out at roughly the same price. All the dishes except the Cottage Pie will freeze well. One word of advice: do not buy cheap, fatty mince. Apart from the fact that it tastes awful, it is false economy, as it cooks down to nothing.

Chilli Con Carne

Serves 20

This dish is another of our best sellers and always popular on a pub menu, although after tasting some of the so-called Chillies on offer - nothing more than red kidney beans in a bit of chillied mince - we wonder how it gained such popularity. Try this recipe, which we were given by an Argentinian acquaintance of ours. Although full of flavour, it is not very hot, but if you want to make it hotter, add more chillies. We add a warning on our menu for customers to beware of the small hot chillies, but even so, some of them still eat them whole and then scream for water!

The original recipe used haricot beans and we think that it tasted better, but in Britain, Chilli means red kidney beans and so we have used those.

1.25 kg (3 lb) red kidney beans
150 ml (¼ pint) olive oil
3 large onions, chopped
6 garlic cloves, crushed
2.25 kg (5 lb) minced beef
1 tbsp thyme
1 tbsp oregano
2 tsp chilli powder
1 tsp cinnamon
1 tbsp ground cumin
90 ml (3 fl oz) red wine vinegar
250 g (8 oz) double concentrate tomato purée
1 x 450 g (15 oz) can tomatoes, chopped
500 g (1 lb) fresh mixed peppers, diced
4.5 litres (8 pints) beef stock or water
250 g (8 oz) fresh, small green chillies
50 g (2 oz) sesame seeds
500 g (1 lb) vegetable chillies
salt

Soak the beans in cold water for 24 hours. Drain the soaked beans and wash them well. Place them in fresh cold water and bring them to the boil. Skim off any scum that forms, then boil rapidly for about 20 minutes to cook the beans and destroy the toxins in them. Wash again.

Heat the oil in a saucepan and fry the onions and crushed garlic. Add the mince and while it is browning, add all the dried spices and herbs. Pour on the wine vinegar, and the tomato purée, tomatoes and diced peppers. Add the beans and cover with stock or water, bring to the boil and simmer for about 30 minutes.

Add the fresh chillies and continue cooking. If the rice looks dry, add a little more water or stock. Once the beans are soft, add the sesame seeds and vegetable chillies and salt if necessary and continue cooking for a further 10 minutes. Serve with wholegrain rice.

Pasticcio Macaronia

Serves 12

The only thing wrong with this dish is its name, which is more of a mouthful than the dish itself! You could try renaming it for your customers but ours tend to order 'that pasta thing'!

90 ml (3 fl oz) olive oil
1 large onion, chopped
5 garlic cloves, crushed
2 tsp nutmeg
2.25 kg (5 lb) minced beef
175 g (6 oz) tomato purée
1 wine glass red wine
4 tbsp red wine vinegar
1 kg (2 lb) buccatini (large bore macaroni)
1.2 litres (2 pints) Béchamel sauce (page 183)
2 eggs, beaten
salt

Heat the oil in a pan and fry the onion, garlic, 1 teaspoon of the nutmeg and the mince until brown. Add the tomato purée, wine and wine vinegar and continue cooking for about 15 minutes. Do not allow the meat to stick.

Cook the macaroni in a pan of boiling, salted water to which a little oil has been added, until it is 'al dente'. Drain really well.

Add half of the Béchamel sauce to the mince mixture, then assemble the dish. Spread half the macaroni in the bottom of an ovenproof dish, cover with the meat mixture and top with the rest of the macaroni. To finish off, mix the remaining nutmeg and two well-beaten eggs into the remaining sauce and pour it over the dish. Bake, uncovered, in a preheated oven at Gas Mark 6/200°C/400°F for about 1 hour. Serve with salad.

Keema Curry

Serves 12

Keema is a dry mince curry. Delicious on its own or with rice, it can also be used as a filling for samosas or in biryani, where it is layered with saffron rice. The recipe contains both small green and black cardamom pods. The small green ones can be a little unpleasant if you crunch one by accident, so we now buy them ready shelled. The large black ones are strange-looking and once caused one of our customers to complain that there was a large black insect in his food. Horrified, we rushed to examine it, only to discover the cardamom - a relief to us, but he was still not really convinced even when we showed him the packet!

150 g (5 oz) ghee or 6 tbsp vegetable oil
3 large onions, choppped
2 tsp ground cinnamon
20 small green cardamom pods
10 large black cardamom pods
2.25 kg (5 lb) minced beef
3 tsp chilli powder
2 tbsp ground cumin
2 tsp turmeric
5 bay leaves
1 tbsp ground coriander
600 ml (1 pint) natural yogurt
250 g (8 oz) frozen peas

Heat the ghee or oil in a large pan and fry the onion until light brown in colour. Add the cinnamon and small and large cardamoms and continue frying for 1 minute. Add the mince, sprinkle with the chilli powder, cumin, turmeric, bay leaves and coriander and stir well. Cook for about 20 minutes over a low heat.

Add the yogurt and peas and cook for a further 10 minutes or until the mince is cooked. Do not allow it to stick.

Cottage Pie

Served 12

This is the alternative to shepherds' pie, so often wrongly named: shepherds' pie is made with lamb; cottage pie is made with beef. This is a very plain version but it is really tasty if you use a good beef stock and really creamy potatoes and cook it for long enough for the flavours to mingle. Nothing is worse than tinned mince topped with instant mash, shoved in a microwave and purporting to be a cottage pie.

2.25 kg (5 lb) minced beef
1 large onion, chopped
75 g (3 oz) cornflour
1.2 litres (2 pints) good beef stock
2.25 kg (5 lb) creamed cooked potatoes, made with milk or a little cream and a knob of butter and freshly ground black pepper
egg or milk wash

In a heavy-bottomed pan, place the mince and onion and allow them to brown. If there is a lot of fat, skim it off. Stir in the cornflour and pour over the stock. Cook for about 45 minutes or until the mince is well cooked. Mash the potatoes with skimmed milk for a more healthy version or a little cream and butter for flavour. Place the mince in a large tray or individual dishes and pipe on the potato. Brush the top with egg or milk wash then finish off in the oven at Gas Mark 6/200°C/400°F for about 20 minutes until the potatoes are brown. If you are going to reheat the pie(s) later in a combi, do not brown the potatoes too much at this stage.

LAMB

Lamb Chops with Orange and Ginger

Serves 12

12 large, lean lamb chops (weighing 125–175 g/4–6 oz each)
300 ml ($1/2$ pint) pure orange juice
grated zest and juice of 1 orange
25 g (1 oz) root ginger, grated
about 1.25 kg (3 lb) puff pastry
salt and freshly ground black pepper

Trim off as much fat as possible from the chops and remove all meat from about the last 5 cm (2 inch) of bone. Mix together the orange juice, zest and ginger with a little salt and freshly ground black pepper. Put the chops in this mixture and leave to marinate in a fridge for about 8 hours, turning occasionally.

Roll out the puff pastry into twelve 15 cm (6-inch) squares and wrap each square around the meaty part of a chop. Bake in a preheated oven at Gas Mark 6/200°C/400°F) for about 20 minutes or in a combi at high power, maximum temperature for 4-5 minutes. One chop should be sufficient serving to make a light and inexpensive meal.

Exmoor Lamb Casserole

Serves 12
Strongly flavoured with lovage, this is a very rich dish ideally served with new potatoes and a little very lightly cooked broccoli.

2.25 kg (5 lb) boned leg of lamb, diced
plain flour for coating
butter for frying
50 g (2 oz) lovage, finely chopped
250 g (8 oz) button onions
1 large onion, chopped
500 g (1 lb) button mushrooms
600 ml (1 pint) dry white wine
600 ml (1 pint) lamb stock
4 bay leaves
a sprig of thyme
300 ml (1.2 pint) single cream
salt and freshly ground black pepper

Lightly coat the diced lamb in flour. In a heavy-bottomed skillet, melt just a little butter. Add the lamb and chopped lovage and stir the meat until it is sealed. Do not allow the meat to stick or the herbs to burn. Transfer to a casserole dish.

Fry the onions and mushrooms, adding a little more butter to the pan if necessary. Pour in the wine, half the stock, the bay leaves and the thyme.The mixture should thicken slightly. Pour over the lamb. Top up with stock until the meat is covered. Bake in a preheated oven at Gas Mark 6/200°C/400°F for about 1 hour. At the end of the cooking time, check the seasoning and thickness, adding salt, pepper and a little flour if necessary. Stir in the cream and cook for a further 30 minutes.

Breast of Lamb on Potatoes

This is such an obvious dish that we were not sure whether to include it or not, but if we feel that the 'Specials' board needs something plain, we make it and it sells well. It is one of those dishes that people no longer bother to make at home and it is amazing how many people remark that they haven't eaten anything like it for years!

In spring, when lamb is at its best and most expensive, people (restaurants included) often ignore the cheaper and sometimes tastier cuts, but pub caterers can take advantage of plain, honest food such as this and be thanked by their customers for doing so.

2 large, lean breasts of lamb (weighing 2.25-2.75 kg/5-6 lb) in total)
2.75 kg (6 lb) potatoes, sliced
2 large onions, sliced
1.2 litres (2 pints) lamb stock
salt and freshly ground black pepper

Ask your butcher to crack the breast bone so that the breasts can be cut into pieces about 5 cm (2 inches) wide. In a shallow, oven-proof dish, layer the potatoes and onions, ending with a layer of potatoes. Barely cover with stock. Place the lamb across the top and bake, sprinkled with salt and pepper, in a preheated oven at Gas Mark 6/200°C/400°F for about 1 hour. The lamp and top layer of potatoes should be brown and crispy. Serve with fresh vegetables.

PORK

Pork makes a delicious and very warming winter dish. The first two recipes, although similar in style, have very different flavours. Both are inexpensive to make and very easy to serve.

Dublin Coddle

Serves 12

For this dish, we use leg or hand of pork – cheaper cuts take much longer to cook. Any herbed sausages (for instance, Lincolnshire or Cumberland) can be used to replace the plain pork sausages we have suggested, but if you use these, leave out the thyme.

- 1 kg (2 lb) lean pork, diced
- 500 g (1 lb) lean bacon, diced
- 1 kg (2 lb) pork sausages, cut into 2 cm (1-inch) pieces
- 500 g (1 lb) mushrooms, cut into quarters
- 2 large onions, chopped
- 1 tsp chopped thyme
- 300 ml ($1/2$ pint) single cream
- 2.75 kg (6 lb) potatoes, peeled and cut into large dice
- water
- salt and freshly ground black pepper

Cover the bottom of a large oven tin with the pork, bacon, sausages, mushrooms, onions, a little pepper and the thyme. Mix well and pour over the cream. Cover with the potatoes, season and add sufficient water nearly to reach the top. Cover with foil and bake in a preheated oven at Gas Mark 7/220°C/425°F for 1 hour. Remove the foil, reduce the heat to Gas Mark 5/190°C/375°F and bake for a further hour until the potatoes are cooked and crispy.

Bakery-style Pork

Serves 12

Bakery-style Pork does need the garlic and herbs to give it its distinctive flavour, so don't be tempted to leave them out.

- 2 large onions, sliced
- 6 garlic cloves, crushed
- 2.75 kg (6 lb) potatoes, sliced
- 3 tbsp chopped oregano
- 1.2 litres (2 pints) chicken stock
- 600 ml (1 pint) single cream
- 24 large, lean slices of belly pork, weighing 2.25–2.75 kg (5–6 lb) in total
- salt and freshly ground black pepper

Mix the onions, garlic and potatoes in the bottom of a large ovenproof dish. Sprinkle the top with half the oregano and cover with the stock and cream. Lay the belly pork on top, season with a little salt and pepper and sprinkle with the remaining oregano. Cover with foil and bake in a preheated oven at Gas Mark 6/200°C/400°F for about 1 hour. Remove the foil and bake for a further 1–1 $1/2$ hours. The belly pork should be very crisp but not burnt. Allow 2 slices per person.

Somerset Pork Chops

Serves 12

- 12 large, lean pork chops, weighing 175–250 g (6–8 oz) each
- 6 crisp eating apples, cored and sliced
- 3 onions, chopped finely
- 375 g (12 oz) mushrooms, sliced
- 1 tbsp chopped savory or sage
- 900 ml ($1 1/2$ pints) dry cider
- 375 g (12 oz) cheese, grated
- 250 g (8 oz) wholemeal breadcrumbs
- salt and freshly ground black pepper

Seal the pork chops either in a non-stick pan or under a hot grill. Cover the bottom of an ovenproof dish with the apples, onions and mushrooms. Season with salt and freshly ground black pepper. Lay the pork chops over the top and sprinkle with savory or sage. Cover with cider. Mix together the cheese and breadcrumbs and sprinkle over the top. Bake in a preheated oven at Gas Mark 6/200°C/400°F for 1–1 $1/2$ hours, until the chops are cooked.

Pork Goulash

Serves 12

- 2.25 kg (5 lb) lean pork
- 4 tbsp oil
- 3 large onions, sliced
- 3 garlic cloves, crushed
- 1 1/2 tsp paprika
- 1.2 litres (2 pints) chicken stock
- 4 tbsp wine vinegar
- 3 tbsp tomato concentrate
- 1 tsp caraway seeds
- 1 tbsp chopped marjoram
- 1 small can of paprikas or pimentos, cut into thin strips
- 600 ml (1 pint) thick yogurt
- salt and freshly ground black pepper

Garnish:
- natural yogurt
- chopped parsley

Trim the meat of all fat and cut it into 5 cm (2-inch) strips or small dice. Heat the oil in a large saucepan and fry the onions and garlic until golden. Add the paprika powder and the pork and stir until the meat is sealed. Reduce the heat, cover the pan and allow to cook for about 5 minutes. Add all the remaining ingredients except the paprikas and yogurt and allow to simmer for about 1 hour. Check the seasoning.

Add the paprikas or pimentos to the goulash, cook for a further 5 minutes, then add the yogurt. Heat to serving temperature. For the best results, serve the goulash with either rice or noodles and garnish with a drizzle of yogurt and sprinkle of chopped parsley.

Malayan Pork Curry

Serves 12

- 2 large onions, chopped
- 50 g (2 oz) root ginger, grated
- 6 garlic cloves, crushed
- 6 tbsp oil
- 2 tbsp ground coriander
- 2 tsp chilli powder
- 2 tsp turmeric
- 1 tbsp paprika
- 1 tbsp cumin
- 2.25 kg (5 lb) lean pork, diced
- 1 x 450 g (15 oz) can of chopped tomatoes
- 2 tbsp tomato purée
- 4 tbsp wine vinegar
- 600 ml (1 pint) water
- 125 g (4 oz) dried diced pawpaw and 125 g (4 oz) dried diced pineapple or 1 x 450 g (15 oz) can of pineapple chunks or 1 small fresh pineapple
- a handful of fresh coriander
- 50 g (2 oz) fresh green chillies
- salt and freshly ground black pepper

Garnish:
- thick yogurt
- chopped fresh coriander

Sauté the onions, ginger and garlic in the oil and add the spices one at a time to cook and bring out the flavour. Add the pork, tomatoes, tomato purée, wine vinegar and water. Bring to the boil, season and simmer for about 1 hour, adding more water if necessary.

Add the fruit (and any juice), the coriander and the fresh chillies. Return to the heat and cook for a further 10 minutes or until the pork is cooked.

Fresh chillies get hotter the longer they are left, so if the curry does not taste very hot at this stage, leave it for at least 1/2 hour before adding any more chilli powder. Serve garnished with a blob of thick yogurt topped with finely chopped coriander and with wholegrain rice.

VEGETARIAN DISHES

In Chapter 4 we looked at the numerous ways in which you can cater for vegetarians merely by replacing an animal product with a vegetable one. Here are a few recipes that are popular with vegetarians and flesh-eaters alike.

Spicy Potato Omelette

Serves 8 as a main course, 12 as a starter
Harissa is red chilli purée which is very hot. Most large stores now stock it.

- 1 kg (2 lb) potatoes, peeled and cut into dice
- 4 large onions, chopped
- 4 garlic cloves, crushed
- 6 tbsp oil for frying
- 12 eggs, beaten
- 3 tsp harissa or chilli sauce
- 1 tbsp chopped parsley
- 1 tbsp chopped coriander
- lemon wedges to garnish

Cook the potatoes in salted water. Drain them well and mash them. Fry the onions and garlic in a little of the oil until they are soft and add them to the potatoes.

Fold the beaten eggs into the harissa or chilli sauce with the parsley and coriander. Slowly mix the sauce into the potatoes.

Heat the remaining oil in two large domestic frying pans (or use one large catering frying pan for a more spectacular result). Divide the mixture between the two and cook on a very low heat for 10–15 minutes. This mixture does have a tendency to burn, so watch it carefully. Once the bottom has set, place the pan under a salamander (or grill) for a further 10 minutes until the top is set and golden-brown.

For best results, serve warm, garnished with lemon wedges, and with a mixed salad.

Spinach and Pease Parcels

Serves 6 as a main course, 12 as a starter
- 1 kg (2 lb) marrowfat peas, soaked overnight in cold water
- 2 large onions, chopped
- 1 kg (2 lb) spinach leaves, chopped finely
- 1 tsp finely chopped hyssop (optional)
- 12 sheets of filo pastry, divided lengthwise
- melted butter, ghee or oil
- freshly ground black pepper

Drain the soaked peas and cook the peas and onions in salted water until they go mushy. Drain off any surplus water and start to 'dry' over a very low heat. Add the chopped spinach and hyssop if used to the peas. The spinach will reduce considerably in volume. Continue to cook until the mixture is firm but moist. Season with a sprinkling of pepper. Leave the mixture to cool.

Place about 3 tablespoons of filling on to each sheet of filo pastry and fold into a rectangle, brushing with melted butter (or ghee or oil for vegans) to seal. The parcels should have several thicknesses of filo all round. Bake in a preheated oven at Gas Mark 8/230°C/450°F for about 15 minutes until golden-coloured.

Boston Baked Beans

Serves 12
Eat your heart out Heinz!

- 1 kg (2 lb) haricot beans, soaked overnight in cold water
- 2.25 litres (4 pints) vegetable stock
- 4 tbsp black treacle
- 4 tbsp wine vinegar
- 2 large onions, chopped
- 8 tbsp tomato purée
- 6 bay leaves
- a sprig of thyme

Drain and rinse the beans. Place them in fresh unsalted water and bring to the boil. If scum forms, drain and wash them and repeat until all the scum has disappeared. Boil rapidly for 10 minutes, then simmer for a further hour. Drain any water from the beans and place them in a large earthenware dish with a tight-fitting lid or use a slow cooker. Add all the other ingredients, stir and bake in a preheated oven at Gas Mark 2/150°C/300°F for 4-6 hours. We cook ours overnight.

Serve with jacket potatoes or Irish Soda Bread (page 182).

Aubergine Slippers

Serves 12

    3 aubergines (to allow 3 slices per portion)
    salt
    Yeast batter:
    250 g (8 oz) flour
    a pinch of salt
    15 g (1/2 oz) butter or margarine
    300 ml (1/2 pint) milk and water mixed
    15 g (1/2 oz) yeast
    a sprinkling of sugar

Cut the aubergines into 0.5 cm (1/4-inch) slices and place in a colander layered with salt for at least 1/2 hour. Wash and pat dry.

Sift the flour with a pinch of salt into a large mixing bowl. Add the butter or margarine to the milk and water and warm slightly. Cream the yeast with a little sugar and 2 tablespoons of the liquid. If using dried yeast, follow the instructions on the packet. Add the yeast to the liquid and leave it until it froths.

Make a well in the flour, pour in the liquid and mix well. Allow to stand for about an hour.

Coat the aubergine slices with the batter and deep-fry until golden. Serve with a yogurt dip or Skorthalia (Garlic Sauce, page 180) and a mixed salad. Courgettes can be cooked in the same way.

Yigantes

Serves 12

    500 g (1 lb) dried butter beans, soaked overnight in cold water
    125 ml (4 fl oz) olive oil
    2 large onions, chopped
    3 garlic cloves, crushed
    2 tbsp chopped parsley
    1 x 450 g (15 oz) can chopped tomatoes
    2 tbsp tomato purée
    2 sprigs of fresh oregano or 1 tsp dried oregano
    salt and freshly ground black pepper

Rinse the beans well. Cover with cold water and bring to the boil. Remove any scum that forms and change the water if necessary. Repeat until the water is clear, then boil for 30 minutes.

Heat the oil in a skillet and sauté the onion and garlic until soft. Add the parsley, tomatoes, tomato purée, oregano and a little seasoning and cook for 10 minutes.

Drain the beans, place them in a casserole dish and pour the vegetable mixture over them. If this does not cover them, add a little water. Mix everything together well, cover and bake in a preheated oven at Gas Mark 4/180°C/350°F for about 1 hour or until the beans are soft.

POTATOES

Perhaps one of the easiest ways to liven up a small menu and create added interest is to switch things around. For example, in a kitchen that only has a small static oven, a griddle and a deep-fryer and a small menu that includes beefburgers, sausages, a simple flan and similar dishes, a caterer may feel that he or she would like to offer a little extra without a drastic reconstruction. One way around this is to vary the type of potatoes. Plain grilled sausages take on a new dimension with O'Brien Potatoes, and a couple of lamb chops with Colcannon Potatoes and fresh broccoli is a meal that very few would fail to enjoy.

Although chips and jacket potatoes will always be popular, it is worth taking a little time to try serving some of the other potato dishes. Convenience foods can sometimes be a little dry, lacking in flavour and needing that added 'zing'. This can be provided by 'spicing' up the veg. There are many types of potato dishes you can try but the four listed below have been chosen not only for their taste but also because they can be kept warm over a session with little deterioration or can be reheated in the microwave.

O'Brien Potatoes

Serves 10–12

Our version is based on an American recipe. It is not exactly a slimmer's delight but our attempts to make it with yogurt have failed.

- butter or oil for greasing
- 2.25 kg (5 lb) potatoes, cut into large dice
- 250 g (8 oz) diced mixed peppers, fresh or frozen
- 1 large onion, chopped
- 4 garlic cloves, crushed
- 75 g (3 oz) grated parmesan cheese
- 2 tsp paprika
- 1/2 tsp chilli powder
- 1 litre (1 3/4 pints) single or whey cream
- a little salt

Use the butter or oil to grease a large oven tin. Put the potatoes in the tin and mix in all the remaining ingredients. Cover with foil and bake in a preheated oven at Gas Mark 7/220°C/425°F for about 2 hours or until the potatoes are soft and creamy. Take care not to overcook them.

Colcannon Potatoes

Serves 10–12

- 2.25 kg (5 lb) potatoes, peeled
- 1.25 kg (3 lb) kale or spring cabbage
- 4 leeks, washed
- 600 ml (1 pint) milk
- 150 ml (1/4 pint) single cream (optional)
- a knob of butter (optional)
- salt and freshly ground pepper

Put the potatoes into salted water to cook. While they are cooking, very lightly cook the kale or spring cabbage and chop it into small pieces. Slice the leeks into slivers (using all the leek), cover with the milk, and cream and butter if used, and simmer until soft. Drain the potatoes, mash them and then beat them until smooth. Add the milk and leeks and the chopped kale or spring cabbage. Continue beating until the mixture is a pale green fluff, and add salt if necessary and a little pepper.

Variation
Any leftovers can be made into potato cakes. Mix the potato with an equal amount of self-raising flour, mould into flat cakes and either shallow fry in a little oil or bake in a preheated oven at Gas Mark 7/220°C/425°C for about 20 minutes.

Garlic Potatoes

Serves 10–12

- butter or oil for greasing
- 2.25 kg (5 lb) potatoes, peeled and sliced thinly
- 8 garlic cloves, sliced very thinly
- 1.2 litres (2 pints) vegetable stock
- 2 onions, sliced thinly

Use the butter or oil to grease a shallow, ovenproof dish. Layer the potatoes and garlic in the dish, finishing off with potatoes, and pour over the stock until it reaches the top of the potatoes. Bake, uncovered, in a preheated oven at Gas Mark 6/200°C/400°F for 1 1/2–2 hours (depending on the type of potatoes). If the top browns too quickly, cover the dish with foil.

Indian-style Potatoes

Serves 10–12
- 50 g (2 oz) ghee or 6 tbsp oil
- 1 onion, chopped finely
- 2 tsp ground cumin
- 1 tsp turmeric
- 1 tsp dried or fresh fenugreek leaves
- 1 tsp chilli powder
- 20 curry leaves
- 600 ml (1 pint) water
- 2.25 kg (5 lb) potatoes, cooked and cut into large dice
- 2 tbsp desiccated coconut

Heat the ghee or oil in a saucepan, add the onion, cumin, turmeric, fenugreek, chilli powder and curry leaves and fry for a few seconds. Add a little water, fold in the potatoes and coconut, and top up with the remaining water. Heat thoroughly and serve, or place in an ovenproof dish and heat through in the oven at Gas Mark 4/180°C/350°F for about 15 minutes.

DIPS AND DRESSINGS

Gone are the days when the ubiquitous bottles of brown sauce or tomato ketchup adorned every British table. One only has to look along the shelves of the local supermarket to see the variety of dressings that are available. However, it is a very simple task to make your own.

Hummus

Serves 12 as a starter
- 500 g (1 lb) chick peas, washed
- 1 tbsp chopped parsley
- 4 garlic cloves, crushed
- 1 tsp paprika (optional)
- 2 tbsp tahini (sesame seed paste)
- 4 tbsp olive oil
- juice of 1 lemon
- a little water
- salt
- Garnish:
- parsley
- black olives

Soak the chick peas overnight in cold water. Cover with water and drain the chick peas, cover them with fresh cold water and cook for about an hour. Add salt to the water and cook for a further 1/2 hour or until the peas are soft. Drain and leave to cool. Place the chick peas, parsley, garlic, paprika if used and tahini in a food processor and start to grind. Drizzle in the oil, lemon juice and a little water which will turn the mixture creamy. Hummus should be very smooth and soft. It will thicken up when left, so add sufficient water to make a thick cream.

Garnish with parsley and black olives and serve with hot pitta bread to scoop the hummus up.

Yogurt and Cucumber Dip (Tzatziki)

Serves 12 as a starter
   600 ml (1 pint) thick natural yogurt
   1 cucumber, peeled and chopped into tiny cubes
   1 small onion, chopped very finely
   2 garlic cloves, crushed
   1/2 tsp finely chopped fresh mint
   2 tbsp lemon juice
   2 tbsp olive oil
   salt and freshly ground black pepper

Mix all the ingredients together, adding a little salt but lots of freshly ground black pepper. Serve very cold with hot pitta bread or with Samosas (page 159) or Falafel (page 161).

Garlic Sauce (Skorthalia)

   6 garlic cloves
   2 slices of bread about 5 cm (2 inch) thick, without crusts, broken into pieces
   600 ml (1 pint) olive oil
   1 tbsp lemon juice
   90–125 ml (3–4 fl oz) water
   salt to taste

Place the garlic and bread in a food processor. Switch on and add the olive oil and lemon juice slowly, as you would if you were making mayonnaise. When mixed in, add the water and add salt if necessary. Chill and serve with Aubergine Slippers or fried or grilled fish.

Tartare Sauce

   50 g (2 oz) gherkins, chopped finely
   25 g (1 oz) capers, chopped finely
   50 g (2 oz) parsley, chopped finely
   300 ml (1/2 pint) mayonnaise

Add all the chopped ingredients to the mayonnaise and mix well. If you wish to make up a large batch, leave out the parsley and store in jars under refrigeration. Serve with fish.

Andalusian Mayonnaise

   600 ml (1 pint) mayonnaise
   3 canned sweet red peppers (pimentos), well drained and chopped
   125 ml (4 fl oz) double cream
   1 tsp crushed ice
   1 tbsp tomato ketchup
   1 tbsp Worcestershire sauce
   1 tbsp brandy
   1/4 tsp paprika
   a pinch of Cayenne pepper
   salt and freshly ground black pepper

Put the mayonnaise in a bowl and add the chopped peppers. In a separate bowl, whisk the cream with the crushed ice followed by the remaining ingredients. Combine the cream and the mayonnaise, mix well and serve. This is delicious with fish and shellfish as a refreshing change from tartare sauce, or with proprietary brands of crispy-coated vegetables.

Raitas

As yogurt-based dips and vegetable salads are deliciously refreshing, they are the ideal accompaniment to hot, spicy food.

The addition of a tandoori paste or powder to a thick natural yogurt will make a very simple raita, as will the addition of a little chilli powder and garam masala.

For a more sophisticated version, diced cooked potatoes, cucumber, radish, tomatoes and fresh chilli flavoured with cumin seeds and fresh coriander can be served with hot pitta bread or poppadums as a light starter.

SIDE SALADS

Coleslaw

Makes about 36 heaped tablespoons
    4 stalks of celery, chopped
    1 small onion, chopped
    500 g (1 lb) white cabbage, chopped finely
    4 carrots, grated
    2 tsp lemon juice
    6 tbsp salad cream
    2 tbsp vegetable oil
    6 tbsp mayonnaise
    salt and freshly ground black pepper

Mix together the celery, onion, cabbage and carrots in a large bowl. Stir in the lemon juice, salad cream, oil, salt and pepper and finally the mayonnaise. Chill well and serve.

Waldorf Salad

Mix equal quantities of diced celery, chopped crisp apples and coarsely chopped walnuts with sufficient mayonnaise to cover. This salad should be served reasonably quickly or the apples will lose their crispness and may discolour. This salad is best made to order.

Tabbouleh

Makes about 36 heaped tablespoons
    250 g (8 oz) bulgar (crushed wheat)
    500 g (1 lb) tomatoes, chopped finely
    375 g (12 oz) onions, finely chopped
    250 g (8 oz) fresh mixed green pepper, chopped finely
    2 garlic cloves, crushed (optional)
    2 tbsp chopped coriander or parsley
    6 tsp olive oil
    juice of 2 lemons
    salt and freshly ground black pepper
Garnish:
    lemon wedges
    parsley or coriander leaves
    black olives

Cover the bulgar with cold water and leave it to soak for about 30 minutes. Drain in a colander then transfer to a muslin or clean tea towel and squeeze out all the water until it is completely dry.

Mix all the ingredients together and season to taste. Chill and serve garnished with a wedge of lemon, parsley or coriander leaves and black olives for added colour.

BREAD, SCONES AND PASTRY

Although it is now possible to buy a wide range of excellent breads, there are times when you either run out or simply feel like a change. Irish Soda Bread or Wholemeal Scones make a delicious accompaniment to soups or, with a moist, tasty filling, they make a healthy alternative for sandwiches.

Irish Soda Bread

Makes 8 scones
This is very easy to make and provides a welcome change. Most soda bread is made with white flour but this wholemeal version is healthier and has much more flavour.

500 g (1 lb) wholemeal flour
1 tsp bicarbonate of soda
1 tsp salt
300 ml (1/2 pint) sour or fresh milk or 150 ml (1/4 pint) natural yogurt and 150 ml (1/4 pint) milk
plain flour for dusting

Mix all the dry ingredients together and make a well in the centre. Pour in nearly all the milk or yogurt and milk and mix with a wooden spoon. It should form a thick dough. The mixture should be slack but not wet and the mixing done lightly and quickly. Add a little more milk if the dough seems too stiff. With floured hands, put the dough on to a floured board and flatten it into a round. Transfer it to a baking tray and make a large cross with a floured knife across the top. This is to ensure an even distribution of heat. Bake in a preheated oven at Gas Mark 5/190°C/375°F for about 40 minutes. Test with a skewer. To keep the bread soft, wrap it in a clean tea-towel.

Wholemeal Scones

Makes 24
250 g (8 oz) wholemeal flour
250 g (8 oz) plain flour
25 g (1 oz) baking powder
125 g (4 oz) butter, cut into small pieces
2 eggs
150 ml (1/4 pint) milk

Sift the two flours and baking powder together and rub in the butter until the mixture resembles breadcrumbs. Make a well in the centre and drop in the eggs. Mix in the milk gradually until the dough is smooth.

Knead the dough lightly and shape it into small, flat rounds or roll it out and use a pastry cutter (plain cutters for savoury scones). Bake for 10 minutes in a preheated oven at Gas Mark 9/220°C/425°F.

Wholemeal Pastry

375 g (12 oz) wholemeal flour
125 g (4 oz) plain white flour
a pinch of salt
125 g (4 oz) margarine, cut into small pieces
about 2–3 tbsp water

Sift together the flours and salt and rub in the margarine until crumbs form. Sprinkle over the water and mix lightly until the pastry easily forms a ball. Leave it to rest for 1/2 hour in a refrigerator before using.

SAUCES

The ability to make a good sauce is a prerequisite for any cook. Even so, you will hear an awful lot of waffle about techniques for making different sauces. Basically, all you are looking for is a sauce which looks right (i.e. has no lumps), tastes right and performs its function of pouring if it is a pouring sauce or coating if it is a coating sauce.

So ignore the purists: if you use a blender or put all the ingredients in the pan at once and you are happy with the results, that is all that matters. Once mastered, the basic sauces are not only an avenue to classic dishes but also a means of further enhancing a basic menu.

Basic White Sauces

> 125 g (4 oz) butter or margarine
> 125 g (4 oz) plain flour
> 1.2 litres (2 pints) milk
> salt and freshly ground black pepper to taste

These quantities make a coating sauce. For a pouring sauce, use 50 g (2 oz) of fat and 50 g (2 oz) flour to the same quantity of milk.

The sauce can be made in one of three ways, as follows:

Roux method
Melt the fat in a saucepan. Add the flour and mix well over the heat until the mixture goes sandy in texture. Do not allow it to brown. Remove the pan from the heat and add a little milk. Return the pan to the heat and allow to cook, stirring vigorously. Repeat until all the milk is used.

Alternatively, when the roux (flour and fat) is taken off the heat, add all the milk, a little at a time to prevent lumps forming. Return the pan to the heat and bring the sauce to the boil slowly, whisking all the time, until it thickens. Season to taste.

Quick method
Place all the ingredients in a saucepan and bring to the boil, whisking continuously.

Blender sauce
Place all the ingredients in a blender or food processor and mix until smooth. Transfer to a saucepan, bring to the boil and simmer until the sauce thickens.

Tips
- Once you have started making a sauce, never leave it - it requires your undivided attention.
- Stir or whisk continuously, making sure that every bit of the sauce gets mixed, e.g. don't forget the angles of the pan.
- If a smooth sauce goes lumpy before it boils, beat it with a whisk.
- If a sauce goes lumpy after it boils, try sieving it or mixing it in a blender.
- To prevent a skin forming, cover the saucepan with tightly fitting greaseproof paper or dot the sauce with tiny flakes of butter.
- For a glossy sauce, add a knob of butter or cream; to make it richer, add an egg yolk.

Béchamel Sauce
Makes 1.2 litres (2 pints)
Peel a small onion and stud it with 2 or 3 cloves. Place this in a pan containing 1.2 litres (2 pints) of milk and heat it to just below boiling point. Leave it to infuse for about 30 minutes. Using the roux method above, make up the sauce with the infused milk.

For more flavour, infuse 1.2 litres (2 pints) of milk with a small onion, a carrot, 1/2 stick of celery, 2 cloves, a bay leaf, a blade of mace, a sprig of parsley and one of thyme and 8 white peppercorns. After simmering, leave for 30 minutes. Using the roux method, make the sauce. Once the sauce is cooked, season it to taste and add 1 tablespoon of cream.

Béchamel Sauce is served with fish, poultry and vegetable dishes.

Onion Sauce
Makes 1.2 litres (2 pints)
When melting the butter for a roux, add 2 tablespoons of finely chopped onions. Do not allow them to brown. Make the sauce in the usual way. Serve with lamb, sausages, Yorkshire pudding or turkey.

Parsley Sauce

Makes 1.2 litres (2 pints)
Add 2 tablespoons of finely chopped fresh parsley to the basic white sauce. This sauce is usually served with fish.

Cheese Sauce

Makes 1.2 litres (2 pints)
While the basic white sauce is still hot, add 50 g (2 oz) of grated cheese and a pinch of nutmeg.

Lemon Sauce

Makes 1.2 litres (2 pints)
Using the basic sauce again, grate in the zest of 1 lemon.

Velouté Sauce

Makes 1.2 litres (2 pints)

    125 g (4 oz) butter or margarine
    125 g (40 oz) plain flour
    1.2 litres (2 pints) white stock (fish, chicken, veal or lamb)
    freshly ground black pepper (optional)

In a heavy-bottomed saucepan, melt the butter and stir in the flour. Cook gently until the mixture turns a pale golden colour. Take off the heat and gradually add the stock. Return the pan to the heat, bring the sauce to the boil and simmer it until it has thickened and has a glossy finish.

Because a Velouté is made with stock, it should not need any additional seasoning, but if you like, a sprinkling of freshly ground black pepper can be added to the finished sauce.

For extra flavour, add a few drops of lemon juice and a spoonful of cream to the finished sauce.

Mushroom Sauce

Makes 1.2 litres (2 pints)
Finely slice about 125 g (4 oz) mushrooms. Lightly fry them in butter and add them to the finished Velouté Sauce together with a little single cream.

Prawn Sauce

Makes 1.2 litres (2 pints)
Make the Velouté Sauce with fish stock and, after cooking, add 125 g (4 oz) of cooked prawns, a little lemon juice and a spoonful of cream to lighten it.

Espagnole (Brown) Sauce

This brown sauce and the Demi-glace Sauce below are used as the basis for many savoury sauces.

    2 rashers of streaky bacon, chopped
    125 g (4 oz) onions, chopped
    125 g (4 oz) carrots, peeled and chopped
    50 g (2 oz) celery, chopped
    50 g (2 oz) mushroom stalks, chopped
    50 g (2 oz) butter, margarine, oil or dripping
    65 g ($2^{1}/_{2}$ oz) plain flour
    1.2 litres (2 pints) brown stock
    25 g (1 oz) tomato purée
    bunch of herbs
    glass of sherry (optional)
    salt and freshly ground black pepper

In a non-stick pan, fry the bacon until the fat is released. Remove from the pan, add all the vegetables and sauté them until they are soft. Remove and drain.

In a heavy-bottomed pan, melt the butter, add the flour and cook until the roux starts to brown. Remove from the heat and gradually add the stock. Bring to the boil and add the vegetables, tomato purée and herbs. Simmer for at least 1 hour, skimming if necessary.

Strain the sauce and season it if required. Add the sherry if used and serve.

Demi-glace Sauce

Makes 1.2 litres (2 pints)
Simmer 1.2 litres (2 pints) of Espagnole Sauce with 1.2 litres (2 pints) of brown stock until it is reduced by half. Skim and strain.

Hollandaise Sauce

Makes 600 ml (1 pint)
Because the egg yolks used in this recipe and the one below for Bearnaise Sauce are not cooked, it is important to ensure that they come from a reputable supplier, i.e. one whose hens have been certified as healthy. If you are unsure, use pasteurised eggs.

- 6 egg yolks
- 1 tsp caster sugar
- 2 tbsp white wine vinegar
- 2 tbsp water
- 2 tbsp fresh lemon juice
- 375 g (12 oz) butter, melted
- a little salt

In a blender, whizz the egg yolks and sugar until they break down (this will take only a couple of seconds). Add the wine vinegar, water and lemon juice. While the machine is still running, drizzle in the melted butter until the sauce thickens. Serve hot or cold.

Hollandaise sauce thickens when cooled.

Bearnaise Sauce

Makes 600 ml (1 pint)
Make up the sauce as for Hollandaise Sauce above but replace the wine vinegar with tarragon vinegar to which has been added 1 teaspoon of finely chopped fresh tarragon.

Tomato Sauce

Makes 1.2 litres (2 pints) of concentrated sauce
This sauce can be made in large batches when both tomatoes and herbs are plentiful and cheap. It will freeze well.

- 1.1 kg (2½ lb) ripe tomatoes
- 2 tbsp olive oil
- 3 shallots or 1 large onion, chopped
- 2 garlic cloves, crushed
- 1 carrot, grated
- 2 tbsp lemon juice
- 1 tbsp chopped fresh basil or tarragon or oregano
- salt

Peel and de-seed the tomatoes if the sauce is to be finished off in a blender; coarsely chop them if the sauce is to be sieved.

Melt the oil in a pan and add the shallots or onion and garlic. Once they start to soften, add the tomatoes, carrot, lemon juice and just a pinch of salt.

Bring to the boil and cover with a tight-fitting lid. Reduce the heat and simmer very gently for about 30 minutes.

Add the herbs and cook very gently for a further 30 minutes. We prefer not to mix herbs in this sauce: basil will give a superb musky taste, tarragon a scented flavour ideal for fish or chicken, and oregano an Italian flavour.

Once cooked, either liquidise the sauce in a blender or run it through a sieve. If it appears too runny, return it to the heat and reduce it.

Sweet White Sauce

Makes 1.2 litres (2 pints)
Follow the basic white sauce recipe but while the sauce is still cooking, add sugar to taste.

To ring the changes, add a tot of rum or brandy, a little grated nutmeg or mixed spice, or the zest of an orange or lemon.

Custard Sauce

Makes 600 ml (1 pint)
- 4 eggs
- 2 tbsp caster sugar
- 600 ml (1 pint) milk or half milk and half cream
- 1 tsp vanilla essence

Beat the eggs with the sugar. Warm the milk in a pan and add it to the mixture. Place the mixture in a double saucepan or a bowl standing over a pan of simmering water and cook, stirring continuously, until the sauce starts to thicken. Test it by running it over the back of a wooden spoon: it should be thick enough to coat the back of the spoon. You must not allow the sauce to boil.

Remove the pan from the heat and add the vanilla essence to taste.

PUDDINGS

In a weight-conscious era, it might be supposed that the sales of puddings would take a nose-dive, but like chips, puddings are now rarely made at home and so part of the 'treat' of eating out is to indulge a sweet tooth.

Unfortunately, to be at their best, puddings do need to be eaten on the day they are made and this is why many caterers like to opt for just an apple pie or ice-cream. To a certain extent, the sale of puddings depends on how they are displayed. If you have not got a cold display unit, you have to rely on a menu description and this limits the choice and variety you can offer.

We have no set sweets apart from ice-cream so we use the cold unit to display those on offer and rely on their visual appeal plus the varying ability of the staff to describe them. Even so, it is very difficult to predict how, or which, puddings will sell.

Liz, who makes our 'sumptuous' puddings, as one guide described them, has provided some of her recipes and tips. We are sure that you will find them absolutely delicious.

Pavlova

Serves 8
Without a doubt, our best seller is a Pavlova, in summer made with fresh strawberries and in winter with home-made lemon curd. A lot of people shy away from Pavlovas, thinking them difficult to make, but do try this recipe. It is most important to weigh the egg whites to get the correct proportions.

>   125 g (4 oz) egg whites
>   190 g (6½ oz) granulated sugar
>   *Filling:*
>   300 ml (½ pint) double or whipping cream, whipped
>   175 g (6 oz) strawberries
>   icing sugar for dusting

Whisk the egg whites until they form stiff peaks, then slowly add the sugar and keep whisking until the mixture shines; it should take no longer than 5 minutes. Divide the mixture into two and pipe it into rounds on non-stick baking parchment. Place in the top of a preheated oven at Gas Mark 7/220°C/425°F for about 20 minutes (do not allow the meringue to brown) then turn the oven down to its lowest setting, removing the tray(s) to the bottom and coolest part of the oven and leave for at least 5 hours. The idea is to dry out the meringues, so if the oven is cool enough, they can be left overnight.

Fill with the whipped cream and fresh strawberries, leaving a few whole strawberries to decorate the top. Dust with icing sugar and voila! the perfect Pavlova!

Danish Spice Cake

Serves 8
This cake is a confection of layers of crisp, highly flavoured, biscuit-like rounds balanced with fresh cream and a chocolate topping. Despite its apparent 'brittle' nature, it cuts quite easily.

>   250 g (8 oz) margarine
>   250 g (8 oz) granulated or caster sugar
>   300 g (10 oz) plain flour
>   25 g (1 oz) cocoa
>   2 heaped tsp mixed spice
>   To assemble:
>   300 ml (½ pint) double or whipping cream, whipped
>   125 g (4 oz) plain cooking chocolate, melted
>   25 g (1 oz) roasted nuts, chopped

Beat the margarine and sugar together until creamy. Sieve the flour, cocoa and mixed spice together and add them to the mixture. Mix to form a soft dough. With cool hands, shape the dough into a sausage and slice it into six equal parts. Roll each piece into an 18 cm (7-inch) round between sheets of greaseproof paper and cling film. The cling film should be on top so that you can see the shape. Prick the rounds with a fine fork and transfer (on the greaseproof paper, cling film removed) on to a baking tray. Place in a preheated oven at Gas Mark 6/200°C/400°F for 8–12 minutes. You have to stand over them as they can easily burn.

As soon as the rounds are cooked, slide them off the tray on to a cool, flat surface before they set. Once cold, the greaseproof paper should just peel off. Spread whipped cream between the layers and top with melted chocolate and chopped roasted nuts.

Variations

For a change, leave out the cocoa and replace the mixed spice with ginger. When finishing, add fresh or tinned pineapple to the cream, top with plain icing to which just a little ginger has been added and decorate with chopped nuts. Liz's favourite is the original base with the mixed spice replaced with cinammon, layered with a thick apple purée and cream and topped with grated chocolate.

Halva - Mama Patsourakou's Recipe

Serves 8
Halva is a semolina pudding popular in Greece and throughout the Middle East. It is usually served cold, cut into wedges. The original recipe contained much more olive oil than our version: we have altered the recipe slightly to make the look and taste more acceptable to the British palate. The type of semolina used is medium-ground, not as coarse as that used in burghul nor as fine as that for the standard semolina pudding.

> 50 g (2 oz) butter
> 4 tbsp olive oil
> 125 g (4 oz) medium-ground semolina
> 175 g (6 oz) almonds, chopped
> 1/2 tsp cinnamon
> 50 g (2 oz) Demerara sugar
> 600 ml (1 pint) water
> 1 x 450 g (15 oz) can of evaporated milk
> 4 tbsp honey
> Decoration:
> toasted almond flakes
> whipped cream (optional)

Melt the butter and oil together in a large saucepan and fold in the semolina until it is coated. Allow it to brown a little but be careful that it does not stick. This is the only difficult part! Once coloured, add the chopped almonds, cinnamon and sugar, mix well and remove from the heat.

In a separate pan, mix the water, evaporated milk and 2 tbsp of the honey, and bring to the boil, pour over the semolina mixture and allow to cook until the mixture has thickened and the semolina has softened. This usually takes 2–3 minutes, depending on the type of semolina used. If the mixture thickens too quickly, add more water. Semolina can vary considerably, some will need more water and honey than others. The mixture should be a thick pouring consistency with a sweet, creamy taste.

While it is still hot, pour the mixture into a pudding basin or bowl. Chill right down and, when cold, turn out on to a serving dish. Dilute the remaining honey with a little water and pour over. Decorate with toasted almonds and whipped cream if liked.

Variations
As a scented alternative, leave out the cinnamon and dilute the coating honey with rose or orange blossom water available from ethnic shops and good delicatessens.

Or serve the Halva with thick Greek-style yogurt to which has been added clear honey. This is a lovely pudding in its own right – topped with chopped toasted almonds, it has a cool and refreshing taste.

Westmorland Tart

Serves 8
This is a real favourite: a rich yet simple-to-make pudding which, unlike some others, is just as good the day after it is made.

> *Base:*
> 250 g (8 oz) digestive biscuits, crushed
> 125 g (4 oz) butter, melted
> *Topping:*
> 250 ml (8 fl oz) water
> 300 g (10 oz) raisins
> 125 g (4 oz) granulated sugar
> 2 tbsp cornflour
> juice of 1/2 lemon and 1/2 orange
> 50 g (2 oz) walnut pieces
> 300 ml (1/2 pint) double or whipping cream, whipped
> 8 walnut halves

Mix together the butter and the crushed biscuits and mould into an ovenproof yet attractive flan-type dish. Bake for 5–10 minutes in a preheated oven at Gas Mark 4/180°C/350°F.

Meanwhile, heat the water to boiling point in a pan, add the raisins and simmer for 3 minutes. Mix together the sugar and cornflour and mix in with the raisins. Bring back to the boil and allow to thicken, stirring all the time.

Remove from the heat and add the lemon or orange juice and walnut pieces. Pour over the biscuit base and leave to cool. Once cold, cover with a thick layer of whipped cream and decorate with the walnut halves. For added flavour, add 1 tablespoon of rum or brandy to the fruit mixture.

Orange or Lemon Bread and Butter Pudding

Serves 8

    6 slices of buttered bread
    orange or lemon marmalade
    50 g (2 oz) raisins or sultanas
    Custard:
    1.2 litres (2 pints) milk
    75 g (3 oz) sugar
    4 eggs
    4 drops of vanilla essence

Spread the bread with the marmalade and press the raisins and sultanas into the slices. Cut the bread into triangles and arrange attractively in an ovenproof dish.

Whisk all the custard ingredients together and pour over the bread. Leave to stand for at least 1/2 hour. Bake for about 1 hour in a preheated oven at Gas Mark 3/160°C/325°F until all the custard has set yet is creamy and the top nicely browned.

Coffee Creams

Serves 8

Apart from being a delicious pudding in its own right, this is an ideal way to use the egg yolks left over from the Pavlovas!

    750 ml ($1^{1}/_{4}$ pints) whipping cream, plus extra for
    decoration
    8 egg yolks
    175 g (6 oz) caster sugar
    6 tsp boiling water
    5 tsp instant coffee granules

In a saucepan, bring the cream nearly to boiling point. Whisk the egg yolks with 75 g (3 oz) of the sugar until creamy. Make a syrup by adding the boiling water to the coffee, then add the remaining sugar. Stir well.

Pour the cream into the egg mixture, then mix in the coffee. Strain through a sieve and divide between eight ramekins.

Preheat the oven to Gas Mark 2/150°C/300°F and prepare a bain marie. Use a shallow oven tray not much larger than the combined width of the ramekins and line it with a thin layer of kitchen paper. This is to stop the dishes moving about. Fill the tray about one-third with water and insert the ramekins (the water should not reach their tops). Bake for about an hour. Allow to cool, then chill well. Decorate with a blob of whipped cream and serve.

Glossary of culinary terms

à la	in the style of
à la carte	menu items which are cooked to order and priced individually
Baste	to moisten food during roasting by spooning over the juices
Beurre manié	equal quantities of butter and flour rolled into small balls and used for thickening
Bind	mix dry ingredients with egg, cream or sauce to hold them together
Blanche	to immerse in boiling water or hot fat for a short time either to loosen tough skins, to retain colour or as a preliminary to cooking or freezing
Blind	a pastry case cooked without its filling (often with baking beans or foil in it to preserve its shape)
Bouquet garni	bunch or bag of parsley, thyme and bay leaves
Braise	sealed meat or vegetables cooked with liquid and additional vegetables
Brown	fry in a little hot fat to seal in the flavour
Carte du jour	menu of the day
Casserole	a stew of meat, fish or vegetables cooked slowly in a low oven for a long time. The lidded dish in which the stew is cooked
Compote	fresh or dried fruit stewed in syrup and chilled
Consommé	a basic clear soup
Cook out	the process of cooking the flour in a soup, sauce or roux
Crêpes	pancakes
Croutôns	squares or cubes of fried bread also known as sippets
Crudités	small segments of raw, fresh vegetables
Dredge	sprinkle with flour or sugar
Dust	dredge lightly
Entrecôte	a steak cut from the sirloin
Escalope	a thin slice
Farce	stuffing
Flake	to separate into slivers
Flan	an open tart
Garnish	decorations or trimmings
Glaze	give a glossy finish to a dish or the residue from meat stock
Grate	reduce to small particles by rubbing against a rough surface
Infuse	steep in hot or cold liquid to extract flavour
Jardinière	vegetables cut into batons
Julienne	vegetables cut into matchstick rods
Lard	to insert strips of bacon or pork fat into meat to moisten it during cooking
Liaison	a thickening or binding
Marinade	a steeping mixture of oil, wine and vinegar with herbs and spices, used to tenderise and flavour
Noisette	a lamb cutlet or chop without the bone
Pickle	preserve in brine or vinegar; that which is so preserved
Poach	cook food at a simmer
Purée	food reduced to a soft consistency by boiling or crushing
Reduce	concentrate a liquid by rapid boiling
Render	melt down fat by slow cooking
Roux	a thickening of flour and fat to which liquid is added to make a sauce
Sauté	toss quickly in fat to seal the outside
Skim	remove fat or scum from the surface of a soup, sauce or boiling liquid, etc.
Steam	cook in the vapours produced by boiling liquid
Stew	cook food slowly in a covered pan or casserole
Zest	oily outside layer of citrus fruits such as lemons, oranges and limes

Index

ACAS 142, 150
accident book 110
Account management 111–22
accountants 115
Acts of Parliament/Regulations
    see also employment law; fire regulations; Health and Safety at Work legislation; hygiene regulations; licensing law
    Food Act 1984 101
    Food Hygiene (General) Regulations 1970 102
    Health and Safety (First Aid) Regulations 1981 110
    Licensing Act 1964 151, 155
    Licensing Act 1988 153
    Offices, Shops and Railways Premises Act 109–10
    Trades Descriptions Act 40
    Wages Act 1986 144
additives, artificial 28
addresses 28, 37, 40, 59, 74, 86, 100, 110, 122, 150, 158
advertising 78–9
agricultural shows 55, 152
all-day opening 16
    Scotland 157
aubergines 26

bacteria 103–5, 106, 107, 167
bain-maries 95–6, 105
banks 122
barbecues 18, 52–9
barley 27
basil 31–2, 34
batters 26
bay leaves 32
Beaton, Mrs 41
bin-liner holders 84, 109
blackboards 75
bookkeeping 115–17
bouillon, ready-prepared 43
bread 25
    soda 27, 182
Brewers' Society 75
British Heart Foundation 22, 28
budgeting 114
burghul 24
butane gas 54
butcher, local 133–4
butter 90
    and vegetarians 38
butter portions 43

Calor Appliances Testing Laboratory 58

Calor gas 54, 55, 56, 58–9, 82, 89, 92, 93
    butane 54
    propane 54, 55, 56
Calor Gas Limited 58–9
canned/bottled food 41
caraway seeds 35
cashew nuts 25
casserole dishes, earthenware 98
casseroling, meat 27
catalytic friers 92
catering colleges 107, 138, 141
CEDA (Catering Equipment Distributors' Association) 80, 83, 87, 100
charities, local 78
cheese, vegetarian 38
cheque cards 111–12
chest freezers 94
chick-peas 23
Chicken Kiev 75
    frozen 43
children 17, 18, 41, 154
Chinese food 24
chips 26–7, 91–2
chives 32
cholesterol 25
chopping boards 97–8, 104, 108
City and Guilds Institute 138, 141, 150
cleaners, industrial 107
cleaning cloths, 106, 107
cleaning the kitchen 107
cleaning materials, toxic 108
Closure
    Emergency 101
    Ordinary 101
coffee, decaffeinated 28
coffee machines 99
coins and notes 82
colour-coding 97, 104
colour on the plate 20
combis 91
complaints 129
computers 121–2, 150
contamination of food 105–6
    cross-contamination 97, 102, 106
    'contracting-out' 149
convenience foods 41–4, 123, 124, 129, 130, 134, 178
cook/chill method 42
cook/freeze method 42
cooked meats 42
cookery competitions 77–8
cooking methods 26–7
cool boxes 57
coriander 33, 34, 35
costume, theme nights 51

cottage industries 14, 134
courgettes 26
couscous 24
cow heel 27
cream 27
    and vegetarians 38
cream portions 43
credit cards 112
crockery 76–7, 82, 98
currency, acceptable 111
curry 36
Customs and Excise 117–22
cutlery 77, 82, 98–9

deep fryers 91–2
deep frying, and fat 26
defrosting frozen food 104
demonstrations of equipment 88
Department of Employment 142, 144, 146, 150
Department of Health and Social Security (DHSS) 149, 150
design services (kitchens) 80
detergents 107
diets, restricted 28
dinner dances 45, 51
dishes, kitchen 96
    for microwave ovens
dishwashers, automatic 94–5, 103, 108
disinfection, kitchen 107
display units 76, 82, 94, 105, 106, 134
dried food 42
drunkenness 154–5

EFTPOS (Electronic Funds Transfer at Point of Sale) 112
eggs
    and bacteria 103
    fresh, in rural areas 134
    and salmonella 105, 185
    and vegetarians 38
electrical equipment, failure 110
electricity bills 114, 117
employment contracts 142
employment law 142–6
entertainment 155–6
Environmental Health requirements 80, 86, 94, 101, 102, 107, 108, 109, 110, 134, 145
equipment 87–100
    cleaning of 107
    dangerous 110
    guards for 109
ethnic shops 36
Eurocheques 112
expenditure 113–5

Index

family rooms 117
fat, removal from meat stock 27, 105
fat fires, procedure 110
fats 24–5, 26
    saturated 24–5, 38
    solid 92
    and vegetarians 38
filo pastry 43, 159
fire drill, staff 110
Fire Protection Association 86
fire regulations 81
first aid kit 110
fish, and bacteria 103
fixed charges, expenditure 114
flans, vegetarian 40, 42
flash point temperatures, oil 92
flies 84, 108
Flour Advisory Bureau 28
flours 25–6
flowers, in garden 18
food bars 76
food poisoning 102, 103, 104
food processors 97
freeze-dried food 42
freezers 93–4
front-of-house area 76–7
frozen food 41
    defrosting 104
functions 45–51
furniture, outdoor 18

games rooms 17
garlic 34
gas leaks 110
gastronorms 89
ginger 35
gourmet evenings 45, 51
grains 24
    in soup 27
gravies
    and bacteria 105
    and vegetarians 38–9
greengrocers 134
grills/griddles 93
guide books 77

halogen lamps 89
halva 24
Health Education Authority 28
Health and Safety at Work legislation 101, 109–10
health food 21, 27–8, 29, 39
heart disease 25
herbs 28–34
    freeze-dried 43
    in the garden 18, 29–33, 34
    storage 34
hot cupboards 95, 105
hygiene
    courses 106–7
    kitchen 102–5
    personal 105–7
hygiene regulations 81, 101–3, 105

income tax, employees' 115, 146–50
infestation treatment 108
inspection of premises 108, 109

kitchen layout 80–6
'knife and fork' service 102
knives
    fish 98–9
    kitchen 97–8
    and soap suds 110
    steak 98
    storage 109
leftovers 105
legislation *see* Acts of Parliament/Regulations; employment law; fire regulations; Health and Safety at Work legislation; hygiene regulations; licensing law
licensing law 151–8
lighting 109
liquefied petroleum gas (LPG) 54, 58
liquidisers 97
location of pub 12–16
    rural 15–16
    seaside and tourists 16
    semi-rural 14
    suburban 14
    urban 12–13

mace 36
magazines, advertising in 78
market research 10–12
Marks and Spencer 41
maternity benefits 145, 150
meat
    and bacteria 103
    and sage 31
    sealing 27
meeting rooms 17
menu, planning the choice provided 21
    individuality 20–1
    problem areas 21
    variety 20
menu, printed
    presentation 75
    sturdiness 76
    truthfulness 75
    wording 76
menu, promotion of 75–9
    advertising 78–9
    blackboards 75
    display unit 76
    publicity 77–8
    signs 75
    Symbol Schemes 75
menu costing 123–6
Microwave Association 90, 100
microwave cooking 26, 27
    dishes, earthenware 96
    ovens 89–90
Middle Eastern dips 40
Middle Eastern food 24
milk
    and bacteria 103

and vegetarians 39
mint 30
modular equipment 85, 88, 93, 96
monosodium glutamate 26, 29
monthly analysis sheet 116
motoring, private 121
moussaka 26

National Insurance 115, 145, 146, 149–50
newspapers, advertising in 78
NLVA (National Licensed Victuallers' Association) 112, 117, 142, 150, 158
nutmeg 36
nuts 25

oil, cooking 92, 93
    flash point temperatures 92
olive oil 25
oregano 33
out-of-season trade 16
outside facilities 18
ovens 89–91
    combination 91
    convection 89
    microwave 89–90
    pizza 89
    static 89
    steam convection 91
    steamers 91

packaged food 42
pans 96
parsley 33, 34
pastry, wholemeal 26
payment, by customers 76
    non-payment 76, 126–7
pension scheme, private 148
pepper 35
peppers 23
pests, 101, 108, 109
petty cash book 116
photographs, functions 49–50, 51
pizza 89
    vegetarian 40
plans, of kitchen 83–6, 103
plants, in garden 18
polyunsaturates 25
portion control 124–5
potassium 26
Potato Marketing Board 28
potatoes 21, 25
poultry 104, 134, 135
power points/supply 83–4, 87
preservatives, artificial 29
pressure cookers, safety of 110
profit calculation 123–6, 131, 133
    ready-reckoner 127
    wine ready-reckoner 62
projection for new pub 10–12, 16, 17
propane gas 54, 55, 56
pub, building
    exterior 16–17, 75
    interior 17–18

Index

outside area 18
Pubcaterer 77–8, 87
Pub Facility Symbols Scheme 75, xvi
public health and hygiene 101–10
publicity 77–8
pulses 23–4
    in soups 27

radiation 90
rates 114, 117
raw food, storage 104
ready-reckoner, profit margins 127
    wine 62
recipes 159–88
    beef 169–72
    bread, scones and pastry 182
    chicken 167–8
    dips and dressings 179–80
    fish 164–6
    lamb 173
    pork 174–5
    potatoes 178–9
    puddings 186–8
    sauces 183–5
    side salads 181
    soups 163–4
    starters 159–62
    vegetarian dishes 176–7
records, business 115, 119
refrigeration 93
    raw food 104
    warm food 105
refrigerators 93–4
reheating food 104–5
'reps' 134, 135, 136
rice 20, 24
    pre-cooked 43
rodents 101, 108
rosemary 32
rotation of stock 131, 133
Royal Institute of Public Health and Hygiene 106, 110

safety
    food 101–9
    at work 109–10
sage 31, 34
salads 23, 181
salmonella 105, 108
salt 26
scones 27, 182
self aggregation 117
self and staff usage 120, 126, 128
semolina 24
separation of raw and cooked food 103–4
service, styles of 76
service charge 76
    and VAT 121
service contracts 87
service standards 140
shopping fatigue 87
shops, local 133–4
silverskins 43

slicing machines 97, 110
small firms 14
Small Firms Advisory Service 122
smoking 106, 143
soda bread 27, 182
sodium chloride 26
soups 26, 27, 39–40, 105, 125, 163–4
'sous vide' method 42–3
spices 34–7
staff 137–50
    age restrictions 145
    clothing 106
    disciplinary procedures 143
    fire drill 110
    income tax 115, 146–9
    interviews 138–40
    maternity pay 145, 150
    meals 126, 131
    meetings 107, 140, 142
    National Insurance 115, 145, 146, 149–50
    personal hygiene 105–7
    private pension schemes 149
    redundancy pay 144, 146
    statutory rights 145–6
    students 147–8
    training 140–2
    uniforms 76, 137
    wages 114, 115, 116, 137, 144–5
    YTS 138, 147
steaming, vegetables 26, 27
stock, meat, removal of fat 27, 105
stock control 133
stock cubes/paste
    ready-prepared 43
    salt in proprietary brands 26
    and vegetarians 38–9
stock pot, permanent 104
stock sheet 130, 133
stocktaking 127–31
storage
    of equipment 108
    of food 93–4, 104
sugar portions 43
sunflower oil 25
suppliers 133–6
    cash and carry 135, 136
    cottage industries 134
    frozen food 134–5
    housewives 134
    local shops 133–4
    specialists 135
sweeteners, artificial 28
SWITCH 112
Symbols Scheme 75

'tab grabber' 84
table linen 77
tarragon 33
tea-towels 108
temperatures
    and bacteria 105
    flash point, oil 92
    food storage 94, 104

wine, serving 66–7
theme nights 45, 51
'theme' pubs 10, 17, 19
thermometers
    dishwashers 108
    fridge 94, 104, 105
thyme 30, 34
tills 111
tobacco 106, 143
toilet areas 109
trade fairs 87
trade publications 87
trading peak 117
trading surplus 115
travellers' cheques 112
    foreign currency 113
'tummy bug', staff 105–6
turmeric 36

uniforms, staff 76, 137

Vacuvin 72
VAT (Value Added Tax) 76, 116, 117–21, 127, 128
vegans 38, 39, 40
vegetables 23
    cooking 27–8
    steamed 26, 27
    vacuum-packed 23
vitamin content 28
vegetarian food 22, 28, 38–40, 176–7
Vegetarian Society 40
ventilation 102, 109
vermin/pest control 108, 109
vitamin content, vegetables 28

wages 114, 115, 116, 137, 144–5
Wages Inspectorate 144–5, 146, 150
waitresses, and food-handling 106
wash-basins 84–5, 102–3
washing of hands 85, 103, 104, 106, 143
washing up 84, 107–8
wastage 126–7, 128, 131
waste disposal 108–9
waste pipes 83–4
water, hot 103, 107
    in toilets 109
wedding receptions 49–50, 152
weekly sheet, sample 116
wine 60–74
    classification 68–9
    profit calculator 62
    profit margins 61
    serving procedure 66–7
    taste guide, red 63–6
    taste guide, white 63, 64–5
    Vacuvin 72
Wine Development Board 74
wounds, septic, staff 105

yogurt 27
YTS (Youth Training Scheme) 138, 147